THE FOREIGN CRITICAL REPUTATION
OF F. SCOTT FITZGERALD, 1980–2000

Recent Titles in
Bibliographies and Indexes in American Literature

The Works of Allen Ginsberg, 1941-1994: A Descriptive Bibliography
Bill Morgan

James A. Michener: A Checklist of His Works, with a Selected, Annotated Bibliography
F. X. Roberts and C. D. Rhine, compilers

The Proverbial Eugene O'Neill: An Index to Proverbs in the Works of Eugene Gladstone O'Neill
George B. Bryan and Wolfgang Mieder, compilers

The Response to Allen Ginsberg, 1926-1994: A Bibliography of Secondary Sources
Bill Morgan

The Literary Index to American Magazines, 1850–1900
Daniel A. Wells

Laura Ingalls Wilder: An Annotated Bibliography of Critical, Biographical, and Teaching Studies
Jane M. Subramanian

Marge Piercy: An Annotated Bibliography
Patricia Doherty

A Topical Index of Early U. S. Almanacs, 1776–1800
Robert K. Dodge, compiler

Joel Chandler Harris: An Annotated Bibliography of Criticism, 1977–1996, with Supplement, 1892–1976
R. Bruce Bickley, Jr. and Hugh T. Keenan

Women and Children of the Mills: An Annotated Guide to Nineteenth-Century American Textile Factory Literature
Judith A. Ranta

Ambrose Bierce: An Annotated Bibliography of Primary Sources
S. T. Joshi and David E. Schultz

Melville's Allusions to Religion: A Comprehensive Index and Glossary
Gail H. Coffler, compiler

The Literary and Historical Index to American Magazines, 1800–1850
Daniel A. Wells and Jonathan Daniel Wells

THE FOREIGN CRITICAL REPUTATION OF F. SCOTT FITZGERALD, 1980–2000

An Analysis and Annotated Bibliography

Linda C. Stanley

Bibliographies and Indexes in American Literature, Number 30

Westport, Connecticut
London

Library of Congress Cataloging-in-Publication Data

Stanley, Linda, 1940–
    The foreign critical reputation of F. Scott Fitzgerald, 1980–2000 : an analysis and
annotated bibliography / Linda C. Stanley.
       p.   cm. — (Bibliographies and indexes in American literature, ISSN 0742–6860 ; no. 30)
    Includes bibliographical references and index.
    ISBN 0–313–30885–3 (alk. paper)
    1. Fitzgerald, F. Scott (Francis Scott), 1896–1940—Criticism and interpretation—History.
  2. Fitzgerald, F. Scott (Francis Scott), 1896–1940—Appreciation—Foreign countries. 3.
Fitzgerald, F. Scott (Francis Scott), 1896–1940—Bibliography. I. Title. II. Series.
    PS3511.I9Z865   2004
    813′.52—dc22   2004044234

British Library Cataloguing in Publication Data is available.

Library of Congress Catalog Card Number: 2004044234
ISBN: 0–313–30885–3
ISSN: 0742–6860

First published in 2004

Praeger Publishers, 88 Post Road West, Westport, CT 06881
An imprint of Greenwood Publishing Group, Inc.
www.praeger.com

Printed in the United States of America

The paper used in this book complies with the
Permanent Paper Standard issued by the National
Information Standards Organization (Z39.48–1984).

10 9 8 7 6 5 4 3 2 1

Contents

Preface

Twenty years after the 1980 volume of *The Foreign Critical Reputation of F. Scott Fitzgerald: An Analysis and Annotated Bibliography* (Stanley, 1980) was published (also by Greenwood Press) and well into a technological revolution in both communication and on-line resources, most of the countries of the world, in Europe as well as in Asia, do not yet have periodical indexes or bibliographies that reliably indicate the scholarly work that has been accomplished in a given year. Britain, Germany and, more recently, France, as it attempts to fulfill the promise of the new *Bibliotheque Nationale de France,* do have useful indexing systems, but Italy does not, despite efforts to update the *Bibliografia sulla letteratura Americana.* Further, the *MLA International Index,* the *Annual Bibliography of English Language and Literature, the Abstract of English Studies,* and *the Essay and General Literature Index* do not include the same sources, nor do all indexes combined represent all the scholarly material written in a given year. The primary reason for the incompleteness of indexes or the lack of indexes at all is that much publishing abroad is conducted within each country's universities, and publications are not distributed throughout. The ultimate reason for the lack of indexes and the lack of scholarly distribution and is no doubt economic.

As with the compiling of the bibliography for the 1980 volume, I have had to make extensive personal contact with Fitzgerald scholars in all countries included here in order to compile a fairly comprehensive bibliography. This volume, then, will provide scholars in the countries included as well as interested scholars throughout the world with a significant representation of the present current scholarly work of Fitzgerald in several countries of Europe, Asia, and North America.

While the 1980 book represented the Fitzgerald scholarship from about 1925 to 1980 in Britain, France, Italy, Germany, and Japan, this current volume on work on Fitzgerald abroad in the past two decades includes as well scholarship on the writer in Denmark, Romania, Russia/Ukraine, India, and Canada. Personal contact proved to be the decisive factor in compiling chapters on Fitzgerald's reputation in Denmark, Romania, Russia/Ukraine, India, Japan, and even Canada. Efforts to locate material in the Serbo-Croatian speaking and other Eastern European countries, in Greece, in Norway and Sweden, in China and in Korea, as well as the Spanish- and Portuguese-speaking worlds proved only partially successful, in that scholars either spoke at conferences or wrote about Fitzgerald's reputation in their countries, but either the bibliographical sources themselves were partially or almost totally unavailable for annotation (Greece, Bulgaria, Serbo-Croatia, China, Korea) or a quest for scholars who might assist with additional sources and comment on their significance remained unfulfilled (Portugal).

The chapters on Britain, France, Italy, and Germany –four of the countries included in the 1980 edition—each begin with an analysis of Fitzgerald's reputation in that country from roughly 1980 until 2000. Although a chapter on Japan was included in the 1980 volume, the Japanese chapter here begins about 1969, the last year Japanese scholarship was available for annotation.in the earlier volume. The chapters on countries not included as separate chapters in the earlier edition—Denmark, Russia and the former countries of the USSR, Romania, India, and Canada, each begin in the year that Fitzgerald was first introduced into that country. Each analysis is based on the annotations in the bibliography as well as on personal contact with scholars abroad. Following the analysis is a list of translations and editions of Fitzgerald's work, arranged chronologically. The bibliography is divided into five sections, with entries arranged alphabetically within each section: Books: Full-Length Studies and Collections, Essays/Chapters/Notes/Conference Papers, Book Reviews/News Articles/Radio Programs, Dissertations, and Teacher/Student Guides and Editions. Most chapters also have a section on American or other Fitzgerald scholarship that has been translated into the language of the country involved.

Because so many of the sources are difficult to obtain and because many are in languages not readily accessible to English-language readers, an effort has been made to write as full an annotation as possible within the confines of space. Longer annotations usually reflect longer or more important work. Each annotation attempts to present as accurate a summary as possible of the writer's point of view. As James L. Harner writes in his *On Compiling an Annotated Bibliography*, published by the Modern Language Association, "Like a shadow, the précis delineates the substance of the body that casts it" (Harner, 1991, 24). Evaluative comments find their way into annotations only where absolutely necessary, as in the annotations composed for several of the Japanese books by scholars in Japan that consist solely of evaluation. Evaluation has been extensive in the analyses, however, both as to the prestige of the particular publication, where known, and to the critical insight or methodology of the writer.

Although French and German are at the command of many if not most scholars, other languages often are not, and therefore, in the interest of consistency, all quotations are in English.

Users of this bibliography may discover that an occasional scholar included in one nation's bibliography is in fact a citizen of another country and/or a professor at a university not located in the country under discussion. Also, there is the anomaly that the current major publisher of German-language translations of Fitzgerald is located in Switzerland. Scholarly goods, as other goods, increasingly cross national borders in our increasingly global society, and I have not been overly concerned to identify, much less to weed out these "impurities." A French periodical deciding to publish the work of a professor from the United States is still reflecting a decision made in France by an editor who believes French readers are interested in the scholar's work on a particular author.

Certainly not the recipients of a final thought but rather the source of my ongoing great gratitude and friendship are the people who have sustained me through the ten-year process of traveling, gathering, compiling, translating, annotating, and analyzing these national bodies of Fitzgerald scholarship: the many scholars abroad, the graduate students at the City University of New York Graduate School and University Center, librarians, faculty who sat on awards committees, grants officers and other staff, Fitzgerald Society members and Greenwood Press staff. I want to mention each of them individually with the intention of expressing a personal note of thanks. First, I include those who directly contributed to the analysis of their country's reception and/or assisted me in locating sources. I proceed geographically according to the arrangement of chapters in the book and include professional titles where I know them.

From Great Britain, Andrew Hook, emeritus Bradley professor of English literature at Glasgow University and author of two books on Fitzgerald (one forthcoming as I write), met me at Glasgow University in 1993 to speak about Fitzgerald and later spoke at the 1996 Princeton Centennial Conference on Fitzgerald's reputation in Britain.

From France, both Jacques Tournier, novelist and translator of *The Great Gatsby* and *Tender Is the Night* and many Fitzgerald short story collections, and Michel Viel, professor of linguistics at Sorbonne IV, who has written several articles on the author, met me in enchanting restaurants in Paris in April 1998 to talk about Fitzgerald in France. Others who assisted include Roger Grenier, novelist, who has also written a Fitzgerald biography into which he interjects his own relationship with the writer, and Roger Asselineau, a Hemingway scholar and emeritus professor of North American Literature and Civilization at the Sorbonne, spoke at the Hemingway/Fitzgerald Conference in Paris in 1994 and has been generous with his own private bibliography of French publications on Fitzgerald. Elisabeth Bouzonviller, University of St. Elienne, has written two books on Fitzgerald, and Jeff Storey, of the University of Nice, has written two essays. Marie-Agnès Gay, University of Jean-Moulin; Pascale Antolin-Pirès, Bordeaux III University, and Pascal Bardet, University of Toulouse, have also each written a book on Fitzgerald. I thank these young scholars for their assistance as well. Also from France, André Bleikasten, University of Strasbourg, a Faulkner scholar, kindly responded to my queries.

From Italy, Donatella Izzo, who is professor of American language and literature at the Istituto Universitario Orientale in Naples, has been of inestimable help with the Italian analysis and has even searched through Roman bookstores for me. She has become a good friend over the years of our e-mail conversations. Sergio Perosa, professor of Anglo-American Literature at the University of Venice, and writer of the 1961 *L'arte di F. Scott Fitzgerald*, the first European work on Fitzgerald translated into English, spoke on Fitzgerald's reputation at the Princeton Centennial Conference. Doc Rossi, professor at John Cabot University in Rome, organized the Rome Fitzgerald Centennial Conference and contributed several papers for this volume. Winnie Bevilacqua, professor at the University of Torino, contributed her preface to an edition of *The Great Gatsby*, and Piero Pignata answered my queries as well as provided newspaper articles.

From Germany, Horst Kruse, emeritus professor of English from the University of Muenster and a leading Fitzgerald scholar, has been a guiding force in the shaping of the German bibliography and analysis. Without his assistance, I shudder even now to think of the German language errors that I would have made. Udo Hebel, Chair, American Studies, Institut für Anglistik und Amerikanistik, Universität Regensburg, spoke about Fitzgerald's German reputation at the First International Fitzgerald Conference at Hofstra University in 1992, the event that got me hooked on this project again.

A Hemingway scholar, Claus Theilgaard, who was listed in the program of the International Hemingway and Fitzgerald Conference in Paris in 1994, graciously scoured libraries and bookstores for me both in Copenhagen and in all the European countries where he vacationed. Claus Secher, professor and head of the department of literary history of the Royal School of Librarianship in Copenhagen, spoke on Fitzgerald's reputation in Denmark at both the Princeton and Nice Conferences and has continued to answer queries on line. His conference presentations contributed significantly to my analysis of Fitzerald's reputation in Denmark.

As for Romania, Virgil Mihaiu, professor at the Academia de Muzica and also poet and jazz musician, has been a most delightful correspondent who performed his poetry and jazz in 2001 at my institution, at Hofstra University, and at several others in the New York metropolitan region. A chapter of Virgil's doctoral dissertation served as the basis for my analysis of the Romanian reputation to the extent that I have given him credit as co-author. Felicia Antip, Romanian journalist, also responded to my queries with several of her articles on Fitzgeraid.

Svetlana Voitiuk, assoc. professor of English at L'viv University in Ukraine, did yeoman's work in securing and annotating the Russian/Ukrainian sources and providing a context for analysis at the international Fitzgerald conferences at Hofstra and Princeton universities in 1994 and 1996 respectively.

In India, Somdatta Mandal, Associate Professor of English at Visva-Bharati University, Santiniketan, has been a powerhouse of assistance in sending me the many volumes to originate in India in celebration of the Fitzgerald Centennial. She also spoke at the Princeton Conference, and I am indebted for her assistance in writing the Indian analysis.

What to say about the incredibly industrious assistance I received from members of the Japanese Fitzgerald Society? Sadao Nagaoka, currently of Teikyo University and former president of the Fitzgerald Society of Japan, whom I first met at the Hofstra Conference, has a bibliography in his home of over 600 items written on Fitzgerald in Japan since the 1930s, and he made many written in English available to me. Most of the annotations here were composed by the writers of the works being annotated because they were unavailable to me for translation and annotation. In order to obtain them, I merely had to send an e-mail request to Seiwa Fujitani, professor and editor of the newsletter of the Fitzgerald Society of Japan, who secured so many summaries of the work of Society members that I had no room to include them all, and I apologize for that. The late Kiyohiko Tsuboi, who taught at Kobe Women's University and was president of the Fitzgerald Society of Japan, spoke on Fitzgerald's reputation at the 1996 Princeton Conference. Yukiko Tokunaga, associate professor, faculty of politics, economics, and law, Osaka International University, studied for a year at the Graduate Center of the City University of New York, and we talked about Fitzgerald in the GSUC cafeteria one April day in 2001. From her, I first learned of Fitzgerald's influence on Haruki Murakami and through Murakami's work on the young people of Japan.

My latest Fitzgerald acquaintance is Michael Nowlin, associate professor of American Literature at the University of Victoria in Canada. Prof. Nowlin has cheerfully posted me several times, giving me a context for the Canadian analysis, a context I reluctantly admit that I needed, despite my proximity to his country. Thanks, Prof Nowlin.

I also need very much to thank the Professional Staff Congress of the City University of New York for making my work possible these ten years with the assistance of seven PSC-CUNY Research Awards. The early awards financed travel to Europe over several summers, and all awards provided funds for students from the Graduate School and University Center of the City University of New York to translate and annotate many of the essays and books written in their own languages. I thank from France, Nathalie Fouyer; from Italy, Giorgio Galbussera; from Germany, Anja Grothe, who also reads Russian and helped me with annotations from Russia and Ukraine; also for assisting with the German, I thank Hanna Hechinger and Joel Wagner. Assisting with the Japanese articles available in this country in Japanese, Keiko Miyajima was most gracious. Annotating the Danish articles was my friend and former colleague, Doris

Asmundsson (professor emeritus, QCC). Also assisting with the Danish was Terese Anthony. GSUC comparative literature doctoral student, Robert Cowan, became my general factotum by virtue of his multi-lingual talents. And Mahwash Shoaib worked for many years entering the bibliography items into the computer.

Marcia Kovler, QCC Inter-library loan librarian became my great pal over many summers of acquiring foreign books and articles from all over the country or allowing me to cry on her shoulder when they weren't available. Mali Daum Katz, director of sponsored programs at QCC, patiently assisted me when PSC Awards went on-line.

Greenwood Press has also patiently waited for this second volume.. I thank George Butler and Elizabeth Potenza, my editors, for going through it with me.

Almost up to her wedding day, Isabel Pipolo formatted the camera-ready copy. I couldn't have found a more efficient and patient formatter than she.

I also must thank the officers of the F. Scott Fitzgerald Society, Jackson Bryer and Ruth Prigozy. If they and Alan Margolies, since retired, hadn't begun organizing and administering the International Fitzgerald Conferences every two years since 1992, I never would have entertained this project nor brought it to conclusion. *The Fitzgerald Society Newsletter* has come to be a valuable source of foreign articles and books written on Fitzgerald.

I also want to thank Sheena Gillespie, chairperson of my department and very good friend, who has been mostly patient with me.

Upon the completion of the first volume in 1980, I felt confident that it was complete and error-free. I have learned subsequently that there will be errors, large and small, in a project of this kind and scope. Any errors are my responsibility and mine alone.

REFERENCES

Stanley, Linda C. *The Foreign Critical Reputation of F. Scott Fitzgerald: An Analysis and Annotated Bibliography.* Westport, CT: Greenwood Press, 1980.

James L. Harner. *On Compiling an Annotated Bibliograph*, Revised Edition. New York: The Modern Language Association of America, 1991.

Introduction

The introduction to the 1980 volume of Fitzgerald's foreign reputation (Stanley 1980) examines the writer's reception in Britain, France, Germany, Italy, and Japan from approximately 1925 to 1980 and determines that it evolved through three stages:

The first and earliest stage, dating from Fitzgerald's first appearance in translation to approximately the time of his American renaissance (the late 1940s), is characterized by an initial lack of comment, either in reviewers' columns or in important studies of American literature. Casual references or negative comments also typify this division. Beginning with the renewed interest in Fitzgerald in America in the 1940s and early 1950s, a second stage in foreign critical reaction set in with isolated critics and reviewers praising Fitzgerald. By the 1960s, perplexed (foreign) scholars were attempting to explain the lack of greater . . . interest in a writer whom American critics regarded so highly. The third stage, still-on going, is a developing recognition by foreign scholars of his contribution to world literature. In the late 1960s and 1970s, scholarly attention has been more frequent and consistent. Critics abroad are beginning to recognize what Michel Fabre has written: 'I believe the current interest will remain because Fitzgerald's best novels are first-rate artistically and will become classics, like Stendhal's or Balzac's" ([Fabre, Jan. 1975] Stanley 1980 xii).

After gathering and analyzing translations and editions of his work, critical studies, and reviews from the 1980s and 1990s, I have sought in this current volume to address, then, whether the interest of 1975, as expressed by Michel Fabre, a now retired eminent French scholar of American literature, has persisted or perhaps even expanded so that Fitzgerald is cited alongside Faulkner and Hemingway, Stendhal and Balzac as a major writer.

The 1980 volume indicated three ingredients necessary to furthering Fitzgerald's foreign reputation: a gifted translator, a respectable publisher, and the support of a leading scholar. Translation in the non-English speaking countries remains a problem two decades later, as the introductions to the various countries' work testify, but significant accomplishments have also been made. Japan has produced multiple translations of most of Fitzgerald's work in an effort to best represent his virtually untranslatable style. France has produced three translations of *The Great Gatsby*, two in the 1990s, both by gifted translators whose work has received favorable reviews: Jacques Tournier (Asselineau, 1 July 1998) and Michel Viel (F116). Fernanda Pivano's translations in Italy have done yeoman's work over the decades, but scholars assert Fitzgerald's works need retranslating. Evgenia Kalashnikov is a major Russian translator who has translated most of Fitzgerald's work, although *The Beautiful and Damned* has not yet been translated into Russian. Romanian readers have been fortunate in Mircea Ivănescu, one of Romania's leading poets, who has translated both *The Great Gatsby* and *Tender Is the Night*. In Denmark, however, *This Side of Paradise, The Beautiful and Damned*, and *The Last Tycoon* still remain to be translated. France, Italy, and Romania have had translated virtually everything Fitzgerald wrote, including, in Italy and France, *The Cruise of the Rolling Junk*.

The publishers of Fitzgerald's work abroad are now for the most part very respectable. In the last two decades, Gallimard and Belmond have published Fitzgerald in France, and the Swiss publisher Diogenes has published most of Fitzgerald's work in German translation. Mondadori has always published Fitzgerald in Italy. In Britain, impressive recent collections of the author's works have been published by the Cambridge and Oxford University Presses. Hudozhestvennaya Literatura and Inostrannaya Literatura, both publishers of the Soviet state, were responsible for encouraging the gifted Evgenia Kalashnikov to translate his work into Russian. In the 1990s, virtually all of Romania's publishers entered the market with translations of Fitzgerald's works. Myriad publishers have also published Fitzgerald in Japan. In Denmark, Gyldendals has sluggishly persisted in publishing the author's work.

As for support by scholars and other writers, well-known and highly-regarded British writer Angela Carter (B90) and esteemed scholar Tony Tanner (B77) have furthered Fitzgerald's reputation in their country. In France, noted novelist Roger Grenier has written on the author (F38), as has novelist and translator Jacques Tournier (F75, F107, F108). Several French scholars, including Michel Viel (F41, F110-F115, F148) and André Bleikasten, the Faulkner scholar (F53, F54), have also written and/or spoken about Fitzgerald. André Le Vot (F40, F85-F90, F133-F135, F175, F176) and Michel Fabre (F164), the foremost Fitzgerald scholars in France two decades ago, continue to speak and/or write about him, and their earlier Fitzgerald work has recently been republished (F36, F39). In 2000, several monographs on Fitzgerald appeared, written by young French academics (F32-F37).

Since the 1960s, Horst Kruse, now retired from the University of Muenster, has been indefatigable in furthering Fitzgerald's reputation in Germany (G57-G61), as has scholar Sergio Perosa in Italy (It45, It46). Italian poet, Anna

Cascella, has both written and spoken on Fitzgerald (It24, It34), while Romanian poet Mircea Ivănescu has both translated and written about him (Ro2, Ro6, Ro32, Ro33). Influential Romanian scholars Dan Grigorescu (Ro31) and Virgil Stanciu (Ro48) have also published significant Fitzgerald studies. In both Denmark and Japan, writers have also led the way: Danish writers Anders Bodelsen (D18), Bo Green Jensen (D22, D23), Klaus Rifbjerg (D26, D27), and Haruki Murakami, the well-known Japanese novelist (J85), have taken it upon themselves to further fellow writer Fitzgerald's reputation in their respective countries. Somdatta Mandal (In5) and Mohan Ramanan (In6) found Fitzgerald's Centennial in 1996 an opportunity each to publish a collection of essays on Fitzgerald by Indian scholars. Novelist Malcolm Lowry's attempt to script a film of *Tender Is the Night* has generated much scholarly interest in Fitzgerald in Canada (C1, C8, C13-16, C21, C26, C30). What is happening to Fitzgerald studies in Russia and Ukraine in the last decade remains unclear.

While inadequate translations of his poetic, polysemic prose will continue to hinder full appreciation of Fitzgerald abroad, efforts to produce improved translations continue unabated. Respected publishers are constantly producing new editions of his work. Distinguished and young scholars both are writing about him. Is Fitzgerald yet considered a classic? The various scholars give differing answers. Andrew Hook cites traces of anti-Americanism in Britain as still hindering respect for Fitzgerald, whose novels, of course, are primarily about America (B67). Horst Kruse in Germany believes Fitzgerald has come into his own although Hemingway and Faulkner still attract more scholars (G57). Roger Asselineau, Hemingway scholar in France, analyzes it this way: Hemingway has received the Pléiade Award, but Fitzgerald has not. Of course, Faulkner hasn't received the Award either, and he is more well-regarded in France than Hemingway (Asselineau, 1998). Virgil Mihaiu writes that Fitzgerald's reputation in Romania is more or less satisfactory but that no work has been done on him as significant as that of Sorin Alexandrescu in his 1969 monograph on Faulkner (Ro39). In Italy, Sergio Perosa claims that Fitzgerald scholars are in between a public that loves Fitzgerald and writers that revere and emulate him, still trying to persuade other scholars about Fitzgerald's worth (It45). Claus Secher argues that Danish scholars who do support Fitzgerald love him intensely because he incorporates their own ambiguous love of America (D30).

How one answers this question about the stature of Fitzgerald abroad also depends on the position one has taken vis à vis recent critical approaches to literature. In the 1980 volume, for example, two opposing trends in European Fitzgerald criticism were cited in an overview of the writer's reception well into the third stage of the late 1960 and 1970s.

> One is the tendency to turn to American works on Fitzgerald for analyses, particularly textual criticism. The second trend is for European criticism to reflect European intellectual preoccupations, such as Marxism and existentialism. In pursuing the second trend, European scholars may contribute

something new, and therefore valuable to the body of Fitzgerald scholarship (Stanley 1980 xii).

This current volume might suggest, then, whether recent European intellectual preoccupations have presented something new and valuable for Fitzgerald studies. In the context of several of the more recent trends in approaches to Fitzgerald's work that are represented here, primarily those of American studies and of the continuing influence of French semiotic and structural as well as post-structural theories, it might be necessary first to reconsider whether the question about Fitzgerald's greatness posed in the first volume will remain a relevant concern. The question "Is Fitzgerald a great author?" has to a considerable extent been replaced by the structuralist/semiotic approach that asks "How successfully can *Gatsby*'s signs and representations be read by other cultures as descriptions of themselves?" And, conversely, the question asked by American studies' scholars: In their responses to Fitzgerald's *oeuvre*, "do foreign scholars reveal new paradigms for thinking about the United States?" (Desmond and Dominguez, 1996, 485). Or a question derived from the various offshoots of post-structuralism: Can the act of reading "write" this literary text? Although the close textual analysis of the new critical approach still characterizes a majority of the articles written on Fitzgerald in the last two decades, it is itself being challenged by foreign scholars influenced by one or more of these recent trends.

While the introduction to each country's reception categorizes current Fitzgerald scholarship according to these trends, some mention here of who might be considered key representatives of each would include the work of the following scholars: From Britain, Geoff Cox (B55), Richard Godden (B60, B61) and Brian Way (B36, B79) critique American commodity culture, Cox and Godden through the critical lens of Jacques Lacan and Louis Althusser. Pascale Antolin-Pirès (F32), Elisabeth Bouzonviller (F34, F35), and Marie-Agnès Gay (F37) have all written book-length studies utilizing the perspectives of various French theorists, including differing combinations of Barthes, Lacan, Foucault, Julia Kristeva, Georges Bataille, René Girard, Philippe Sollers, Girard Genette, and P. Hamon.

In a 1985 work in Italy, Paola Cabibbo and Donatella Izzo, influenced by structural and semiological analysis, read *Gatsby* as pointing both backwards to modernism and forward to post-modernism (It23). Lacan and Althusser have influenced Bernd Herzogenrath in Germany in his interpretation of Gatsby's desire for Daisy as that for an enchanted object (Lacan's object a) (G44). Udo Hebel borrows from Derrida, Barthes, Foucault, Kristeva, Pfister, and Genette in his discussion of textuality and intertextuality in *This Side of Paradise* (G23). In an American Studies vein, Tilman Höss describes *Gatsby* as a parable of the American Dream in a consumer society (G25), and Jens Peter Becker has written three articles on Fitzgerald and American popular culture of the 1920s (G33-G35). In Romania, Virgil Stanciu was influenced by Greimas and Courtes of the French school of semiology in writing his sophisticated study of Fitzgerald's work (Ro48).

Several articles from India by Vijay Sharma (In52) and Sherine Upot (In55) reflect feminist theory, narratology studies and post-structural work, while Prasenjit Biswas (In13) and V. C. Harris (In23) use Barthes and Derrida respectively. Japanese scholars have produced a very large body of essays using an American Studies approach, many on gender, several on the new economy of the 1920s, others on urbanization and its discontents, still others on consumption, accumulation, commercialism and the lure of financial success. Others in this vein include essays on class, on the search for identity, and on the societal effects of new inventions like the automobile and the telephone. Canadian scholarship features articles on race, class, and sexual identity, including Keith Fraser's well-known article on the ambiguity of sexual identity in *The Great Gatsby* (C5) and Michael Nowlin's on the relationship between modernism and feminized men (C18).

In conclusion, Fitzgerald's work lends itself to the global explosion of American studies, and both India and Russia are seeking to find their cultures revealed in American literature, including Fitzgerald's. His porous novels provide space to be "written" by readers. Whether new forms for looking at American culture will emerge from Fitzgerald studies is not yet fully realized. Donatella Izzo's and Michael Nowlin's comments about younger scholars being more interested in ethnic, African-American, and women writers (Izzo, 16 Sept. 2001 and Nowlin, 8 Sept. 2003) are balanced by the several young French scholars who have utilized French post-structural theory to produce monographs on Fitzgerald's work (F32-36). Continued university study is assured in all countries included here.

As for popular acceptance in these countries, scholars in Germany, Denmark, Romania, and Japan continue to cite the impact of the 1974 Jack Clayton film of *The Great Gatsby* on the average citizen (G57, D30, Ro39, J85). Piero Pignata in Italy asserts that in the past decade, Fitzgerald has been the object of newspaper articles that go unrecorded even in the computer era (Pignata, 1995). In his paper at the Princeton Centennial Conference, Andrew Hook presents a computer-assisted study of the numerous mentions of Fitzgerald in British journals and newspapers read by the university-educated segment of society, indicating the author has permeated the cultural consciousness of Britain (B67).

Fitzgerald's reputation has improved and/or solidified over the past two decades, and indications for the future seem to be reassuring. Even as critical thought and literature itself move in new directions, the more seminal scholarship written on Fitzgerald in the last twenty years suggests his work will have a permanent place in world literature because it is both a profound cultural critique of American culture as American culture continues to become more globally pervasive and also great artistically as it proves endlessly responsive to critical approaches, be they textual study, area study, or study of the more theoretical structural, semiological, post-structural and psychoanalytical bents. Even the societal upheavals and change in Russia, Romania, and India have found scholars susceptible to the depths in Fitzgerald's work. Perhaps no final decision will ever be made about Fitzgerald's "greatness" because his work like the world's work is simply too protean to be encapsulated in any formula that denotes stasis, even the stasis of being placed in the pantheon of the great.

This volume too must remain porous, with an introduction but no conclusion. Reader, write your own evaluation of Fitzgerald's global greatness as you read the efforts expended here by scholars in countries representing a broad swath of the planet.

REFERENCES

Asselineau, Roger. Letter to author. 1 July 1998.

Desmond, Jane C. and Virginia R. Domínguez. "Resituating American Studies in a Critical Internationalism." *American Quarterly* 48:3 (Sept. 1996): 485.

Fabre, Michel. Letter to author. Jan. 1975.

Izzo, Donatella. E-mail to author. 16 Sept. 2001.

Nowlin, Michael. E-mail to author. 20 June 2003.

Pignata, Piero. Letter to author. 29 Oct. 1995.

Stanley, Linda C. *The Foreign Critical Reputation of F. Scott Fitzgerald: An Analysis and Annotated Bibliography.* (Westport, CT: Greenwood Press, 1980.

Parenthetical citations to entry numbers refer to annotated references.

BIBLIOGRAPHY

Britain

In his Introduction to his *Contemporary Criticism*, Malcolm Bradbury characterizes the approach of British literary critics of the 1960s: "the British critic," he writes, "is primarily an empiricist," concerned with giving "a personal and detailed response to a given text or writer, as opposed to the abstract substantialism of an aesthetic or a poetics" (Bradbury, 1970, 27). The British critic lays stress on "entering sympathetically into a work, and on the imaginative power of literature to lead him towards experience and insight" (Bradbury, 1970, 27). For this critic, literature is a source of moral and cultural values, a judgment which reflects the influence of F. R. Leavis and the *Scrutiny* school. As a result, well into the third period of Fitzgerald criticism abroad (1960-1980), British critics did not show much interest in Fitzgerald, who was considered to offer little in the way of moral values. They concluded that *The Great Gatsby* gives rise to intellectual doubts even if on the level of poetry "the resolution achieved is wholly satisfying" (Millgate, 1962, 336).

Furthermore, the British considered their literature and culture far superior to that of the United States; American culture and literature were quite foreign to them. As Andrew Hook, emeritus Bradley professor of English literature at Glasgow University, has said, "Today we tend to underestimate completely just how entrenched and determined was the traditional British prejudice and hostility towards every aspect of American culture" (B69). Although by the 1960s, as in other European countries, British interest in Fitzgerald had begun to expand, it would take another two decades before this interest increased substantially.

Since 1980, when well-known British writer Angela Carter proclaimed *The Great Gatsby* "the most perfect romance . . . of high capitalism" (B90), British criticism has entered a new phase, shifting from an emphasis on values to a critique of capitalism and other aspects of contemporary culture. Prof. Hook attributes the shift to the introduction of cultural studies courses: "When courses in American Studies and American Literature at last began to appear over a generation ago in British universities—and in many of the old polytechnics and colleges, they proved tremendously popular. Students were eager to read American authors, to learn about American life and society. Fitzgerald answered both demands. Hence he always appeared in the new courses, a regular set-text" (B69).

The number of editions of Fitzgerald's work that has been published in Britain between 1980 and 2000 supports Hook's contention that Fitzgerald has been more widely accepted in that country. As opposed to the 18 editions published in the 1960s and 1970s, 25 new editions of his fiction, essays, poems and sayings have appeared in this latest period: one of *Gatsby*, five of *Tender Is the Night*, five short story collections, two of *The Crack-Up*, and one each of *This Side of Paradise*, *The Beautiful and Damned*, *The Love of the Last Tycoon*, *Trimalchio*, his poems, and his sayings.

Over 50 British books and essays have been written on Fitzgerald in this period including three monographs, a collection of essays, a four-volume collection of critical assessments from Britain and the United States, and a study of this assessment. In addition, 11 books written in the United States have also been published in Britain as well as a translation of the biography by André Le Vot, the French Fitzgerald scholar.

Thirteen of the 40 British monographs and essays written in this period focus on *The Great Gatsby*; seven on *Tender Is the Night*; three or four on each of his other novels, *The Crack-Up*, and the stories. While British scholars continue to take traditional critical approaches to his work—emphasizing biographical details or questions of influence, for example—several of the critical works are written from an American studies vantage point: e.g., on class, gender, popular culture, and/or cultural history.

Two of the authors of the articles who write from this area studies approach, Geof Cox (B55) and Richard Godden (B60, B61), cite the influence of French Marxist theorist Louis Althusser on their work. Althusser came to the attention of British scholars through his influence on *Screen*, the British film journal, which appeared in the early 1970s and came to be immensely influential. *Screen* sought, after Althusser, to theorize "the encounter of Marxism and psychoanalysis on the terrain of semiotics" (Heath, 1981, 201). The question posed by Althusser's work is "How does a people come to subject themselves to the dominant ideologies of their societies?" He uses the image of a child seeing his identity in his reflection in a mirror from Jacques Lacan's psychoanalytic theory of the mirror stage of development. Likewise, individuals see their identities as reflected in the signs and social practices of the culture in which they live. Subjection to these images makes them subjects while at the same time constituting them as free agents in making choices (Althusser 1971). An ensuing debate over whether individuals have a choice or not in how they respond to the signs of their culture led the Open University in Britain to offer a popular culture course that enrolled over 5,000 students between 1982 and 1987.

In his essay, "Literary Pragmatics: A New Discipline (B55)," Geof Cox sees culture itself as a potential major commodity of a nation's economy. Literary pragmatics thus include social expectations as well as linguistic constraints on the communication situation. The varying language levels of the British editions of *The Great Gatsby* enhance class differentiation. Thus, Cox claims that all readings of *Gatsby* are distorted by the ideology of commodity culture (B55). Brian Way sees *Tender Is the Night* as a passionately imaginative critique of capitalism (B36, B79). In two essays on Fitzgerald's novels published in 1990 in his *Fictions of Capitalism: The American Novel from James to Mailer*, Richard Godden is also concerned with the economic implications of Fitzgerald's novels. In "*The Great Gatsby*, Glamour on the Turn," Godden asserts that while Nick is romanticizing Gatsby, Gatsby indicates that he himself understands that he is merely a commodity in a capitalist society when he asserts of Daisy that "Her voice is full of money" (B60). In "Money Makes Manners Make Man Make Woman: *Tender Is the Night*, a Familiar Romance?" Godden says the novel is "balanced between residual and emergent economic forms." Fitzgerald uses the figure of the psychiatrist, a "professional guardian of the unthinkable," as his protagonist because the "history of what a class finds unthinkable is one measure of how that class maintains its integrity despite economic transition. As economic forces dismembered individuals, psychoanalytic theory was developed to explain how the subdivided person held together. For Fitzgerald, then, the psychiatrist is guardian of both the subconscious and the bourgeoisie. Dick loses interest in himself as an individual because he recognizes himself as a subject produced by forces in the capitalist society which he has come to despise (B61).

In his 1995 essay on gender in a society in transition, "Newnesses of Beginning: The Violent Phantasies of Willa Cather and F. Scott Fitzgerald," Ian Bell claims that fantasies about and actual damage to the female body in both novels result from a need to contain sexual threat by characters in a society debating immigration, assimilation, and the status of Native Americans. Nick Carraway, in a search for origins, sees women as nurturers and resorts to "wonder" both to "aestheticize the material bases" and to mark the possibility of new beginnings, just as Gatsby restructures his origins by rejecting his patrilineal heritage. But breasts are ravaged in both novels by "the colonizing instinct which seeks the authority of origination" (B50).

Four books and essays are primarily biographical or comment on the autobiographical elements in Fitzgerald's work. A. Robert Lee writes that Fitzgerald's reincarnations of himself in his own novels reappear in stories about him in the writings of others and also in the characters of other fiction (B30, B68, B69). Andrew Hook says of Fitzgerald that he "discovered that the kind of man he was, and the kind of writer he needed to be, were difficult to reconcile. The recognition and exploration of this problem then becomes a unifying subtext in a great deal of his writing" (B66). Through Fitzgerald's letters to Maxwell Perkins, Arnold Goldman traces the waxing and waning possibility of a Fitzgerald autobiography (B62). And Harold Weatherby publishes his mother's account of her girlhood friend, Zelda Fitzgerald (B113).

Although Marc Dolan is an American scholar, the Cambridge University periodical *Journal of American Studies* published his essay "The (Hi)story of their Lives: Mythic Autobiography and 'The Lost Generation'" in 1993. From a cultural history vantage point, Dolan sees autobiography as a "rhetorically constructed account of the relation of narrated past to narrating present within the life of a particular individual." He finds a structural similarity in the stories of members of the Lost Generation who, like Fitzgerald in *The Crack-Up*, begin their accounts in the "heady" days after the war, skip the middle section that corresponds to their post-war experience, and conclude with the despondency following the onset of the Depression. They elided this middle period because it didn't evoke an individual response but rather a collective one as Americans responded to technological advance and a growing consumer society (B57).

Three studies focus primarily on the influence of other writers on Fitzgerald and two others on his influence on other writers. Harold Beaver believes *Tender Is the Night* is Fitzgerald's most Jamesian fiction (B49). Owen Dudley Edwards argues that the final female rejection of Anthony in *This Side of Paradise* was undeniably influenced by George Ponderevo in H. G. Wells's novel *Tono-Bungay* and the fall of Uncle Teddy Ponderevo influenced Fitzgerald in *The Great Gatsby* (B58). And Paul Bourget, the 19th century French writer, in his book *Outre-Mer,* wrote of the American "deification of woman . . . as a supreme glory of the national spirit" and, according to Jackie Vickers, influenced Edith Wharton in framing the character of Lily Bart and through his reading of her novel, Fitzgerald saw possibilities for his characterization of Nicole Diver (B78). Still others mention his influence by or on other writers in passing: Poe, Hawthorne, James, Conrad, Spengler, Keats, Willa Cather, Frank Norris, T. S. Eliot.

Three other scholars trace Fitzgerald's influence on three American writers. Jeffrey Hart believes Mark Goodman in writing *The Legend of Hobey Baker* was influenced by *The Great Gatsby,* as Baker was a Princeton graduate whom Goodman presents, like Gatsby, as a gentleman *manqué* (B65). Norman Macleod sees enough correspondences between *Goodbye, Columbus* and *The Great Gatsby* to indicate that Philip Roth was influenced by Fitzgerald's novel (B71). And David Seed asserts that David and Rilda Westlake in Carl Van Vechten's *Scenes from Contemporary New York Life* are based on Scott and Zelda (B75).

Other traditional criticism in this period includes John Coyle's mythic study "Meaulnes, Gatsby and the Possibilities of Romance" in which he sees Alain-Fournier's novel *Le Grand Meaulnes* and *The Great Gatsby* as "parallel exercises in . . . writing a romance in a post-romantic age" (B56). Tony Tanner, in his introduction to the Penguin Twentieth-Century Classics edition of *Gatsby,* remarks that the novel is "word-perfect and inexhaustible. [It] is, I believe, the most perfectly crafted work of fiction to have come out of America." Much of his essay examines Fitzgerald's craft through a New Critical lens (B77). David Monk writes that Fitzgerald was "painstakingly aware of the weight stylistics effects, in their own right, can bear" (B73). Asserting that Fitzgerald's *Post* stories contain self-parody, Brian Harding claims they are radical (B64). Finally, in his monograph, Thomas Stavola claims that "Erik Erikson's psychoanalytic theories, rooted in the belief that personal growth and communal culture are inseparable, have seemed to offer a uniquely appropriate means for examining the American identity crisis of Scott Fitzgerald and those of the major male characters in his four completed novels" (B34).

While this British criticism, particularly that in the American studies tradition, does contribute fresh visions of Fitzgerald's work, whether it "decenters" what has been written in the United States, as Jane C. Desmond and Virginia R. Domínguez suggest in their 1996 "Resituating American Studies in a Critical Internationalism?," is open to opinion (Desmond and Dominguez, 1996, 485). Certainly, its impression on Great Britain has been substantial, particularly Godden's work which Nicolas Tredell selects to discuss in his 1997 Columbia Critical Guide, *F. Scott Fitzgerald: "The Great Gatsby"* (B35). However, Andrew Hook does not think that there has been a radical change in the traditional British critical estimate of Fitzgerald: "British critics are not now saying that Fitzgerald is a twentieth-century heavyweight, like Joyce, or Kafka, or Thomas Mann. Certainly, *Gatsby* has gained almost universal recognition as a novel of extraordinary beauty, and *Tender Is the Night* is admired as a novel of power and emotional intensity" (B67). He does believe, however, that the change in Fitzgerald's reputation is not so much a matter of a major critical revaluation as that he has become a part of normal British cultural consciousness.

For a paper presented at the Centennial Conference on Fitzgerald at Princeton in 1996, with the assistance of the new information technology, Hook examined British newspapers with a generally more educated readership for references to Fitzgerald. As a result of his research, he concludes that "Fitzgerald has become a standard British author [in] that he has become an almost automatic point of reference for significant areas of American life and society: the New America of the 1920s, the glamour of Jazz Age America; . . . the writer best able to sum up some aspect of American experience in a single phrase or sentence—in all of these areas and more, Fitzgerald has become a kind of touchstone, almost inevitably summoned for reference or allusion when any of these topics are in question" (B67).

REFERENCES

Althusser, Louis. "Ideology and Ideological State Apparatuses." *Lenin and Philosophy and Other Essays.* London: New Left Books, 1971.

Bradbury, Malcolm. "Introduction: The State of Criticism Today." *Contemporary Criticism.* New York: St. Martin's Press, 1970.

Desmond, Jane C. and Viriginia R. Dominguez. "Resituating American Studies in a Critical Internationalism." *American Quarterly* 48.3 (Sept. 1996): 475-490.

Heath, Stephen. "Jaws, Ideology and Film Theory." *Popular Television and Film* (1981): 201.

Millgate, Michael. "Scott Fitzgerald as Social Novelist: Statement and Technique in *The Great Gatsby.*" *Modern Language Review* (July 1962): 335-339.

Parenthetical citations to entry numbers refer to annotated references in this chapter.

EDITIONS

B1. Fitzgerald, F. Scott. *This Side of Paradise.* Collins, 1921. Reprinted: Collins, 1923, 1927; Grey Walls Press, 1948; *The Bodley Head Fitzgerald,* Vol. III, 1960, 1961, 1965, 1969; Penguin, 1963, 1965, 1967, 1970, 1974; Ed. Patrick O'Donnell. Twentieth Century Classics, 1990, 1997; Ed. James L. West. Cambridge Edition of the Works of F. Scott Fitzgerald, 1995, 1996; Everyman's Library, 1996; Dover, 1996; Modern Library. Random House (Bailey Distrib.), 1997.

B2. Fitzgerald, F. Scott. *The Beautiful and Damned.* Collins, 1922. Reprinted: Collins, 1922, 1925; *The Bodley Head Fitzgerald,* Vol. IV, 1961, 1967, 1983 (Revised); Penguin, 1966, 1971, 1974; Twentieth Century Classics, 1989; Ed. Alan Margolies. Oxford World's Classics. Oxford UP, 1998. xxvi, 359.

B3.   Fitzgerald, F. Scott. *The Great Gatsby*. Chatto and Windus, 1926.
       Reprinted: 1927; Grey Walls Press, 1948, 1949; Penguin, 1950, 1954,
       1958, 1961, 1962, 1963, 1964, 1966, 1967, 1968 (twice), 1969 (twice);
       Twentieth Century Classics, 1990; Eds. David Crystal and Derek Strange.
       Penguin Authentic Texts, 1991 and 1992; Penguin Popular Classics,
       1994; *The Bodley Head Fitzgerald*, Vol. I, 1958, 1960, 1963, 1966, 1967,
       1970, 1983 (Revised); Folio Society, 1968; Ed. Matthew Bruccoli,
       Cambridge Edition of the Works of F. Scott Fitzgerald; Cambridge UP,
       1991, 1995 (Cambridge Literature 5); Everyman's Library, 1991; Dent,
       Everyman's (Ed. Jeffrey Meyers), 1993; New Longman Literature, 1991;
       Longman Fiction 5, 1993; Macmillan Stories to Remember, 1992 (Ed.
       Mary Tomalin); Abacus: 1992; Wordsworth Classics, 1992; Bloomsbury
       Classics, 1994; Compact, 1994; Ed. Ruth Prigozy. Oxford World's
       Classics. Oxford UP, 1998. xiv, 151; Essential Penguin Series.
       Penguin, 1998. 176.

B4.   Fitzgerald, F. Scott. *Tender Is the Night (original version)*. Chatto and
       Windus, 1934, 1936; Grey Walls Press, 1948; *The Bodley Head
       Fitzgerald*, Vol. II, 1959, 1961,1965, 1969, 1983 (Revised); Revised
       version: Grey Walls Press, 1953; Penguin, 1955, 1958, 1961, 1963, 1964,
       1966, 1968, 1970, 1974, (Twentieth Century Classics) 1989, 1998;
       Tender Is the Night: A Romance. London: Penguin Books, 1982, 1986;
       Folio Society, 1987; New Longman Literature, 1993; Ed. Jeffrey Meyers,
       Dent Everyman, 1993; Wordsworth Classics, 1994; London: Samuel
       Johnson, 1995; Dent, Everyman Library, 1996; Penguin Popular
       Classics. Penguin, 1997. 400.

B5.   Fitzgerald, F.Scott. *The Crack-Up*. Falcon Press, 1947. *The Bodley Head
       Fitzgerald*, Vol. I, 1958, 1965, 1968, 1971, 1983 (Revised); Penguin
       (Twentieth Century Classics) 1990.

B6.   Fitzgerald, F. Scott. *The Last Tycoon*. Grey Walls Press, 1949 (twice);
       Penguin, 1960, 1962, 1963, 1965, 1968 (Twentieth Century Classics)
       1990; *The Bodley Head Fitzgerald*, Vol. I, 1958, 1960, 1963, 1966, 1970,
       1983 (Revised); *The Love of the Last Tycoon: A Western*. Ed. Matthew
       J. Bruccoli. Cambridge: Cambridge UP, 1993, 1994; London: Little
       Brown, 1994; Abacus, 1995.

B7.   Fitzgerald, F. Scott. *The Diamond as Big as the Ritz and Other Stories*.
       Penguin, 1961, 1963, (Twentieth Century Classics) 1990; E. Asia,
       Wordsworth Classics, 1994; Dover Publications, 1998. 160.

B8.   Fitzgerald, F. Scott. *The Diamond as Big as the Ritz*. Ed. E. Hare.
       Travelman Science Fiction Series, No. 2. Travelman Pub., 1998. 26.

B9.   Fitzgerald, F. Scott. *Stories of F. Scott Fitzgerald, 5 Volumes*. Penguin,
       1962-68. Reprinted: Vol. I (*The Diamond As Big As the Ritz*) 1965,
       1967, 1969, (Twentieth Century Classics) 1990; Vol. II (*The Crack-Up
       and Other Stories*), 1965, 1968, (Twentieth Century Classics) 1990; Vol.
       III (*Pat Hobby Stories*) 1967, 1970, 1974, (Twentieth Century Classics)
       1992; Vol. IV (*Bernice Bobs Her Hair*) 1968, 1974, 1989, (Twentieth
       Century Classics) 1989; Vol. V (*The Lost Decade and Other Stories*)
       1968, (Twentieth Century Classics) 1991.

B10.   Fitzgerald, F. Scott. *As ever, Scott Fitzgerald: Letters between F. Scott
       Fitzgerald and his literary agent, Harold Ober, 1919-1940*. Ed. Matthew
       J. Bruccoli, assisted by Jennifer McCabe Atkinson. London: Woburn
       Press, 1973.

B11.   Fitzgerald, F. Scott. *The Price Was High: The Last Uncollected Stories
       of F. Scott Fitzgerald*. Ed. Matthew J. Bruccoli. London: Quartet, 1979.
       xx, 785; (Picador Ed.) Pan Books, 1981.

B12.   Fitzgerald, F. Scott. *The Bodley Head Scott Fitzgerald*. London: Bodley
       Head, 1983. Revised edition, 6 vols.

B13.   Fitzgerald, F. Scott. *Short Stories of F. Scott Fitzgerald: A New
       Collection*. Ed. Matthew J. Bruccoli. New York; London: Scribner's,
       1989. xix, 775. London Edition. Abacus: 1992.

B14.   Fitzgerald, F. Scott, and Zelda Fitzgerald. *Bits of Paradise: 21 New
       Stories*. Penguin (Twentieth Century Classics) 1990.

B15.   Fitzgerald, F. Scott. *The Fantasy and Mystery Stories of F. Scott
       Fitzgerald*. Ed. Peter Haining. London: Hale, 1991.

B16. Fitzgerald, F. Scott. *Love in the Night: For a Romantic*. London: Ebury,
      1994; Phoenix, 1995.

B17. Fitzgerald, F. Scott. *The Sayings of F. Scott Fitzgerald*, Ed. Robert
      Pearce. London: Duckworth, 1995.

B18. Fitzgerald, F. Scott. *Babylon Revisited. The Screenplay*. Carroll & Graf
      Publishers, 1996. 192.

B19. Fitzgerald, Zelda. *The Collected Writings*. Intro. Mary Gordon. Ed.
      Bruccoli, Matthew J. NY: Scribners; Toronto: Markwell Macmillan
      Canada, 1991. xxvii, 480.

B20. Fitzgerald, F. Scott. *The Rich Boy and Other Stories*. Phoenix, 1998.
      256.

B21. Fitzgerald, F. Scott. *Trimalchio: An Early Version of* The Great Gatsby.
      The Cambridge Edition of the Works of F. Scott Fitzgerald. Cambridge:
      Cambridge UP, 2000. xxii, 192.

B22. Fitzgerald, F. Scott. *Flappers and Philosophers*. Ed. James L. W. West
      III. The Cambridge Edition of the Works of F. Scott Fitzgerald.
      Cambridge: Cambridge UP, 2000. xxxi, 398.

BOOKS: FULL-LENGTH STUDIES AND COLLECTIONS

B23. Bradbury, Malcolm. *The Modern American Novel*. Oxford: Oxford U.
      Press, 1992.

More than most, Fitzgerald is essentially a social novelist. The historical
development of America in the 1920s, moving from glittering excitement to
danger, was his own psychiatric curve; the political reassessment of the '30s was
the match for his own endeavor to put his spiritual house in order. Such
identifications were so potent exactly because Fitzgerald always chose to live
them as such, making his literary experimentation part of the period's social and
sexual experimentation, making the style of his life an essential component of
the style of his art. This made his work itself appear innocent, his writing seem/

short of formal skill. It has taken time for us to see that there was much more, and that the innocent performer of the '20s became, in his mature work, one of the finest of modern American novelists. After *The Beautiful and Damned*, Fitzgerald's sense of his immersion in his times increases, just like his character Dick Diver in *Tender Is the Night* who feels compelled to risk his own sanity and intelligence in order to understand and redeem the crisis consciousness of others. With *The Great Gatsby* this mixture of involvement and understanding reaches an extraordinary balance. Gatsby is a dandy of a desire that has been redirected from its human or material object of fantasy, a dream of retaining a past moment in an endless instant of contemplation. It is a symbolist tragedy about the struggle of the symbolic imagination to exist in lowered historical time, and about that symbol's inherent ambiguity, its wonder and its meretriciousness.

B24.   Chambers, John B. *The Novels of F. Scott Fitzgerald.* New York: St Martin's Press; Basingstoke: Macmillan, 1989. x, 212.

What has never been seriously considered is the possibility that everything Fitzgerald wrote was drawn from a firm intellectual center; that he had a consistent point of view which determined all his fiction. Even though he only formulated this analysis near the end of his life, Fitzgerald consistently exhibited a wise and tragic sense of life. In *This Side of Paradise,* the ironic vision exists on three levels: Amory's finally realizing the gap between his perception and his experiences; his coming to see struggle as worthwhile; and his also realizing that life will continually offer disappointment. Likewise, the organization in *The Beautiful and Damned* is based upon a coherent ironic point of view. Thus, these early works should be viewed as being much closer to *The Great Gatsby* and *Tender Is the Night* than any double vision theory has so far allowed. *The Great Gatsby* then is not a startling advance from earlier novels. The "double vision" of both Amory and Gatsby makes Fitzgerald's pessimistic tragic vision possible. This deeper double vision is consistently conveyed in all novels through the imagery. The biographical approach that stresses feeling over intellect is even more inhibiting in reading *Tender Is the Night.* However, the sad tone is not the result of a subjective melancholia but is the artistic consequence of Fitzgerald's ironic vision, which actually lightens what could otherwise have been unrelieved pessimism.

B25.   Claridge, Henry, ed. *F. Scott Fitzgerald: Critical Assessments.*
      Fitzgerald in Context: Memories and Reminiscences. Vol. 1.
      Robertsbridge, UK: Helm Information Ltd., 1992. xix, 452.

Fitzgerald was not a prolific writer, so that he is, in the final analysis, a major, rather than a great, writer.   /

B26. Claridge, Henry, ed. *F. Scott Fitzgerald: Critical Assessments. Early Writings: This Side Of Paradise, The Beautiful and Damned, The Vegetable, 66.* 4 vols. Robertsbridge, UK: Helm Information Ltd., 1992. ix, 499.

B27. Claridge, Henry, ed. *F. Scott Fitzgerald: Critical Assessments. Tender Is the Night, The Last Tycoon, The Crack-Up,* and *The Short Stories.* 4 vols. Robertsbridge, UK: Helm Information, Ltd., 1992. ix, 531.

B28. Claridge, Henry, ed. *F. Scott Fitzgerald: Critical Assessments. General Perspectives: Fitzgerald and Other Writers.* 4 vols. Robertsbridge, UK: Helm Information, Ltd., 1992. vii, 495.

B29. Hook, Andrew. *F. Scott Fitzgerald.* London; New York; Melbourne; Auckland: Edward Arnold, 1992.

Fitzgerald discovered that the kind of man he was and the kind of writer he needed to be were difficult to reconcile. The recognition and exploration of this problem becomes a unifying subtext to a great deal of his writing, and thus no voice, not even that of Hemingway or Faulkner, speaks to us from their generation more clearly than Fitzgerald's. His reputation as a major American author has been developed and sustained by the ever-increasing popularity of the concept of the American Dream. His early credentials of youth, beauty, and success were not those of a great writer and he was not taken seriously, but rather considered, like Robert Burns, a "heaven-taught ploughman" and as intellectually weak. *The Beautiful and Damned* is however remarkable as an advance on *This Side of Paradise* in terms of structural unity, characterization, and consistency of tone. In *The Great Gatsby,* involvement and detachment coexist in the text and the contradictions and confusion of the earlier novels disappear. Through *Tender Is the Night* and into *The Last Tycoon,* Fitzgerald shows a continuing awareness of the problems inherent in the roles of man and artist. His voice is a living voice which allows a partial triumph over the exigencies of life.

B30. Lee, A. Robert, ed. *F. Scott Fitzgerald: The Promises of Life.* London: Vision Press; New York: St. Martin's Press, 1989.

Lee, in his Introduction to this book of essays, calls the author's claims "more various" than the Jazz Age he is most often identified with, and makes note of his sense of irony. Elizabeth Kaspar Aldrich writes in her essay "'The most poetical topic in the world': Women in the Novels of F. Scott Fitzgerald," that "To conflate the life and the work is to violate a sacred tenet of New Criticism," committing an intentional fallacy. Further, she maintains that Fitzgerald, in documenting the Jazz Age, was a "sociologist of the finest accuracy and the weightiest authority." The final female rejection of Amory Blaine in *This Side of Paradise* was influenced by George Ponderevo's *Tono-Bungay*, according to Owen Dudley Edwards in "The Lost Teigueen: F. Scott Fitzgerald's Ethics and Ethnicity;" H.G. Wells was an undeniable influence on *The Beautiful and Damned* and *The Great Gatsby*. Harold Beaver, in *"Tender Is the Night*: Fitzgerald's Portrait of a Gentleman," calls the novel Fitzgerald's most thoroughly Jamesian fiction. Herbie Butterfield ("'All Very Rich and Sad': A Decade of Fitzgerald Stories") finds that of all the stories Fitzgerald wrote between 1919 and 1929, only "Babylon Revisited" ranks, as do those by James, Kipling, Conrad, Joyce, Lawrence, and Hemingway, as the finest of its age. In the character of Monroe Stahr, asserts Robert Giddings (*The Last Tycoon*: Fitzgerald as Projectionist"), Fitzgerald draws on American cultural history to provide a symbolic texture to his theme. Giddings cites the author's influences: Irving Thalberg (MGM executive and the "original" of Stahr), Henry Adams, Andrew Jackson, and Abraham Lincoln. Essays by Andrew Hook, A. Robert Lee, Brian Harding, and John S. Whitley round out this collection. (See also under individual essays.)

B31. Le Vot, André. *F. Scott Fitzgerald: A Biography*. London: Allen Lane, 1984. Paris: Julliard, 1979. 459.

See under France (F40).

B32. Matterson, Stephen. *The Great Gatsby*. Basingstoke: Macmillan Education, Ltd., 1990. xiii, 80. Macmillan's Critical Debate series.

Common critical approaches to the novel include the mythic (such as American or Romantic), the Formalist (symbolism, reliability of narration), the authorial perspective (the importance of short stories within the text), the socio-historical (the critique of the American Dream), and the question of characters (such as Gatsby as Trimalchio). *Gatsby* was co-opted by the society it criticized, its film versions making it look like romantic nostalgia or merely a 'school text.' *Gatsby* is very much a man's book in which women are victimized and dehumanized by obsessive men. Often neglected is the anti-Romantic view of time and the Romantic dream, evidence that Nick, not Gatsby, is haunted by time.

B33. Pearce, Robert. *The Sayings of F. Scott Fitzgerald*, ed. Robert Pearce. London: Duckworth, 1995.

Fitzgerald's writings are among the most readable and memorable in twentieth-century literature.

B34. Stavola, Thomas J. *Scott Fitzgerald: Crisis in American Identity.*
      London: Vision Press, 1979. 176.

Erik Erikson's psychoanalytic theories, rooted in the belief that personal growth
and communal culture are inseparable, offer a uniquely appropriate means for
examining the American identity crisis of Fitzgerald and those of the major male
characters in his four completed novels. *American* here implies a naïve but not
deterministic belief in the limitless material promises of American life and the
rejection of all forms of deprivation in view of the limitless resources the land
seemed to offer. But inherent in this romantic vision of life is a critical
deficiency, an anti-historical bias that hoped to live unaffected by the scales of
traditional values that have ordered life in other societies. Fitzgerald's life,
especially his complex relationship with his wife, Zelda, both exemplifies and
exposes the limitations of this kind of social faith. Unlike Fitzgerald himself, the
heroes of his completed novels almost entirely fail in their individual pursuits of
identity, love, and maturity. In each case their psychological backgrounds have
left them ill-equipped to succeed at work and intimacy. Fitzgerald roots these
various failures both in the weaknesses of the individuals and in a more
fundamental weakness in the American belief in unlimited possibility. In
contrast, Fitzgerald tried to order his life according to the more traditional norms
of "honor, courtesy, and courage."

B35. Tredell, Nicolas, ed. *F. Scott Fitzgerald: The Great Gatsby.* Columbia
      Critical Guides. New York: Columbia UP, 1997. 189.

A historical anthology of the critical reception of *Gatsby* from 1920 to 1990,
through primary sources and commentary, and an effort to locate current
"growth points" in *Gatsby* studies. Early responses to *Gatsby* ranged from
dismissal to praise. The novel was compared to, among others, *The Turn of the
Screw* and *The Good Soldier*. Isabel Patterson called it a "fascinating trifle."
H.L. Mencken described it as a "glorified anecdote" but, like other reviewers of
the time, found Fitzgerald much matured, though still superficial. The book also
received similarly mixed reviews in Britain. The publication of *Tender* sparked
new critical interest in *Gatsby*; contrasts and comparisons were made. In 1941
Dos Passos called *Gatsby* "one of the few classic American novels;" new
attention to the novel was raised by the publication of *The Last Tycoon*. Both
Alfred Kazin and Arthur Mizener, in the late 1940s, were instrumental in
establishing for Fitzgerald a more positive, posthumous reputation. In the '50s,
spearheading a surge in Fitzgerald studies, Lionel Trilling presented Fitzgerald
as an heroic, quintessentially American figure. *Gatsby* began to be seen as an
"evaluation of the American dream." Later, narrative techniques were
extensively explored. By 1958, author and novel had been definitively rescued
from obscurity. By the early '60s, an increasing acceptance of *Gatsby* in
England was evidenced. In both the U.K. and the U.S. a growing agreement on

the stature of *Gatsby* created a climate in which other aspects of the novel could receive fuller attention: optical motifs, internal structure, patterns, unity. Civil Rights-motivated criticism challenged Fitzgerald's representation of ethnic minorities. Leslie A. Fiedler's 1967 account opened up "issues about the representation of women and sexuality," which would be largely expanded in the '70s. Challenges to the accepted readings of the '50s emerged; psychoanalytic approaches to *Gatsby* were explored. A "comparative critical inertia" marked the '80s. The '90s saw a "range of fresh approaches" to *Gatsby*, combining structuralism, post-structuralism, deconstruction, post-modernism, and information and chaos theory in the criticism of Patti White; textual detail with popular culture in Ronald Berman; "strongly gendered aesthetic discourse" in the work of Frances Kerr. These three signal that there is a broad scope for future Fitzgerald and *Gatsby* interpretations.

B36. Way, Brian. *F. Scott Fitzgerald and the Art of Social Fiction.* London: Arnold; NY: St. Martin's; 1980. xi, 171.

Fitzgerald's work enables us to understand particular dimensions of American life but only if we fully appreciate what he is doing. He is not so much the chronicler of the failure of the American Dream as a novelist of manners of a certain social group, its 'dreams, processes of thought, and deeper psychology." His work is informed by the Protestant ethic and his concept of the artist influenced by James and Wharton. Like James, he felt that social fiction can be poetic. His early work is not a failure because it reveals his development as a writer. Through its scenic construction, *The Great Gatsby* conveys subtlety of character and social interaction. Its larger themes of American civilization and the romantic sensibility are "balanced and contracted" by a poet's precise attention to detail. In *Tender Is the Night* Fitzgerald's reading of Marx is evident in the theme of exploitation by the moneyed classes. *The Crack-Up* writings are "artistically stunted and emotionally dead," while in *The Last Tycoon*, Stahr embodies the superb professionalism Fitzgerald had come to admire in the Hollywood of the 1930s. In this novel, Fitzgerald is at the height of his powers.

British Editions of American Studies and Collections

B37. Bruccoli, Matthew J. *Fitzgerald and Hemingway: A Dangerous Friendship.* London: Deutsch, 1996.

B38. Bruccoli, Matthew J. *New Essays on The Great Gatsby.* Cambridge: Cambridge UP, 1985. viii, 120.

B39. Bruccoli, Matthew J. *Scott and Ernest: The Authority of Failure and The Authority of Success*. London: Bodley Head, 1978.

B40. Bruccoli, Matthew J. *Some Sort of Epic Grandeur: The Life of F. Scott Fitzgerald*. London: Hodder & Stoughton, 1981.

B41. Bryer, Jackson R. *New Essays on F. Scott Fitzgerald's Neglected Stories*. Columbia; London: Missouri UP. xi, 363.

B42. Mangum, Bryant. *A Fortune Yet: Money in the Art of F. Scott Fitzgerald's Short Stories*. New York; London: Garland, 1991. xix, 233. London Edition.

B43. Mellow, James. *Invented Lives: Scott Fitzgerald and Zelda Fitzgerald*. Boston: Houghton; London: Souvenir Press, 1985.

B44. Meyers, Jeffrey. *Scott Fitzgerald: A Biography*. Basingstoke: Macmillan; NY: Harper Collins, 1994. xiv, 400.

B45. Moore, Benita A. *Escape into a Labyrinth: F. Scott Fitzgerald, Catholic Sensibility, and the American Way*. New York; London: Garland, 1988. iv, 358. London Edition.

B46. Roulston, Robert and Helen H. Roulston. *The Winding Road to West Egg: The Artistic Development of F. Scott Fitzgerald*. Lewisburg, PA: Bucknell, UP, 1995; London: Associated Universities Presses, 1995. 208.

B47. Stanley, Linda. *The Foreign Critical Reputation of F. Scott Fitzgerald*. Westport and London: Greenwood Publishing Co., 1980.

ESSAYS/CHAPTERS/NOTES/CONFERENCE PAPERS

B48. Aldrich, Elizabeth Kaspar. "'The Most Poetical Topic in the World': Women in the Novels of F. Scott Fitzgerald." *F. Scott Fitzgerald: The*

Promises of Life. Ed. A. Robert Lee. London: Vision Press; New York: St. Martin's, 1989. 131-156.

What is particularly challenging to criticism of Fitzgerald's work is how little we seem to be able to avoid saying that his female characters 'are all Zelda' one way or the other, for the highly public and well documented career of his marriage served always as addendum to or even gloss on the work. Immortality conferred or exploitation committed, Fitzgerald's use of Zelda in his fiction, like his non-literary advertisements of their life together, amounted to an extraordinary kind of collaboration, one which calls for the most careful reconsideration—a positive challenge—of the relationship between text and context and how we interpret it.

B49.   Beaver, Harold. *"Tender Is the Night*: Fitzgerald's Portrait of a Gentleman." *F. Scott Fitzgerald: The Promises of Life.* Ed. A. Robert Lee. London: Vision Press; New York: St. Martin's, 1989. 61-73.

Tender Is the Night is Fitzgerald's most thoroughly Jamesian fiction, with European-style settings, overwhelmingly or scarcely American characters, its theme of a vampire draining the energy out of her husband, and its initial point of view. The 61 chapters, divided into three books, are arranged Jamesianly, as dramatic moments whose scenic design was to suggest a philosophy of history, 'a cultural clue to the meaning, the moral development, of an era.' The novel is not so much 'psychological' in the Freudian sense as modeled on *Vanity Fair*, with a narrator constantly obtruding his own epigrammatic commentary.

B50.   Bell, Ian F. A. "Newnesses of Beginning: The Violent Phantasies of Willa Cather and F. Scott Fitzgerald." *The Insular Dream: Obsession and Resistance.* Ed. Kristiaan Versluys. Amsterdam: VU University Press, 1995. 242-260.

As in *Medea*, damage to the female body is to be understood in a context of sexual danger in *The Great Gatsby* and in *The Professor's House*. Fitzgerald and Willa Cather chose to construct fantasies of origin based on the needs of the protagonists. These fantasies include a "sense of ravage to the female body in an effort to contain sexual threat and to allow its modified expression." Carraway's oscillation between attraction and repulsion goes beyond narrative knowingness to suggest a need for the romance he dooms to failure. Distance is key—as a voyeur, Nick's phrasing is snobbish and fanciful, going beyond mimicry of Gatsby's speech. "Wonder" is crucial, perhaps the most crucial in Carraway's vocabulary. The reality of Daisy's presence diminishes her wonder. Maintaining the distance of the vision is paramount. The sequences about female sexuality are particularly exemplified in Carraway's repulsion by female body perspiration and in Myrtle's sensuality. He "maternalizes his fantasy to read origin as part of a natural process."

B51.   Bender, Bert. "'His Mind Aglow': The Biological Undercurrent in
       Fitzgerald's *Gatsby* and Other Works." *Journal of American Studies* 32.3
       (1998): 399-420.

Fitzgerald's interest in evolutionary biology shaped his work to a great extent. He was concerned with interrelated biological problems: the question of eugenics as a possible solution to civilization's many ills as evidence in *This Side of Paradise* when Amory and Burne Holiday discuss whether "the light-haired man is a higher type" and in Tom Buchanan's fear of the rise of the colored races in *The Great Gatsby*. Fitzgerald was also influenced by the linked principles of accident and heredity, as influenced by Ernst Haeckel's *The Riddle of the Universe at the Close of the Nineteenth Century* (1900), as we see in *Gatsby* by his use of the words "accident" or "accidental" to describe Gatsby's knowledge that he was in Daisy's childhood house by a "colossal accident" and his use of the word to describe the movement of Gatsby's dead body as an "accidental course with its accidental burden." God seems an accident too as in his description of the billboard with the eyes of Dr. Eckleburg who "sees everything" but then sinks down "into eternal blindness." Finally, Fitzgerald was influenced by the revolutionary theory of sexual selection according to Darwin in his insistence that the female was the power to select the superior male and the male must struggle to be selected. Gatsby is doomed because he ignores the laws of sexual selection which depend on money and heredity sufficient for ornamental display and brute power, both of which Tom Buchanan possessed through an accident of birth.

B52.   Bradbury, Malcolm. *The Modern American Novel.* New ed. Oxford:
       Oxford UP, 1992. 83-93.

More than most, Fitzgerald is essentially a social novelist. The historical development of America in the 1920s, moving from glittering excitement to danger, was his own psychiatric curve; the political reassessment of the '30s was the match for his own endeavor to put his spiritual house in order. Such identifications were so potent exactly because Fitzgerald always chose to live them as such, making his literary experimentation part of the period's social and sexual experimentation, making the style of his life an essential component of the style of his art. This made his work itself appear innocent, his writing seem short of formal skill. It has taken time for us to see that there was much more, and that the innocent performer of the '20s became, in his mature work, one of the finest of modern American novelists. After *The Beautiful and Damned*, Fitzgerald's sense of his immersion in his times increases, just like his character

Dick Diver in *Tender Is the Night* who feels compelled to risk his own sanity and intelligence in order to understand and redeem the crisis consciousness of others. With *The Great Gatsby* this mixture of involvement and understanding reaches an extraordinary balance. Gatsby is a dandy of a desire that has been redirected from its human or material object of fantasy, a dream of retaining a past moment in an endless instant of contemplation. It is a symbolist tragedy about the struggle of the symbolic imagination to exist in lowered historical time, and about that symbol's inherent ambiguity, its wonder and its meretriciousness.

B53.   Butterfield, Herbie. "'All Very Rich and Sad': A Decade of Fitzgerald Short Stories." *F. Scott Fitzgerald: The Promises of Life*. Ed. A. Robert Lee. London: Vision Press; New York: St. Martin's, 1989. 94-112.

During the 1920s, Fitzgerald must have had a larger readership for the dozens of stories he published in various magazines than for his novels, ten of which rank as the third peak of his literary achievement alongside *The Great Gatsby* and *Tender Is the Night*. They range from fantasies, reminiscent of Poe's Arabesques and Hawthorne's allegories ('The Diamond as Big as the Ritz') to Joycean epiphanies ('Absolution') to Jamesian nouvelles ('The Rich Boy'). Their voices are at once awed and ironic, their style at once sumptuous and melancholy and always marvelously cadenced, their substance a highly charged and well founded critique of the world of the rich and the adventures of the capitalist economy. The critique is all the more telling because it is regularly also a self-criticism able to effectively demonstrate the attraction and allure of that money-mesmerized ethos.

B54.   Claridge, Henry. Introduction. *F. Scott Fitzgerald: Critical Assessments*. Ed. Henry Claridge. 4 vols. Robertsbridge, UK: Helm Information Ltd., 1991.

Fitzgerald is not a prolific writer, so that he is, in the final analysis, a major, rather than a great, writer.

B55.   Cox, Geof. "Literary Pragmatics: A New Discipline: The Example of Fitzgerald's *The Great Gatsby*." *Literature and History* 12.1 (Spring 1986): 79-96.

Literary pragmatics includes social expectations and norms as well as linguistic constraints on communication situations. This is based on the Althusserian view that distortions of representations begin over an imaginary relationship to the world before it is in our signifying practices, or the way language is used. Social class is an important constraint on the reader. Also, the packaging of a text as a commodity affects our reading of it; thus, a book's dust jacket is part of its meaning. The importance of social class is seen in the preparation of *The Great Gatsby* for different educational levels. College versions are prepared not for a common language base, but for a differentiated one. These legitimize the class differentiation of high capitalism. Culture is a major commodity in the development of an economy. Thus, all readings of *The Great Gatsby* are distorted by the ideology of the commodity culture.

B56. Coyle, John. "Meaulnes, Gatsby and the Possibilities of Romance."
   Essays in Poetics: The Journal of the British Neo-Formalist School 12.1
   (Apr. 1987): 15-40.

The two books are parallel exercises in writing a romance in a post-romantic age. In both, tension between realism and romanticism is embodied in the relationship between narrator and hero. Nick writes for a more ironic age than that of *Le Grand Meaulnes*, but the narrators of both books seek to impose order, Nick through common sense. And in both books, a stranger interrupts this order. *The Great Gatsby* argues for the virtues of a "romantic readiness" and "extraordinary gift for hope." For all the doubts of the narrators, they are still drawn in by the glamour of "protracted adolescent idealism." "Different as these testaments are, they each point to acts of duty undertaken in hope." *Gatsby* is not so much a romantic novel as a realist romance.

B57. Dolan, Marc. "The (Hi)story of Their Lives: Mythic Autobiography and
   'The Lost Generation.'" *Journal of American Studies* 27.1 (1993): 35-56.

Historians have objections to the use of formal autobiographies as primary sources of historical evidence, including the unverifiable quality of inner experience, problems posed by integrating verifiable events with the unverifiable, the possibility that narrative presents a false view of history, the obscuring literariness of narrative, and the frequent distance of the narrator from the events described. The new cultural history, however, stresses the textual nature of historical knowledge and draws on the insights of the methodologies of both anthropology and literary criticism. Autobiography must be read as personal and tribal myth, such as the numerous memoirs of Americans in 1920s Paris, the most influential being Cowley's *Exile's Return*, Hemingway's *A Moveable Feast*, and Fitzgerald's *The Crack-Up*, largely responsible for the myth of the "Lost Generation" and a valuable, mythic testimony of their own experience of the 1920s. Fitzgerald's mythic narrative had a clear protagonist, a clear beginning, and a very clear end—but the middle stretches remained oddly murky. The signified journey of all these narratives is from the false perception of cultural homogeneity through an illusive sense of cultural uniqueness to a renewed commitment to cultural pluralism. Historical experience may prove, in practice, to be as much of a myth as "the Lost Generation." But if we seek to know what a given historical period like the 1920s "felt like while it was happening," then we must recover each of the mythic life-stories of that period and measure them against each other, in the hopes of discovering palpable, resonant, historically significant patterns.

B58. Edwards, Owen Dudley. "The Lost Teigueen: F. Scott Fitzgerald's Ethics and Ethnicity." *F. Scott Fitzgerald: The Promises of Life*. Ed. A. Robert Lee. London: Vision Press; New York: St. Martin's, 1989. 181-214.

Due partly to the devotion of Edmund Wilson and others and due partly to the postwar "'20s cult' which yearned for liberation in manners, sexual relations and human integrity, the 1950s responded to Fitzgerald with an enthusiasm far beyond any reflected in the sales of his books during his lifetime. However, while the cult passed, Fitzgerald's popularity did not wane as critics found Fitzgerald to owe less to Henry James and H.G. Wells than had been asserted.

B59. Giddings, Robert. "*The Last Tycoon*: Fitzgerald as Projectionist." *F. Scott Fitzgerald: The Promises of Life*. Ed. A. Robert Lee. London: Vision Press; New York: St. Martin's, 1989. 74-93.

The assertion that Fitzgerald wrote best when writing about his experiences and observations of the Jazz Age has produced the problem of determining whether he was the master or servant of his materials. In the case of Fitzgerald's modeling of Monroe Starr on Irving Thalberg in *The Last Tycoon*, however, the author has not only kept but mastered his imaginative distance, giving the reader 'the history of a consciousness.' The novel goes beyond the creation of a 'maybe great' character, beyond any one figure or phase of American history, into a vision of how Art, as Fitzgerald conceived it, might 'project' History itself.

B60. Godden, Richard. "The Great Gatsby, Glamour on the Turn." *Fictions of Capitalism: the American Novel from James to Miller*. Cambridge: Cambridge UP, 1990. 290. Rpt. of "*The Great Gatsby*: Glamour on the Turn." *Journal of American Studies* 16 (1982): 343-71.

Gatsby stands as a parable of the relationship between leisure class capital and the industrial base that it criminally exploits and ignores. In Gatsby's hands, his house, his car, his suit, his smile, take on theatrical properties, with which he "displays the repressive 'inner emptiness' of reified forms." As both producer and product he is potentially aware of what he has done to create himself and why; he has "Brechtian skills" that allow him to feel himself to "be a commodity."

B61. Godden, Richard. "Money Makes Manners Make Man Make Woman: *Tender Is the Night*, A Familiar Romance?" *Literature and History* 12.1 (Spring 1986): 16-37.

The "history of what a class finds unthinkable is one measure of how that class maintains its integrity despite economic transition." Victorian-age repression leads Dick to keep the door to Nicole's unconscious locked. As a result, she is not cured but becomes a consumer self. Dick is not a failure because he is "aware of his position within a sexual and economic trauma." The Althusserian distinction: he "loses interest in himself as an 'individual' because he recognizes himself as a 'subject,' that is, as something subjected to and produced by and productive of forces that he learns to despise." The process of reading and re-reading *Tender Is the Night* provides what Late Capitalism must deny: history—a history, from drawing-room to Hollywood, of the very thing that would revoke history—commodity.

B62. Goldman, Arnold. "F. Scott Fitzgerald: the 'Personal Stuff.'" American Studies: *Essays in Honor of Marcus Cunliffe*. Eds. Brian H. Ried and John White. New York: St. Martin's Press, 1991. 210-30.

Few have valued Fitzgerald's non-fiction as did Marcus Cunliffe who found the essays to constitute a legitimate strand of thematic concern and stylistic development. The unadorned, monosyllabic paratactic prose, echoing Hemingway's, is a remarkable departure from Fitzgerald's ordinary style, even in correspondence. Fitzgerald had wanted to create a testament out of his various scattered 'personal' material because some of it had attracted positive attention, but feared that is might appear to be a collection of 'what the cat brought in.' Perkins admonished him to rewrite the book as 'a volume of reminiscence,' and Fitzgerald eventually voiced his feelings against the autobiographical book. Despite everything, with more understanding and support from peers he might have synthesized social comment and analysis with personal involvement and self-revelation, particularly the writer's estate.

B63. Gross, Dalton and Mary-Jean Gross. "F. Scott Fitzgerald's American Swastika: The Prohibition Underworld and *The Great Gatsby*." *Notes and Queries* 41/239 (Sept. 1994): 377.

The fact that Meyer Wolfsheim's enterprises is called the Swastika Holding Company shows not that Fitzgerald had a prescient awareness of Nazism, but that he was associated with the prohibition underworld of New York City nightlife, which also used the symbol.

The Promises of Life. Ed. A. Robert Lee. London: Vision Press; New York: St. Martin's, 1989. 113-130.

Fitzgerald's assertion to Zelda that he had even brought 'radicalism' to the *Saturday Evening Post* is problematic. In some of the stories on the themes of love and marriage the gestures towards romance that were made 'for the trade' were undercut by ironies of characterization and plot. The disparity between what we are allowed to see of character and what is obviously dictated by the machinery of the plot makes for an obvious implausibility that subverts the norms on which the fiction depends. There is a tendency towards self-parody in the commercial fiction that has radical implications.

B65. Hart, Jeffrey. "'Out of it ere night': The WASP Gentleman as Cultural Ideal." *The New Criterion* 7.5 (Jan. 1989): 27-34.

The idea of the gentleman, based on the British and not continental model, has been since the eighteenth century the only persisting social ideal in American culture. Fitzgerald's gentlemen *manqués* represent a tribute to the now eviscerated ideal, though they are usually tragic figures undone through illusion or weak character. Fitzgerald was fascinated with the legendarily doomed American-gentleman figure Hobey Baker, whom he may have seen as the last Edwardian. Quite probably the long line of American gentlemen ran out during the period following World War II, when W.A.S.P. American aristocrats, untitled of course but solidly established, temporarily shaped the world. The American governing class was highly permeable, but certainly identifiable.

B66. Hook, Andrew. "Cases for Reconsideration: Fitzgerald's *This Side of Paradise* and *The Beautiful and Damned*." *F. Scott Fitzgerald: The Promises of Life.* Ed. A. Robert Lee. London: Vision Press; New York: St. Martin's, 1989. 17-36.

Some have argued that as a writer, Fitzgerald has to be seen as sharing in that experience of failure which occurs thematically so frequently in his fiction, his reputation sustained only by the one unqualified success of *The Great Gatsby*, that *This Side of Paradise* and *The Beautiful and Damned* are two immature pieces of writing, scarcely worthy of regard as serious novels. Yet Fitzgerald's assessment of them was accurate. According to Fitzgerald, the former is "selective" like *Gatsby*. He felt the latter to be "full and comprehensive" like *Tender Is the Night*, and the strength of the book indeed lies precisely in its dense accumulation and weight of detail and not at all in any profundity of philosophical or interpretative scheme. While not great novels, the two books demand closer attention.

B67.   Hook, Andrew. "Scott Fitzgerald's Current British Reputation," F. Scott
        Fitzgerald Centennial Conference, Princeton U., 21 Sept. 1996.

Fitzgerald's scholarly reception in Britain is still highly qualified as the British
only like Americans who become British. He has become part of the cultural
consciousness, however, a touchstone, in fact, for cultural topics in publications
for the educated.

B68.   Lee, A. Robert. "'A quality of distortion': Imagining *The Great Gatsby*."
        F. Scott Fitzgerald: The Promises of Life. Ed. A. Robert Lee. London:
        Vision Press; New York: St. Martin's, 1989. 37-60.

Gatsby deserves its critical and popular success. Nick's telling amounts to a
consummate parody of 'authoritative' first-person narration, a 'distortion' in the
sense of a plausible but dramatic lie of autobiography. He can never tell his
story only as he feels and remembers it, or even recovers from it, in this sense
paradoxically a 'truer' account than a supposed objective retelling of the facts of
the case. Nick's distortion, however, points less to the surreal or grotesque than
to the sublime, referring us to the larger mythic frame of the story, Gatsby's rise
and fall as emblematic drama. Nick offers a final and embracing act of
remembrance, that of a pristine 'dream' America, a new found land as yet still
clear of carelessness and money and even glamour.

B69.   Lee, A. Robert. Introduction. *F. Scott Fitzgerald: The Promises of Life*.
        Ed. A. Robert Lee. London: Vision Press; New York: St. Martin's, 1989.
        7-16.

Lee, in his Introduction to this book of essays, calls the author's claims "more
various" than the Jazz Age he is most often identified with, and makes note of
his sense of irony. Elizabeth Kaspar Aldrich writes in her essay "'The most
poetical topic in the world': Women in the Novels of F. Scott Fitzgerald," that
"To conflate the life and the work is to violate a sacred tenet of New Criticism,"
committing an intentional fallacy. According to Owen Dudley Edwards in "The
Lost Teigueen: F. Scott Fitzgerald's Ethics and Ethnicity;" H.G. Wells was an
undeniable influence on *The Beautiful and Damned* and *The Great Gatsby*.
Harold Beaver, in *"Tender Is the Night*: Fitzgerald's Portrait of a Gentleman,"
calls the novel Fitzgerald's most thoroughly Jamesian fiction. Herbie Butterfield
("'All Very Rich and Sad': A Decade of Fitzgerald Stories") finds that of all the
stories Fitzgerald wrote between 1919 and 1929, only "Babylon Revisited"
ranks, as do those by James, Kipling, Conrad, Joyce, Lawrence, and
Hemingway, as the finest of its age. In the character of Monroe Stahr, asserts
Robert Giddings (*The Last Tycoon*: Fitzgerald as Projectionist"), Fitzgerald
draws on American cultural history to provide a symbolic texture to his theme.
Giddings cites the author's influences: Irving Thalberg (MGM executive and the

"original" of Stahr), Henry Adams, Andrew Jackson, and Abraham Lincoln. Essays by Andrew Hook, A. Robert Lee, Brian Hardin, and John S. Whitley round out this collection.

B70.   MacDonald, Niall. "The brevity of youth: F. Scott Fitzgerald's *Tender Is the Night.*" *The English Review.* 8.2 (Nov. 1997). 22-24.

The symbolism and settings contribute to the overall themes of the tragic nature of the brevity of youth and the difficulty of sustaining long-lasting relationships as people change. Fitzgerald said that 'an author ought to write for the youth of his generation.' The events in *Tender Is the Night* transcend time and place. The use of contrasting settings show change in Dick as he experiences and appreciates his youth's tragic fate.

B71.   Macleod, N. "A Note on Philip Roth's *Goodbye, Columbus* and Fitzgerald's *The Great Gatsby.*" *The International Fiction Review* 12:2 (Summer 1985): 104-107.

Enough correspondences exist between the two novels to indicate that Roth was influenced by Fitzgerald's novel. The most explicit allusion is when Roth describes Brenda Patimkin as "the King's daughter." Both novels tell of the crowded events of a single summer, both heroes are imaginative orphans, and both stories start when a major protagonist is introduced to an alien social milieu through a cousin. Neil as well as Gatsby repays old-fashioned hospitality by seducing the daughter. In both novels, socially distinct areas exist side by side. Roth's novel is a prequel to *Gatsby* in that it echoes the story of Gatsby and Daisy in Louisville. Neil's loss of Brenda reviews exactly the sense of loss which motivates Gatsby to recapture "the freshest and best."

B72.   Meyers, Jeffrey. "Scott Fitzgerald and the English." *London Magazine* Oct./Nov. 1992: 31-44.

There is more to Fitzgerald's hostile attitude toward the English than his first biographer, Arthur Mizener, suggests. His attitude stems from myriad factors including preconceived ideas about England from his youth, English writers and tourists he met abroad, unsuccessful love affairs with English women, uneasy relations with English publishers, and disappointing reviews and book sales in England. Nevertheless, he had a great deal in common with Evelyn Waugh: both writers failed as undergraduates, wrote for Hollywood, and became depressed alcoholics, for starters. As innate conservatives, they recorded the social nuances and spirit of the 1920s through social satire and defined the sophisticated rebellion of the postwar generation by expressing the themes of disillusioned idealism.

B73. Monk, David. "Fitzgerald: The Tissue of Style." *Journal of American Studies* 17.1 (1983): 77-94.

Fitzgerald's obsession with style implies a counterforce to impermanence. Given the unsummonability of deep emotion at will, he at a low ebb felt that this stylistic emphasis condemned him to a treadmill of technical variations. His commitment to 'great and moving experiences' and not the disguises which trick them out is persuasive. Fitzgerald takes his stand with the great body of Romantic Decadent belief which insisted on the primacy of emotional intensity and on the 'organic' literary form true to it. His best work in the short story genre—'Babylon Revisited' and 'Financing Finnegan'—are memorable not for narrative but for stylistic evocation of mood and atmosphere, which comes back to the preeminence of emotional intensity. Throughout his five novels, Fitzgerald was learning to balance style and lifestyle, and it is in the analysis of the characteristic craft that an abiding interest lies. Fitzgerald's failures are such only by the highest standards, and more can be learned even from his local flaws than by his more facile successes.

B74. Newby, Peter T. "Literature and the Fashioning of Tourist Taste." 130-41. *Humanistic Geography and Literature: Essays on the Experience of Place.* Ed. Douglas C. D. Pocock. Totowa, NJ: Barnes & Noble; London: Croom Helm, 1981. 224.

Scott and Zelda's move to the Mediterranean in the Summer of 1924, due partly to financial pressures, undoubtedly influenced where New York society chose to spend the summer. The publication of *Tender Is the Night* in 1934 was a decided encouragement to the growth of a summer Mediterranean season. At the opening of the novel the author remarks that the French Riviera had "become a summer resort of notable and fashionable people," whereas "a decade ago it was almost deserted after its English clientele went North in April." Fitzgerald' influence is due to the fact that he captured and correctly interpreted social change, both in his novel and in his own lifestyle, and in so doing helped to create a new tourist fashion.

B75. Seed, David. "Party-going: The Jazz Age novels of Evelyn Waugh, Wyndham Lewis, F. Scott Fitzgerald and Carl Van Vechten." *Forked Tongues?: Comparing Twentieth-Century British and American Literature.* Eds. Ann Massa and Alistair Stead. London: Longman, 1994. 117—34.

An inadequate amount of attention has been paid to 1920s party-going novels because of the moral confusion felt on the part of many critics between the superficial social worlds depicted and the supposed quality of the novels. The responses of Americans Fitzgerald and Van Vechten and Englishmen Waugh and Lewis to the decade following the First World War, which functions as a major reference point in this fiction, grow out of contrasting historical circumstances and put quite different emphases. While Van Vechten saw himself as the chronicler of an age which had ended and accordingly applied methods of scenic depiction, Fitzgerald investigates the pathos growing out of the failure of his party-givers. His narrative perspectives are characteristically those of a witness elegiacally recording the passing of these social events. In contrast with both these writers, Waugh, Lewis—and for that matter their contemporary Aldous Huxley—vigorously satirize their party-goers, ridiculing the postures of postwar nihilism and exploring the social ferment taking place in this period.

B76.   Swann, Charles. "A Fitzgerald Debt to Keats? From 'Isabella' into
       Tender Is the Night." Notes and Queries 37.4 (Dec. 1990): 437-48.

Fitzgerald's description of Nicole and Rosemary's shopping spree in *Tender Is the Night* may be inspired by stanzas XIV and XV of Keats's 'Isabella.'

B77.   Tanner, Tony. Introduction. *The Great Gatsby*, by F. Scott Fitzgerald.
       London: Penguin Books, 1990.

There are parallels between Gatsby's and Petronius's Trimalchio. The latter is obsessed with a green ball and passing time, while the former is obsessed with a green light banishing time. Or is this version Nick's even more than it is Gatsby's? Trimalchio served eggs stuffed with a baccafacio, a small bird, considered quite a delicacy. The eggs in *Gatsby* are filled with disgusting, aborted, still born things. While from the perception of the wingless, West and East Egg look similar, the novel is concerned with dissimilarities as well as resemblances, but are the inhabitants of both eggs perhaps not more similar than different? Certainly, Fitzgerald's radiance is only glittering when it is about to dim? Nick is a spectator in search of a performer. "Whatever the motivation for his writing, he has still delivered a work of art; and there can never be any unraveling of the motives than lie behind the making of a work of art." *The Great Gatsby*, "with something of the lean yet pregnant economy of a parable . . . is word-perfect and inexhaustible. It is, I believe, the most perfectly crafted work of fiction to have come out of America."

B78.   Vickers, Jackie. "Women and Wealth: F. Scott Fitzgerald, Edith Wharton
       and Paul Bourget." *Journal of American Studies* 26.2 (Aug. 1992):
       261-3.

Wharton complained that in *Outre-Mer* Bourget was too eager to see Americans as deifying women and relating them to the power of the dollar, yet a decade later Wharton had constructed her own "living orchid" in the person of *The House of Mirth*'s Lily Bart. Laurence Selden, characterized as a connoisseur, appreciated Lily's appearance and struggles to relate it to the American financial structure identified by Bourget. A generation later in *Tender Is the Night*, Fitzgerald approaches that same relationship between wealth and those beautiful women who are both its justification and its end product. Wharton read all her friend Bourget's work, and Fitzgerald read Wharton. It is within this nexus of reading that we find the trajectory of Fitzgerald's most compelling perceptions of the nature of women and wealth.

B79. Way, Brian. "Fitzgerald and the Art of Social Fiction: *The Great Gatsby*." *American Fiction: New Readings*. Ed. Richard Gray. London: Vision Press, 1984; Totowa, N.J.: Barnes & Noble, 1983. 150-64. Rpt. of title chapter in Brian Way, *Fitzgerald and the Art of Social Fiction*. (See No. B38.)

B80. Whitley, John S. "'A Touch of Disaster': Fitzgerald, Spengler, and the Decline of the West." *F. Scott Fitzgerald: The Promises of Life*. Ed. A. Robert Lee. London: Vision Press; New York: St. Martin's, 1989. 157-180.

Fitzgerald's pessimism originates in Romantic poets such as Keats and social realist writers like Frank Norris. He had, from his earliest days as a writer, a very strong sense of decline and decay, a sense neither originated nor changed, only enhanced, by the influence of Oswald Spengler—particularly the second volume of *The Decline of the West*. A prominent aspect of his "touch of disaster" was his treatment of women and the related themes of sex and motherhood.

BOOK REVIEWS/NEWS ARTICLES/RADIO PROGRAMS

B81. Bawer, Bruce. "Fairyland." Rev. of *Invented Lives: F. Scott Fitzgerald and Zelda Fitzgerald*, by James Mellow. *The London Review of Books* 7.8 (2 May 1985): 17-18.

To Fitzgerald, the ritual of courtship was not "a matter of love between a man and a woman but of competition between man and man." Mellow's book is full of evidence suggesting "a strong homosexual component" in the work of Fitzgerald.

B82.   Beaver, Harold. Rev. of *New Essays on 'The Great Gatsby,'* ed. M. J. Bruccoli. *Yearbook of English Studies* 19 (1989): 354-5.

This new series is too short and too idiosyncratic to be useful to students. The series editor presents the "muddled insight" that "works of art generate many different kinds of interpretation." The result is a "hybrid free-for-all." Introduction by Bruccoli, essays on *Gatsby*; the odd-essay-out is Kenneth E. Eble's, *"The Great Gatsby* and the Great American Novel."

B83.   Bellflower, Robert. Rev. of *New Essays on 'The Great Gatsby,'* ed. M. J. Bruccoli. *Review of English Studies: A Quarterly Journal of English Literature and the English Language* 39.154 (1988): 333-4.

The purpose of the new series is to reappraise texts and their critical assumptions. Four or five new essays have been written by both established critics and promising younger scholars. The *Gatsby* essays are not especially "stimulating," except for novelist George Garrett's "accomplished appreciation of Fitzgerald's style."

B84.   Blythe, Ronald. "Fitzgerald's dream-men." Rev. of *The Price Was High: The Last Uncollected Stories of F. Scott Fitzgerald*, ed. Matthew J. Bruccoli. *Listener* 102 (15 Nov.1979): 685-6.

A collection of stories, most written for *The Saturday Evening Post*. Not Fitzgerald's finest, but reading him "in bulk, reading the dozen fine things, and the masses of plot and dialogue that he could never have waned to write, his professional slog and inspired hours are, in this context, equally intriguing from our point of view."

B85.   Bradbury, Malcolm. "Tender Tragedy." Rev. of BBC2 serial presentation of *Tender Is the Night. Observer Magazine* (15 Sep. 1985): 27-8.

American finance and casting (this is a co-production between the BBC and Showtime), and British "finesse and high production standards" combine to make this a quality production suited to television. It is more suited even than the movie version to dramatizing the novel: it has "wide dramatic space, a long storyline, a glow from the past,, a strong period feel, continued relevance."

B86.   Bradbury, Malcolm. "The Wound and the Bow." Rev. of *F. Scott Fitzgerald*, ed. M. J. Bruccoli. *New Statesman* (27 Oct. 1978): 549.

Hemingway hated Fitzgerald's weaknesses, particularly those he exposed in "The Crack-Up." Bruccoli reminds us that their friendship began on an odd balance, when Hemingway was still virtually unknown. Still, their friendship is a "modern fable," here re-analyzed and set straight.

B87. Bradshaw, David. "Old facts, new lives." Rev. of *F. Scott Fitzgerald: A Biography*, by André Le Vot, and *Invented Lives: F. Scott and Zelda Fitzgerald*, by James Mellow. *Times Literary Supplement* (2 Aug. 1985): 857.

Le Vot's main strength is his "meticulous meticulous evocations of the physical and cultural topographies" of Fitzgerald's life. The book has "stylishness and poise." It took its author 20 years of research, during which time, unfortunately, Turnhill's Milford's and Bruccoli's biographies were published. Mellow's "racy patois" is "as vivid in its own way as Le Vot's more elegant homage. Still, either fulfills what must be the purpose of a major biographical project— wither to resuscitate an interesting but neglected subject, or to reappraise someone of prominence in the light of new data.

B88. Carabine, Keith. Rev. of *New Essays on The Great Gatsby*, ed M. J. Bruccoli. *Notes and Queries* 34.4 (Dec.1987): 575.

Apart from George Garrett's "idiosyncratic" "Fire and Freshness: A Matter of Style in *The Great Gatsby*," Bruccoli's collection of five short essays "fails to fulfill any of the series' aims." Bruccoli's introduction is "bitty," and the four remaining essays are "dull and straightforward accounts of the 'long shadow' of the novel upon its successors; of the 'tragic note of aspiration'; of the theme of 'illusion'; and of the history behind Fitzgerald's desire to write 'the great American novel.'"

B89. Carabine, Keith. Rev. of *Scott Fitzgerald: Crisis in American Identity*, by Thomas J. Stavola. *The Modern Language Review* 76 (1981): 947-8.

An Eriksonian study of the psycho-histories of Fitzgerald, his protagonists, and Zelda that "consciously accepts and reworks the clichés of Fitzgerald criticism." Fitzgerald was an Eriksonian because he was aware of how his own and his characters' "identity crises" are complicated by their relation to American culture. The Eriksonian grid of development fits Amory Blaine but "grotesquely deforms" Gatsby, the great function of which he sees as "the source in childhood of Gatsby's past." Stavola fails to realize that raw experience of life does not teach an artist how to integrate material into art, and correspondingly, fails to do justice to either Erikson or Fitzgerald.

B90. Carter, Angela. *"The Great Gatsby." Observer* (24 Feb. 1980): 34, 37.

The Great Gatsby is the "most perfect romance of capitalism." It is also the most Balzacian of all American novels, and certainly the only "authentic" story of a sentimental education. If Daisy won't leave her adulterous husband to retain self-respect, then she will "scarcely be regenerated by the renewed offer of Gatsby's pure heart."

B91.   Claridge, Henry. Rev. of *F. Scott Fitzgerald*, by Andrew Hook. *Notes and Queries* 41.2 (June 1994): 281-82.

Hook's volume "has much to commend it. It is clearly written, jargon-free, unpretentious, and makes a concerted effort to see Fitzgerald's work, notably the fiction, in its totality." The author argues for the value of the first two novels, and their "elegant style, psychological and emotional honesty, and a freshness of point of view." Hook's account of *The Beautiful and Damned* is "consistently informed and perceptive." He believes the key to the success of *The Great Gatsby* is in its narrative form and his account of this form is "intelligent, particularly in the discussion of the complex task that Fitzgerald gets Nick Carraway to perform." Hook is a more invigorating critic of the last two novels. A reader who wants an "intelligent overview of Fitzgerald's achievement can do little better than begin here."

B92.   Claridge, Henry. Rev. of *F. Scott Fitzgerald: A Study of the Short Fiction*, by J. Kuehl. *Notes and Queries* 40 (March 1993): 123-24.

Extended treatment is accorded to Kuehl's list of Fitzgerald's best stories, which reflects a conventional view: "The Ice Palace," "May Day," "The Diamond as Big as the Ritz," "Absolution," "Winter Dreams," "The Rich Boy," "Babylon Revisited," and "Crazy Sunday." Kuehl finds similarity between "Absolution" and Joyce's stories, in that it echoes Joycian conflict "between sexual repression and sexual expression." Internalization is pursued in his treatment of "Babylon Revisited," which allowed Fitzgerald to "internalize the conflict between the two sides of the protagonal nature," and that of "opposing landscapes" (Europe and America). Kuehl pursues this discussion of "internalization," seeing it as a method through which "first-person observers and third-person consciousness helped Fitzgerald merge private and public phenomena." In Parts II and III, brief extracts from other critics on Fitzgerald are an important addition.

B93.   Coren, Michael. "The Other Side of Paradise (Life & Works)." *London Sunday Times* Section 6 (16 Dec. 1990): 5. BHI.

An assessment written on the 50th anniversary of Fitzgerald's death. According to Mencken, "He was the amalgam of all the geniuses of all the children in America." Stephen Vincent Benet: "This is not a legend, this is a reputation—

and, seen in perspective, it may well be one of he most secure reputations of our time."

B94. Cox, Geof. "Three Literary Figures: Thomas Edison, Scott Fitzgerald and *The Great Gatsby.*" Rev. of *F. Scott Fitzgerald: A Biography,* by André Le Vot. *Essays in Poetics: The Journal of the British Neo-Formalist School* 10.2 (Sep. 1985): 28-34.

David Nye's *The Invented Self* is one attempt to deconstruct a figure in the American dream (Thomas Edison), and *The Great Gatsby* is another. Earlier biographies of Edison created a self for him that was as fictional as Gatsby. Le Vot's biography of Fitzgerald is presumably of the type Nye would attack, as Le Vot has no truck with deconstruction. Fitzgerald felt trapped by the image of the Jazz Age, but the image is so compellingly developed that *Gatsby* is seen as a tragedy of romance rather than a powerful critique of American capitalism. The importance of *Gatsby* is the way in which it figures forth the tension between truth and ideology." The significance of this escapes Le Vot, who sees no duplicity of meaning. One must look for both truth and ideology in the language that *Gatsby* describes.

B95. Dingley, R.J. "Review of *Forked Tongues? Comparing Twentieth-Century British and American Literature.*" Eds. Ann Massa and Alistair Stead. *Notes and Queries* (1996): 372-3.

In a "ragbag" collection of essays purportedly on the "curious and compelling differences between British and American writing in the twentieth century," David Seed's essay on party-going in the fiction of the Jazz Age is at least interesting.

B96. Dunn, Douglas. "Courtly diversions." Rev. of *Poems 1911-1940*, ed. M. J. Bruccoli. *Times Literary Supplement* (29 Jan. 1982): 101.

Amory Blaine recognizes that he'll never be anything but a mediocre poet because he's not enough of a sensualist. *This Side of Paradise* was written in modernist prose that had no counterpart in Fitzgerald's poetry. His practice of poetry was "an incidental and perhaps even sentimental pastime," a "high-spirited, sometimes melancholy diversion."

B97. Dyer, Geoff. "Classic Thoughts: A Touch of Class on the Riviera. Geoff Dyer on the degradation and poise of F. Scott Fitzgerald's *Tender Is the Night.*" *The Independent* (8 May 1993): 28.

Tender Is the Night is saturated by the aftermath of World War I. Fitzgerald was entranced by the poise of the wealthy, yet aware of the degradation of those who toil for their way of life. "In failing, Dick is somehow fulfilling his destiny."

B98. Egan, Sue. Rev. of *F. Scott Fitzgerald and the Art of Social Fiction*, by
        Brian Way. *Notes and Queries* 28 (Oct. 1981): 465-6.

"Social fiction is a heavily weighted term and, to an expert, Way appears to be fighting his material." He defines social fiction on Fitzgerald's own, shifting, ground. Way never balances his initial concentration on Fitzgerald's place in literary tradition with a sufficiently detailed examination of the relationship between author and contemporary events. A short-coming of the book is Way's reluctance to provide a "more incisive analysis of social context." As a result, this book is a "suggestive yet inadequate location of Fitzgerald's social fiction within a social framework."

B99. Gallafent, Edward. Rev. of *F. Scott Fitzgerald: The Great Gatsby*, by
        John S. Whitley. *The Yearbook of English Studies* 10 (1980): 357-8.

The Great Gatsby is a "great world novel." Gatsby, like great Romantic writers, seeks to transform the real world into something "new and dynamic." Yet Mr. Whitley assumes much too easily that the real can be found in Nick Carraway's perspective. Nick is compared to Marlow in *Heart of Darkness*, and to Melville's Ishmael. Whitely damages his own argument by claiming too much. Narrative schemes have some similarities but are also vastly different.

B100. Hamilton, Cynthia S. Rev. of *New Essays on The Great Gatsby*, ed. M. J.
        Bruccoli. *Journal of American Studies* 22.2 (1988): 306-8.

"Haphazard." Bruccoli's introduction only hints at his encyclopedic and deep understanding of Fitzgerald. The essays are disappointing, though two rise above the rest. George Garrett discusses the stylistic accomplishment of *Gatsby* with "sensitivity and understanding." Susan Resnick Parr's "The Idea of Order at West Egg" argues that Gatsby, Daisy and Nick "all knowingly turn away from reality. . . ." This essay hints at the "richness of Fitzgerald's layered narrative."

B101. Johnston, Sheila. "American Bad Dream." Rev. of BBC2 serial
        adaptation of *Tender Is the Night*. *The Listener* 114 (19 Sept.1985): 29.

Dennis Potter's screenplay follows the "chronological sequence of the revised edition." It's focus is psychological, and the cast for the most part conveys the complex sensibilities behind the characters. Nicole, played by Mary Steenburgen, overshadows Dick with "hard-edged brilliance" but the "poetic splendor" of what Dick accomplishes is impossible for television to capture.

B102. Lodge, David. "Fitzgerald's Fear of the Flesh." Rev. of F. Scott
*Fitzgerald: Critical Assessments. Vol. 4, General Perspectives:
Fitzgerald and Other Writers,* ed. Henry Claridge. 4 vols.
Robertsbridge, UK: Helm Information, Ltd., 1992. 405-408.

Fitzgerald was strongly influenced in his youth by Catholic influences at home
and at school. These are "most plausible" in his attitudes toward sexuality in
This Side of Paradise and *The Beautiful and Damned.* "Fear of the destructive
power of sex and of women. . .persists in Fitzgerald's mature work but in more
subtle and complex forms." "Absolution," written as a first chapter to *The Great
Gatsby,* is therefore of "crucial interest." Fitzgerald eliminates any religious
assertions with Gatsby's early life, but they are the source of his dream. The
effect is that Gatsby is a much more mythical and enigmatic figure.

B103. McNeil, Helen. "Dream Factory." Rev. of *The Price Was High: The
Last Uncollected Stories of F. Scott Fitzgerald,* ed. M. J. Bruccoli. *New
Statesman* 5 (Oct. 1979): 520.

Fitzgerald was "the finest natural stylist in American literature," yet he didn't
write stories to "buy time for writing the novels, he wrote them to destroy the
novels, because the novels were the life he was busy destroying."

B104. Mullen, Richard. "A Portrait of F. Scott Fitzgerald: Chronicler of the
Manners and Moods of the Jazz Age." *Listener* 114 (12 Sep. 1985): 15-
16.

Despite the fact that early fame contributed to an unstable personality, Fitzgerald
is a superb storyteller with a poetic gift for language, and *Tender Is the Night* is
most important work. Although he once remarked that the novel was a
'confession of faith,' he later stated 'I guess I am too much of a moralist at heart
and really want to preach at people in some acceptable form rather than to
entertain them.'

B105. Norman, Philip. "Great Scott." *Sunday Times Magazine* (26 Oct. 1997):
16-17, 19, 21, 23.

This essay is the first in a series of imaginary conversations between Sunday
Times writers and remarkable figures of the 20th century. Here Fitzgerald is
supposed to be 38-years-old. Fitzgerald anticipated the 20th-century disease
nostalgia, the *Esquire* essays of 1936 set off the age of confessional journalism,
and showed that anyone can reinvent himself totally and get away with it. "You
take all this more personally than I did," Fitzgerald said. Fitzgerald's most
magical power was enthusiasm.

B106. Oates, Joyce Carol. "The Authority of Failure: Scott Fitzgerald's Progress from Voice of the Jazz Age to Hemingway's Butt." Rev. of *The Love of the Last Tycoon: a Western,* by F. Scott Fitzgerald, ed. Matthew J. Bruccoli, and *Scott Fitzgerald: A biography,* by Jeffrey Meyers. *Times Literary Supplement* 4840 (5 Jan. 1996): 3-4.

Fitzgerald was the "most minor" of the "major" American writers. The most serious flaw of *Tender Is the Night* is that Fitzgerald "seems not to have known whether the novel would be ironic, or romantic." The choice of Cecilia as narrator was a "fateful choice" because of her "intellectually limited position." *The Far Side of Paradise* by Arthur Mizener is "still the most compelling of the numerous accounts, with a dramatic freshness that time has not dulled." Jeffrey Meyers's biography *Scott Fitzgerald* is a sort of *Reader's Digest* of biographies.

B107. *Off the Shelf: Tender Is the Night* by F. Scott Fitzgerald. BBC World Service. London, 24 September 1996.

This is a serialization of parts of the novel. According to the correspondent, on September 24, 1996 the speaker used an "inept semi-Texas accent and even tried some Australian for the father pulling his son out of Dick's sanitorium."

B108. Rhodes, Kate. Rev. of *The Winding Road to West Egg: The Artistic Development of F. Scott Fitzgerald.* Eds. Robert Roulston and Helen H. Roulston. *Journal of American Studies* 30.2 (1996): 305-6.

This critical study takes a diagrammatic approach to Fitzgerald's work before *The Great Gatsby.* It spends time describing his plots and little time on engaging in deep textual analysis. Even in the epilogue, the authors describe plots in the novels written after *The Great Gatsby* rather than commenting on the evident patterns of his pre-*Gatsby* work. The work does comment on his relationships with his various editors in some detail.

B109. Stevenson, Randall. Rev. of *F. Scott Fitzgerald,* by Andrew Hook. *Journal of American Studies* 28.1 (1994): 112-13.

Despite the contrary impulse of much recent theory and criticism, Hook sees Fitzgerald's life and art as too closely allied to "deconstruct." His views are fairly orthodox except for his attack on the myth that the first two novels are immature. He sees them as having "achieved power," although by admitting they are "uneven, structurally loose, sometimes sentimental and self-indulgent" he undermines his argument. The volume does at least thoroughly introduce familiar ideas, sometimes even developing them further. A concise, helpful introduction to the novelist.

B110. Symons, Julian. "A gift for hope." Rev. of *Some Sort of Epic Grandeur: The Life of F. Scott Fitzgerald*, by M. J. Bruccoli. *Times Literary Supplement* 26 Feb. 1982: 221-2.

Bruccoli's biography contains more facts than the others but many we don't need or wish to know. Further, his style is graceless, but the final result justifies the enterprise. *This Side of Paradise* and *The Beautiful and Damned* are "very bad." In *The Great Gatsby*, Fitzgerald shows "exquisite tact and effective understatement." The book is also a structural triumph. In *Gatsby*, Fitzgerald "found the proper approach for his genius, the right story to accommodate it."

B111. Townsend, Roy. Rev. of *Scott Fitzgerald: The Promises of Life*, ed. A. Robert Lee. *Journal of American Studies* 24.3 (1990): 471-2.

Harold Beaver's analysis of *Tender Is the Night* does not justify his sympathy or the weighty symbolism of the novel's "relative failure." The only story of Fitzgerald's to put him in the league of James, Kipling, Conrad, Joyce, Lawrence and Hemingway, is "Babylon Revisited." *The Great Gatsby* is a masterpiece despite its "translation of living woman to symbol."

B112. Vaux, Anna. "The discontented flapper." Rev. of *Zelda Fitzgerald: The Collected Writings*, ed. M. J. Bruccoli. *Times Literary Supplement* (25 Dec. 1992): 18.

Zelda's articles bolster the Scott and Zelda myth. Her stories are brief and not very good sketches of their life, but *Save Me the Waltz* is a "funny and frank and weird" book. Zelda's language provides the book with its "peculiarly heightened atmosphere and its luminously childlike manner." Her Jazz Age is more surreal than Scott's, and far more comically bizarre. Zelda had a greater sense of humor about things turning out badly than Scott. "What is clear is that being married to Scott is what Zelda's life was about."

B113. Weatherby, Harold L. Introduction. "Zelda Fitzgerald." *PN-Review* 15.6 (1989): 8.

Recollection of Zelda by her school classmate Weatherby's mother. Zelda was different from us even in high school in that she was unsupervised. She was amiable, kind, happy-go-lucky, uninhibited, and undisciplined. She followed her own interests to the neglect of duties. She was calm, soft-spoken, and even-tempered, but she "talked lots." Zelda dressed in hand-me-downs, was a little shocking, and started going steady with Scott when we were seniors in high school and he was based at Camp Sheridan. When she returned to Montgomery years later after being in a mental institution, she looked old, haggard, unkempt, and listless. There was instability in the Sayre family generally.

B114. Whitley, John S. Rev. of *Some Sort of Epic Grandeur: The Life of F. Scott Fitzgerald*, by M. J. Bruccoli. *Journal of American Studies* 17 (1983): 145-7.

The grandeur of Fitzgerald's life came precisely from his belief in the validity of the Romantic dream, and his effort to transform himself into a creative artist who would represent the *zeitgeist* of his era.

B115. Wood, Michael. "Wonder." Rev. of *The Love of the Last Tycoon: A Western*, ed. Matthew Bruccoli; *The Great Gatsby*, ed. Matthew Bruccoli; Rev. of *Scott Fitzgerald: A Biography*, by Jeffrey Meyers. *The London Review of Books* 16.21 (1994): 26.

Some of the prose in *The Great Gatsby* ("So he waited, listening for a moment longer to the tuning fork that had been struck upon a star") is written as if "Conrad had been reading *True Romance* and was working for Disney."

DISSERTATIONS

B116. Chambers, J. B. "F. Scott Fitzgerald and the Idea of the Novel." Diss. Univ. of Newcastle-upon-Tyne, 1985.

B117. Cooper, S. W. "Moral Values and Developing Technique in the Early Work of F. Scott Fitzgerald." M.A. Thesis. Univ. of Birmingham, 1975/76.

B118. Gould, R. H. "The Romantic Vision of F. Scott Fitzgerald." Ph.D. Thesis. Univ. of Leicester, 1977.

B119. Rowe, Joyce A. *Equivocal Endings in Classical American Novels: The Scarlet Letter, The Adventures of Huckleberry Finn, The Ambassadors and The Great Gatsby.* Cambridge: Cambridge UP, 1988. ix, 161.

B120. Sangari, K. "The Ironic Passions: Henry James and F. Scott Fitzgerald— A Study." Diss. Univ. of Leeds, 1979.

B121. White, R. L. "Fitzgerald's Women." M.A. Thesis. Univ. of Kent, 1974.

TEACHER/STUDENT GUIDES AND EDITIONS

B122. Altena, I. *Notes on F. Scott Fitzgerald's The Great Gatsby.* London: Methuen Educational, 1976. Study-Aid Series.

B123. Colomb, Stephanie, ed. *The Great Gatsby.* Harlow: Longman, 1991. xix, 185.

B124. Fitzgerald, F. Scott. *The Baby Party and Other Stories.* London: Penguin, 1995. 96.

B125. Fitzgerald, F. Scott. *The Beautiful and Damned.* Ed. M. Tarner. Heinemann Guided Readers. Heinemann E.L.T., 1992.

B126. Fitzgerald, F. Scott. *Bernice Bobs Her Hair and Other Stories.* Ed. Pamela Davies. Nelson, 1995.

B127. Fitzgerald, F. Scott. *The Diamond as Big as the Ritz and Other Stories.* Longman Structured Readers, 1974; Oxford (Progressive English Readers), 1994.

B128. Fitzgerald, F. Scott. *The Great Gatsby.* Ed. Margaret Tarner. Heinemann Guided Readers. Heinemann Educational (New Windmill Series)1987, 1992. Oxford Progressive Readers, Grade 4, 1994.

B129. Fitzgerald, F. Scott. *The Ice Palace and Other Stories.* Large Print Books. Transaction Pubs. 1998. 256.

B130. Handley, Graham. *Brodie's Notes on F. Scott Fitzgerald's The Great Gatsby and Tender Is the Night.* London: Pan Books, 1989. Revised edition 1990.

B131. Parkinson, Kathleen. *F. Scott Fitzgerald, The Great Gatsby.* London: Penguin Books, 1987.

B132. Parkinson, Kathleen. *F. Scott Fitzgerald, Tender Is the Night.* Harmondsworth: Penguin, 1986. 104.

B133. Ping, Tang Soo. *York Notes on The Great Gatsby*. Beirut: York, 1980. 71.

B134. Schwenker, Gretchen L. *York Notes on Tender Is the Night*. Beirut: York, 1984. 78.

B135. Tarner, Margaret. *The Great Gatsby*. London: Heinemann Educational, 1979.

B136. Tomalin, Mary. *The Great Gatsby*. London: Macmillan, 1992.

B137. Whitley, John S. *F. Scott Fitzgerald: The Great Gatsby*. London: Arnold, 1976. 64. (Studies in English Literature, 60)

France

Considerable progress has been made in the French contribution to Fitzgerald scholarship in the past two decades. In 1979, André Le Vot published his *Scott Fitzgerald*, a biography of the writer, which was widely praised and translated into several languages, including English (Ro16). Le Vot's volume has become the Fitzgerald biography of choice for many Europeans, although it is now curiously out of print in the original French (F40). Le Vot, a now retired Américaniste, has since the late 1960s fulfilled for Fitzgerald the role of championing major scholar that Maurice Coindreau, Camus, Sartre, and Gide were able to fulfill for Hemingway and Faulkner at an earlier time. In 1969, Le Vot published his first major critical work on Fitzgerald, *Gatsby le magnifique*, which came out in a subsequent edition in 1979 (F39). Although retired, he has continued to guide French perceptions of Fitzgerald's career, including writing several pieces for the edition of *Le Magazine Littéraire* (F85, F86, F87, F89) celebrating the Fitzgerald centennial and also an essay in *europe: revue littéraire mensuelle*, a monthly literary magazine, arguing for the influence of *À la récherche du temps perdu* on Fitzgerald's writing of *Gatsby* (F88).

Another much-esteemed French writer and critic to champion Fitzgerald has been Roger Grenier, author of 30 novels, essays, and stories and an influential work on Chekhov. Grenier first read and admired Fitzgerald in the 1950s and subsequently in the 1960s wrote prefaces for the Gallimard editions of *The Crack-Up* and *This Side of Paradise* (Grenier, 1963, 1965). More recently, in 1995, he wrote a biography of Fitzgerald for Gallimard's *l'un et l'autre* series with the avowed purpose of correcting the French view of Fitzgerald (F38).

The Great Gatsby and *Tender Is the Night* have also found an excellent new translator in novelist Jacques Tournier. His 1985 translation of *Tender Is the Night* was particularly well received by the critics and has sold well over 100,000 copies in France (F2). Of its success, he writes, "I believe that it can be explained on two different planes. First, it is a novel that occurs nearly entirely in France, principally on the Côte d'Azur, and it gives this region an extremely surprising image for readers of today, for in 1925-30, the beaches were practically deserted because tanning was not à la mode. There is a nearly documentary aspect to the description in the novel of these years of the immediate *après guerre* which for us correspond to the years Art Deco, that gives an image of Paris, more the right bank than the left. But this aspect does not suffice to explain the value of the novel, which is essentially the narrative itself, the characters of Nicole and Dick, the disintegration which underlines the book, and the perfection of the writing" (Tournier, 4 June 1998).

Tournier writes that due to the "force of existence" with which Fitzgerald created him, Gatsby has in France become a type, as Tartuffe, Rastignac and Emma Bovary have long been types (Tournier, 4 June1998). Still, his 1996 translation of *Gatsby* has not sold well nor has it even garnered many reviews (F1). He cannot explain the reason for *Tender*'s success and *Gatsby*'s relative failure, other than that *Tender* is "more French." It is also possible to surmise that it may have to do with the fact that between 1991 and 1996 three different translations of *Gatsby* appeared in bookstores. In 1991, L'Âge d'homme brought out a new translation of the novel, for which the publisher, thinking that it was in the public domain, did not obtain the permission of the Fitzgerald heirs and so was subsequently forced to remove it from the bookstores (F1). This translation by Michel Viel, a linguistics scholar at Paris IV who has written many articles on Fitzgerald and edited collections of others, was well-received by Roger Asselineau, another Sorbonne Américaniste and Hemingway scholar (F116). Then, in 1993 and 1994, with the Viel translation still on the shelves, new printings of the original Llona translation of 1926 appeared (F1). By 1966 when Tournier's authorized translation replaced Llona's, it may simply have been lost in the shuffle, both with reviewers and in bookstores. However, Tournier's translation has appeared in a Livre du Poche edition, and Elisabeth Bouzonviller, the author of a book on Fitzgerald published in 2000 (F34), believes it finally does justice to Fitzgerald's writing (Bouzonviller 9 July 1999). In an interview for the Centennial Edition of *Le Magazine Littéraire*, Tournier speaks passionately of translating *Gatsby* in the celebration by *Le Magazine Littéraire* of the Fitzgerald centennial, offering the reader many insights into Fitzgerald's writing of the novel as well as the difficulties in translating it (F75)

Various Américanistes from French universities have offered varying descriptions of the current state of affairs of Fitzgerald's reputation in France. André Bleikasten, of the Université de Strasbourg, a Faulkner scholar who wrote an article on Fitzgerald for the *Magazine Littéraire* Centennial edition, writes that "to my knowledge, there has not been much academic research done in France on Fitzgerald since André Le Vot. . . . My impression is that Fitzgerald still has his devotees in France. He is certainly not as highly ranked as Faulkner. . . . But he is clearly doing better than his contemporaries Hemingway, Dos Passos, or Steinbeck, . . ." (Bleikasten, 23 Jan. 1998).

Roger Asselineau, now retired from Paris IV, responded to Bleikasten's estimation:

It's very difficult to assess his reputation by comparison with that of Hemingway, as you will see. I may be partial, but I disagree with Bleikasten. Scholars like him, of course, prefer Faulkner who supplies them with rich Happy Hunting Grounds, but the general reader prefers the real hunting grounds described by Hemingway in a less tortuous manner. There is no doubt that he is more popular than Fitzgerald despite the latter's subtle art, and Dos Passos, though Sartre ranked him very high, and Steinbeck. Hemingway is the only one of them who has been included in the Pléiade, and his Oeuvres Romanesques in two volumes sell very well indeed and have been several times reprinted. He has attracted talented translators—unlike Fitzgerald [Jacques Tournier excepted!] (Asselineau, 1 July 1998).

Bleikasten's comment about the lack of academic research cannot go without challenge. While comparative statistics on the quantity and quality of Hemingway and Faulkner research being done in France are not readily available, still, when Fitzgerald work is compared with itself over the decades and even within the past twenty years, the amount of academic research is sizable and growing and, more significant, is of increasingly high quality. If Fitzgerald's reputation suffers in France, it may be because France does not have yet a thorough indexing system for its scholarly work. More has been written on Fitzgerald in France than perhaps most French scholars know.

To compare the number of translations and scholarly publications on Fitzgerald in France in the 50 years between 1926 when Gatsby was first translated and the late 1970s with the amount of translations and scholarship accomplished in the last two decades alone is to reveal a significant trend: 11 translations as opposed to 13 earlier ones; 47 editions compared to 22 in the first five decades; 56 essays published while only 42 were written in the previous fifty years; three book-length studies as opposed to two; and 12 dissertations compared to two until the late 1970s.

In the 1980s and the 1990s, work on Fitzgerald continued to expand: five articles were written between 1979 and 1985 and 12 in the last five years of the twentieth century. Dissertations increased from one in the first six years to five between 1995 and 2000. Collections of essays have also increased from two between 1986-1995, and two in the years between 1996 and 2000 alone.

Translations in this period include not only Tournier's retranslations of Gatsby and Tender, but also of several collections of short stories, including those in The Price Was High [known as the Love Boat series] (F27), his poetry in Mille et un navire [A Thousand and One Ships] (F30), and La ballade du rossignol roulant [The Cruise of the Rolling Junk] (F28). Larry Phillips's edition of Fitzgerald's comments on writing and his and Zelda's correspondence have also been translated (F21).

In addition to the publication of André Le Vot's and Roger Grenier's biographies, the 1969 Armand Colin volume containing André Le Vot's study of

Gatsby and Michel and Geneviève Fabre's study of *Tender Is the Night* (Le Vot and G. and M. Fabre 1969) was reissued in two volumes, Le Vot's in 1979 as mentioned above (F39) and the Fabres's in 1989 in response to *Tender Is the Night*'s having been placed on the *agrégation* exam (F36). The critical approach in these volumes, as in the majority of the essays written during these past two decades, has been most influenced by American New Criticism. While in their 1978 *Les Américanistes: New French Criticism on Modern American Fiction*, Ira D. and Christiane Johnson find that the contributors to their volume are "directly, obliquely, or negatively" affected by recent criticism in France, which they emphasize as being "at present in a very fertile and ebullient period," they also recognize that "being Américanistes, French scholars are aware of much of English and American criticism." In fact, as they say, "In the 1950s what shook the French out of the prevailing academic criticism (historical, biographical, and sociological) was the influence of the American New Critics" (Johnson, 1978, 8).

Elisabeth Bouzonviller, in her *Francis Scott Fitzgerald,* published in 2000 in France, stresses the polysemic quality of Fitzgerald's prose (F34) which perhaps expresses best the continuing use of the New Critical lens. Indeed, most of the recent and current books and articles trace patterns of imagery in *Gatsby* and *Tender Is the Night*. Seemingly, there is an infinite supply of such patterns in Fitzgerald's work and each individual scholar's close reading uncovers a different pattern. Even in his biography, André Le Vot devotes a considerable section to an analysis of Fitzgerald's use of color imagery, particularly yellow and blue (F39). Other imagery studies include Fitzgerald's use of bodily description in *Gatsby* and *Tender* (F60), his use of Greco-Roman cosmological imagery in *Gatsby* (F66) and multiple place descriptions in *Tender* as suggestions of mental space (F74).

Many discussions of imagery are in the context of modernist themes arising out of nineteenth-century occurrences: Fitzgerald's pattern of juxtaposing pastoral versus urban imagery in *Tender* is seen as ultimately traceable to the defeat of rebel armies at Appomatox and hence the defeat of the pastoral ideal (F96). Images of advertising in *This Side of Paradise* are mourned as a triumph over humanistic values (F62). Time imagery is presented as either influenced by Proust or parallel to his concept of lost time (F88). Many French scholars continue to pursue the mythology of the American Dream, while others persist in claiming that this aspect of *Gatsby* eludes most French scholars. Still other studies of imagery do so in pursuit of socio-political and psychoanalytic themes.

Of course, the French have their own tradition of close reading in the *explication de texte* exercises for students studying for the *agrégation* exams. In one collection, Michel Viel asks four Américanistes to comment on the final pages of *Gatsby* and in so doing "proved" that even four expert readers would explicate the imagery of the text in four very different ways (F41).

Donatella Izzo, an Americanista at the L'Istituto Universitario Orientale in Naples who has written about the modern/postmodern narratology of *Gatsby*

(It33), conjectures that "It is true that French academic critics seem to be very new critical in their approach, despite the fact that most new theoretical approaches in United States scholarship have come from France. . .I guess it depends on the structure of academia there, where both examinations and doctoral dissertations have to follow a very precise normative pattern based on a close-reading approach, which probably translates straight into the books and articles academics publish" (Izzo, 27 Mar. 2000).

Despite the new critical influence on Amèricanistes beginning in the 1950s, Roland Barthes identified the four main "philosophies" of French criticism in the 50s as existentialism, Marxism, psychoanalysis and structuralism (Barthes 1963). While in the French Fitzgerald criticism of this earlier period and extending into this current stage, examples of all four philosophies can be found, only the latter three have continued to influence French Amèricanistes writing into this fourth period. For example, French scholars continue to mention E. M. Cioran's 1952 essay in which he described Fitzgerald's crack-up as "a Pascalian experience without Pascal's spirit" (Cioran, 1 Oct. 1952, 44), although most are more willing than he to give Fitzgerald credit for a Pascalian spirit as well. Social critics now concede the subtlety of his criticism of capitalism. One essay takes a structuralist approach, seeing Gatsby as an epic genre. Jean Bessière, a critic who wrote a psychoanalytic study in 1972 (Bessière) wrote another for the *Magazine Littéraire* centennial edition (F51).

The British scholar, Nicolas Tredell, in his research on American scholarship for his 1997 Columbia Critical Guide on *Gatsby* has found that beginning in the 1990s French literary theories have begun to affect *Gatsby* scholarship in America (B35). This is strangely true of French scholarship on Fitzgerald as well. Elisabeth Bouzonviller's doctoral dissertation, published by Sententrion in 2000, utilizes the various critical approaches of Barthes, Lacan, Foucault, Kristeva, Georges Bataille, René Girard, and Philippe Sollers (F34). Ms. Bouzonviller has also published a second book based on her dissertation written for the wider audience of the Voix américaines'collection, the editor of which is Marc Chénetier, one of France's most well-known Améicanistes, who has also written a recent article on Fitzgerald (F62). A brief summary indicates the scope of her work: Through his silences, lack of realistic detail, hazily defined characters, revelations to the limit of what consciousness permits, and apparently baseless anguish, Fitzgerald suggests zones of darkness and breakage to which his post-war society but also humanity in general is prey. Bouzonviller sees the postmodern themes of rupture, fissure, and fragmentation and the Lacanian emphasis on deferral of desire as coexisting with the modernist tensions between order and disorder and unity and fragmentation and also with the modernist use of the quest pattern and mythic archetypes. His writing is a unique exercise that enabled him to express the unknowable in an art through which he aspired to create fusion (F34).

One of Bouzonviller's dissertation advisers, Prof. François Pitavy, a Faulkner scholar at the Université de Bourgogne in Dijon, provides the first reaction to her work by writing that while he has never "felt fitzgeraldian," reading her dissertation has changed his mind, as it has led him to see not 'this side of Fitzgerald' but the other Fitzgerald, who wrote to explore violence and mental breakdown, in fact what Melville called in Hawthorne 'the power of blackness' . . . This is a dissertation that leads one to reread Fitzgerald closely" (F141). Prof. A. Duperray, professor of American literature at Provence University, notes that the book "successfully revitalizes the various approaches to this endlessly fascinating work which were rather outdated" (F127). Donatella Izzo, of Istituto Universitario Orientale in Naples, agrees: "It's as if this were a new and different Fitzgerald from the one I studied almost twenty years ago, and one that still interests me in different ways—I'm glad I had this opportunity to rediscover him from a new angle" (Izzo, 16 Aug. 2001).

Two other young French scholars, Pascale Antolin-Pirès and Marie-Agnès Gay, have also published books on Fitzgerald reflecting the new French theoretical approaches. In *L'Objet et ses doubles. Une relecture de Fitzgerald*, Antolin-Pirès draws on semiotics in her analysis of the semantic double-meaning of objects in Fitzgerald's novels at the expense of their objective existence, seeing them as representing both ontological and poetic quests, thus providing for human identity (F32). In *Epiphanie et fracture: l'évolution du point de vue narratif dans les romans de F. Scott Fitzgerald*, Marie Agnès Gay analyzes Fitzgerald's manipulation of the narrative voice in this study located at the conjunction of a stylistic analysis and the study of the linguistic and pragmatic references of the narrative voice as these bear on thematics (F37).

What to conclude then at this juncture between centuries about Fitzgerald's reputation in France? In the last 20 years, translated and retranslated, analyzed endlessly both as to biography and to work, his centennial celebrated not only by the *Magazine Littéraire* and Grenier's biography but also by Van Cleef and Arpels's "Un diamante Gros Comme le Ritz" ("A Diamond as Big as the Ritz") gala featuring Sharon Stone, a Salon du Livre homage by noted Américanistes (Peterhansel, 25 July 1996), and by Roger Grenier's radio program at the Festival d'Avignon (Grenier, 17 Jan. 1998), Fitzgerald is now, as novelist and director of *Le Figaro* editorial board Franz-Olivier Giesbert has indicated, "studied in all colleges and universities" (Giesbert, Mar. 1998). But what finally will confirm for the French Michel Fabre's conviction expressed two decades ago that Fitzgerald along with Balzac and Stendhal is a classic (Fabre 1975)? A Pléiade edition? Certainly, but according to Roger Asselineau, Faulkner has yet to appear in that esteemed series, and he is revered in France (Asselineau, 1 July 1998). The prognosis for Fitzgerald's ultimate acceptance by the French as a classic writer, based on the several standards mentioned, appears excellent.

REFERENCES

Asselineau, Roger. Letter to the author. 1 July 1998.

Barthes, Roland. *Times Literary Supplement.* 1963.

Bessière, Jean. *Fitzgerald, la vocation d'échec.* Paris: Larousse, 1972.

Bleikasten, André. Letter to the author. 23 Jan. 1998.

Bouzonviller, Elisabeth. E-mail to the author. 9 July 1999.

Cioran, E. M. "Physionomie d'un effondrement: l'expèrience pascalienne d'un grand romancier américain." *Profils* I (Oct.1952): 44-52.

"Un diamant Gros Comme le Ritz." Van Cleef & Arpels Joailliers event announcement, faxed by Jérôme Yager to Ruth Prigozy, co-chair of Fitzgerald Society, September 1996.

Fabre, Michel. Letter to the author. 1975. See also 1980 ed. p. 14.

Giesbert, Franz-Olivier. Letter to the author. Mar. 1998.

Grenier, Roger. "Préface." *La Fêlure.* Paris: Gallimard, 1963; "Préface." *L'Envers du Paradis.* Paris: Gallimard, 1965.

Grenier, Roger. Letter to the author. 17 Jan.1998.

Izzo, Donatella. E-mail to the author. 27 Mar. 2000.

Izzo, Donatella. E-mail to the author. 16 Aug. 2001.

Johnson, Ira D. and Christiane. *Les Américanistes: New French Criticism on Modern American Fiction.* Port Washington, NY, London: Kennikat Press, 1978.

Le Vot, André. *"The Great Gatsby."* and Michel and Geneviève Fabre.*"Tender Is the Night." Francis Scott Fitzgerald.* Collection U2. Paris: Librairie Armand Colin, 1969. For Annotations, see L. Stanley, *The Foreign Critical Reputation of F. Scott Fitzgerald.* Westport, CT: Greenwood, 1980. 20-21, 23-24.

Peterhansel, Andra. Letter to the author. 25 July 1996. Peterhansel attended the event; participants included P. Y. Pétillon, J. Tournier, F. O. Giesbert, R. Grenier, A. Bleikasten, and Jasmina Reza.

Tournier, Jacques. Letter to the author. 4 June 1998.

Parenthetical citations to entry numbers refer to annotated references in this
chapter.

TRANSLATIONS/EDITIONS

F1.   Fitzgerald, F. Scott. *Gatsby le magnifique* [*The Great Gatsby*]. Trans.
        Victor Llona. Paris: Collection Européene, Kra Édit, 1926. Reprinted
        Paris: Editions du Sagittaire, 1946 (Preface, Edouard Roditi); Le Club
        français du livre, 1952 (Preface, André Bay), 1959; Grasset, 1962
        (Preface, Antoine Blondin, Bernard Frank, Jean-François Revel), 1968;
        Livre de poche, 1962 (same Prefaces); Editions Rombaldi, 1969; Le Club
        de la femme, 1969; Livre de poche. Le Sagittaire, 1973; France-Loisirs,
        1974; Le Livre de poche 900. LGF, 1983; Grasset, 1993. 256; Trans.
        Michel Viel. Lausanne: L'Age d'homme, 1991; Trans. Jacques
        Tournier. Paris: Grasset, 1996; Livre de poche, 1997.

F2.   Fitzgerald, F. Scott. *Tendre est la nuit* [*Tender Is the Night*]. Trans.
        Marguerite Chevalley. Paris: Stock, 1951 (Preface, André Bay).
        Reprinted Paris: Delamain et Boutelleau, 1951; Brussels: Les Editions
        Biblis, 1953; Lausanne: Ed. Rencontre, 1965, 1971; Paris: Stock, 1961,
        1967, 1973; Paris: Livre de poche, 1969 (original version); France-
        Loisirs, 1973; Flachette, 1974; Librairie générale française, 1974. Trans.,
        intro. and notes by Jacques Tournier. Belfond, 1985; Le Livre de poche
        6722. LGF, 1990. 476; In *Fragments de Paradis: "Love Boat" et 63
        autres nouvelles; "Tendre est la nuit."* Trans. Jacques Tournier and
        Nicole Tisserand. Paris: Omnibus, 1998.

F3.   Fitzgerald, F. Scott. *Le dernier nabab* [*The Last Tycoon*]. Trans. André
        Michel. Paris: Gallimard, 1952; Trans. Suzanne Mayoux. Du monde
        entier. Paris: Gallimard, 1976. 218. Preface Edmund Wilson;
        Gallimard, 1988. 246.

F4.   Fitzgerald, F. Scott. *La fêlure* [*The Crack-up*]. Trans. Dominique Aury
        and Suzanne Mayoux. Preface, Roger Grenier. Paris: Gallimard, 1963;
        Folio 1305; Gallimard, 1981. 512.

F5.   Fitzgerald, F. Scott. *Un diamant gros comme le Ritz* [*A Diamond as Big as the Ritz*]. Trans. Marie-Pierre Castelnau and Bernard Willerval. Paris: Laffont, 1963; Preface, Malcolm Cowley, 1973; Classiques pavillons. Laffont, 1984. 576; Livre de poche 3658; LGF, 1984. 731.

F6.   Fitzgerald, F. Scott. *Les heureux et les damnés* [*The Beautiful and Damned*]. Trans. Louise Servicen. Paris: Gallimard, 1964; Folio 1583; Gallimard, 1984. 512.

F7.   Fitzgerald, F. Scott. *L'envers du paradis* [*This Side of Paradise*]. Trans. Suzanne Mayoux. Paris: Gallimard, 1964; L'imaginaire 27. Gallimard: 1978.

F8.   Fitzgerald, F. Scott. *La longue fuite* [*The Long Way Out*]. Trans. Marie-Pierre Castelnau and Bernard Willerval. Lausanne: La Guilde du livre, 1964.

F9.   Fitzgerald, F. Scott. *Histoires de Pat Hobby, et autres nouvelles* [*Pat Hobby and Other Stories*]. Trans. Marie-Pierre Castelnau and Bernard Willerval. Preface, John Dos Passos. Paris: Laffont, 1965; New ed. *Histoires de Pat Hobby* [*The Pat Hobby Stories*], 10/18, 1997.

F10.   Fitzgerald, Francis Scott. *Lettres de F. Scott Fitzgerald.* Trans. J. & L. Bréant. Du monde entire. Gallimard, 1965. 648.

F11.   Fitzgerald, F. Scott. *Les enfants du jazz* [*The Children of Jazz*]. Trans. Suzanne Mayoux. Paris: Gallimard, 1967; Folio 1052. Gallimard, 1978. 436.

F12.   Fitzgerald, F. Scott. *Le légume* [*The Vegetable*]. Trans. and Adaptation by Jean Louis Abadie. Paris: Laffont, 1972; Théatre 515. *Avant-scène*, 1973. 50; *Le légume ou le president devenu facteur* [The V*egetable or from President to Postman*]. Trans. Charles Dantzig. Paris: Les Belles Lettres, 1996. 243.

F13.   Fitzgerald, Zelda. *Accordez-moi cette valse* [*Save Me the Waltz*]. Trans. Jacqueline Remillet. Paris: Laffont, 1973.

F14.   Fitzgerald, Francis Scott. *Eclats du paradis [Fragments of Paradise]*.
       Trans. Jean Queval. Contes et nouvelles. Julliard, 1977. 341

F15.   Fitzgerald, Francis Scott. *Le pirate de haute mer [The Offshore Pirate]*.
       UGE, 1981. 320.

F16.   Fitzgerald, Francis Scott. *Histoires de Pat Hobby [The Pat Hobby
       Stories]*. Trans. Bernard Willerval. 10/18. 1418 Domaine étrangere.
       UGE, 1981.

F17.   "Huit lettres de Scott et Zelda Fitzgerald, 1930-1940 [Eight Letters of
       Scott and Zelda Fitzgerald]." *Nouvelle Revue Française* 363 (April
       1983): 24-44.

F18.   Fitzgerald, Francis Scott. *Love Boat*. Ed. Matthew J. Bruccoli. Trans.
       Jacques Tournier. Belfond, 1983. 326.

F19.   Fitzgerald, Francis Scott. *Le garçon riche [The Rich Boy]*. Classiques
       pavillons. Laffont, 1984. 430.

F20.   Fitzgerald, Francis Scott. *Lettres à Zelda et autres correspondances
       [Letters to Zelda and Other Correspondence]*. Trans. and ed. Tanguy
       Kenec'hdu. Eds. M. J. Bruccoli and Margaret M. Duggan. Du monde
       entire. Gallimard, 1985. 400.

F21.   Fitzgerald, F. Scott. *De l'écriture [On Writing]*. Ed. and intro. Larry W.
       Phillps, Trans. Jacques Tournier, Preface Franz-Olivier Giesbert.
       Editions Complexe, 1985. xi, 123;. Le regard littéraire 48. Complexe,
       1991. 144.

F22.   Fitzgerald, Francis Scott. *Entre trois et quatre [Between Three and
       Four]*. Trans. Hervé Proulx. Livre de Poche. Belfond, 1986. 340.

F23.   Fitzgerald, Francis Scott. *Fleurs interdites [Forbidden Flowers]*. Trans.
       Nicole Tisserand. Livre de Poche. Belfond, 1988. 366.

F24.   Fitzgerald, Francis Scott. *Fragments du paradis* [*Fragments of Paradise*]. Trans. Jacques Tournier. Littérature étrangère. Livre de poche. Belfond, 1991. 400.

F25.   Fitzgerald, Francis Scott. *Love Boat.* Trans. Jacques Tournier. . Bibliothèque Belfond. Belfond, 1991. 350.

F26.   Fitzgerald, F. Scott. Excerpt from The Great Gatsby. *Les Grands Classiques de la littérature anglaise et américaine.* Paris: Hachette, 1992.

F27.   Fitzgerald, Francis Scott. *Love Boat: et autres nouvelles* [*Love Boat: and Other Stories*]. Trans. Jacques Tournier. Ed. and intro. M. J. Bruccoli. Livre de poche, 9531. LGF, 1992. 406.

F28.   Fitzgerald, F. Scott. *La ballade du rossignol roulant* [*The Cruise of the Rolling Junk*]. Trans. Jacques Tournier. Belfond, 1993.

F29.   Fitzgerald, F. Scott. "Une centaine de faux départs [A Hundred False Departures]"—un texte inédit de F. Scott Fitzgerald." Trans. Jacques Tournier. *Magazine Littéraire* 341 (Mar. 1996): 54-60.

F30.   Fitzgerald, F. Scott. *Mille et un navires* [*A Thousand and One Ships*]. Ed., trans. and foreword by Patrick Hersant. Paris: Les Belles Lettres, 1996. 157.

F31.   Fitzgerald, F. Scott. "Descriptions de filles [Descriptions of Young Women]." *L'Infini* 61 (Spring 1998): 27-38.

BOOKS: FULL-LENGTH STUDIES AND COLLECTIONS

F32.   Antolin-Pirès, Pascale. *L'Objet et ses doubles: une relecture de Fitzgerald* [*The Object and Its Doubles: A Rereading of Fitzgerald*]. Lettres d'Amèrique(s). Bordeaux: Presses Universitaires de Bordeaux,

2000. 242.

Fitzgerald's novels abound with traditional and modern objects whose invasive presence betrays their critique of early twentieth-century American materialism, as well as their strategic role in plot resolution. The object discourse is subjective and metaphorical while revealing its heuristic function and consciously affirming that man is incapable of controlling machines but can reestablish order and meaning in modern society. While for Fitzgerald, the object is more representative of its function than of its signification, he puts emphasis on the semantic game: the object's double meaning. For instance, sign-objects, such as cars, houses, radios, gramophones, and papers represent mechanical as well as poetic techniques. In *The Great Gatsby* and *The Beautiful and Damned* cars represent not only the modernization of American society in the '20s but also liberation and alienation, and in *The Last Tycoon*, the elevator suggests the downfall of the characters. In each novel, constant interruptions all through the story manifest the semantic role of objects at the expense of their mere representation. The sign-objects, as languages but not systems of exchange, represent the difficulty of a mechanical society in which communication dies because of its excess. The characters that seem to suffer from a lack of identity rely heavily on the sign-object to acquire an identity. For Fitzgerald, the collection of objects—to which he adds social, economic and personal values—can no longer be objective for they would loose their heuristic role. Collecting plays a significant role in the dialectic system for it is precisely the lack of something that gives rise to the desire. Fitzgerald's objects are less innocent than they seem, representing ontological and poetic quests.

F33.   Bardet, Pascal. *De la lumière verte à la vallèe des cendres: exploration de l'espace symbolique dans Great Gatsby de F.S. Fitzgerald* [*The Green Light and the Valley of Ashes: Exploration of Symbolic Space in F. Scott Fitzgerald's The Great Gatsby*]. Paris: Editions Rivé Droite, 1994. 86.

American culture is founded on movement, such as that from Puritan to pioneer to immigrant. To be an American is to elevate oneself above the limits fixed by regional identity. This faculty of reproducing the atmosphere of a place and reattaching it to characters and plot is the mark of a literary talent. In *The Great Gatsby* space is used symbolically to reunite the city, the country, and the suburb in a microcosmic universe, a veritable Fitzgerald symbol for a global vision of America. The East evokes the present, but the West is for Nick the future and for Gatsby the past. In the end Nick presents East and West as two facets of the same reality, that of an America in decline which is searching for its equilibrium. In the pastoral convention, harmony between man and nature is reestablished, but Fitzgerald denounces it through his ironic manner.

F34. Bouzonviller, Elisabeth. *Francis Scott Fitzgerald ou la plénitude du
      silence* [*Francis Scott Fitzgerald or the Plenitude of Silence*]. Thèse a la
      carte. Villeneuve d'Ascq: Presses Universitaires du Septentrion, 2000.
      477.

Calling on Barthes, Lacan, Foucault, Bataille, Sollers, Cioran, and Kristeva,
Bouzonviller argues that Fitzgerald suggests zones of darkness and breakage to
which his post-war society, but also humanity generally, is prey and that he
aspired to create fusion by writing of the unknowable and the hidden. Fitzgerald
does violence to his texts and describes the act of writing with violent
metaphors. Literary creation is born of the alliance of sexuality and death, of
eroticism, and a search for the sacred. Limit (and its geographical and
psychological dissolution) and frontier, both essential elements of Americanism,
are fundamental to the creation of the author. Human beings appear as
essentially divided, but they also offer an interior space, a source of innumerable
and unexpected discoveries which the author as hero will explore. Fitzgerald
foreshadows the vogue of psychoanalysis with characters who seek to deny their
origins and create themselves anew, yet denial is impossible for the American
family in which both maternal and paternal roles undergo profound mutation.
Unbeknownst to most French critics, the pleasure and eroticism of the text,
however, is situated in the fractures of wandering and individual failure which
are the source of the characters' existences. For Fitzgerald, writing affirms the
force of a creation welling up from disequilibrium and tirelessly interrogates the
shadowy psychological zones of which the author has presentiments. At the
heart of this combat, the Fitzgeraldian heroes lead quests proper to each but
which have universal echoes.

F35. Bouzonviller, Elisabeth. Francis Scott Fitzgerald: Écrivain du
      déséquilibre [Francis Scott Fitzgerald: Writer of Disequilibrium]. Belin:
      Paris, 2000. 128.

An adaptation for a wider audience of the author's *Francis Scott Fitzgerald ou
la plénitude du silence*. Like Conrad, Fitzgerald refuses the directly observable
in order to provoke emotional reactions in the reader. He also evokes the
reader's imaginative capacities for his writing is characterized by an
"extraordinary polysemie." His work becomes then an endlessly creative
entanglement which offers to the reader some presumptions of sense but never
definitive conclusions. The imprecision of his writing reflects his exploration of
the mysteries of being, particularly as revealed in the war between the sexes and
the need of the hero for fusion with the loved woman as a way of discovering a
part of himself he feels to be missing. Fitzgerald also explored the American
need for self-creation and the need to deny one's birth leading to a crisis in the
family and the roles of the parents, particularly of the missing father. Although

maternal imagery abounds, actual female characters are not maternal but predatory. As a result, adult infants dominate his work. Society itself is in crisis: the urban savagery after the war fundamentally split the structure of the individual. The writer sacrifices himself so that healing will take place.

F36.   Fabre, Michel et Geneviève. *Tendre est la nuit*. Paris: Armand Colin, 1989. Re-ed. of Le Vot, André, Fabre, Michel et Geneviève, *Gatsby le Magnifique* et *Tendre est la nuit*. Avec une présentation de Bernard Poli, éd. Colin, 1969.

The destiny of *Tender Is the Night* has not been a happy one in France. A better translation, one which will not eliminate three percent of each sentence, is needed to convey "the rich ambiguity of a prose" nearly as good as Conrad's or Proust's. The Fabres give an in-depth discussion of the themes and architecture of the novel between which there is a "profound unity." "Each movement of *Tender Is the Night* is composed of structures which are combined in more complex ensembles": cyclical structures of reparation and degradation and quest and escape, and linear structures of rise and fall. Some "great principles" arise from these structures—the chain of events, the repetitions and contrasts, symmetry and selection, reversals—as well as more subtle processes such as reflections and mirrors, and the usage of parody or burlesque, irony or symbol. "One discovers in this novel a veritable obsession with composition," as if Fitzgerald were giving life itself form and structure.

Cowley's version helps throw Rosemary's view into better focus and makes Dick's romanticism seem more understandable, but it lacks the suspense of the original. The complexity of life is reflected in the complex narrative devices of the novel in which Fitzgerald employs Conrad's theory of "chronological muddlement." Time destroys Dick who early knew too much hope, while it can only elevate Nicole from her miserable childhood. "As and when Dick loses his magic gift of arresting time or refuses to exercise it, his personality declines and thus his prestige." Not really an idealist, Dick has betrayed his father's values. His talent appears to him to be a perversion, a way of getting along with a world he hates. "He should have revolted," for the "ally of the rich becomes their victim." Dick dramatizes the principle that the individual is alone not only because he is isolated but also because his efforts to integrate himself constitute a kind of alienation. There are many mistakes in *Tender Is the Night*, but they "don't mar the novel."

F37.   Gay, Marie-Agnès. *Epiphanie et fracture: l'evolution du point de vue narratie dans les romans de F. Scott Fitzgerald Etudes Anglaises* [*Epiphany and Fracture: The Evolution of the Narrative Point of View in the Novels of F. Scott Fitzgerald*]. 102. Paris: Didier, 2000. 328.

Like Faulkner and Hemingway, Fitzgerald understood the potential in manipulating narrative voice. Point of view plays different roles in his novels, not only as foundation, but as support of intrigue. It is via the bias of the point of view, that Fitzgerald consciously shares his apprehension and disillusionment with the reader. This is a study of stylistics, thematics, and linguistic and pragmatic references of the narrative voice. The chronological study of Fitzgerald's novels allows us to single out the steps of this process. While his early novels show two similar viewpoints, his later works epitomize the fracture and subsequent imprisonment of the narrative point of view. Through the viewpoint of one character Fitzgerald depicts the downfall of another. In so doing, he establishes a distance between the author and the protagonist. Moreover, Fitzgerald offers his reader juxtaposed narrative voices in conjunction with his own viewpoint in order to maintain the ambiguity in the story. Fitzgerald wants to affirm his detachment and mastery over his characters, when in fact, his narrative strategy betrays both a lack of distance and his narcissism. In *Tender Is the Night*, the viewpoint determines the justification of the thematic strategy vis-à-vis the rupture within the novel. Fitzgerald aims at showing that the narrative voice is vulnerable, inadequate and subject to disappearance. The theme of appearance and disappearance of the narrative voice mirrors not only the wandering of the protagonists but also that of the reader. Fitzgerald's voice moves from an early optimism present in his early novels to a more pessimistic point of view in his later works.

F38.   Grenier, Roger. *Trois heures du matin, Scott Fitzgerald* [*Three O'Clock in the Morning*]. Paris: Gallimard, 1995.

This book consists of over 40 short impressionistic pieces which, as a whole, seek to correct the French view that Fitzgerald's earlier work was not as successful as the later novels by tracing the reactions of French critics and thinkers such as E.M. Cioran, Maurice-Edgar Coindreau, Claude Roy, Romain Gary and Jean Seberg. Grenier states that he hopes in this collection of essays "to seek out the man behind the legend, and above all the writer behind the man." Cioran had found that *The Crack-Up* was the only Fitzgerald success, and an absurdity at that. Coindreau, who arrived at Princeton the year after Fitzgerald left, was told nightmare stories of the insufferable student. Roy compared Fitzgerald to an acrobat who never showed so much talent as when he missed. He found that the later works when Zelda was crazy and Scott was out of fashion the most successful. The piece *"Le Jardin d'Allah"* concerns Fitzgerald's dealings with MGM, highlighting the author's discomfort with Hollywood's high Jewish quotient. Grenier's long-term admiration for Fitzgerald's work culminates at the collection's end in personal reminiscences about being among the small circle of French admirers in the 1950s who clung to Fitzgerald as the representative of worlds now gone.

F39. Le Vot, André. *Gatsby le Magnifique*. Paris: Armand Colin, 1979. Re-
      ed. of Le Vot, André, et Fabre, Geneviève et Michel. *Gatsby le*
      Magnifique, Tendre est la nuit, avec une présentation de Bernard Poli, éd.
      Colin, 1969. Out of print.

Le Vot presents an in-depth study for the French student of the themes and
techniques of *The Great Gatsby*, "one of the richest texts of American
literature." While the dialectic of *The Great Gatsby* stems from the American
classical tradition, Fitzgerald's use of a Conradian narrator to objectify Gatsby's
subjective experiences gives the novel universal significance. Fitzgerald
underlines his attempt to achieve universality in his description of Gatsby as
Trimalchio.

Fitzgerald presents his secondary characters more vividly than his heroes:
"psychological truth supports that the former are seen from the outside while the
latter are apprehended in terms of their interactions." Fitzgerald's presentation
of the Daisy-Gatsby relationship is intuitively correct. Nick has a weak
character. Infatuated by Daisy, he identifies with Gatsby's love and therefore
attempts to help him win her; "it is thus that the irreversible mechanism of the
action is put into motion." His weakness constantly reveals itself: he yields to
Tom by going to his Manhattan tryst and, at the end, shakes his hand; he judges
Gatsby's parties only when Daisy does; like a reassuring big dog, he listens to
others' loves and quarrels; he consents to read *The Rise of the Colored Empires*;
he ruins both the girl in the Middle West and Jordan; finally Nick is
reproachable only because he makes such claims for his honesty. He is a
Flaubertian, not a Jamesian innocent. Flaubert's character tends to deceive those
whom, in his foolishness, he thinks wish to abuse his ignorance, whereas James'
innocents remain innocent even though they become victims of society. Nick
certainly is not a victim of society. He worships Gatsby for his dream; the sense
of his own existence disappears as Gatsby's adventures absorb him. He is
"desperate to accede to a superior order of perception which would reconcile the
heterogeneous elements of the world."

The scene between the actress and her director is reminiscent of the scenes on
Keats' urn; Fitzgerald, like Keats, was searching for a world beyond time. Like
Joyce, Fitzgerald defines his characters by a familiar gesture, a way of speaking
or of dressing: his characters are neither ideograms nor allegorical silhouettes.
"Fitzgerald's originality is in his use of material detail to sense a moral reality."
As with Joyce, his choice of details is not a definition or a limitation but rather
an enlargement of reality. At moments *Gatsby* is like *Portrait of the Artist as a*
Young Man. Like Proust, Fitzgerald gives his primary characters traits of his
secondary characters. He also uses Dostoyevsky's method of the double. Unlike
Holden Caulfield and Huck Finn, Nick uses literary language to exorcise reality,
but, in the end, also as a catharsis. Nick the commentator and Nick the
participant have different languages. He uses simple, but negative, language in

speaking to others; he saves his sarcasm for the reader. Beyond this level of realism is the "radiant universe where all is order and beauty." The language describing these moments of transcendence forms an "esthetic of adhesion." These narrative and lyrical modes are dialectical: that of civilization versus the pastoral. Only in Gatsby's memory is the dichotomy between dream and reality merged. *Gatsby* is reminiscent of both tale and legend. Gatsby's love for Daisy marks the intrusion of the fairy tale on the legend: for, in the legend, the exemplary hero seeks to transform the world, the women are usually a hindrance. "Therefore the meeting with Daisy suspends provisionally the high ambitions of Gatsby." Like Galahad, Gatsby follows a grail, but as in the fairy tale, the goal is Daisy. Unlike the fairy tale, Gatsby's "perilous quest" was not recognized by the king or society, and so he must go outside the law.

F40. Le Vot, André. *Scott Fitzgerald*. Paris: Julliard, 1979. 459. New York: Doubleday & Company, 1983; London: Allen Lane, 1984; Harmondsworth: Penguin, 1985.

Fitzgerald's fascination with young women of a higher social standing, and with "defeat and renunciation," was more European than American, even as he became the spokesman for a new American attitude. He reinvented Henry James's romantic and cultivated but failed American woman, creating female characters who were bold, independent, and invulnerable. There are Pascalian echoes in the maturity and gravity he achieved; without them he would still have identified himself with the America Gertrude Stein said had gone from barbarity to decadence without passing through civilization. In Fitzgerald's spiritual biography, *Gatsby*, the author identified himself with a double character who on one hand disavows his mutilating lineage and asserts being literally a self-made man and on the other tries to dispel his worst fears by miring himself in impotence and renunciation. While satire and lyricism are the major themes of the book, light and color are used to create "climates of the soul." Icons—such as Dr. Eckelburg's eyes—are another important expressive force in this and other Fitzgerald works, as is popular music, which extends the "suggestive power of forms." Living in and loathing Rome, Fitzgerald wrote "The Adjuster," an exploration of xenophobia, which he ascribed to a "peculiarly American lag." More at home in Paris, he became critical of "unenterprising" American tourists and but would eventually use the admiration for America he instilled in his friend André Chamson in his own description of the "essence of America." *The Crack-Up* was greeted in France on one side by E. M. Cioran as a second-rate effort that didn't go deeply enough into its own failure and on the other by Michel Déon as the most appalling confession of failure yet dared to be made.

F41. Viel, Michel. Avant-propos [Foreword]. *Figures libres, figures imposées: L'explication de texte en anglais (fiction)* [*Free Forms,*

Imposed Forms: The Explication of the Text in English (Fiction)]. Ed.
Michel Viel. Paris: Hachette, 1993.

This book is a kind of handbook of *explication de texte* in English. The editor
asked five French scholars of American literature to select five works in their
field to explicate. He also imposed on them the explication of the last page of
Gatsby. Through comparisons of the compulsory texts, this proved that
explication de texte does not lead to uniformity while at the same time it does
lead to common themes and arguments.

French Translations of American Studies and Collections

F42. Bruccoli, Matthew J. *F. Scott Fitzgerald, une certaine grandeur épique*
      [*F. Scott Fitzgerald: Some Sort of Epic Grandeur*]. Ed. Henri Marcel.
      La Table Ronde, 1994.

F43. Bruccoli, Matthew J. *Scott Fitzgerald, sa vie, sa gloire, sa chute* [*Scott
      Fitzgerald: His Life, His Glory, His Fall*]. Trans. Solange Schnall and
      Christian Mégret. Vertiges, 1985.

ESSAYS/CHAPTERS/NOTES/CONFERENCE PAPERS

F44. Antolin-Pirès, Pascale. "Fitzgerald's Lists as 'Lexical Playfields' in
      Tender Is the Night." Paper delivered at the 5th International F. Scott
      Fitzgerald Conference. Université de Nice, 29 Jun. 2000.

F45. Audhuy, Letha. "The Waste Land Myth and Symbols in *The Great
      Gatsby*." *Études Anglaises* 33.1 (1980): 41-54.

The parallels between Eliot's *The Waste Land* and *The Great Gatsby* go much
further than has been noticed; Fitzgerald, "consciously and unconsciously, drew
upon the Waste Land as a whole, to the point of making it the informing myth of
his novel." Its permeation is clear in the coherent, intricate network of
significant details and allusions: the setting, view of modern society, characters
(Daisy as both hyacinth girl and Philomela) and use of the grail legend (owl eyes
as Tiresias, Gatsby as Fisher King, sun-god, life symbol).

F46. Auffret-Boucé, Hélène. *"The Great Gatsby." Figures libres, figures
      imposées: L'explication de texte en anglais (fiction)* [*Free Forms,*

Imposed Forms: The Explication of the Text in English (Fiction)]. Ed.
Michel Viel. Paris: Hachette, 1993. 121-125.

The Great Gatsby is a fugue: the theme—Gatsby's ideal, and the counter-theme—Nick's adventure, make a muted return, suffering the adjunction of a coda with the final sentence opening on another story—that of mankind's dream. The textual locus bears the stigmata of the past so deeply that it becomes legendary. A nocturnal lighting is chosen in which Gatsby's house slips back into nothingness. Thus, in the empty setting, endowed again with its initial virginity by dreams, the desire founding the adventure and the whole work makes its subtle and surreptitious comeback. The prism of Nick's memory rejects confrontation with other memories. Thus, he has a privileged reading in which he sees Gatsby's enemy as Time itself. The story of Gatsby, a victim of his dream, is exemplary. The utopian illusion of the Garden of Eden as both regained and effaced time, is a shared one. Nick compels his reader to acknowledge that nothing but his own story has been told. Such is the masterly poetic closure of *The Great Gatsby*.

F47.   Ballard, Michel. "Commentaire No. 10." *Le commentaire de traduction anglaise* [*Commentary on Translation into English*]. Collection 128. Paris: Nathan, 1993. 90-97.

The purpose of the book is to demonstrate for students in their first year of university that translation from another language is not easy, that, in fact, it is a difficult, complex operation. The author proposes a systematic exposure to translation and ways to analyze it, to acquire the vocabulary and some theory. He uses Llona's (1926) and Viel's (1991) translations of *The Great Gatsby* and discusses the differences between them, commenting on which is nearer in meaning to the original and on differences between English and French in general. For example, both translators render the passive English into the active with an indeterminate subject, again a tendency of French. Both also render the gerund, such as "being a politician," in the infinitive, but Llona's verb "politicailles" is more pejorative than Viel's "faire de la politique."

F48.   Bardet, Pascal. "A Short Trip Abroad: The Riviera as Another Version of America." Paper given at the Fifth International Fitzgerald Conference, Nice, 30 June, 2000.

No international theme exists in Fitzgerald's fiction, only his characters' alienation from their environment. Fitzgerald himself had no great interest in France, its writers, its culture; his so-called "international" fiction, reflecting this disinterest, tells the same story of Americans drifting in a perpetual "Noplace, USA." Exile was merely a means to further analyze one's Americanness. Characters were all doomed to suffer eventual emotional bankruptcy in Europe and then return to America. Like his "American" stories, Fitzgerald's "European" stories confront a failure of American idealism.

F49.   Bayle, Thierry. "Splendeurs et misères [Splendors and Miseries]." *Magazine Littéraire* 341 (Mar. 1996): 40-41.

In this interview, novelist Roger Grenier, explains why, since World War II, despite the French reverence for Faulkner, he has admired Fitzgerald. "What I loved about Fitzgerald was a certain charm. I read everything he wrote and that was written about him. He is a remarkable writer. The skill in the construction of *The Great Gatsby* is without precedent." In 1996, Grenier and Antoine Blondin were sent to cover the Winter Olympics in Cortina d'Ampezzo. This journey evoked the trip that Fitzgerald and Budd Schulberg took in *The Disenchanted*, and Grenier wrote a story "Les jeux [The games]" published in *La salle de rédaction*, for which he owed a debt to Shulberg's account, as only Blondin recognized. Fitzgerald's incarnation of the American Dream is an aspect of Fitzgerald which escapes the French critics for the most part. Fitzgerald wrote to capture the disorder of his life, to lose nothing. To lose nothing is important for a writer. He must deliver all, put all in literature, hide nothing. To lose no one, most of all not himself. Fitzgerald, as he himself said, deserves a small immortality.

F50.   Bessière, Jean. "F. S. Fitzgerald, univers littéraire, univers américain [F. S. Fitzgerald: Literary Universe, American Univerise]." *europe* 74.803 (Mar. 1996): 8-22.

The emblematic nature of Fitzgerald's work, representing the play between the individual and American society, is presented through allegorical argument, the emblematic and allegorical serving as checks to each other. Fitzgerald is also a critical writer in his sense that both experience and reflection have two sides: in his first two novels, aestheticism and egotism are also means of imposing individual liberty. In the last three novels, revolt is presented as an increasingly problematic and complex alternative challenge to the individual's lack of freedom. His work is also reflexive, his dialogue polemical in his characters' search for a truce with reality in order to live their lives. The world constitutes his characters; his characters constitute the world. Fitzgerald's dualities introduce us to the idea of "another America," a universe of moral affirmation in the Henry James tradition. Many of the characters are mute in an attempt to express the sense of a lost moral reality. Despite the muteness of the characters, the moral verities represent an American universe Fitzgerald took care to represent through seasonal imagery in *Gatsby* and *The Last Tycoon*, a universe that is a composite of New York City and the midwest, of the Cote d'Azur, Switzerland, and upstate New York.

F51. Bessière, Jean. "Les pleurs de Gloria [The Tears of Gloria]." *Magazine Littéraire* 341 (Mar. 1996): 47-50.

Fitzgerald's original contribution to an understanding of our experience of the world is in his "anthropological concept of sadness." Sadness, which is both outside of history yet does not separate itself from the experience of time and history because it is in itself this duality, proves the contradictory nature of reality, of human community and of private life. Fitzgerald saw contemporary life as neurotic, with sadness and weeping such as that of Gloria in *The Beautiful and Damned*, as symbols of that proof, of consciousness, and of lucid exposition of the public neurosis. Sadness affirms man's belonging to the human family at the same time that he is suffering. Social neurosis finds a remedy, a strength, in sadness. In *The Great Gatsby*, Nick interprets the life of Gatsby under both the sign of sadness and the sign of that which permits man to imagine the framework through which he is called to realize himself in his historicity. In *Tender Is the Night* the alliance of the amorous and psychoanalytic themes notes explicitly the social and individual pathologies, but, also, by the indissociable sadness of the amorous theme, represents this framework in which man is called upon to realize himself.

F52. Bessières, Michel. "Avec Gatsby, Long Island a gardé tout son chic [With Gatsby, Long Island Has Remained Chic]." *Le figaro magazine* Aug. 12, 1994: 100-105.

I visited Long Island's North Shore in 100°F weather, appropriate for doing research on *The Great Gatsby*, in which the heat and humidity were nearly liquid. I traveled to Port Washington to meet the members of Manors and Millionaires, whose purpose is to revive abandoned "Gold Coast" mansions from the turn of the century for display by inviting New York City decorators to refurbish them. In between visiting each of 16 "denuded" mansions, I interject Fitzgerald's critique of the rich who built these homes. Later, while driving me to Great Neck to visit the house Fitzgerald lived in while beginning to write *Gatsby*, Nelson de Mille, author of *Gold Coast*, told me the north shore of Long Island has not in fact changed much since the 20s. De Mille, as it turned out, doesn't like Fitzgerald much, except for the last three paragraphs of *Gatsby*. I plead for Gatsby, particularly for the green light: "It is perhaps thanks to the green light that I am a writer; it signifies that I must force myself to become what I truly wish to become."

F53. Bleikasten, André. "La gloire du vaincu [The Glory of the Vanquished]." *Magazine Littéraire* 341 (Mar. 1996): 32-34.

Without his failures, Fitzgerald would not have become a legend. While his writing reveals intellectual paucity, uncertain spelling, and uneven syntax, he proved he had the intelligence of a novelist through his treatment of the romantic, which, while indispensable to fairy tales, dreams, and illusions, is also indispensable to the novel, having lured the great novelists from Cervantes to Flaubert. He pushed the freshness of his imagination in a prodigious capacity to marvel, but it was also the engine of his lucidity. Lucidity is perhaps nothing more than the bitter comfort of sensible souls and the alibi of the flabby in literature as well as life. Yet Fitzgerald's lucidity is not only the grimace of Narcissus, and in *The Crack-Up* he pushed it to the limits of the confessional. *The Crack-Up* is a journey into nothingness according to the formula of Cioran: "the evocation of a pascalian experience without Pascal's spirit." Fitzgerald recognized he was neither a hero nor a saint but an ordinary man who was also an extraordinary writer. "With his courage and his patience of poverty and in spite of all that blocked his vision, he raised himself one more time to write and was faithful to his endeavor to his last breath."

F54.   Bleikasten, André. *"The Great Gatsby." Figures libres, figures imposées: L'explication de texte en anglais (fiction) [Free Forms, Imposed Forms: The Explication of the Text in English (Fiction)]*. Paris: Hachette, 1993. 141-145.

Like the first, the final chapter is about Nick as much as about Gatsby. Hardly a word on the final page is not used earlier in the novel; the words acquire symbolic weight through repetition. Unlike the Dutch sailors, Gatsby attempted to impose his own aesthetic vision upon a world whose beauty had been cheapened and corrupted. The language of equivocal sexuality and erotic and venal overtones indicates the greedy dream of lawless possession of the first settlers. Nick realizes that Gatsby's dream, the American dream, the dream of humanity has been engulfed by history but that "the final irony is that the lessons of the past are never learnt, that no amount of disillusion can ever cure man of hope."

F55.   Bonnet, Michèle. "Le 'moi' divisé dans *Tender Is the Night* [The Divided "Me" in *Tender Is the Night*]." *Americana* 5 (1990): 57-69.

The crux of Dick Diver's tragedy is the division of his personality, the "unhappy conflict between two selves, between two exigencies, one dictated by a social, civilized, idealistic self, the other by some desire long repressed of a more primitive self, which finishes by taking the upper hand as is shown not only in the personal destiny of Dick Diver but in the evolution of all those who surround him." I am interested first in the fact that idealists' dreams take form isolated from reality. A fundamental theme of the novel is that the self of repressed desires lurks behind the self that dreams of an ideal world. The animal metaphors throughout the novel function as signs of irrationality, amorality and triumph of libido for both Dick and Nicole. Sometimes Dick sees himself as the hero of a tragedy, with an incomprehensible destiny. Much is made of his corruption by wealth and the wealthy. All the fathers in the novel are discredited for one reason or another, especially the fathers of America, whose values were all destructive in the end. Dick's story is the story of a man deceived by fathers who would nourish and love him, but who were unconscious or hypocritical, and gave him a task impossible to fulfill. Not a pioneer's dream but the decadent world of Rome, the supreme father.

F56. Bouzonviller, Elisabeth. "The Frontiers that Artists Must Explore . . ." Paper given at the 5th International Fitzgerald Conference, Nice, July 4, 2000.

Wavering between great pride in his writing potential and complete self-deprecation, Fitzgerald managed, most probably without being aware of it, to reach and grasp what constitutes and troubles the human being as he strives in a violent universe reflecting his own divided self. Fitzgerald's works express "the power of blackness," an exploration of the human mind and a quest for "the meaning of the act of writing." His emphasis on man's "dark other side" in his writing reflects his own fear, of sexuality, of madness, of death. In approaching dark areas through words, Fitzgerald reaches beyond language and reason.

F57. Bubloz, Eric. "La double vision de F. Scott Fitzgerald [The Double Vision of F. Scott Fitzgerald]." *Études des Lettres* (2 Jan. 1979): 41-53.

Both dream and reality are positive and negative in Fitzgerald's stories and novels. Music and moonlight imagery heightens the positive onset of dream when boy meets girl. Similarly, in *Gatsby* space and time are abolished. The dream cannot survive the human condition, however, and thus begins to negate reality through alcohol, money, cynicism, Hollywood. Even the aspects of the positive dream—such as the negation of time and space—become negative and trap the dreamer. Reality weighs most not on Gatsby so much as on Wilson. In "A Diamond as Big as the Ritz," on the other hand, the capacity for wonder is essential for life. The two negative visions, both the one of the dream and the one of reality, produce ghosts, like Wilson. The positive vision of reality responds to the negative conception of the dream or illusion in "Family in the Wind" and "Lees of Happiness." "Babylon Revisited" illustrates best a positive vision of reality and a rejection of the "nightmare that could pass for a dream." In Fitzgerald, there is no middle ground between dream and reality.

F58. Carlet, Yves. *"The Great Gatsby." Figures libres, figures imposées: L'explication de texte en anglais (fiction) [Free Forms, Imposed Forms: The Explication of the Text in English (Fiction)]*. Ed. Michel Viel. Paris: Hachette, 1993. 127-133.

The last chapter is less an account of the facts of Gatsby's death than a half-outraged, half-mournful testimony, a painful quest for an elusive phantom, a strident post-mortem plea in favor of Gatsby's greatness, and an attempt at recovering 'the colossal vitality of his illusion.' It is one of the most unexpected finales in American literature. The tone is half-elegiac, half-eerie wistfulness. The unusual force of the ending results from its zoomlike effect—blowing up a starry-eyed bootlegger to an archetypal follower of a grail. The fading of the vision that eclipses Gatsby's house is the dominant trope for the final dirge, a jeremiad for the betrayal of America's promise. The American incarnation of the romantic vision raises insoluble problems of complicity and rivalry between inner and outer space, of total control and loss of this control.

F59.   Cashill, Jack. "The Keeper of the Faith: Mogul as Hero in *The Last Tycoon*." *Revue Française d'Études Américaines* 9.19 (February 1984): 33-38.

The Last Tycoon is a novel of capitalism as much as a novel of Hollywood. The American democratic beliefs of a beneficent and constructive life for the individual and a rational, virtuous order for society as well as faith in the idealism of industrial America are expressed in George Santayana's portrayal of the "Millionaire." Like Santayana's depiction, Monroe Stahr, the only capitalist to be accorded heroic status by his creator, is industrious, productive, purposeful in terms of the common good, ethical, independent of political forces, and prudent in his acquisition of material goods and use of leisure time. Stahr's work represents industry not exploitation; he is an artist, an individual, and has a "transcendent sense of "Great Purposefulness." He is both more and less than a democratic hero, however, "because the people who depend on him, depend on him too much." He is a capitalist hero but a tragic hero as well. The novel is elegiac for an America of the past.

F60.   Chard-Hutchinson, M., and C. Raguet Bouvard. "L'évolution de la problématique de la corporéité dans *The Great Gatsby* et *Tender Is the Night* [The Evolution of the Problematic of Corporality in *The Great Gatsby* and *Tender Is the Night*]." *Revue Française d'Études Américaines* 16.55 (Feb. 1993): 83-93.

In both *The Great Gatsby* and *Tender Is the Night*, Fitzgerald uses images of the body to convey character and theme. In *The Great Gatsby*, character is represented by fragments of the body, while in *Tender Is the Night*, the body is an obsessive presence (Tommy Barban). In *The Great Gatsby* the fragmentation of the body represents the gap between appearance and being itself. The body in both novels is unstable (George Wilson), becomes unstable (Myrtle Wilson) or disappears (Gatsby through death, Dick through moral decline and displacement). Nick as narrator serves to provide a moral cohesion despite dominance of Tom's body, while in *Tender Is the Night* there is no such moral frame and the dominating body of Tommy Barban is ascendant. The coherence of both texts depends on the disappearance of the protagonists. In *The Great Gatsby*, Nick give transcendental meaning to the American Dream through Gatsby's corporeal liquidation, while in *Tender Is the Night*, Dick is left in upstate New York to meditate on the decaying body of America.

F61. Charyn, Jerome. "Scott l'insaisissable [The Insensible Scott]." *Magazine Littéraire* 341 (Mar. 1996): 19.

Louise Brooks knew best how to observe Scott and Zelda: "what dominated was the lightning intelligence of Zelda." They saw the universe only as reflected in their own mirror. Beyond portraits of his country and his time, there is a poetry, an exactness of the sentence, an incisive rhythm that places itself outside of all convention or all historic actuality. Gatsby and Stahr are dreamers exalted by unearthly power as was Fitzgerald himself. The "crack-up" of Scott is the very lucid lament of a writer endowed with a profound sense of style. His most beautiful works are the emblem of the wounded self of the child-man who liked the noise of money and described with such a penetration the emptiness behind this noise, the sadness behind the fraudulent racket of the American dream.

F62. Chénetier, Marc. "L'enfer du paradis" [The Hell of Paradise]. *europe* 74.803 (Mar. 1996): 3-7.

Introduction to a collection of essays celebrating the centennials of Fitzgerald and Dos Passos. The French translation of *This Side of Paradise* as the Hell or torment of Paradise emphasizes ambivalence or failure rather than suggests a desire, even an impatience for the achievement of an Edenic dream. The novel mirrors a clearly delineated decade of polarities and contradictions, a decade that opened up more oppositions than it resolved. With the birth of modern American capitalism in the '20s, an era of signs was inaugurated. Semiotics replaced the Moloch of accumulation, the value of exchange triumphed over the value of use. Tensions thus generated between present values and the values of the past are illustrated in Fitzgerald's and Dos Passos's works. Where Dos Passos borrows the tensions of jazz in the structure of his novels, Fitzgerald utilized its strident, jumpy, sad moods. Dos Passos writes of the break-up of society into two nations, Fitzgerald of the failure of being. Dos Passos is a literary cubist, Fitzgerald a revealer of riven characters. This was not the first nor the last time that the greatest writers took it upon themselves to commit treason against the dream, to say the hell with paradise.

F63. Costaz, Gilles. "Yasmina Reza: la détresse et la bonté [Yasmina Reza: Distress and Goodness]." *Magazine Littéraire* 341 (Mar. 1996): 51.

Unlike most authors, Fitzgerald has moved Reza to tears "with a solitude behind each word that conveys a compassion for the universal order." In stories collected in "A Diamond as Big as the Ritz," "the extraordinary solitude of the human condition has rarely been as well expressed. One is in the heart of a distress not purely terrestrial." The light tone is deceptive. Despite the surface themes, his stories convey existential anguish. In the "Babylon Revisited" stories, no character is the king of himself, yet Fitzgerald's characters are good, exceptionally good; for example, husbands love their wives. Fitzgerald influenced her in writing *The Passage of Winter.* "There has not passed a year when I have not reread a story of Fitzgerald, of Yourcenar, and of Borges." Fitzgerald treats daily wounds as great tragedies, which is difficult to do. It is in the face of material the most insignificant that he is great for then he is uniquely himself.

F64.   Danon-Boileau, Laurent, and Marie Christine Lemardeley-Cunci. "Espace louche: à propos de *Tender Is the Night* [Dubious Space in *Tender Is the Night*]." *L'espace littéraire dans la littérature et la culture anglo-saxonnes.* Ed. Bernard Brugière. Paris: Presse de la Sorbonne Nouvelle, 1995. 13-17.

While Nicole is depicted as one of the flowers in her garden in *Tender Is the Night,* she is in fact a disturbing copy of nature, with an extremely complex relation to it. Nicole's transgression of the psychic incest taboo in marrying her psychiatrist is not made explicit but suggested through the insistent recourse to artifice. The garden reveals Nicole's fragility as the reverse of the psychiatric clinic. The fundamental conflict of the book is the disjunction of thought which indicates the sadness of Nicole. She moves forward through detours of negation in her "lovely grassless garden;" in this image, is the literary space. Finally, the parallelism of that which exists and that which doesn't is in the sentence "Five small houses had been combined to make the house, and four destroyed to make the garden." By juxtaposing the emptiness of the absence and the fullness of the nonexistent, making of the hiatus itself a design, but without articulating it, Fitzgerald leaves the imprint of Nicole's failure and her madness. Nicole thus knows only the ambiguity of space.

F65.   Dezon-Jones, Elyane. "Gatsby le Magnifique à la recherche du temps perdu [The Great Gatsby in Search of Lost Time]." *Proust et l'Amérique: La Fiction américaine à la recherche du temps perdu.* Paris: Nizet, 1982. 55-88.

Both Marcel and Gatsby are searching for an absolute, whether personified by a woman or a place, "which has no form or color," and both find absolute time through the art of the novel. While all Fitzgerald's novels and stories are concerned with lost time, *The Great Gatsby* is the most perfect example of a quadruple search for lost time: that of Fitzgerald, that of Gatsby, that of Nick, and that of the audience—that is, the author, narrated, narrator, and reader. Gatsby's quest is for a lost adolescence which in America had been obliterated by the war. Having only a name, Gatsby has not behind him the sins of accumulated time which supports the long elaboration of an authentic personality. In a certain sense Fitzgerald succeeded in the creation of a masterwork, in realizing his dream of eternity, in helping each reader to rediscover lost time.

F66. Dixsaut, Claire. "La galaxie Gatsby [The Gatsby Galaxy]." *europe*
       74.803 (Mar. 1996): 23-32.

Fitzgerald "renews the tradition that makes of the pantheon of the ancients a universe of reference for Anglo-Saxon literature." Greco-Roman mythology associates the sky and the stars with the gods, according to their power. In Gatsby this celestial mythology reveals the fundamental nature of his characters: their power, their emotions, and their rapport with the gods—and therefore their opportunity for fulfillment. The logic of the celestial system of metaphor affects the structure of the novel. The nine chapters refer to the nine planets, the names of the divinities in the Roman pantheon: Chapter 1: Nick, the messenger of the gods; 2: Myrtle, or Venus; 3: Gatsby's mansion, the Earth; 4: Mars, Gatsby's armored death car; 5: Jupiter, Gatsby as sun-god; 6: Dan Cody, Saturn, father of Jupiter, is the god of inexorable death; 7: through Uranus, the god of seasons, Nick becomes adult; 8: Neptune, god of ocean, and Gatsby dies in his pool; 9: Pluto, or Wolfsheim as Mephistopheles.

F67. Gay, Marie-Agnès. "Vision and Loss in *Tender Is the Night*." Paper
       delivered at 5th International F. Scott Fitzgerald Conference. Université
       de Nice, 28 Jun. 2000.

F68. Gerbaud, Colette. "Amérique et féminité, ou le rêve, l'or et la nuit dans
       Tender Is the Night [America and Feminity, or the Dream, the Gold and
       the Night in *Tender Is the Night*]." *Americana* 5 (1990): 81-96.

In *Tender Is the Night*, femininity represents America, to which the author has an bitter yet loving attachment. The female characters "prevail in color, vigor of character, action, and function in the relational world of the novel" and "carry the weight of the decadence of a civilization." In spite of her fragility, however, American woman has an astonishing resistance, an unbelievable energy that causes her to triumph in the war of the sexes. Success of all kinds is associated with women, but Fitzgerald's women are unlike the mature women of the frontier. Real but incomplete women look in vain for a satisfactory definition of their role in a land of artists who treat them as goddesses or bitches. Both male creator and female creation have lost the connection between the conscious and the subconscious; femininity is treated instead as an exterior reality. *Tender Is the Night* is a "voyage-into-night book," for man who must be guided by his anima has no map for it so he must depend on the woman. If the woman disintegrates, so does the man. America is presented as an enchanted garden of the Extreme Occident containing apples of gold, objects of all human dreams, and promising riches to the hero who seeks it from the East. Western dreams divide rather than unify as in the East. The end of the dream corresponds to the beginning of the knowledge of the sun.

F69.   Giesbert, Franz-Olivier. "Éloge du Fitzgéraldisme [Praise for
        Fitzgeraldism]." *Magazine Littéraire* 341 (Mar. 1996): 18.

Our imagination would be something restful and boring without Fitzgerald. We would miss drunkenness, nostalgia, luxurious cars, the ecstasy of failure, and mad nights on the French Riviera. God created Fitzgerald injured, too fragile to conquer the world that retired before him. His midwestern boyhood dreams remained with him until the end. He was not killed by misery or failure, but saved by them. It is because of his congenital ineptitude that he is the dirty kid that we would like to remain. The rage that resounds in "A Diamond as Big as the Ritz" is equal to the imprecations of Leon Bloy or Karl Marx. Like many great artists, Fitzgerald sacrificed himself to his work and created until he died.

F70.   Giesbert, Franz-Olivier. Préface. *De l'écriture* [*On Writing*]. Ed. Larry
        W. Phillips. Trans. Jacques Tournier. Éditions Complexe, 1985. xi, 123.

What would American literature be without Fitzgerald? We would miss his faults, his suicidal longings, his presentiment of disaster. *The Great Gatsby* and *Tender Is the Night* are his two great works; in the rest we find the best and the worst. Sometimes he is frankly bad, but it was on his disaster and his weaknesses that he constructed his work. He transformed his failure into success, his success into failure. "He is always on the wire, but suddenly he loses his balance and falls. This is why he touches us. His embarrassments enhance him, his fragility is his strength." It is paradoxical that he has become the incarnation of the American Dream. This *"personage Baudelairien"* had much with which to succeed. But with all his successes, "melancholy always had the advantage." He died in the "same solitude as Mozart." It is just that he is now considered one of the giants of literature. First, for his natural art, second, for his transparence, and finally for his characters who are always seeking to transcend their class.

F71.   Hays, Peter L. "Undine in US: Wharton's Attack on American Greed."
        Études Anglaises 47.1 (1994): 22-31.

The Great Gatsby is a satirical novel of manners as is *The Custom of the Country*. Both novels use satire to depict a corrupt America. Both novelists criticize a commercialized urban culture where financially powerless women trade on their physical charms to succeed.

F72.   Hays, Peter and Pamela Demory. *"Nostromo* and *The Great Gatsby."* *Études Anglaises* 41.4 (Oct-Dec. 1988): 405-417.

Fitzgerald's favorite Conrad novel was *Nostromo* which possibly influenced his writing of *The Great Gatsby*. Both novels are about the corruption of a dream through unawareness of the taint that materialism brings, a materialism that infects the entire country in which each novel is set. Gatsby and Gould are idealists who make their lives into fairy tales in order to justify the means taken to achieve them. Gatsby and Nostromo assume new names, achieve great wealth, and are naïve more than shrewd, masterful not crafty, more generous than those who use them. Both believe in their Platonic conceptions of themselves: one is a charming rascal, the other an elegant young roughneck. Nostromo has a talent for the imaginative task, Gatsby a gift for hope, a romantic readiness. Both are courageous, hard-working, determined. Both novels treat history as cyclical and repetitive. In the theme of corruption by wealth, they are most in alignment: Gould, Gatsby, even Nick rationalize their corruption, but none sees his own complicity clearly.

F73.   Hersant, Patrick. Foreword. *Mille et un navires* [*A Thousand and One Ships*]. Ed. and Trans. Patrick Hersant. Les Belles Lettres, 1996.

Fitzgerald the poet is the same as the disenchanted singer of the Lost Generation, who saw the favorable aspects of the Riviera and loved life with so much eagerness. He is the same dandy who exalted nostalgia as a profession of faith in *This Side of Paradise*. One will discover, perhaps, in these poems a less familiar aspect. If his poetry doesn't have the depth of his novels, still it doesn't take itself seriously. Unlike Lawrence and Hardy, who estimated their poetry above their fiction, Fitzgerald wrote his poems with detachment, a lightness that in the end saves them. In a minor mode, we love them for what they are— joyous, insouciant, and even in moments of great melancholy lacking in gravity.

F74.   Hubner, Patrick. "Le génie du lieu dans *Tendre est la nuit* [The Genie of Place in *Tender Is the Night*]." *Americana*. Presses Université de Paris-Sorbonne 5 (1990): 97-107.

The multiplication of place in *Tender Is the Night* affirms a particular magic tied to a definition of mental space, reflecting the nomadic and unstable life of the Divers. Travel of the characters takes on geographic and mental, realistic and poetic, autobiographical and dreamed dimensions in a trembling dialectic. A rapport is established between the nocturnal enchantment of décor and the characters, and, more significantly, between the microcosm and macrocosm, the limited world of man and object with the universe. Place becomes the expression of human anguish tied to nature and tinted with a melancholy light. To this confused geography of intellect and desire, Fitzgerald added the scheme of the decline of the West in Rome, marking the end of Dick's fragile dream of grandeur that Rosemary had evoked. America is only a margin into which Dick disappeared with little trace. The vertical plunge unites a vertical dizziness with the aquatic element, which emphasizes the idea of the downfall of the couple and that of a descent into the unconscious. The motif of a promontory rejoins that of a precipice as a symbolic frontier between life and death.

F75.   Hurtin, Jean. "Jacques Tournier: en retraduisant *Gatsby* [Jacques Tournier: In Retranslating *Gatsby*]." *Magazine Littéraire* 341 (Mar. 1996): 26-29.

Translating *The Great Gatsby* is difficult because the writing is an enclosed, poetic text that plays with symbols and images. For example, does one translate "yellow cocktail music" as "sweet cocktail music"? This novel poses problems of which the solution goes beyond the words themselves. It is impossible not to believe that Fitzgerald has simply assembled words that evoke for him images of a fragile and also very powerful way of life. He is a writer who allows himself to be pushed by the joy of words and takes risks but always lands on his feet. One risks ridicule or excess in translating the language of Fitzgerald's very powerful and humorous imagination. One cannot translate, for example, the play on words in his guest list. There are moments when the rhythm is more important, when the writing is literally musical. For example, he was struck by words of one syllable but how can they be conveyed in French? "Old sport" is untranslatable because it both conveys Gatsby's snobbery and holds him up to ridicule. His editor chose "*cher vieux*" which is anonymous, discrete.

F76.   Intissar-Zaugg, Brigitte. "*Tendre est la nuit* ou le rêve d'un ailleurs [*Tender Is the Night* or the Dream of an Elsewhere]." *europe* 74.803 (Mar. 1996): 44-54.

There is a parallel between the created sentimental world of Hollywood and Dick's created world. Dick plays a perpetual role due to his need to be loved by others and Rosemary plays one because she is an actress by profession who confuses the created and the real. The multiplicity of places frequented reveals the profound malaise of Americans come to Europe in pursuit of a dream, in quest of a future, in order to collect some morsels of a crumbling world. Dick is in transit between a past which he flees and a future which flees him. Rejecting America, rejected by Europe, he finds himself nowhere.

F77. Johnson, Christiane. "Daughter and Father: An Interview with Mrs. Frances Scott Fitzgerald Smith." *Études Anglaises* 29 (1976): 72-5.

Scottie Fitzgerald Smith granted this rare interview because the interviewer was French and she had just returned from "a very pleasurable" trip to France. Mrs. Smith has a charm that is fitzgeraldian in its elegance, lack of snobbery, warmth, ease, intelligence and perception. She says that Fitzgerald took 10 years to finish *Tender Is the Night* because you can't write about one country while you are in another. His love of football was "a romanticized view of what he really wanted to do. . . . I think he lived almost entirely within his own mind." She adds that "He was terribly interested in why people came to this country," and that he "was not so much aware of money but of accomplishment." "I think Daddy was very disappointed by the lack of intellectualism in American life." She believed that her father reflected this fascination with accomplishment in his youth, but that later he did think a great deal of F.D. Roosevelt. She thinks that her father's reputation became so great "because we have so few good writers in this country. . . we have not got the splendors of Western Europe."

F78. Johnson, Christiane. "F. Scott Fitzgerald et Hollywood: Le rêve Américain dénaturé [F. Scott Fitzgerald and Hollywood: The Perverted American Dream]." *Revue Française d'Études Américaines* 9.19 (February 1984): 39-51.

For Fitzgerald the contradictions inherent in American life stem from the disjunction between the national dream and its perversion in reality. In *The Last Tycoon*, Fitzgerald ascribes to Hollywood the characteristics of the frontier whose traits he parodies because the myth of success is stronger there than ever, now founded on rigid conformity, the ruggedness of its beginning succeeded by excess, and the violence of the Old West replaced by the social violence of the film industry. Here he wanted to reattach Hollywood to the past, Eastern principles of the nation from which it had detached itself geographically and by its future-oriented way of life. Fitzgerald was one of the first to note that film insinuates itself into the lives of citizens by procuration of the adventures of the films and the lives of the stars. Cinema cultivates narcissism and anesthetizes faculties of judgment so that it becomes difficult to make distinctions between authenticity and artificiality. The irony revealed by Fitzgerald is that Hollywood created a new American Dream, founded on a search for pleasure and happiness in which illusions are subordinate to material reality.

F79. Johnson, Christiane. "F. Scott Fitzgerald or the Ambivalence of America." *Cahiers Charles V* 8 (1986): 83-97.

In his fiction, Fitzgerald reveals his ambivalence toward traditional morality, tempering and qualifying his ethical views by understanding and sensibility.

America itself confuses the material and the spiritual, appearance and reality and also tends to project into the past with its old values or into the promise of the future and ignore the unsatisfactory present. These polarities are reflected in the contrasts and contradictions in his fiction which "are due to the constant passage from the conscious to the unconscious, from the search for ethics to the search for happiness.

F80.   Johnson, Christiane. "*The Great Gatsby*: The Final Version." *Fitzgerald Hemingway Annual*, 1976: 109-115.

The last page of *The Great Gatsby* gives the novel a mythical dimension that is characteristic of American literature. Fitzgerald has prepared us for this dimension all through the novel with elegiac passages. The desire to be united again with nature as a mother's breast is "the buried cause of America's attraction to its pastoral past." Gatsby's dream is the American dream and "his tremendous and misled hope becomes that of mankind." Fitzgerald evokes American history as well as images of darkness in these last paragraphs, imbued with gestural quest motifs. Man is both acting and acted upon in the contradictory ambiguity of an "orgastic future" that "recedes." In *The Great Gatsby*, Fitzgerald evokes the whole human condition "and this seems to us its greatest value: the breadth of its vision lending it an archetypal quality."

F81.   Kaspi, André. Présentation. *The American Dream*. Paris: Hatier, 1992.

This collection also includes short stories by Dos Passos, O. Henry, Henry Miller, James Thurber, John Steinbeck, William Saroyan and Ray Bradbury. Is the American Dream the result of a puritanical ideology which exalts predestination and underlines the pact that God made with his most deserving creatures?   Does it express only the desires of the middle class which industrialization and urbanization created? The image of the American Dream lives—whatever it actually is, diminishing social tensions and inspiring hope in those who have little. It erases social injustice, the insufficiency of individuals, the consequences of heredity, and the effects of education. Social mobility in the United States has never been as easy as Horatio Alger wanted us to believe. But the level of life is superior to that of the rest of the world. "An American is one who believes in the American Dream."

F82.   Kenec'hdu, Tanguy. Avertissement du traducteur [Foreword]. *Lettres à Zelda et autres correspondances* [*Letters to Zelda and Other Correspondence*], by Francis Scott Fitzgerald. Eds. M. J. Bruccoli and Margaret M. Duggan. Du monde entier. Paris: Gallimard, 1985. 400.

The American editor of Fitzgerald's letters exaggerates in pretending that Fitzgerald's spelling was that of an illiterate; rather, it was simply mediocre.

These spelling anomalies may be of some psychological interest, but the translator must necessarily be disinterested in them. On the other hand, typographic anomalies have been respected. Scott and Zelda often wrote to each when drunk or deranged and so the letters often lack logic, and since their correspondence is very private, it is a mixture of high literary style with familiar, even vulgar terms. A major obstacle is that English does not distinguish between the personal and impersonal use of the "you" pronoun, and the translator must decide when the relationship is sufficiently close to use it. Titles of Fitzgerald's works not yet translated into French by French publishers have been left in the original because a literal translation risks ending in nonsense.

F83.   Kundu, Gautum. "Inadvertent Echoes or 'An Instance of Apparent Plagiarism'? Cather's *My Ántonia*, *A Lost Lady* and Fitzgerald's *The Great Gatsby*." *Études Anglaises* 51.3 (1998): 325-37.

Fitzgerald credited Willa Cather's influence, even in a letter to Cather herself. Many critics have noted similarities in their narrative techniques but there are also striking similarities of language, structure, and theme. One critic notes Fitzgerald's use of Cather's first novel, *Alexander's Bridge* in *Gatsby*, particularly as the genesis of the green light. However, *My Ántonia* and *A Lost Lady* touch on some of the same vital matters as *Gatsby*: the myth of the American Dream and its defilement and desolation, a near-pastoral nostalgia for the past, and the East-West polarity. Further, both of Cather's novels are narrated by a sensitive observer as is Nick. In both Cather and Fitzgerald, the American Dream is seen as shifting from moral regeneration and bright expectation to dissolution through materialistic ideology. In *My Ántonia*, as in *Gatsby*, the West assumes the significance of a universal symbol of stability and flux.

F84.   Lagayette, Pierre. *"The Great Gatsby."* Figures libres, figures imposées: L'explication de texte en anglais (fiction) [Free Forms, Imposed Forms: The Explication of the Text in Englishn (Fiction)]. Ed. Michel Viel. Paris: Hachette, 1993. 135-140.

The endings of *The Great Gatsby*, *This Side of Paradise*, and *The Beautiful and Damned* open timeless perspectives that partly deny their conclusive function. In *Gatsby* three stories end: Gatsby's, Nick's and a chapter in human history. Through his prose, Fitzgerald attempts to impose the reconstructed order of art on the chaos of a crumbling postwar world. Gatsby's house now has a dreamlike quality, standing like a broken icon of the past. In the movement backward to the pre-mansion days, the novel is an anti-celebration of material progress. As Nick refuses to hear and therefore consider other accounts of the events leading to Gatsby's death, the reader, really, has no other alternative than to follow him as guide. Nick's conjectures can be seen as "the product of accumulated ignorance or as ontological nescience, the mystery of the irrecoverable past and of the unpredictable future." The only hope is in a stubborn challenge of art against mortality, of love against erosion of time.

F85.   Le Vot, André. "Bibliographie—Fitzgerald en Français [Bibliography— Fitzgerald in French]." *Magazine Littéraire* 341 (Mar. 1996): 52.

Bibliography of translations of Fitzgerald's works and several scholarly analyses.

F86.   Le Vot, André. "Chronologie [Chronology]." *Magazine Littéraire* 341 (Mar. 1996): 20-25.

Chronology of main events of Fitzgerald's life.

F87.   Le Vot, André. "Les années parisiennes [The Parisian Years]." *Magazine Littéraire* 341 (Mar. 1996): 34-39.

Fitzgerald's two years in Paris were the central kernel of a brief life, accelerating a process of maturation which caused him to pass from a dionysiac vision of the feast to a tragic sense of life which found expression in his '30s writing. He fluctuated between a modest way of life and the lifestyle of those in Paris who became his closest friends—Hemingway and Gerald Murphy. Until 1930, the two antithetical destinies of the brilliant worldly man and the professional writer solicited his imagination. After 1926 they incarnated opposing aspects of his conception of himself: Murphy, the "old dream" of the complete man which had always haunted him and Hemingway's resolve, rigor and athletic wisdom. As a result, he could no longer recover the solitude and the determination he had in writing *Gatsby*. Liberty had become license. But he never truly felt at home in Paris, unlike Hemingway and Murphy. In *Tender Is the Night*, Paris is an unreal city, a mirage, a zone of irresponsibility, which encouraged his tendency toward self-destruction. But far from alienating Fitzgerald from America, the strange land reinforced his Americanness, his identification with his native land. Thus, in France he wrote *Gatsby* and conversely finished *Tender Is the Night* in Baltimore.

F88.   Le Vot, André. "Les intermittences du baiser: Fitzgerald et la Recherche du temps perdu [The Discontinuities of the Kiss: Fitzgerald and The Search for Lost Time]." *europe* 74.803 (Mar. 1996): 33-43.

The Great Gatsby was written in France in the Autumn of 1924 at the same time that the English translation of two volumes of Proust's *À la recherche du temps perdu* appeared. A series of resemblances between the two works concerning women's love solicits our attention. The authors use the same objects to suggest analogous situations of which the symbolic functions are too similar to be coincidental, particularly the ceremony surrounding the kiss: the status of "connoisseurs" in kissing, the delayed kiss, kisses that effect the future. All the couples in Fitzgerald and Proust are founded on the betrayal of the women and the jealousy of the men. In Fitzgerald, the terms of the kiss obey a hierarchical identity climbing the scale from the conventional (Nick & Jordan) to the romantic (Gatsby & Daisy) to the symbolic (star & director). The function of the kiss is to release a moment of incarnation and of knowledge.

F89.   Le Vot, André, ed. "Le registre 1924: l'année de *Gatsby* [The Register 1924: The Year of *Gatsby*]. *Magazine Littéraire* 341 (Mar. 1996): 30-31.

A reproduction of the page from Fitzgerald's *Ledger* written from Sept. 1923 to Sept. 1924 in which he recounts events occurring simultaneous to writing the novel. Also translated into French.

F90.   Le Vot, André and Townsend Ludington. "Repères chronologiques [Bench Marks]." *europe* 74.803 (Mar. 1996): 144-48.

Key events in Fitzgerald's life, concluding with publication of Arthur Mizener's biography in 1951.

F91.   Llona, Victor. "Why I Translated *The Great Gatsby*." *Michigan Quarterly Review* 32.1 (Winter 1993): 132-35. Rpt. of Victor Llona, "Pourquoi jái traduit *Gatsby le magnifique*," *Nouvelles Littéraires* (12 Feb. 1927): 6.

The Great Gatsby is a "curious and moving" novel which reveals both a great talent and the United States to the French reader. *This Side of Paradise* indicated to critics that an "original and fascinating" talent had appeared, "audacious" even among such "adventurous pioneers" as Dreiser and Anderson. *The Beautiful and Damned* reassured his admirers that "the talent continued to hold its promise." *Gatsby* is the coup, affirming a "complete mastery, a perfect equilibrium." The novel dramatizes "the *danse macabre* of a funny little society who danced a saraband to the jingle of dollars, whipped without mercy by the horsewhip of intoxication." The characters are real, if extravagant, an "extravagance which seems natural enough if one knows Americans well. . . . But the small blue Anglo-Saxon flower is not completely withered," as it flourishes in Gatsby's heart. Fitzgerald does not wish to reform this society, however, for he finds in it a rich vein needed for his art.

F92.   Lozano, Maria. "Les voies du silence [The Ways of Silence]." *europe* 74.803 (Mar. 1996): 55-64.

The critical cliché that Fitzgerald's work falls into two distinct domains—the serious novels and the commercial stories—creates a divorce between mythical and historical perspectives, the chasm of silence separating the observer from the world in which he lives forever alienated, in a mode of ironic imagination nearer to Kierkegaard than to the romantics to whom Fitzgerald loved to compare himself. While the stories have neither the tight structure nor the audacity of image of *The Great Gatsby*, it is erroneous to dismiss them as merely commercial. This young boy leaves the midwest for the East in flagrant contradiction of the foundational myth modern, and his displacement leads to his inevitable fall into history. The myth and history do not mix, even in the sophisticated and dissociative techniques of jazz. Women—whose wealth in made possible by midwestern factories—devour their Pygmalions here, entangled in a macabre dance. "A Diamond as Big as the Ritz," "The Ice Palace," and "The Rich Boy" are three avatars of the initial scene of seduction in "Absolution": a dream of possession in the first, a dream of love in the second, and a dream of the writer in the third.

F93.   Meral, Jean. "Aspects Parisiens de la grande migration [Parisian Aspects of the Great Migration]." *Paris, dans la Littérature Américaine.*, Paris: Editions du CNRS, 1983. 171-94.

The Paris of Fitzgerald is different from that of Hemingway. Certainly Fitzgerald is more Right Bank, but Hemingway is not only Left; he is more extended, nearer to the intimate experience of the novelist than is Fitzgerald. Fitzgerald gave economic and poetic significance to the rites of women shopping in Paris. Rosemary and Nicole together symbolize the splendor of wealth integrated into the passion for beauty. Several Fitzgerald characters participate in "Le Fête," the joyous atmosphere of the Parisian 1920s, usually in dissipation. Night is palpable in *Tender Is the Night* and the opposition between day and night corresponds to Fitzgerald's affinity for nocturnal scenes.

F94.   Pauwels, Marie-Christine. *"The Great Gatsby." Figures libres, figures imposees: l'explication de texte en anglais (fiction) [Free Forms, Imposed Forms: The Explication of the Text in English (Fiction)]*. Paris: Hachette, 1993.

André Le Vot in his brilliant study shows the color red as being permanently associated with danger for Gatsby and its dominant tone is chosen to describe the world of the Buchanans. Nick refuses contemporary assessments of Gatsby, yet he describes the house at the end, as at the beginning, as a fake. A feeling of hesitancy and confusion pervades the first three paragraphs of the last page, written in a voluntarily constrained and syncopated rhythm which emphasizes action over emotions. Words with ironic overtones and numerous negatives abound, particularly in conjunction with the verb "to hear." Choice of verbs expresses movement and the transient quality of the passage. The mood changes as Nick sprawls on the beach and meditates. Nick's thoughts pass gradually from the temporal to the timeless. The rhythm becomes lyrical and melodic. The appeal now to the senses and the emotions is intensely evocative.

F95. Pétillon, Pierre-Yves. "Francis Scott Fitzgerald: Le mirage de la fille d'or [Francis Scott Fitzgerald: The Mirage of the Golden Girl]." *Magazine Littéraire* 331 (April 1995): 86-88.

America, in its solitude and relative savagery, did not lend itself to the sentimental education genre so dependent on the social theater of the old world whose cities are heirs to scenes of the Court, of its pomp, its joys, and its reflection. Then came James, Wharton, and Fitzgerald and gave us the icons of American literature. The attraction of the poor young man to *la fille d'or* is erotic and social. What is fascinating in Zelda, Daisy, and Nicole is their aplomb, their casualness, the arrogance that results from a wealthy background, and their ease in the world from which the hero feels excluded. Gatsby doesn't want Daisy as much as he wants to see himself through her eyes, to be co-opted magically into her circle. The paradox is that the magic aura of money exists only in the eyes of those who don't have it. Sentimental, Dick had believed himself to be the elegant, aristocratic double of Nicole. *Tender Is the Night* is the most Marxist of American novels in its depiction of the permanence of the class one is born into.

F96. Pétillon, Pierre-Yves. "L'arrière-saison des adieux [The Autumn of Good-byes]." *Magazine Littéraire* 341 (Mar. 1996): 42-44.

If Fitzgerald has transformed his novel into a 'national autobiography' it is because he has perceived the neurosis of America in his own nervous instability. There are two wars in *Tender Is the Night*: the First World War and the American Civil War. The Civil War gave birth to the capitalist boom of 1872-1892, and the 1920s were a remake of this period. Abe North represents Abe Lincoln but his victory degenerates into the degeneration of the après-guerre. Dick Diver represents Ulysses S. Grant who invented the war of extermination of 1914-18 and the most sordid era of corruption in America prior to the 1920s. The defeat at Appomattox was the defeat of an entire nation, of pastoral America. What triumphed was Chicago with its great barons of industry, one of whom violated his own daughter, as in the two incestuous situations in the novel. America indulged in a national fantasy in the 1920s as the nation sought refuge from modernity and its mutilations in the nursery.

F97.   Pétillon, Pierre Yves. *Histoire de la littérature américaine. Notre demi-siécle 1939-1989* [*The Story of American Literature. Our Half Century 1939-1989*]. Libraire Arthéme Fayard, 1992. passim.

The great year of modernism was 1925: *Manhattan Transfer* by Dos Passos, *The Great Gatsby*, and Alan Lock's *The New Negro*.

F98.   Phillips, Larry W. Présentation [Introduction]. *De l'écriture* [*On Writing*]. Ed. Larry W. Phillips. Trans. Jacques Tournier. Éditions Complexe, 1985. xi, 123.

This volume assembles the reflections and observations that Fitzgerald made throughout his life on the problems of the writer. André Le Vot is correct in his biography of the writer that Fitzgerald had "a need to share what he had learned." The reader will discover that his counsel is varied and profound.

F99.   Saporta, Marc. "Scott Fitzgerald en son temps [Scott Fitzgerald in His Times]." *Americana* 5 (1990): 71-79.

While Fitzgerald anticipated leisure civilization in the ambiguity of success, he is not an authentic representative of his epoch. In the 1950s and '60s he reappeared as his foresight predicted the success and the resulting disenchantment of these decades. Fitzgerald was interested neither in social nor psychological realism but in the spiritual. He responded to the aspirations of his readers by writing about millionaires and princesses as though they represented the population, but his focus on marvelous and condemned human beings was because "the cruel romanticism inherent in Western humanity satisfies itself only in the tears of a princess." The rich may exercise their mastery over society but not their own lives; they know life yet achieve only a mortal desperation. Dick Diver's "process of demolition" does not originate with Fitzgerald; there are many reasons for his and Fitzgerald's autodestruction, although they are saved by their dignity. Fitzgerald's dignity has contributed greatly to safeguarding his literary importance, for "certain manners live, even when the moral has fled the field. Give thanks for his grace."

F100.   Sarotte, Georges Michel. *Comme un frère, comme un amant* [*Like a Brother, Like a Lover*]. Paris: Flammarion, 1976. *Male Homosexuality in the American Novel and Theater from Herman Melville to J. Baldwin.* Trans. from the French by Richard Miller. Anchor Press/Doubleday, 1978. 212-228.

This is the first comprehensive, systematic analysis of male homosexuality in American theatre and fiction. Fitzgerald's protagonists, like the author, are narcissistic sissies or "prehomosexual." They are chronic hero-worshippers in an attempt at self-virilization. Their love for women is narcissistic. Just as Fitzgerald and Zelda were both androgynous, so are Amory and Isabella, Anthony and Gloria, Nick and Jordan, Dick and Nicole. Gatsby and Tom are very similar in their virility, rough beauty and wealth, which is why Daisy moves from one to the other so easily. Gatsby is so much like Tom, that had Fitzgerald attempted to describe him in more detail, he would have had to omit one of them. However, he also possesses the qualities of the men who, like Nick, adore him—the smile and charm—and so is a narcissistic projection of his creator, much closer to him than Tom Buchanan. Dick is so linked with Nicole that when she has sexual relations with Tom, she enables Dick to achieve a homosexual union with his hero, Barban. Although apparently heterosexual, Fitzgerald's feminine-masochistic protagonists love women only insofar as the women bring them closer to their heroes.

F101. Stéphane, Nelly. "Chercheuses d'or et croqueuses de diamants [Gold Diggers and Diamond Devourers]." *europe* 74.803 (March 1996): 132-143.

The rapprochement between Fitzgerald and Dos Passos on female characters is suggestive. Despite great differences, both writers emerge from an experience which enlarges the dimensions of creation to mythic proportions. Each female character is exemplary, individual, but the opposition of gold diggers and diamond devourers occurs. Fitzgerald's characters aspire to success, power, money, happiness as do Dos Passos's, but equally to something more hidden, impalpable, the realization of their personalities. Fitzgerald's novels are autobiographical, even to the point of self-justification, and his female characters represent him as much as do his males. His protagonist suffers a grave humiliation of some kind and prestige and riches are refused him or are the price of labor, a price he does not want to pay. For Dos Passos, men and women belong to an ordinary humanity of laborers who know best ephemeral success. Fitzgerald's characters belong to a universe of false appearances, of lies, of illusion, and of poetry and dreams.

F102. Storey, Jeff. "Roger Grenier's *Trois Heures du Matin*: Subjective Fitzgerald Biography and the Quest Leitmotif *Chez les Français*." Paper delivered at The 5th International F. Scott Fitzgerald Conference, Université de Nice, 30 June 2000.

F103. Storey, Jeff. "Style and the Figure of the Author: F. Scott Fitzgerald's Textual Identity and the Role of Rhetoric and Borrowed Narrative Technique in Its Construction." *Cycnos 14.2*, 1997. 127-41.

Using rhetoric to seduce the reader, Fitzgerald makes even disagreeable characters like Dick Diver gain the reader's sympathy. Having Nick Carraway refer to himself as "I," Fitzgerald further seduces the reader by allowing him to believe that "I" refers to Fitzgerald himself. Fitzgerald believed that maintaining his personal identity within the text was crucial to seducing the reader and that a realistic style, more than content, contributed to this. He borrowed the narrative techniques of realistic authors—Conrad and Flaubert—for *Gatsby* and *Tender* because their narrative structures allowed room for the author to assert his individuality. The borrowing, kept in the background, enhanced his own presence in his work.

F104. Taylor, Marcella. "The Unfinished American Epic: Fitzgerald's *The Great Gatsby* and the Twenties." Preface Barbara Smith Lemeunier. Aix-en-Provence: Université de Provence, 1982: 65-78.

By creating two characters to form one protagonist in *The Great Gatsby*, Fitzgerald was able to construct a novel with the texture, scope, structure, and archetypal impulse of the epic, a literary genre that balances the mythical and the historical. Nick is the poet narrating the exploits of a cultural hero: Menelaus seeking to recover Helen from Paris. The city is the underworld in which the two battle scenes are played out. However, Gatsby's final protecting of Daisy and his death are a parody of the heroic gesture. Unlike Achilles, Gatsby replaces his goal with its symbol. Nick is the true Son of God because he realizes what Gatsby does not. The structure of the novel emerges in the tension between downward and upward movement. Nick as Gatsby's double parallels his journey, but complicates his downfall; Gatsby dies, Nick goes home—a double epic dénouement. However in the traditional epic, the dying order gives rise to a new order. Because the new order does not arise in Gatsby, the novel as epic is unfinished for neither protagonist frees himself from the outdated myth.

F105. *"Tendre est la nuit* au festival d'Avignon [*Tender Is the Night* at the Festival of Avignon]." *Magazine Littéraire* 341 (Mar. 1996): 44.

The radio station France Culture celebrated the Fitzgerald centennial with an original six episode radio program by Roger Grenier that evoked *Tender Is the Night*, its Swiss and Riviera settings, its wealthy Americans and the sanitoriums they inhabited.

F106. Tissot, Roland. "Pour une nouvelle carte du *Tendre* de Francis Scott Fitzgerald [For a New Map of Francis Scott Fitzgerald's *Tender*." *De la littérature à la lettre: Poésie, Fiction, Arts (Domaine anglophone)* [*From Literature to the Letter: Poetry, Fiction, Arts (English-speaking*

Domain)]. Eds. Adolphe Haberer and Josiane Paccaud-Huget. Lyon: Presses Universitaires de Lyon, 1997. 149-161.

Despite appearances, *Tender Is the Night* is the antithesis of Keatsian romanticism for it produces a theatre of cruelty, which plays with chaos. The novel's voyages are references to an ideological project: desired, put to work, then completely rejected, reflecting the profound identity crisis of the postwar world. The romantic ideal is a sociological and ontological accomplishment of the American Dream, but rather than the passionate pilgrims of innocents abroad, these are nihilistic waifs of disaster. World War I introduced through the universality of its subversion an epistemic break in spirit and language. The voyagers on the Borgesian map of the novel trace their interior itinerary to a subjectivity which attempts to articulate closure and opening. At the heart of *Tender Is the Night* one hears the song of the nightingale, a song of the anguish of a tenderness lost forever. Thus in the ways of the writer, it is a question of a possible journey to the end of night of his unconscious desire, at the risk of losing himself.

F107. Tournier, Jacques. Introduction. *La ballade du rossignol roulant* [*The Cruise of the Rolling Junk*]. Trans. Jacques Tournier. Belfond, 1993.

In 1924 Fitzgerald published in *Motor* magazine ten songs which recount his and Zelda's 1,200-mile odyssey from Westport, Connecticut to Montgomery, Alabama in their first car, a second-hand Marmon, which failed to survive the trip. It is the only text in which Zelda appears without any kind of mask. Under the deliberately free and easy writing and Fitzgerald's characteristic modesty, one feels the taste for being elsewhere which bound them together and above all the fascination this Southern belle held for the young midwesterner, and how she had attracted him to her. Perhaps here is the first sketch of the destiny of their relationship.

F108. Tournier, Jacques. Préface. *Fragments de paradis* [*Fragments of Paradise*]. Trans. Jacques Tournier. Paris: Omnibus, 1998.

Fitzgerald's stories are better than generally thought. The stories are to his novels what studies and preparatory designs are to the painter. They have a grace of improvisation that touches nearer to his personal universe than do his novels. The menace of failure dominates the stories despite the happy ending required by *The Saturday Evening Post*. In fact, the endings are like a pirouette, so much so that they appear unconvincing. On the other hand, *Tender Is the Night* is a novel of abdication. Zelda was Fitzgerald's temptation and he knew the first time he kissed her that he had abandoned an imaginary paradise for an earthly one, on the other side of paradise, toward which one veers when the

Angel with the sword has forbidden entry. He sought this paradise through words all his life, through memory and forgetfulness, present and past time, to recognize in the surrounding air that which he had breathed another time for, as Proust wrote, "one would be able to provide himself this profound sensation of renewal only if one had breathed this air once before."

F109. Varet-Ali, Elizabeth. "The Unfortunate Fate of Seventeen Fitzgerald Originals: Toward a Reading of the Pat Hobby Stories on their Own Merits Completely." *Les Cahiers de la nouvelle.* 14 (1990): 87-110.

The Pat Hobby Stories are unique in Fitzgerald's work because of his persistent use of satire and his pathetic main character. Critics too often see them as autobiographical and dismiss them as the work of a broken-down writer, even though they were written contemporaneously with *The Last Tycoon*. Given a fair reading they yield a range of analyses on another vein in Fitzgerald and throw light on the stage of development that his views had come to at the end of his life. The part they played in Fitzgerald's regained confidence of 1939 cannot be underestimated. They gained him time and confidence for his novel. The universally human Pat is "stubbornly alive" as he struggles for his own identity, never giving up hope. For his author, he represents the debasement wrought by Hollywood and in his caricature of the Hollywood script writer, Fitzgerald sought to divest both Hollywood and California of their illusory "escape magic" and to focus on their "debasement" of human talent and negation of art, culture, and integrity.

F110. Viel, Michel. "Abecedaire Philologique" [Philological ABCs]. *Études de linguistique et de littérature en l'honneur d'André Crepin.* Eds. Danielle Buschinger and Wolfgang Spiewok. Serie Wodan, Band 20. Reineke: Greifswald, 1993.

In this "literary and linguistic miscellany," six letters are about *The Great Gatsby*. "D" represents "Danilo" or the "Order of Danilo" imprinted on the medal bestowed on Gatsby by Montenegro. Bruccoli indicates Nick reads a Latin text when in fact it is in Cyrillic. Nor could the inscription have been placed on a two-faced coin. "H" is for Fitzgerald's "Hesitation" over whether the ramifications of Ella Kaye's treatment of Dan Cody "were common property of the turgid journalism of 1902." "I" refers to the "orgastic" v. "orgiastic" debate in reference to the final page. "J" stands for "Jackson Stonewall Abrams" one of Gatsby's guests whom Victor Llona in 1926 dubiously translated as "George Washington Cohen." "K" or "k v. t" recounts the editing of "kike" to read "tyke." Is this censorship, good intentions, or poor taste? "U" cites the "urban" versus "urbane" debate. Why wouldn't Jordan have the distaste for the concrete of the urbanite? One of Fitzgerald's major themes is the distinction between the provincial and the urban.

F111. Viel, Michel. "Advertissement du traducteur [Foreword]." *Gatsby le Magnifique*. Trans. Michel Viel. L'Age d'homme, 1991. 159.

This new French translation is based on the original 1925 edition and the corrections of the second edition sanctioned by Fitzgerald. In dubious cases, corrections are noted but not made or accompanied by a question mark.

F112. Viel, Michel. "Gatsby et ses invités en traduction [The Rendering of Proper Names, Titles, and Allusions in the French Translations of *The Great Gatsby*]." *Les langues modernes* LXXXIX.1 (1995): 39-50. Rpt. in *F. Scott Fitzgerald: New Perspectives*. Eds. Jackson R. Bryer, Alan Margolies, and Ruth Prigozy. The University of Georgia Press, 2000: 115-119. Earlier version delivered as paper at the First International F. Scott Fitzgerald Conference, Hofstra University, 1992.

In French, Gatsby is referred to as "magnificent" rather than "great." West Egg becomes "the Western Egg" in the Llona translation. Possible French translations for proper names could be "Mademoiselle Cauchon" for "Miss Haag," "Madame Ulysse Lesueur" for "Mrs. Ulysses Swett," or "la famille Sangsue" for "the Leeches."

F113. Viel, Michel. "Les lectures de Mrs. Wilson dans *The Great Gatsby* [Myrtle Wilson's Reading Matter in *The Great Gatsby*]." *Études anglaises* 50.4 (1997): 434-441. Earlier version delivered as paper at Hemingway/Fitzgerald International Conference, Paris, 1994.

Five of the seven main characters in *Gatsby* are readers. Nick reads for business; Jordan reads for pleasure; Tom reads for instruction; Gatsby reads "for appearances," but has a full library; Myrtle reads for fun. The fact that Nick reads from *Simon Called Peter*—a naughty, "popular theology" novel against which Fitzgerald bore a grudge—while Tom and Myrtle are convening in the next room, is no coincidence. Several small details in *Gatsby* may originate in this book. Myrtle reads *Town Topics*, a gossip and society magazine that may have influenced Fitzgerald in his drawing up of *Gatsby*'s guest lists. The further, narrower comparison of literature to trash is a complement to comparisons of *Gatsby* to other "good" literature.

F114. Viel, Michel. "Notes on the Origin of Gatsby's Guest List." *F. Scott Fitzgerald Society Newsletter* 3 (1993): 6-8.

For his guest list, Fitzgerald drew his inspiration from the English satirist of the 18th century, Christopher Anstey, author of *The New Bath Guide*, an epistolary novel in verse that went through 30 printings between 1766 and 1830 and was reproduced in Fitzgerald's time in collections of British poets, in anthologies, or in dictionaries of quotations. Such similarities as the hosts both being newcomers, the major characters meeting their fate in the pool, Anstey's line "How he welcomes at once all the World and his Wife" and Fitzgerald's "the world and its mistress returned to Gatsby's house" indicate Anstey's influence.

F115. Viel, Michel. "Translations as Help and Object in the Study of *The Great Gatsby*." Paper delivered at the Fifth International F. Scott Fitzgerald Conference, Nice, July 3, 2000.

"Indirect stylistics" are used to determine how different translations of *Gatsby* reflect on the original. Problems and ambiguities arise in the consistency of the translation of individual words, in the translators' choice of tense, in using grammar to translate meaning. Having two translations of *Gatsby* to compare raises further questions about expansion, sentence hierarchy, and metaphor.

BOOK REVIEWS/NEWS ARTICLES/RADIO PROGRAMS

F116. Asselineau, Roger. Rev. of trans. of *Gatsby le magnifique* by Michel Viel. *Études Anglaises* 45.1 (Jan-Mar. 1992): 116.

The Llona translation is very mediocre even though Fitzgerald found it marvelous. Viel produced the translation that the novel merits, a version without fault and which reads well. It follows the text of the original edition but indicates in appendices some interesting corrections that the author had intended to make. Viel consulted the original in the Princeton University Library. Few translators have such scruples.

F117. Barelli, M. "Littérature: 'Gatsby' vu par Roger Grenier [Literature: 'Gatsby' seen by Roger Grenier]." Rev. of *Trois heures du matin: Scott Fitzgerald* [*Three O'Clock in the Morning: Scott Fitzgerald*], by Roger Grenier. *Nice-Matin* 13 Oct. 1996: n.p.

More than a simple biography, Grenier's book retranscribes a life through subjective accounts "such as memory invents them, our imagination recreates them, our passion animates them." Grenier is looking for the man behind the legend and the writer behind the man.

F118. Baroche, Christiane. "Un charme nostalgique" [A Nostalgic Charm]. *Quinzaine Littéraire* (15-31 Jan. 1984): 24.

Hemingway's stories are dated beside Fitzgerald's. Fitzgerald's flappers are "fresh, living, ready to seduce the young wolves of today. . . . Into this material of living flesh, the master worker slips his inimitable song, this writer who seems to touch nothing in a perfect décor, and who jostles softly, who capsizes, who through others, without ceasing, taps the poor beating heart."

F119. Bayle, Thierry. "Poésie et thèatre [Poetry and Theater]." Rev. of *Mille et un navires* [*A Thousand and One Ships*] and *Un legume* [*The Vegetable*], by F. Scott Fitzgerald. *Magazine Littéraire* 341 (Mar. 1996): 50.

Fitzgerald is not a Shelley or a Milton. This conventional translation of *A Thousand and One Ships* does not help in refurbishing the poetic coat of arms of a great American novelist. The plot and dialogue of *The Vegetable* are of heartbreaking mediocrity. Neither his poetry nor his play add anything to Fitzgerald's glory.

F120. Bona, Dominique. "Fitzgerald: une légende dorée et sulfureuse [Fitzgerald: A Gilded and Sulphurous Legend]." *Figaro* 3 Feb. 1986: n.p.

"Resuscitated as a salamander, reprinted, retranslated, reread, Fitzgerald has never appeared more seductive or, more incongruous, more modern. *The Great Gatsby* and *Tender Is the Night* still have an extraordinary youth—it is the Fitzgerald miracle." Bruccoli worked to decipher this miracle and after reading 500 dry pages, we no longer ignore anything Fitzgerald wrote. The biography gradually achieves the dramatic level of a tragedy. Fitzgerald mixes with his charm and weakness an extraordinary force of character. Egotistical but infinitely generous, immoral and puritanical, ambitious and honorable, all these contradictions resolve themselves in his inventive and non-conformist work. This very American biography renews the inspired tradition of Maurois and Troyat of not separating the man and his work. Divested of his frivolous legend, not of his poetry, he is clothed in the light of "some sort of epic grandeur."

F121. Bosquet, Alain. "Aimer ou ne pas aimer Scott Fitzgerald? [To Love or Not to Love Scott Fitzgerald?]" Rev. of *Trois Heures du Matin: Scott Fitzgerald* [*Three O'Clock in the Morning: Scott Fitzgerald*], by Roger Grenier. *Le Figaro Littéraire* 14 Dec. 1995: n.p.

Biography does not respond to the simple and primordial question whether one must love the work and the man. There is without a doubt honesty and depth in this meticulous work on a mythical writer, on whom one has never ceased to lean for a half century, without putting him in conversation, perhaps because objectivity is inoperative before his questionable incarnation of the Lost Generation. Grenier's sentiments include attachment, mistrust, admiration, pity, some distrust, and a sort of fatality. He loves Fitzgerald in spite of himself, finds some excuses, and then decides to love him because of his contradictions. An indefinable charm emanates from Fitzgerald; it is a sensation of fatality, seductive nearly involuntary, nearly ethereal.

F122. Bott, François. "Conversation tardive avec Scott Fitzgerald [A Belated Conversation with Scott Fitzgerald]." Rev. of *Trois heures du matin: Scott Fitzgerald* [*Three O'Clock in the Morning: Scott Fitzgerald*], by Roger Grenier. *Le Monde des Livres* 10 Nov. 1995: n.p.

Grenier speaks very well of Fitzgerald, understands him, and owns him in a way, a long time after his death. This happens between writers sometimes, in these belated conversations in which the silence allows them access to the passage of time. There is a tremendous amount of charm in the portrait and the brief studies in this volume. It is as though, under the edge of the legend, he refound and rendered the melancholy of Fitzgerald's "poor dreams of celestial happiness," which were transfigured by the literature.

F123. Braudeau, Michel. Rev. of *"Fragments du paradis"* [*Fragments of Paradise*], by F. Scott Fitzgerald, and *"De l'ecriture"* [*On Writing*], by F. Scott Fitzgerald. *Le Monde* 6 Dec. 1991: 24.

A better collection of Fitzgerald's stories. These seven stories are the last to be published, and are happily excellent stories. Larry Philips has regrouped some citations of Fitzgerald's about writing, about the novelist's craft, from his correspondence for the most part, and notably from his letters to his daughter Scottie.

F124. Cariguel, Olivier. Rev. of *Trois heures du matin: Scott Fitzgerald* [*Three O'Clock in the Morning: Scott Fitzgerald*], by Roger Grenier. *L'Oeil-de-Boeuf* 8 (Jan. 1996): n.p.

The old Proustian debate of the *Contre Sainte-Beuve* celebrated by the radical separation between the writer's creative and social selves is here assumed and exceeded, which constitutes the ambition of the collection *L'un et l'autre*. Outside of the traditional plodding biography, it proposes subjective essays animated by the intimate place of the essayist-biographer and his secret hero. In sum, the story of a complicity without complacency, in which imagination and passion have a place. In the course of short, thematic chapters carving the creative course of Fitzgerald's life as cinematic sequences, Grenier retraces Fitzgerald's early frenzied efforts to fashion a character on paper. He loves his characters, and thanks to them, he pushes the caricature to the extreme and finds a *modus vivendi*, a terrain of understanding acceptable to himself. Grenier locates the journey from and to the labyrinth where Fitzgerald created his characters. By using himself, Zelda, and others as models, Fitzgerald falls into the confusion of an author in quest of a character, to amend a famous title of Pirandello.

F125. Couturier, Maurice. Rev. of *Scott Fitzgerald: The Promises of Life*, ed. A.R. Lee. *Études Anglaises* 43.1 (1990): 128-.

This volume accords a sizeable place to the historical, social, and ethnic context in which Fitzgerald's characters evolve, but the book is more a series of distinct essays than a coherent interpretation of the work. Taken individually, the articles are interesting, but do not shed a truly original light on this oeuvre already so abundantly dissected and analyzed.

F126. Crom, Nathalie. "F. Scott Fitzgerald, une scintillante 'touche de désastre'" [F. Scott Fitzgerald: A Scintillating 'Touch of Disaster']. Rev. of *Love Boat et 63 autres nouvelles, Tendre est la nuit* [*Love Boat and 63 Other Stories/Tender Is the Night*], by F. Scott Fitzgerald. *La Croix l'événement* 22 June 1998: n.p.

This volume confronts us simultaneously with the profound charm and the limitations of the Fitzgerald universe. He has neither the inspiration of Faulkner nor the creative esthetic of Dos Passos, but his greatest attributes were a careful attention to his epoch, a capacity to know and render the spirit of the times with great subtlety; a honed gift painting life such as it is, made of weak emotions and of sensation more often than of high drama, of smiles more than shouts of laughter, of discrete despair more than elevations of tone.

F127. Duperray, A. Rev. of *Francis Scott Fitzgerald ou le plénitude de silence*, by Elisabeth Bouzonviller. Letter to E. Bouzonviller, 2000.

A professor of American literature at Provence University, Prof. Duperray writes that the book "renews successfully the various approaches to this endlessly fascinating work as they were rather outdated."

F128. Durand, Dominique. "Une entreprise de démolition [A Demolition Project]." Rev. of *Trois heures du matin: Scott Fitzgerald* [*Three O'Clock in the Morning: Scott Fitzgerald*], by Roger Grenier. *Le canard enchaîné* 13 Dec. 1995: n.p.

Grenier states he loves neither eccentrics nor alcoholics; however, he does love Fitzgerald, whose "taste for catastrophe seems innate more than acquired." If Fitzgerald admired the rich, Hemingway was largely responsible for it. Fitzgerald's attitude toward Paris was that of Henry James. Both think of the frontier, although Scott preferred the Right Bank—the Ritz not *La Coupole* or the *Deux-Magots*. Jean Seberg who named her cat Gatsby was also touched by disaster. Grenier knew and loved Romain Gary and Jean, and comments that their romanticism is not far from that of Fitzgerald and Zelda.

F129. Frank, Bernard. "Que faire? Que dire?: Les deux simplets [What to Do? What to Say?: The Two Simpletons]." *Le Nouvel Observateur* 20 Dec. 1995: n.p.

Does this count as a good book about an American writer dead for half a century? *Trois heures* was motivated by a defunct passion. Fitzgerald has only written some small things. Both he and Hemingway are simpletons in depth and form. According to Angelo Rinaldi, puerility, arrogance, and lack of culture form a menage à trois for Fitzgerald.

F130. Hays, Peter L. "Bruccoli's *Gatsby.*" *Études Anglaises* 50.4 (Oct.-Dec. 1997): 442-45.

The only college text version of *The Great Gatsby* available in America from Simon and Schuster is based on Matthew J. Bruccoli's Authorized Text. Three inadvertent errors that Bruccoli has restored or left uncorrected are distracting: "Wolfshiem" should have been changed to "Wolfsheim" as previous editors have done even though the *ie* spelling is possible if uncommon; "retina" should have been changed to "pupil" or "iris" as "retina" is not visible to the naked eye; and "dashboard" should have been replaced by "running board" as Gatsby could not have gracefully balanced "himself on the board (dashboard) of his car with "that resourcefulness of movement that is so peculiarly American."

F131. Homassel, Anne-Sylvie. "Hollywood dans le miroir de la mort [Hollywood in Death's Mirror]." *Magazine Littéraire* 341 (Mar. 1996): 45-46.

Bruccoli's reedition of *The Last Tycoon* is more austere and more disjointed than Edmund Wilson's. Nevertheless, although tenuous and badly pieced together, the novel is a miraculous text of an American Lazarus. Fitzgerald sought to create in Monroe Stahr an American more convincing in the role than Gatsby, Blaine or Diver. Rooted in the depths of the decline of the West, Fitzgerald gave Stahr the radiance of obscure and distant divinities, although the incompleteness of the novel leaves incomplete the mythic crystallization of Stahr, who will never be to literature what *Citizen Kane* is to cinema. But of all the major writings of Fitzgerald, there is a unique and properly cinematic perception of light and of moment here. Fitzgerald's radiance is missing from Kazan's film. Nathaniel West's *Day of the Locust* is the best Hollywood novel, but why oppose them; one clarifies the other. West had a vigor, a taste for the unusual and for color, an onirism of which Fitzgerald is devoid. But their object is the same: Hollywood is the mirror of death.

F132. Le Clec'h, Guy. "Scott Fitzgerald retrouvé [Scott Fitzgerald Refound]."
    Figaro 24 May 1985.

The new translation of *Tender Is the Night* is complete and excellent, but as
Fitzgerald is a master of style, it is not as good as the original. *Letters to Zelda*
constitutes the other side of *Tender Is the Night*. Scottie wrote to the author:
"My father adored France. I found it extraordinary that he never learned French.
Perhaps it presented itself that he would have had to confront some problems
that he would rather avoid. But then how was he able to recommend the
translation of Andrè Chamson's *Les Hommes de la route*? He read Stendhal and
recommended to me to read Flaubert. After, he said to me, you will never be the
same."

F133. Le Vot, André. "Aide-Mémoire [Manual]." Rev. of *Trois heures du
    matin, Scott Fitzgerald [Three O'Clock in the Morning: Scott Fitzgerald]*,
    by Roger Grenier. *Magazine Littéraire* 341 (Mar. 1996): 41.

Despite Fitzgerald's adolescent affections, occasional bad form and spelling,
and despite Grenier's own preference for Faulkner, he loves Fitzgerald for his
very qualities: hard won maturity, fraternal compassion, and passionate love of
literature. In this *L'un et l'autre* collection Grenier maintains he discovered
Fitzgerald in an epoch in which he was able to believe himself one of
Fitzgerald's rare admirers this side of the Atlantic. In fact, in 1958 he wrote a
radio script on Fitzgerald in which Romain Gary and Jean Seberg also
participated. The autobiographical text by Grenier that prefaces the 1963
translation of *The Crack-Up* was a forerunner of *Trois Heures*, which is an
anthology of chosen anecdotes and reminiscences. It is a "syncopated montage
of short citations and of scenes which constitute Fitzgerald himself."

F134. Le Vot, André. "Fitzgerald Révisité [Fitzgerald Revisited]." Rev. of
    *Lettres à Zelda et autres correspondances [Letters to Zelda and Other
    Correspondence]* and *Tendre est la nuit [Tender Is the Night]*, by F. Scott
    Fitzgerald. *Magazine Littéraire*. April 1985: 71-72.

Only 20 of 360 pages of this volume contain letters to Zelda, or 15 letters. Still,
Zelda is the heart of the work as 16 of her letters to Scott, letters of harrowing
tenderness are included. They were written between 1931 and 1934, the most
unhappy years of the couple when Zelda sunk into and struggled in her madness,
made a balance sheet of the past and tried to find an outlet in writing stories and
her novel *Save Me the Waltz*. One imagines the difficulty with which such a text
confronts the translator; an underlying network of complex images, the slightest
lapse compromising the harmony of the whole. The 1951 translation is frankly

unacceptable. Jacques Tournier respects the integrity of the text and retains the 1934 version with its superb opening. There are moments of pleasure in his version which reads generally with ease, but also unhappily some approximations and some weaknesses.

F135. Le Vot, André. "Le Metier d'écrire [The Occupation of the Writer]." Rev. of *De l'écriture [On Writing]*, by F. Scott Fitzgerald. *Magazine Littéraire* 341 (Mar. 1996): 48-49.

Philips' collection of comments and aphorisms is a sort of counterpart to Roger Grenier's in the domain of the art of writing and the mílieu of the writer. Excerpted from letters, notebooks, essays, the writings are a collection that would suffice without doubt to dissipate the equivocations and place in perspective all aspects, as appealing as misunderstood, of his talent.

F136. Marissel, André. Rev. of *Scott Fitzgerald*, by André Le Vot. *Esprit* Mar. 1980: 176-7.

This is an absolutely magnificent work that is more than a biography in that it associates the history of the Fitzgeralds, this epoch of US history, and the life of the writer. Le Vot legitimizes the myth while demystifying it, justifying it while explaining its extraordinary attraction. In Drieu La Rochule, in Aragon, in Nimier and Mourissen, one can perhaps find a "spiritual family" of Fitzgerald. If he had lived, would Fitzgerald have chosen a political ideology as Drieu and Aragon? An ideology recognized in France? Nothing is less sure. A hypothesis: Fitzgerald would represent the concern of the new lost generation, already nostalgic for a society of abundance, terrified by the "crisis" but plunging into terror with the delight of the suicidal.

F137. Mertens, Pierre. "Histoire d'un rescapé [The Story of a Survivor]." Rev. of *Trois heures du matin: Scott Fitzgerald [Three O'Clock in the Morning, Scott Fitzgerald]*, by Roger Grenier. *Le Soir* 13 Dec. 1995: n.p.

Though Fitzgerald said a good biography could not be written of a good writer, Grenier's, in its way, is excellent. Without evoking other recent Fitzgerald biographers such as Bruccoli and Le Vot, Grenier renders Fitzgerald's charm transparent from the first few pages. Antoine Blondin in his "Certificate of Studies" said he was "nearer to Ariel than Caliban." Gertrude Stein's comment that Fitzgerald would be remembered when many of his contemporaries had been forgotten is true in Europe which has recently "done much to reinstate his true dimension. . . . One is not astonished that Roger Grenier, admirer of Chekhov and Pascal Pia, has put feet in the footprints of this disenchanted enchanter."

F138. Mikriammos, Philippe. "La place d'un familier" [The Space of a
    Familiar]. Rev. of *Trois heures du matin: Scott Fitzgerald* [*Three
    O'Clock in the Morning: Scott Fitzgerald*], by Roger Grenier. *La
    Quinzaine Littéraire*. 16-31 Jan. 1996: n.p.

Grenier speaks familiarly of Fitzgerald, a sign of long acquaintance. He has
"harmonized" Fitzgerald's life just as a jazz riff sloughs itself off into a long,
harmonious blues. Grenier attempts nothing new and Fitzgerald's life is a
standard, but he replays the life. For example, Fitzgerald worked harder that it
appears on Bruccoli's definitive version of *The Great Gatsby*. Grenier also
rectifies the image of Fitzgerald's last days as a alcoholic: if one reads the letters
of this period, one can see that he was methodical and organized. Fitzgerald had
an inexhaustible reserve; only death kept him from writing.

F139. Neuhoff, Éric. "La paradis selon Fitzgerald [Paradise According to
    Fitzgerald]." Rev. of *Fragments de paradis* [*Framents of Paradise*], by
    F. Scott Fitzgerald. *Madame Figaro* 4 Apr. 1998: n.p.

Tender Is the Night is simply one of the most beautiful novels in the world.
There is nearly no waste in the texts.

F140. Nourissier, François. "'Scott et Roger': une amitié ['Scott and Roger': A
    Friendship]." Rev. of *Trois heures du matin: Scott Fitzgerald* [*Three
    O'Clock in the Morning: Scott Fitzgerald*], by Roger Grenier. *Le Figaro
    Magazine* 25 Nov. 1995: 187.

Grenier's is one of the best books in the collection *L'un et l'autre*. The writer is
subjective, in dialogue or polemic with his model, confusing as much as he
interrogates his subject. He is severe with the man but he respects the writer. All
the novelists who knew him have noted that as soon as he spoke of his métier he
became precise, sharp, passionate. "Neither critical essay, nor biography, nor
polemic, this unclassified and refined book is the record of a posthumous
friendship."

F141. Pitavy, F. Official Report on *Francis Scott Fitzgerald ou le plénitude de
    silence*, dissertation by Elisabeth Bouzonviller. 2000.

American literature professor at University of Bourgogne in Dijon and President
of M. Bouzonviller's dissertation jury, Pitavy wrote "this is a dissertation that
leads one to reread Fitzgerald closely." It enables one "to see not this side of
Fitzgerald but the other Fitzgerald who wrote to explore violence and
breakdown, in fact what Melville described in Hawthorne, 'the power of
blackness.'"

F142. Planes, Jean-Marie. "Scott Fitzgerald: cruelle est la nuit [Scott
    Fitzgerald: Cruel Is the Night]." Rev. of *Trois heures du matin: Scott
    Fitzgerald* [*Three O'Clock in the Morning, Scott Fitzgerald*] by Roger
    Grenier. *Quest* 17 Dec. 1995: n.p.

The Fitzgerald legend has always annoyed us. Can his work, like that of
Stendhal and Proust, correct the impression produced by his extravagant
admirers? "Life is naturally a process of demolition" goes the epigraph to one
of his novels. The interest of this essay is to restore to Fitzgerald a moving
human dimension and a complex, contradictory, multiple truth. Grenier—
painter, doctor, confessor—insists on the sentiment of exclusion from which his
model suffers, counts the frustrations of the one who never could console
himself for not having been a hero at Princeton. He underlines the sincerity of
Fitzgerald. Grenier salutes Fitzgerald for aiding others with his counsel and
using his influence on their behalf. Finally, Grenier convinces us to love "this
small midwestern provincial."

F143. Polch-Ribas, Jacques. "Un Américain pas tranquille [An Untranquil
    American]." Rev. of *Trois heures du matin: Scott Fitzgerald* [*Three
    O'Clock in the Morning, Scott Fitzgerald*], by Roger Grenier. *La Presse*
    7 Jan. 1996: n.p.

Scott Fitzgerald is probably the American writer most discussed by the critics,
whether American, English, or French. One reproaches him for nearly
everything: his precocious celebrity, the repetitive plots of his stories, his bad
grammar, and static dialogue. He cannot, however, be all bad. I confess that
each time I open *The Great Gatsby* to Chapter Two, my Proustian madeleine
rendezvous with me. This book is passionate. It is a way of seeing, in each
moment and over time, in each aspect of Scott, Zelda, and their daughter, their
magnificence, misery, sadness, and madness.

F144. Rinaldi, Angelo. "Un garçon à la noce [A Boy at the Wedding]." Rev. of
    Trois heures du matin, Scott Fitzgerald [*Three O'Clock in the Morning:
    Scott Fitzgerald*], by Roger Grenier. *L'Express* 30 Nov., 1995: 125.

As an example of the superiority of the image to the work, Borges cited Byron,
who is now read only by graduate students searching for a dissertation topic. For
the twentieth century, Borges would have chosen Fitzgerald as an example. It is
urgent to repair such negligence, for the writer pursued an astonishing
posthumous career, which the essay of M. Grenier, by his talent, is going to
revive. To attach oneself, as do his heroes, to wealth, to young gallants, is in
itself neither a fault nor a crime. The error is not to achieve a distance which
permits one to touch the universal in the human. To go beyond that is the mark
of a superior intelligence. Grenier, who is truthful, cites a letter from Fitzgerald

written on his arrival in Europe in 1921 deploring the defeat of Germany and the immigration to America of various European nationalities. Such puerility, arrogance and lack of culture form a ménage à trois with Fitzgerald who wrote *The Great Gatsby* as the Abbé Prévost, who was a polygraphic soul, wrote *Manon Lescault*.

F145. Roy, Claude. "Portrait d'un Maître: Fitzgerald par coeur [Portrait of a Master: Fitzgerald by Heart]." Rev. of *Trois Heures du Matin, Scott Fitzgerald* [*Three O'Clock in the Morning: Scott Fitzgerald*], by Roger Grenier. *Le Nouvel Observateur* 27 Dec. 1995: 66.

To love someone is to understand them best. Grenier is the sympathetic critic of Camus, Pascal, and Chekhov. For Scott Fitzgerald, author of *Tender Is the Night*, he has "the friendship of which one dreams in life, that of an affectionate observer, who knows our qualities but perceives our faults, does not reproach us for our stupidity, but merely raises his eyebrows, does not scold us, but mutters in a low voice, rejoices in our successes and makes little noise over our defeats. Fitzgerald is the author of some very beautiful works and some moving short stories. He also is the author of a valuable axiom: "Life is naturally a process of demolition," which is true of his novels. But the life of an author is a process of extension. Fitzgerald loved the life of his characters as did Grenier. But Grenier lived another imagined life in America, the friend of Fitzgerald and his circle. This is not a book of critical essays but a book of memories.

F146. Saint Vincent, Bertrand de. "On réédite ses nouvelles. Scott Fitzgerald, le désenchanté [One Reedits His Short Stories: Scott Fitzgerald, the Disenchanted]." Rev. of *Fragments de paradis, Love Boat et 63 autres nouvelles, Tendre est la nuit* [*Fragments of Paradise, Love Boat and 63 Other Short Stories, Tender Is the Night*] by F. Scott Fitzgerald. *Le Figaro Magazine* 28 Mar. 1998: n.p.

The stories shine each in its own way: natural, easy, and melancholy.

F147. Vallée, Jean-François. "Francis Scott Fitzgerald: un rêve américain" [Francis Scott Fitzgerald: An American Dream]. Sep. 25, 1996. 2 hour film.

Featuring interviews with Fanny Myers Brennan, Honoria Murphy Donnelly, Eleanor Lanahan, Frances Ring, and Budd Schulberg.

F148. Viel, Michel. Review of Bruccoli (Cambridge) Edition of *The Great Gatsby*. *Études Anglaises*. 45.4 (1992). 483-85.

The conditions under which the novel was originally published were not the best: on one hand, Fitzgerald made major changes to the proofs, on the other, the publication was rushed by an editor who hoped for high sales. Thus the original version is full of mistakes. For a long time, Matthew J. Bruccoli has attempted to restore Fitzgerald's *œuvre* to its full authenticity. However, this edition from Cambridge University Press is more than the working in of Bruccoli's published preparatory research, for it includes a lengthy introduction concerning the genesis, editing, the circumstances of the work's publication, as well as the much enriched and more precise text itself.

F149. Vitoux, Frédéric. "De 'Love Boat' à *Tendre est la nuit*: Fitzgerald le magnifique [From 'Love Boat' to *Tender Is the Night*: The Great Fitzgerald]." *Le nouvel observateur* 12 Mar. 1998: n.p.

The question of Fitzgerald is always financial. His stories can be classified according to the hero's stratagems for attempting to attain money. Some poor young men become rich, others pretend to be rich, there are those who plunge into poverty, or the rich who pretend to be poor, the rich who live as poor, and the poor who live as rich. However, Fitzgerald did not merit Hemingway's disdain for being an opportunistic, materialistic merchant of his talent; in spite of or because of, this monetary imperative, these stories are the most true, the most delicate, the most sensible and even the most harrowing of his work. There is a miraculous grace in these stories. Grouped chronologically and culminating in *Tender Is the Night*, they enable the reader to follow the precocious disenchantment of the writer.

F150. Vuilleumier, Jean. "Scott Fitzgerald dans la nuit noire de l'âme [Scott Fitzgerald in the Black Night of the Soul]." Rev. of *Trois heures du matin, Scott Fitzgerald* [*Three O'Clock in the Morning: Scott Fitzgerald*], by Roger Grenier. *24 Heures* 5 Dec. 1995: n.p.

Grenier, author of 30 novels, essays, stories, and *Regardez la Neige qui tombe* about Chekhov, gives testimony about Fitzgerald whom he finds no less captivating than Faulkner, although he thinks Faulkner the best American writer. Grenier affirms his interest more in the work than the legend. Fitzgerald compensated for the harmony of one word by the roughness of the following. *Trois heures du matin* is perhaps a conscious allusion to St. John of the Cross.

F151. Wolfromm, Jean-Didier. "Rêves américains [American Dreams]." Rev. of *Love Boat et autre nouvelles* [*Love Boat and Other Short Stories*]. *Magazine Littéraire* 202 (Dec. 1983): 64.

Contained here are 14 previously unpublished stories translated with finesse and intelligence. The short story is dear to the Anglo-Saxons and seems to have been created for the talent of Fitzgerald. Fitzgerald is a virtuoso talent because he works by strong demand, giving concerts to great applause in the US.

DISSERTATIONS

F152. Antolin-Pirès, Pascale. "Le discours des objets dans l'œuvre de F.S. Fitzgerald [The Discourse of Objects in the Work of F.S. Fitzgerald]." Diss. Bordeaux 3, 1998.

Fitzgerald's objects are both real and poetic, both representational and reflexive. More poetic and reflexive than signs of the real, his objects form a gap between signifier and the signified, thus speaking the language of desire..

F153. Bardet, Pascal. "'Not in the guidebook': departs et derives. Itineraires Fitzgeraldiens. ['Not in the Guidebook': Departures and Drifts, Fitzgeraldian Journeys.]." Diss. Paris 3, 1997.

The American's search for his own identity is most visible in his unsuccessful search for a home. Whether the search is in the city, the American South, or in Europe, the American is alienated from his environment.

F154. Bouzonviller, Elisabeth. "Francis Scott Fitzgerald ou la plenitude de silence [Francis Scott Fitzgerald or the Plenitude of Silence]." Diss. Lyon 2, 1998.

Fitzgerald's prose offers a vast potential for the reader's imaginative grasp of the unconscious, the inner void. Through its lack of explanation and realism, his prose remains in the unknown and unanalyzed. Through his writing, imbued with a raging violence hidden behind highly social conventions, he also expresses what troubles the inner being in a universal way. The inexpressible and unavoidable inner void is felt in that never fulfilled longing for unity which is endlessly conjured up by the writer.

F155. Gay, Marie-Agnes. "Etude stylistique du point de vue narratif et de son evolution dans les cinq romans de F. Scott Fitzgerald [A Stylistic Analysis of the Narrative Point of View and Its Evolution in F. Scott Fitzgerald's Five Novels]." Diss. Lyon 3, 1994.

Fitzgerald's third-person novels parallel point of view and theme, while his first-person novels make the point of view a theme in itself. Movement across novels is from the epiphanic and fragile point of view in *Gatsby* to fragmentation of the point of view in *Tender is the Night* to imprisonment of point of view in *The Last Tycoon.*

F156. Liny, Marie-Pierre. "Le mythe Mediterraneen dans la fiction Americaine de l'entre-deux-guerres" [The Mediterranean Myth in American Fiction Between the Two Wars]. Diss. Paris 3, 1996.

This analysis focuses on the social, historical and cultural causes of a reinforcement of the Mediterranean myth in US fiction between the world wars, specifically Fitzgerald's *Tender Is the Night*; Hemingway's *The Sun Also Rises, A Farewell to Arms,* and *For Whom the Bell Tolls*; and Thornton Wilder's *The Cabala* and *The Woman of Andros*. What emerges from these texts is the quest for a golden age, an acknowledgement of the failure of the rituals aiming at the recovery of a lost mythical Mediterranean past, and survival of the myth through the very attempt to destroy its illusion.

F157. Storey, Jeff. "Scott Fitzgerald: Figures autobiographiques et mythiques [Scott Fitzgerald: Autobiographical and Mythical Figures]." Diss. Université de Nice-Sophia Antipolis, 1999.

TEACHER/STUDENT GUIDES AND EDITIONS

F158. Fabre, Geneviève and Michel. *'Tender Is the Night' de F. Scott Fitzgerald* [*'Tender Is the Night' of F. Scott Fitzgerald*]. Intro. Bernard Poli. Paris: Armand Colin, 1989. 168.

F159. Fitzgerald, Francis Scott. *Premier mai; Absolution; Retour à Babylone* [*May Day; Absolution; Babylon Revisited*]. Trans. M. P. Castelnau and B. Willerval. Ed. A. Le Vot. Bilingue 49. Aubier-Flammarion, 1972. 308; 1992. 310.

F160. Fitzgerald, Francis Scott. *The Diamond as Big as the Ritz and Other Stories.* Longman Structural Reader. Paris: Armand Colin, 1985.

F161. Fitzgerald, Francis Scott. *Pat Hobby and Orson Welles: and Other Short Stories.* Ed. Martine Skopan. Le Livre de poche 8604; Lire en anglais. LGF, 1988.

F162. Fitzgerald, F. Scott. "Babylon Revisited." *Americans in Paris.* Ed. Michel Viel. Annot. by Pierre Lagayette. Preface by Sim Copan. Series Lire en version originale. Domaine anglo-américain. Ed. Michel Viel. Paris: Hatier, 1990. 1-30.

F163. Fitzgerald, F. Scott. "Three Hours Between Planes." *Love Stories.* Ed. Martine Skopan. Intro. by Patrick Poivre d'Arvor. Series Lire en version originale. Domaine anglo-américain. Ed. Michel Viel. Paris: Hatier, 1991. 31-41.

F164. Fitzgerald, F. Scott. "The Homes of the Stars." *Hollywood Stories.* Ed. Claude Grimaf. Intro. Jean Tulard. Series Lire en version originale. Domaine anglo-américain. Ed. Michel Viel. Paris: Hatier, 1991. 103-114.

F165. Fitzgerald, Francis Scott. *The Cut-glass Bowl.* Intro. and notes Ivan Deïdda, collab. Jennifer Michaudon. (Référence, 6) Ellipses-Marketing, 1992. 63.

F166. Fitzgerald, Francis Scott. *The Great Gatsby.* (Easy readers D.) Bordas, 1992. 112.

F167. Fitzgerald, F. Scott. "The Third Casket." *The American Dream.* Ed. Régine Hollander. Intro. by André Kaspi. Series Lire en version originale. Domaine anglo-américain. Ed. Michel Viel. Paris: Hatier, 1992. 1-21.

F168. Fitzgerald, F. Scott. "In the Holidays." *Crime Stories.* Ed. Marie-Christine Pauwels. Intro. by Jerome Charyn. Series Lire en version originale. Domaine anglo-américain. Ed. Michel Viel. Paris: Hatier, 1992. 33-44.

F169. Le Vot, André. F. S. *Fitzgerald, Nouvelles* [*F.S. Fitzgerald: Short Stories*]. Bilingue Aubier-Flammarion, 1972.

F170. Le Vot, André. *Gatsby le magnifique* [*The Great Gatsby*]. Intro. Bernard Poli. Colin, 1979.

F171. Taane, Éric. "Texte 8: F. Scott Fitzgerald, *The Great Gatsby. L'explication de texte: Méthode et pratique (domaine anglais)* [*The Great Gatsby. The Explication of the Text: Method and Practice (English language)*]. HU Anglais Littérature. Ed. Michel Viel. Paris: Hachette Livre, 1997: 142-157.

Italy

Donatella Izzo, a leading Americanist in Italy who has written on Fitzgerald and Henry James, writes that Fitzgerald is better known in Italy today than some other American writers, including James, "because he's so 'American,' and of course Italian culture has been deeply interested in things American since the 1930s" (Izzo, 16 Aug., 2001). At the Fitzgerald Centennial Conference at Princeton University in 1996, Sergio Perosa, another leading Italian Americanist, analyzed what he sees as the two stages that Fitzgerald's reputation in Italy has passed through: from the 1940s to the 1970s and subsequently to the present. He unifies the thirty years from 1940-1970 according to four "difficulties" that the reception of Fitzgerald encountered in Italy during that period (It45).

The first and main concern Perosa sees as a problem of translation. Fernanda Pivano's translations are beautiful, he says, but they have little to do with Fitzgerald's own language and culture. Donatella Izzo interprets the problem with Pivano's translations as her having placed "emphasis more on the culture than on the language—I mean, more on Fitzgerald as representative author of the twenties, portrayer of the jazz age and so on, than on his formal and linguistic abilities—and that probably helped in making her work sound very cursory at some points. . . . I would say that one of the reasons for the continued reprinting of her translations is her being so well-known as a literary and cultural figure, more than any evaluation of the intrinsic qualities of her translation (Izzo, 20 Apr. 1998).

As the second difficulty faced during this period by those seeking to elevate Fitzgerald to what they see as his rightful place in Italian estimations, Perosa cites scholars' insistence, following the lead of first-generation Americanists Cesare Pavese and Elio Vittorini, and perhaps Pivano's translations, on interpreting Fitzgerald as merely representative of the jazz age, rather than as a socially-committed writer. A third difficulty was that while Antonioni made

Fitzgerald into a cult figure through his film *La Notte* and while writers, including those of the neo-avant garde, praised him for his art, they weren't politically correct in terms of the leftist politics of the time.

Finally, the fourth problem Perosa cites was that in Italy, even more than in other countries, Fitzgerald continued to receive competition from what were seen as the socially-committed American writers Dos Passos, Caldwell, Steinbeck and Sinclair, at least among the left reading public and socially-committed critics; from Hemingway, who had lived in Italy and written about it; and from Faulkner, who was seen as a more authentically tragic writer. Both Hemingway and Faulkner were also praised for their stylistic experimentation and modernist themes.

Fitzgerald's reputation has evolved in the last two decades, particularly among academic scholars. Americanists in Italy have felt strongly that, with new scholarly and linguistic expertise, new translations should be undertaken, and Perosa attempted to complete such a project in time for the Italian Fitzgerald Centennial celebration in 1996. His effort was thwarted by the European Union, however, because the new Union copyright laws stipulate that seventy-five years must elapse before new translations can appear, which in Fitzgerald's case would be 2014. Before the Union acted to stop new translations though, Tommaso Pisanti did retranslate *The Great Gatsby* in 1989, which was reprinted in 1993 (It2).

Perosa says that new scholarly expertise has ceased to stress Fitzgerald's popular legend and also ceased to overly praise Hemingway and the politically conscious American writers of Fitzgerald's time. This annotated bibliography of translations and editions of Fitzgerald's works and of scholarship about him written since the late 1970s and papers presented at the Rome Centennial Conference in 1996 reveals the current emphases of Italian scholars on Fitzgerald's work (Perosa, Sept. 1996).

In 1994, a printout acquired from the University of Milan bookstore listed new translations and in-print editions of all of Fitzgerald's novels and short story collections. Subsequent investigation indicates that all novels and several short story collections have been reprinted well into the 1990s, except for *Tender Is the Night*. New translations include, in addition to Tommaso Pisanti's *Il grande Gatsby* [*The Great Gatsby*], 1989, also *I taccuini* [*The Notebooks*], 1980 (It16); *Il prezzo era alto* [*The Price Was High*] Vol. I , 1981, Vol. II, 1982 (It17); *Tenera è la notte* [*Tender Is the Night*] Version 2, 1984 (It1); *La crociera del rottame vagante* [*The Cruise of the Rolling Junk*], 1985 (It18); *Festa da ballo* [*Dance Party*],1987 (It19); *I racconti di Pat Hobby* [*The Pat Hobby Stories*], 1990 (It20); *Troppo carina per dirlo a parole e altri racconti,*1994 (It21); and *Maschiette e filosofi* [Flappers and Philosophers], 1997 (It22).

Five books have also been written about Fitzgerald in this period and are fairly evenly distributed throughout: Barbara Nugnes's *Invito alla lettura di F. Scott Fitzgerald* [*Invitation to a Reading of F. Scott Fitzgerald*], 1977 (It26);

Sangiuliano's *Il mito America: Hollywood e Fitzgerald* [*The American Myth: Hollywood and Fitzgerald*], 1983 (not available for annotation); Paola Cabibbo and Donatella Izzo's *Dinamiche Testuali in* The Great Gatsby [*Textual Dynamics in* The Great Gatsby], 1984 (It23); Angelo Cecchini's *La casa senza tetto. Il 'narcisismo ' nell'opera e nella personalità de Francis Scott Fitzgerald* [*The House Without a Roof: Narcissism in the Work and Personality of Francis Scott Fitzgerald*], 1988 (It25); and Anna Cascella's *I colori di* Gatsby*: Lettura di Fitzgerald* [*The Colors of* Gatsby*: A Reading of Fitzgerald*], 1995 (It24). German writer Kyra Stromberg's biography of Fitzgerald was also translated into Italian in 1998 (It27).

In her book Nugnes is highly complimentary, arguing that the limited scope of Fitzgerald's people and places should not be interpreted as reflecting the scope of his thought. According to Nugnes, Fitzgerald is, in fact, interested in the universal and in his work imbues life with rich signification (It26).

Angelo Cecchini's *La casa senza tetto: Il 'narcisismo' nell'opera e nella personalità de Francis Scott Fitzgerald* is a Freudian study of the author in which he concludes that "Narcissism in Fitzgerald and in his characters is not an adolescent stage but an alienation from reality in all its aspects, an inability to love and to 'participate' in society and in reality in general." While he is obviously interested in Fitzgerald, his study runs counter to the positive conclusions of other critical work and to current critical methodologies (It25).

Cabibbo and Izzo's book, *Dinamiche Testuali in* The Great Gatsby, broke new ground in its time as the authors see Fitzgerald as both a modernist and a precursor of postmodernism. His novel anticipates postmodernism, reflects postmodern narratology techniques and at the same time is a high modernist mythical novel (It23). As Izzo now reflects,

> Our book was, at the time it was published , a challenge to current American criticism of Fitzgerald, since it engaged a method of structural and semiological analysis mostly drawn from French sources, at a time when Fitzgerald was still being read in traditionally thematic terms. Our aim was then to place his work in the context of both high modernism and post-modernism, a move which has been repeatedly performed on a variety of authors since then, but was comparatively original at that time. . . . (Izzo, 27 Oct. 1997).

Cabibbo and Izzo's book remains one of the major contributions of foreign scholarship to Fitzgerald studies. For a presentation at the 1984 Rome Conference of the European Association for American Studies, the authors made many of their book's arguments in an English language presentation, and the paper was published in a collection by the Free University Press in Amsterdam (It33). How many Fitzgerald scholars in the English-speaking world may have read it cannot be gauged, but Nicolas Tredell indicates that by the 1990s American scholars writing on Fitzgerald finally had begun to reflect the influence of French theorists (B35). Furthermore, Izzo has just recently published a book on Henry James in English for an American university press, a reflection of the increasingly global distribution across borders of intellectual work (Izzo, *Portraying the Lady*).

Anna Cascella is a well-known Italian poet, and her book *I Colori di Gatsby: Lettura di Fitzgerald* is a thorough analysis of the color symbolism in *The Great Gatsby*. Although much work has been done on the meaning of the colors in this novel [see André Le Vot's biography on the color yellow (F40), Sachs on the use of white (It59), and Vatanpour on the prevalence of metallic colors (It60)], Cascella sees pink and gray as representing the main paradigm of the novel in their opposition and complex interplay (It24). Cascella also presented a paper at the Rome Centennial Conference on "Alcuni riflessioni su *The Last Tycoon*," indicating the extent of her interest in and support of Fitzgerald (It34).

In addition, 28 articles, introductions or forewords, book chapters, and papers have been published or presented. Of this number, four are articles, five are book chapters, 10 are introductions or forewords, and nine are conference presentations. Twice as many were written in the 1980s as the 1990s, although Fernanda Pivano's introductions to five of her translations have been reprinted in the late 1980s and the 1990s. The nine 1996 Rome Centennial Conferences presentations also reflect interest well into the end of the century.

When queried as to the reason why five books might have been written about Fitzgerald and only four articles, Donatella Izzo writes,

> After the demise of *Studi Americani* and before the advent of *Acoma* (which, however, is more militantly socio-historical in approach and surely less interested in modernist classics) virtually no journals devoted to American studies have existed in Italy (*R.S.A. Journal* being a partial exception—but then it's only been published since 1990 and even then at desultory intervals and also *Letterature d'America*, which publishes one issue a year on Anglo-American literature and culture.). So it's finally easier to publish a small book—departments usually fund scholarly publications—than to wait for a literary journal to accept and print your article (Izzo, 16 Aug. 2001).

The essays and book chapters represent various approaches to and conclusions about Fitzgerald's work. Several are, in part at least, biographical [Bevilacqua (It29), Conetti (It37), Fink et al (It40) and Pivano in the several introductions to her translations (It49, It50, It51, It53)], but even these move away from biography to speak of *Gatsby* as a modernist text and Fitzgerald as aware of the social dynamics of his time (Pivano, despite what the detractors of her translations say). Other articles focus on *Gatsby*'s intertextuality and the doubling theme (It28), the Bakhtinian chronotopes of the breakdown of the idyll and of the carnival in *Gatsby* (It30), and the use of montage as a technique in *Gatsby* (It39).

In a more new critical mode, Viola Sachs is concerned with the symbolism of clothes in *Gatsby*, particularly in white clothes which symbolize racial purity although "various passages in the book suggest that Gatsby may be passing for white" (It59). Vatanpour too writes about the colors in *Gatsby*, the metallic colors that represent money (It60).

Other writers focus on *The Last Tycoon*. Bottalico establishes that the novel rests on two myths: the primordial myth of Eros and the modern myth of Hollywood, with the latter unexpectedly suggesting hope for a new life (It31). Cecovini sees Fitzgerald as having great moments, but also as applying his extraordinary craft without much feeling. Hemingway, Faulkner, Steinbeck, Capote are "more substantial narrators" (It35). Citati and de Strobel agree that the novel would have been, if finished, formally accomplished, but "a 'dry and still' one, lacking his previous graceful talent" (It36).

Only two articles even mention *Tender Is the Night*, either as a critique of culture or for its style. Fink et al claim that in *Tender* Fitzgerald attempts to achieve greater structural and stylistic complexity but loses his capacity for mythical synthesis (It40). Citati and de Strobel, on the other hand, do think that the best quality of both *Gatsby* and *Tender* is that they are narrated in a "fragmentary, personal, but always fascinating way" (It36). Conetti's take on his style is that it is "reminiscent of the linear but highly personal logic of a child. This also explains his constant success when his role as the best interpreter of the Twenties has long vanished: Fitzgerald was able to represent every age that he went through, from adolescence to adulthood, thus reaching out to all readers by expressing the same emotions they have experienced at some time in their life" (It37).

Finally, Iain Halliday compares Pivano's and Pisanti's translations of *Gatsby*, using translation theory to suggest that in translation, poetry may be gained as well as lost (It43).

Perosa says that new scholarly expertise, such as Cabibbo and Izzo's interest in narratology and post-modernism, has moved scholars away both from Fitzgerald's popular legend and reputation and from overpraise of Hemingway and the proletarian writers of the 30s and 40s. As for Fitzgerald's current reputation in Italy, Perosa is perplexed that while there now is interest in *The Great Gatsby* and *The Last Tycoon* for their tautness and the latter also for, along with the Pat Hobby stories, its portrayal of Hollywood, there has been very little work done on *Tender Is the Night*, which, in his opinion, is the most profound analysis of American culture that Fitzgerald produced (It45).

Izzo suggests that "Young Italian scholars are not very interested in Fitzgerald: while they are probably ready to pay him lip service as a classic, they tend to direct their attention either to contemporary writers (preferably ethnic and/or avant-garde) or to non-canonic, out-of-the-way figures that can be 'discovered' or rediscovered for the Italian academic world. Of course, this is closely connected to what goes on in the US, where not accidentally, virtually all young Italian scholars have studied." Ironically, in assuming that Fitzgerald is a classic and then moving on, these younger scholars have crowned him but still, for the most part, have not studied, appreciated, and written about his work.

(Izzo, 16 Aug. 2001).

The print-out from the University of Milan in 1994 indicates the range of Fitzgerald texts available to university professors for their curriculum. Piero Pignata, who has also written on Fitzgerald, indicated in 1996 that he was "to assist at a meeting in Bergamo where a special session on Fitzgerald and Hollywood is due" (Pignata, 10 Jan. 1996). Donatella Izzo recently taught *The Great Gatsby* in a course at Istituto Universitario Orientale in Naples. Finally, the variety of universities represented by the 1996 Rome Centennial Conference presenters attests to the wide reading of Fitzgerald in Italian universities.

And again, as elsewhere in Europe, the long-range effect on Italian popular culture of Jack Clayton's film of *The Great Gatsby* cannot be overstated. As Izzo says, "Gatsby as a synonym for the rich, luxurious, and excessive and/or for the lost elegance and glamour of the Twenties—certainly seems to have become familiar to the Italian media [probably, mostly by way of the movie]" (Izzo 2001). Many reviewers in this period responded to the translation of *The Cruise of the Rolling Junk* for its emphasis on "the American theme of travel and the symbolic aura of the automobile," two preoccupations of popular culture. That the book was widely reviewed in the popular media indicates both the extent of Fitzgerald's reputation and his permeation of popular culture" (It45).

Perosa concludes that in Italy there is currently "a split between popular culture interest on the one hand and artists like Anna Cascella on the other with scholars in the middle still trying to establish Fitzgerald's reputation" (It45).

REFERENCES

"Fortunes and Misfortunes in the Life and Times of F. Scott Fitzgerald," Centennial Conference, Rome, 10-11 Oct. 1996.

Izzo, Donatella. E-mail to the author. 27 Oct. 1997.

---. E-mail to the author. 20 Apr. 1998.

---. E-mail to the author. 16 Aug. 2001.

---. *Portraying the Lady: Technologies of Gender in the Short Stories of Henry James*. Lincoln and London: U of Nebraska P, 2001.

Pignata, Piero. Letter to the author. 10 Jan. 1996.

Parenthetical citations to entry numbers refer to annotated references in this chapter.

TRANSLATIONS/EDITIONS

It1.   Fitzgerald, F. Scott. *Tenera è la notte* [*Tender Is the Night*]. Trans. and
        preface by Fernanda Pivano. Turin: Einaudi, 1949, 1957, 1973, 1978,
        1980; Milan: Mondadori, 1958, 1967, 1972, 1986; *Il Grande Gatsby*
        [*The Great Gatsby*], and *Tenera è la notte* [*Tender Is the Night*] (Versions
        1 & 2) Milan: Club degli Editore, 1984.

It2.   Fitzgerald, F. Scott. *Il grande Gatsby* [*The Great Gatsby*]. Trans., ed.
        and intro. by Fernanda Pivano. Milan: Mondadori, 1950, 1958, 1961,
        1964, 1965, 1968, 1974, 1978, 1986, 1988, 1989; *Il grande Gatsby* [*The
        Great Gatsby*] and *Tenera è la notte* [*Tender Is the Night*] (Versions 1 &
        2) Milan: Club degli Editore, 1984;. Trans. Tommaso Pisanti. Turin:
        Mondadori, 1989, 1993.

It3.   Fitzgerald, F. Scott. *Di qua dal Paradiso* [*This Side of Paradise*]. Trans,
        ed. and intro. by Fernanda Pivano. Milan: Mondadori, 1952, Reprinted
        1961, 1964, 1968, 1969, 1980, 1990; Milan: Garzanti, 1988; Rome:
        Newton Compton, 1996.

It4.   Fitzgerald, F. Scott. *Belli e dannati* [*The Beautiful and Damned*]. Trans.
        Fernanda Pivano. Milan: Mondadori, 1954, 1972, 1973, 1978, 1992,
        1996; Trans. Pier Francesco Paolini. Rome: Grandi Tascabili
        Economici, 1998. 312.

It5.   Fitzgerald, F. Scott. *Gli ultimi fuochi* [*The Last Tycoon*]. Trans. Bruno
        Oddera. Ed. Fernanda Pivano. Milan: Mondadori, 1959, 1962, 1968,
        1974, 1977, 1986, 1990, 1997.

It6.   Fitzgerald, F. Scott. *Basil e Cleopatra. Due racconti* [*Basil and
        Cleopatra: Two Stories*]. Trans. Domenico Tarizzo and Cesare Salmaggi.
        Milan: Il Saggiatore, 1960; *I racconte di Basil e Josephine* [*The Stories of
        Basil and Josephine*]. Trans. Giulia Fretta, Giorgio Monicelli, and Bruno
        Oddera. Milan: Mondadori, 1976, 1997.

It7.   Fitzgerald, F. Scott. *L'età del jazz e altri scritti* [*The Jazz Age and Other
        Stories*]. Trans. Domenico Tarizzo. Ed. E. Wilson. Intro. by Fernanda
        Pivano. Milan: Il Saggiatore, 1960, 1966; Club degli editori, 1963;
        Milan; Mondadori, 1990.

It8.   Fitzgerald, F. Scott. *Ventotto racconti [Twenty-eight Stories]*. Trans.
         Bruno Oddera. Milan: Mondadori, 1960, 1981. 2 vols.

It9.   Fitzgerald, F. Scott. *28 racconti [28 Stories]*. Trans. Bruno Oddera.
         Preface, M. Cowley. Milan: Mondadori, 1960, 1995.

It10.   Fitzgerald, F. Scott. *Postino o presidente? [Postman or President? [The
         Vegetable]*. Trans. Domenico Tarizzo. Milan: Il Saggiatore, 1962.

It11.   Fitzgerald, F. Scott. *Crepuscolo di uno scrittore [Afternoon of an
         Author]*. Trans. Giorgio Monicelli. Milan: Mondadori, 1966, 1967,
         1990, 1992.

It12.   Fitzgerald, F. Scott. *Racconti dell'età del jazz [Stories of the Jazz Age]*.
         Trans. Giorgio Monicelli and Bruno Oddera. Milan: Mondadori, 1968,
         1980, 1990, 1996.

It13.   Fitzgerald, F. Scott. *Il diamante grosso come l'Hotel Ritz [The Diamond
         as Big as the Ritz]*. Trans. Bruno Oddera. Milan: Mondadori, 1969,
         1974.

It14.   Fitzgerald, F. Scott. *Romanzi [Novels]*. Trans. Fernanda Pivano and
         Domenico Tarizzo. Ed. Fernanda Pivano. Milan: Mondadori, 1972,
         1983.

It15.   Fitzgerald, F. Scott and Zelda. *Lembi di Paradiso. Racconti di F. Scott
         Fitzgerald e Zelda Fitzgerald [Edges of Paradise: Stories of F. Scott
         Fitzgerald and Zelda Fitzgerald]*. Trans. Vincenzo Mantovani and Bruno
         Oddera. Milan: Mondadori, 1975, 1995, 1997.

It16.   Fitzgerald, F. Scott. *I taccuini [The Notebooks]*. Trans. A. Pajalich and
         Domenico Tarizzo. Ed. M. J. Bruccoli. Turin: Einaudi, 1980.

It17.   Fitzgerald, F. Scott. *Il prezzo era alto [The Price Was High]*. 2 vols.
         Intro. by M. J. Bruccoli, Vol. 1; Postscript by Fernanda Pivano, Vol. 2.
         Milan: Mondadori, 1981, 1982.

It18. Fitzgerald, F. Scott. *La crociera del rottame vagante* [*The Cruise of the
       Rolling Junk*]. Ed. and trans. R. Cagliero. Palermo: Sellerio di
       Giorgianni, 1985. 1996, 1997. Rome: Editori Riuniti, 1997.

It19. Fitzgerald, F. Scott. *Festa da ballo* [*The Dance*]. Ed. S. Petrignani.
       Rome: Theoria, 1987. 53.

It20. Fitzgerald, F. Scott. *I racconti di Pat Hobby* [*The Stories of Pat Hobby*].
       Ed. and postword by Ottavio Fatica. Rome: Theoria, 1990, 1996. 192.
       Editori Riuniti, 1996.

It21. Fitzgerald, F. Scott. *Troppo carina per dirlo a parole e altri racconti*
       [*Too Cute for Words and Other Stories*]. Intro. by Enrico Groppali.
       Trans. Bruno Oddera. Milan: Mondadori, 1994.

It22. Scott Fitzgerald. *Maschiette e filosofi* [*Flappers and Philosophers*].
       Rome: Newton Compton, 1997.

BOOKS: FULL-LENGTH STUDIES AND COLLECTIONS

It23. Cabibbo, Paola, and Donatella Izzo. *Dinamiche Testuali in The Great
       Gatsby* [*Textual Dynamics in The Great Gatsby*]. Rome: Bulzoni
       Editore, 1984. 168.

This study is a search for elements anticipating postmodernism, such as
oppositions, discontinuities, and fragmentation that hint at an elliptical subtext.
Thus *The Great Gatsby* can be inserted in the tradition of 'experimental' fiction,
as a link between the 19th century artistic anti-mimesis of Flaubert and James
and later modernist fiction. The use of many contradictory metaphoric structures
at once explodes the idea of one unifying pattern and points toward a
postmodern critique of the very concepts of the individual, history, and
causality. The point of view of the narrator and of all characters is limited and
highlights the problematic status of seeing and being seen; yet, unlike in the
typical modernist gaze, the characters in *The Great Gatsby* are unable to sustain
a coherent unifying perspective. In his idealization of Gatsby, Nick is reflecting
his own initiation into the world, but the author suggests that whereas Gatsby is
destroyed by his romantic quest, Nick becomes by the end the real "low-key
hero" of the novel, an anticipation of the postmodern hero who accepts chaos

and its possibilities rather than trying to impose order and meaning on it. The element that best shows the postmodern traits of the novel is its portrayal of time; the modernist negation of the linearity of time is reflected in the desire to "repeat the past" and in the simultaneous wish to erase past errors and start anew, thus binding the personal quest to the historical dimension of the nation's dream.

It24.   Cascella, Anna. *I colori di Gatsby: Lettura di Fitzgerald* [*The Colors of Gatsby: A Reading of Fitzgerald*]. Rome: Lithos, 1995.

This is an analysis of color symbolism in *The Great Gatsby*, conducted by looking both at the presence of material objects of a particular color and at evocations of the different nuances of light and darkness in the novel. The main paradigm can be found in the opposition and complex interplay of pink and gray. Vivid colors dominate the social scene, but they are often evoked in their absence, as in the case of the lilac trees, which are not in full bloom because their season is long past. Silver and gold are a constant presence in the novel, alluding to Gatsby's status as a knight in search of his personal grail: they are fragments of the old world of romance and of Gatsby's short-lived idyll with Daisy, that he desperately tries to recreate with parties, expensive and shining cars, and glittery suits of bright colors. Yet gray is always lurking nearby, in the form of dust or fog, asserting the impermanence of things, their slow decay, revealing the other side of the dream. This contradiction is finally embodied in the "green light," the most significant symbol of the novel: it stands for Gatsby's undying attachment to his own dream, which is nonetheless unattainable and always receding in the distance.

It25.   Cecchini, Angelo. *Casa senza tetto. Il "narcisismo" nell'opera e nella personalità de F. Scott Fitzgerald* [*House without a Roof: 'Narcissism' in the Work of F. Scott Fitzgerald*]. Pisa: ETS, 1988.

Narcissism in Fitzgerald and in his characters is not an adolescent stage but an alienation from reality in all its aspects, an inability to love and to "participate" in society and in reality in general. Freud's second definition of narcissism, an intermediate form between auto-eroticism and love, as opposed to the more common uses of narcissism as simply egocentric, vain or exhibitionist, applies to Fitzgerald's characters. The narcissist can love only the present, past, or future idealization of himself and is thus alienated by his incapacity to transcend the limits of his own subjectivity ("the house without a roof"). Amory and Rosalind achieve some understanding, yet this awareness of alienation is not testimony to an acquired maturity on the part of Amory. Anthony and Gloria triumph over unbearable reality but remain narcissists. Gatsby's and Daisy's relationship consists of their only participation in the world. Dick and Nicole are unable to sustain sincere relationships with others. In *The Pat Hobby Stories* and

The Last Tycoon, Fitzgerald tries to confess his own alienation in the first person.

It26. Nugnes, Barbara. *Invito alla lettura di F. Scott Fitzgerald* [*Invitation to the Reading of F. Scott Fitzgerald*]. Milan: Mursia, 1977. 148.

Fitzgerald has been accused of caring only for the young and rich, of having no culture, and of having nothing to say. Though he did see life not as an idea but as a drama and a spectacle, this vision evoked symbols of concrete, immediate, and sensible emotions of ambiguity, contradiction, and the complexity of the human experience that are on a par with Poe, Melville, and Hawthorne. Despite the limited scope of the people and places he made his subjects, Fitzgerald was interested in the universal and imbued life with rich signification. Fitzgerald makes the Romantic's idealization of youth and dream of perfection into something distinctly modern and American, his subjects debutante balls instead of Grecian urns. The application of religious metaphors to his work is useless, for Fitzgerald's ironic and tragic world is one of spiritual and material divisions.

It27. Stromberg, Kyra. *Zelda e F. Scott Fitzgerald* [*Zelda and F. Scott Fitzgerald*]. Trans. Giuseppe Cospito. Milan: Pratiche, 1998.

See German Books, G29.

ESSAYS/CHAPTERS/NOTES/CONFERENCE PAPERS

It28. Bacigalupo, Massimo. "Doubling in *The Great Gatsby*." *Quaderni Del Dipartimento Di Lingue e Letterature Straniere Moderne* [*Notebooks of the Department of Modern Foreign Languages and Literatures*] 10 (1998): 213-32.

The Great Gatsby is striking in both structure and texture. The novel contains many correspondences to other literature: Hawthorne's "My Kinsman, Major Molineux" (Robin and Nick both are initiated into reality through the fall of the major character); Melville's *Moby Dick* (Ahab's and Gatsby's single-mindedness); and "Bartleby the Scrivener" (in particular for "the story of the story,") and in general for their central characters becoming sacrificial victims of a crass society, and for the "high pathetic key" of their endings. "Nick *is* Gatsby," a classic doubling, the two living by reflecting each other, experiencing parallel affairs that end more or less simultaneously. Jordan is a minor replica of Daisy: both are dishonest, both decamp, leaving "vast carelessness" behind. Wilson and Tom are husbands who discover their wives' infidelity at the same time. Gatsby and Myrtle are both from poor backgrounds and seek to elevate themselves. Myrtle's apartment is a small replica of Gatsby's mansion. Both have "intense" or "colossal vitality." Both make lists. As for texture, the wisdom and certainty of tone stand out as both compassionate and dispassionate.

It29.   Bevilacqua, Winifred Farrant. Introduction. *The Great Gatsby,* by F.
        Scott Fitzgerald. Reading Classics. Genoa: Cideb, 1994: lx-lxvii.

The Jazz Age was one of the most brilliant decades of the twentieth century in literature for Modernism reached its peak during this period. In their attempt to convey a vision of the social breakdown and repudiation of the American Dream in the 1920s, the Modernist writers produced work of great beauty and vitality. Of all the writers of this period, Fitzgerald most brilliantly captured the tone and temper of the Jazz Age because of his dual romantic and moralistic visions. Characteristics of Modernist fiction include a subjective and more limited point of view, the rejection of a strictly chronological narration for a series of scenes, a unique style of clarity and magical suggestiveness, economy and richness of texture, the coexistence of surprise and a sense of inevitability, and, finally, in establishing objective correlatives, all characteristics of *The Great Gatsby*. The classic quality of *The Great Gatsby* is due to the balanced perfection of its overall design.

It30.   Bevilacqua, Winifred Farrant. "Provincial Idealism and the
        Carnivalesque: Chronotopes in *The Great Gatsby*." Fortunes and
        Misfortunes in the Life and Times of F. Scott Fitzgerald (1896-1940):
        Centennial Conference, Rome, 10-11 Oct. 1996.

The novel's narrative shifts from one conceptualization of time and space to another which generates reformulations of fundamental ideas about identity, society, and morality. The two Baktinian chronotopes that interact dialogically in Fitzgerald's novel are those of the destruction of the idyll—the breakdown of the image in harmony with nature—and of the carnival—a temporary, atypical removal from the normal progression of biographical or historical time which flows according to its own laws and during which life is shaped according to a certain pattern of play, as at Gatsby's parties. Another distinct feature of the carnival is its ritual dismemberment as in Myrtle's death.

It31.   Bottalico, Michele. "The Illusion of Myth: Hollywood in *The Love of the
        Last Tycoon*." Fortunes and Misfortunes in the Life and Times of F.
        Scott Fitzgerald (1896-1940): Centennial Conference. Rome, 10-11 Oct.
        1996.

Matthew Bruccoli's critical edition of Fitzgerald's last novel raises some valid doubts about Edmund Wilson's edition of the work. Unfinished texts should be left autonomous, particularly when they form a discernible whole as does this book, which Bruccoli calls by the last title Fitzgerald gave it: *The Love of the Last Tycoon: A Western*. This title establishes the two myths on which the novel rests: the primordial myth of Eros, symbolizing the internal cohesion of the universe and the forces of attraction which impel the elements of nature to unite, and the modern myth of Hollywood, which was too close to Fitzgerald for him to have been able to perceive it as such. In the novel, the myth of Hollywood ends up acquiring a new significance, as if this last resort had become the starting point of a new life.

It32. Cabibbo, Paola, and Donatella Izzo. *"The Great Gatsby*: Mise en oeuvre du désoeuvrement" [*The Great Gatsby: Putting Inaction into the Work*]. *Anglistica* [*Anglistics*] 23.1 (1980): 7-27.

Chapter 1 of Cabibbo and Izzo's book *Dinamiche testuali* in *The Great Gatsby*. See Entry It23 above.

It33. Cabibbo, Paola, and Donatella Izzo. "Looking Backward, Looking Forward: A Postmodern Reading of *The Great Gatsby's* Modernism." *Social Change and New Modes of Expression: The United States, 1910-1930*. Eds. Rob Kroes and Alessandro Partelli. European Contributions to American Studies X. Amsterdam: Free University Press, 1986.

One of the collected papers from the 1984 Rome Conference of the European Association for American Studies, this article summarizes the contents of *Dinamiche Testuali*, the book published by the authors in 1984. See Entry It23.

It34. Cascella, Anna. "Alcuni riflessioni su *The Last Tycoon*." Paper presented at Centennial Conference. Rome, 10-11 Oct. 1996.

It35. Cecovini, Manlio. "Il libro non finito [The Book Doesn't End]." *Escursioni in Elicona* [*Excursions in Elicona*]. Trieste: Lint, 1990. 201-05.

Looking at a book before the author has been able to approve its final version, such as Fitzgerald's *The Last Tycoon* or Hemingway's *A Moveable Feast*, gives the reader privileged insight into the writer's craft and its evolution. Fitzgerald's value as a narrator is uncertain: he has great moments, which can be observed even in single sentences that are particularly expressive, but he may also be just endowed with an extraordinary craft that he applies to his subject matter without much feeling. Fitzgerald's position is difficult to determine, as it seems to be inextricable from the social climate of the roaring Twenties, unlike the positions of later, more substantial American narrators such as Faulkner, Steinbeck, and Capote.

It36.   Citati, Pietro, and Maria de Strobel. "Francis Scott Fitzgerald." *I Contemporanei—Novecento Americano [Contemporaries—19th Century American]*. Ed. Elémire Zolla. Vol. I. Rome: Lucarini, 1982. 759-773.

The very different social backgrounds of Fitzgerald's parents influenced Scott throughout his life, causing him frustration over his social position, especially in grade school and college. Zelda's restlessness and excessive desire to be admired disturbed his artistic and personal balance, forcing him to keep trying to secure a financial position; on the other hand, Zelda's complex personality gave him material for his work. Scott helped Zelda finish her novel, in hopes of finding some relief from her psychological condition, with no durable success. The writer died in Hollywood just as he was finding a new personal balance in the relationship with Sheilah Graham and experiencing a new creative period. Fitzgerald's novels are perfect and objective works of art, whereas in the short story his genius is constrained and limited. The most distinctive traits of his genius are the naturalness that pervades his novels, the lightness of touch, the ability to express every fleeting moment in the most poignant way. Fitzgerald narrates in a fragmentary, personal, but always fascinating way. The last phase of his career represents the descending parabola, in which he tragically tries to substitute dedication for lost inspiration. *The Last Tycoon*, even if finished, would have been a formally accomplished novel, but a dry and still one, lacking his previous graceful talent.

It37.   Conetti, Lidia. Introduzione. *Il diamante grosso come l'Hotel Ritz [The Diamond as Big as the Ritz]*, by F. Scott Fitzgerald. Trans. Bruno Oddera. Milan: Emme, 1974. Milan: Mondadori, 1993: 5-15.

Fitzgerald shows early on in his experiences as a child, then in college, and finally in the army, many of the distinctive traits that will characterize his personality throughout his life: total self-absorption, the need to impress others, even the propensity to alcohol abuse. On the other hand, the writer is also influenced by the values of the southern gentleman inherited from his father. His works are always a reflection of his experience; his peculiar style is an emotional language which is reminiscent of the linear but highly personal logic of a child. This explains his constant success even when his role as the best interpreter of the Twenties has long vanished. Fitzgerald is able to best represent every age that he himself goes through, from adolescence to adulthood, thus reaching out to all readers by expressing the same emotions they have experienced at some time in their lives.

It38.   Etheridge, Chuck. "*Tender Is the Night*, The Novel of Romance, the Novel of Manners, and the Modern Tragedy." Fortunes and Misfortunes in the Life and Times of F. Scott Fitzgerald (1896-1990): Centennial Conference, Rome, 10-11 Oct. 1996.

From the point of view of both English and American literary critics, one cannot write a novel that upholds the social order as the most important thing while at the same time upholding the self-reliant individual as being the thing of greatest value. Henry James reflects the American critical assumption that the novel of manners is impossible in American culture. Fitzgerald's work embraces this paradox, especially in *Tender Is the Night,* and exploits the dramatic tension between these two fundamentally incompatible modes of creating modern tragedy. Dick a natural idealist who wants to be the greatest psychologist that ever lived, in his early years almost the personification of Emerson's 'Man-Thinking,' determined to chart a genuinely new course, and in fact was lucky enough to be well on his way to doing so. Dick is Emerson's American Scholar in dramatic form, using his study as preparation for future action. Dick persists, despite warnings from his European colleagues and friends that he cannot remake the world in order to make it acceptable for him to wed his schizophrenic patient, Nicole. He is destroyed by holding on to an individual vision despite the presence of valid social mores. His innocence becomes ignorance with frightening consequences. He cannot recover his romantic vision within the world of manners represented by Nicole's wealthy family, and the strain begins to tear him apart. In a literary sense, his end is tragic; at every step of the way he has sown the seeds for his own destruction.

It39. Fink, Guido. "'Inesprimere l'esprimibile': tre romanzi americani del 1925" [To Inexpress the Expressible: Three American Novels from 1925]. *RSA Journal* 2 (1991): 37-52.

This essay compares *The Great Gatsby* to Dreiser's *An American Tragedy* and Dos Passos's *Manhattan Transfer.* Even though their relation to Modernism differs greatly, the novels show some common traits which seem to be in part motivated by the ubiquitous modernization of the American way of life. Dos Passos is the most modern in his portrayal and embracing of the masses, whereas Fitzgerald mostly isolates his characters from the urban crowd. The similarities among the three novels are more evident on a narrative level, in a series of technical features highly influenced by cinematic language: the use of various degrees of elliptical and fragmentary structure; the presence of apparently 'unimportant' elements next to the ones that are considered the core of traditional narration; the insistence on the gaze and its function in shaping the perspective; the automobile as theme and symbol of freedom, speed, and modernity. The most explicit connection of the three novels to cinema is the idea of montage as a technique, as it had been theorized by Eisenstein; parallel to the loss of importance of montage with the end of silent movies, there is a return of the technique in literature. In Fitzgerald, Nick is constantly trying to reconfigure things and people according to his own perception; his inability to recapture the fading dream once Gatsby is dead, as well as similar incongruities and discontinuities in Dreiser and Dos Passos, make the three novels examples of modernist texts, which contain within themselves the paradoxical impossibility of linear narration.

It40.   Fink, Guido, Mario Maffi, Franco Minganti, and Bianca Tarozzi. "Francis Scott Fitzgerald: miti e successi del fallimento" [Francis Scott Fitzgerald: Myths and Successes of Failure]. *Storia della letteratura americana [History of American Literature].* Florence: Sansoni Editore, 1991: 252-6.

Fitzgerald's early production can be read under the sign of the transparent presence of autobiographical elements, and constitutes an eminently emotional exploration of his literary project. Yet, behind the romantic myth of success and youth it is already possible to see the emptiness, the abyss. It is eventually with *The Great Gatsby* that he gains lasting fame as one of the great American novelists. In *Tender Is the Night* he attempts to achieve a greater structural and stylistic complexity, while somehow losing the capacity for mythical synthesis. Although not as experimental as Gertrude Stein's, Fitzgerald's writing is nonetheless modernist in its problematic staging of the conflict between art and life; much of his production lies within the success-failure parabola presented with particular attention to mythical figures, the sensuality of images, and the use of irony.

It41.   Giorcelli, Cristina. "Fitzgerald and Rawlings via Wharton." Fortunes and Misfortunes in the Life and Times of F. Scott Fitzgerald (1896-1940): Centennial Conference, Rome, 10-11 Oct. 1996.

Edith Wharton is the point of reference between the younger artists Fitzgerald and Marjorie Kinnan Rawlings, particularly *Ethan Frome*, the characteristics of whose three stark protagonists can be seen in Fitzgerald's and Rawlings's characters.

It42.   Golino, Enzo. "Scott's Story . . . 'Io sono un marxiano' [Scott's Story . . . 'I am a Marxist']." *La Repubblica Cultura.* 28-29 Dec. 1980. 16.

Fitzgerald's claim that he is essentially Marxist is consonant with his pronouncement that he is a typical product of his moment in time. In reality, "the beautiful and damned" are "beautiful and alienated," not damned to Hell, but alienated by the spasmodic desire for a hotel as big as the Ritz.

It43.   Halliday, Iain. "Two Gatsbys: Translation Theory as an Aid to Understanding." Fortunes and Misfortunes in the Life and Times of F. Scott Fitzgerald (1896-1940): Centennial Conference, Rome, 10-11 Oct. 1996.

A middle course between the empirical and the hermeneutical is possible in examining the translations of *The Great Gatsby* into Italian by Fernanda Pivano (1950) and Tommaso Pisanti (1989) in terms of Fitzgerald's awareness on the one hand of potential multiple points of view and on the other of the inevitable limits of fixed ideas. Translation is an aid to understanding but some loss always results both in the intralingual, the phenomenon of writing, as well as the interlingual, the translation of a text into another language. Nick invites the reader to translate. Various comparisons of the two translations contribute to understanding Fitzgerald's text. For example, "'The poor son-of-a-bitch'," he said" is alternately translated as "'povero bastardo'," disse" and "'Poveraccio!' disse." Is the rougher, less affectionate *bastardo* more correct or is the sympathetic tone of *poveraccio* more in keeping with the way one sees Gatsby? To paraphrase and revolutionize Robert Frost, sometimes poetry is what is *gained* in translation, *gained* in interpretation.

It44. Kezich, Tullio. "Scott's Story . . . Lo scrittore nella Fabbrica dei Sogni [Scott's Story . . . The Writer in the Factory of Dreams]." *La Repubblica Cultura*. 28-29 Dec. 1980. 16.

Fitzgerald saw Hollywood as an impiegato of the "Factory of Dream." He never understood cinema and cinema never understood him. Despite his altercations with film industry colleagues like producer Joseph L. Mankeiwicz, Fitzgerald did enjoy some of his time there, and had his first stable relationship with a woman since Zelda was committed in 1930. Films of Fitzgerald's work have in fact fared better than those of Hemingway or Faulkner.

It45. Perosa, Sergio. "Fitzgerald's Current Reputation in Italy": F. Scott Fitzgerald Centennial Conference, Princeton U, 21 Sept. 1996.

See Chapter Introduction.

It46. Perosa, Sergio. "Fitzgerald Studies in the 1970's." *Twentieth-Century Literature: A Scholarly and Critical Journal* 26.2 (1980): 222-46.

American scholarship on Fitzgerald in the 1970s had the remarkable result of securing a well-defined position for him alongside other twentieth-century writers.

It47. Pivano, Fernanda. "Francis Scott Fitzgerald." *America rossa e nera*. Milano: Il Formichiere, 1964.

Fitzgerald's career starts with the commercially constructed success of *This Side of Paradise*, which will prove harmful for his later accomplishments, giving him a sense of early failure when his later books do not sell as many copies as his first novel. His glamorous life with Zelda costs him not only an incredible amount of money, but also emotional exhaustion and restlessness that he tries to quench with alcohol. In order to keep up with the expenses he writes "too many short stories" and publishes them even when he is not satisfied with them. Zelda's mental illness puts the final strain on their life, and every attempt to mend the situation with trips and distractions proves disastrous; Scott's own health and mental state are rapidly declining, as he records in *The Crack Up*, one of his best works. His last years in Hollywood are a succession of professional and personal humiliations; he dies leaving unfinished one of his masterpieces, *The Last Tycoon*, forgotten by almost everybody and with a sense of personal failure.

It48.   Pivano, Fernanda. "Fitzgerald e la sua denuncia sociale" [Fitzgerald and His Social Denunciation]. *Mostri degli anni Venti* [*Exhibitions of the Twenties*]. Milan: Mondadori, 1976, 1986. 137-52.

My intention here is to reverse the stereotype that sees Fitzgerald primarily as the herald of the Jazz Age, a sentimental writer who profited from the clamor and revolution of manners that involved the youth of the time. There is in him another important dimension, namely the awareness of the social dynamics of his time and the corruption of money, a "poison without any possible antidote." His critique is much more powerful and meaningful thanks to his own obsessive fascination with wealth and his final defeat by the mechanism of commercialism. All his main characters, from Amory Blaine, to Jay Gatsby, to Dick Diver, are destined to lose their initial moral and physical integrity under the pressure and the temptation of money. The fictional topic has clear autobiographical roots: Fitzgerald will never overcome his sense of inferiority to his "aristocratic" friends, who were born into wealth and comfort and never had to work; his books expose both this category and the *parvenus* with equal ruthlessness, showing the all-pervading corruptive power of money.

It49.   Pivano, Fernanda. Introduzione [Introduction]. *Belli e dannati* [*The Beautiful and Damned*]. Trans. Fernanda Pivano. Milan: Mondadori, 1954, 1972, 1973, 1978, 1992, 1996. viii-xxxii.

The novel presents a generational conflict typical of the 1920s: Anthony Patch embodies the Jazz Age with its cult of money and success, while his grandfather is a representative of the values of the Victorian past. The novel was first serialized in *Metropolitan Magazine* with a different, 'happy' ending imposed by the publishers; it was later published with a radically different ending, to which Zelda contributed. The couple in the novel are of course inspired by biographical events from Scott and Zelda's life, although they are highly manipulated to give Scott's own interpretation of their relationship and his sense of what they might become, rather than what they actually were at the time.

Thus, the protagonists also represent a whole generation, for whom money, beauty, and fame are the only values, as superficial as they are. The novel also suggests the conflict between Fitzgerald's early and disproportionate commercial and critical success and his life-long insecurity about his own real literary talent.

It50. Pivano, Fernanda. *"Il grande Gatsby"* [*The Great Gatsby*]. *Mostri degli anni Venti* [*Exhibitions of the Twenties*]. Milan: Mondadori, 1976, 1982. 112-115.

In this introduction to *The Great Gatsby*, Pivano claims that the two main accomplishments of the novel are its critique of the hypocrisy of materialist society and its concise and intense style. The story, as it is often the case in Fitzgerald, is inspired by autobiographical events, and many of its characters reflect such an origin; the writer, who never writes about sex, only about love, portrays in the idealized and stylized figure of Daisy his own attitude of worship towards Zelda; Gatsby stands also for Scott himself, especially in his sense of being excluded from the society of the rich and respectable. The novel works also on a more social level as it expresses the futility of the American dream as it is embodied in the enthusiasm of the roaring Twenties.

It51. Pivano, Fernanda. Introduzione [Introduction]. *Racconti dell'età del jazz* [*Stories of the Jazz Age*]. Milan: Mondadori, 1980. 5-11.

The short stories anticipate crucial themes of Fitzgerald's later novels and are also an important technical exercise for the writer. The topic of the corruption of money is especially important in "The Diamond as Big as the Ritz," in which it is presented with stylized exemplarity; in the novels it will be developed more in depth in its social and psychological implications. Other stories are important above all because they give Fitzgerald the chance to experiment with narrative techniques; in some, he even anticipates Dos Passos's juxtaposition of multiple perspectives.

It52. Pivano, Fernanda. "Le versioni di *Tenera è la notte*" [The Versions of *Tender Is the Night*]. *Mostri degli anni Venti* [*Exhibitions of the Twenties*]. Milan: Mondadori, 1976, 1986. 126-36.

There are at least three unpublished and two different published versions of *Tender Is the Night*, all of which went through several revisions. The original core of the novel, entitled *The World's Fair*, is the story of Francis Melarky, a young man who travels through Europe with his mother and eventually kills her; although the story will change radically, many episodes and characters are retained in the later versions with only a few changes. The title then changes to *The Drunkard's Holiday*, and the novel becomes the story of director Lew Kelly and his wife Nicole. The third version sees the appearance of Dick Diver as the main character; in addition, the figure of Nicole is more clearly modeled on Zelda and her psychological condition, and Rosemary is introduced as a point of view character. The title is originally *Doctor Diver's Holiday*, and then finally *Tender Is the Night*; it is yet a different version to be published for the first time in *Scribner's Magazine* in the winter of 1934. Fitzgerald was not entirely satisfied with this version, nor with the one published as a volume, and in many letters complained about the great number of mistakes and saw the non-chronological structure of the novel as a serious defect. It is only in 1951 that Malcolm Cowley edits a version, based on Fitzgerald's notes, which rearranges radically the succession of the episodes; yet the use of Rosemary and the initial mystery about Dick and Nicole's story adds to the suspense and effectiveness of the novel.

It53.   Pivano, Fernanda. *"Tenera è la notte"* [*Tender Is the Night*]. *Mostri degli anni Venti* [*Exhibitions of the Twenties*], Fernanda Pivano. Milan: Mondadori, 1976, 1986. 122-25.

This brief introduction to *Tender Is the Night* reconstructs the circumstances of the writing of the novel: the summers of the late Twenties spent by the Fitzgeralds between the Riviera, Switzerland, and Paris; Zelda's incipient mental illness, and Scott's long and difficult elaboration of the book. The plot of the novel is a flirtation with disaster: the integrity of the promising psychiatrist is corrupted by the money and the cynicism of the rich, while Nicole progressively gets better as Dick plunges into alcoholism. Such a negative portrayal of the corruption of wealth, paired with Fitzgerald's own dedication and effort to finish the novel, make the book an expression of faith in courage, dignity and above all work as the only true meaning of life.

It54.   Pivano, Fernanda. "Zelda e la sua colpa di essere nata donna" [Zelda and Her Fault in Being Born a Woman]. *Mostri degli anni Venti* [*Exhibitions of the Twenties*]. Milan: Mondadori, 1976, 1986. 153-59.

This brief essay is a portrait of Zelda Fitzgerald, based on the biography by Nancy Milford, and a visit to Scottie made by Pivano in 1956. Zelda is a victim, not so much of Scott, but of the social expectations and the limits imposed on a woman in the 1920s. Both Zelda and Scott are prisoners of the Jazz Age myth, partly created by themselves, which becomes a gilded cage that will condition the rest of their lives. Zelda's fabled eccentricity is less a truth than a cliché created out of the anecdotes of the early months of their marriage and their reckless life. In her behavior, she was trying to live all the lives she was denied as a woman: this pattern will return with her attempts to find a creative expression in painting, dancing, writing.

It55. Placido, Beniamino. "Scott's Story . . . Danzando sul ponte del Titanic
       [Scott's Story . . . Dancing on the Bridge of the Titanic]." *La Repubblica
       Cultura.* 28-29 Dec. 1980. 16.

The years following World War II involved an accelerated cultural recuperation.
Now, with the publication of Fitzgerald's notebooks, almost 50 years after the
war, that recuperation has all but vanished and the must-read American literature
is not Melville and Fitzgerald, but Chandler and Hammett. We now read
Fitzgerald to see the cadaver of the '30s lurking behind the glitter of the '20s,
and in that same way we read his notebooks. We read in Fitzgerald the authority
of failure, which, in Hollywood, was partially due to his inability to understand
the new role of the intellectual that came out of the crises of 1929 and the
introduction of forces like the Federal Writers Project. Fitzgerald, as de
Tocqueville said of Americans, loved money and courage. His writing gives us
pause to reflect on his personal affirmation, professional role, and social
identity.

It56. Quinn, Patrick J. M. "Lamia in Love": The English Decadent Legacy in
       The Beautiful and Damned. Fortunes and Misfortunes in the Life and
       Times of F. Scott Fitzgerald (1896-1940): Centennial Conference, Rome,
       10-11 Oct. 1996.

Generally, critics conclude that *The Beautiful and Damned* is immature, its
structure shapeless, and the characters unsympathetic. The English Decadents, to
whom Fitzgerald refers several times in the novel, were similarly criticized. In
the novel, in fact, Fitzgerald utilizes the Decadents' revolt against the
industrialized way of life, their accent on the ideal and the transcendent nature of
reality, their abhorrence of the activity of the everyday mundane world, and their
emphasis on urban life. He also attaches to Anthony Patch his own obsession
with the *femme fatale* due more to his reading of Swinburne and other English
Decadent writers than to his experience with Zelda. Fitzgerald's association
throughout the novel of female predators with animal imagery is clearly rooted
in the English Decadent tradition. Fitzgerald refers to Swinburne at the
conclusion of the novel as Anthony muses about the death of poetry: "Beauty, as
the sum of several beautiful parts, reached its apotheosis in Swinburne. It can't
go any further."

It57. Rossi, Doc. "Fantasties and Fools: Allegory in Fitzgerald's Short
       Stories." Fortune and Misfortune in the Life and Times of F. Scott
       Fitzgerald (1896-1940): Centennial Conference, Rome, 10-11 Oct. 1996.

Fitzgerald crossed the boundaries of the real and the fictive to take the reader to
a third area that, like the crook comedies that inspired Basil Duke Lee to write
The Captured Shadow, opened out into a world much larger and more brilliant

than themselves. Fitzgerald suggests allegorical interpretation through fragmentation and parody. His characters are not usually personifications of abstract qualities, but their names are often peculiarly appropriate, revealing the selection and combination of elements that characterize them in relief against what has been left out. Readers are drawn in two directions—to the characters, settings, and events themselves, and to the ideas or significance they are intended to convey. The energy of attraction and repulsion runs throughout his work creating a dynamic that puts choice firmly in the hands of the reader, if not forcing him or her to make a choice, then at least suggesting that one needs to be made.

It58.   Rubeo, Ugo. "F. Scott Fitzgerald e *The Crack-Up*: Frammenti per un'
         autobiografia" [F. Scott Fitzgerald and *The Crack-Up*: Fragments for an
         Autobiography]. *Identità e scrittura: Studi sull'Autobiografia Nord-
         Americana* [*Identity and Writing: Studies in North-American
         Autobiography*]. Eds. Anna Lucia Accardo, Maria Ornella Marotti and
         Igina Tattoni. Intro. by Maria Ornello Marotti. Rome: Bulzoni, 1988.
         77-89.

These three pieces are not so much essays as an autobiographical tale in three parts, in which Fitzgerald uses a new form based on a mixture of fiction and personal narrative. In the first part the author adopts a double perspective—as both character and narrator, sometimes using the first person and sometimes looking at himself from the outside—to make a parallel with *The Great Gatsby*. This allows Fitzgerald to look at himself from a vantage point, distancing himself from his life so far and from what has caused his crisis; it is both a refusal of his former self and the beginning of a regeneration. The narrative past is substituted by the present tense, which erases his former self and leaves the subject in a sort of moral waste land. At this point, the last part of the work leads to a reevaluation of writing as the only tenable position for the subject. This attitude will offer the author the model for a reasoned and fruitful use of autobiographical elements in his later works.

It59.   Sachs, Viola. "The Symbolism of Clothes in Mythic American Texts:
         Fitzgerald's *The Great Gatsby* and Hawthorne's *The Scarlet Letter*."
         Abito e Identità: Ricerche di storia letteraria e culturale [*Press and
         Identity: Research in Literary and Cultural History*]. Ed. Cristina
         Giorcelli. Rome: Associate Editrice Internazionale, 1999. 49-61.

Compared to the rich depiction of characters' clothing in European literature, American novels lack detail. Clothing rather is perceived in conjunction with complex symbolic clusters in which it reveals racial, religious, and sexual identities. Daisy is associated with white and yellow, the colors of Easter, of regeneration and resurrection, of whitewashing the sordid past of pioneers like

Dan Cody, for white refers to the racial construction of American identity. Gatsby's clothes, his white suit also reflect his racial identity but various passages in the book suggest that Gatsby may be passing for white. Tom accuses him of being a "Mr. Nobody from Nowhere" and predicts the coming intermarriage between black and white.

It60. Vatanpour, Sina. "The American Dream and the Meretricious Game of Money and Love in Fitzgerald's *The Great Gatsby.*" *Letterature d'America* [*Literature of America*] 50 (1993): 71-87.

Money is more mythical than real in *The Great Gatsby*. Mineral substances such as jewels and gold generate forms, colors and other patterns which create the texture of the characters, space and time in the novel. Script money is associated with counterfeiting, lying, adultery, fake identity, manipulating games and fictitious writing. For Gatsby, who believes in the American dream, commercial undertaking, speculation and bootlegging replace the gold rush. The change from mineral riches to money coincides with the corruption of the true values of the American Dream. Gatsby's white flannel suit, silver shirt and gold tie recognize Daisy's colors but only superficially. He is counterfeit. Nick goes East to learn about the bond business and make his fortune. Instead, he decides to write a book about false bonds in which he finds careless people together. Thus, both narrator and writer are counterfeiters.

It61. Villari, Lucio. "Scott's Story . . . Belli, dannati, soprattutto disperati [Scott's Story . . . Beautiful, Damned, Above All Hopeless]." *La Repubblica Cultura.* 28-29 Dec. 1980. 16.

The fact that Fitzgerald does not remember when he wrote certain things is indicative of his absorption in his writing, as evidenced in his recently published notebooks. One can no longer read Fitzgerald with the levity with which we read him years ago, for, with the benefit of hindsight, we see the disillusionment with which Fitzgerald's generation came of age. Fitzgerald's entire biography is dominated by the world wars.

BOOK REVIEWS/NEWS ARTICLES/RADIO PROGRAMS

It62. Albinati, Edoardo. "In cerca di emozioni Zelda e Fitz attraversano l'America su una vecchia carcassa" [In Search of Emotions: Zelda and Fitz Crossing America in an Old Wreck]. Rev. of *La crociera del Rottame Vagante* [*The Cruise of the Rolling Junk*], by F. Scott Fitzgerald. *Paese Sera* 3 Oct. 1985: n.p.

In *The Cruise of the Rolling Junk* Fitzgerald uses an overexcited tone, a style which is similar to the humor of Jerome K. Jerome, a hyperbolic accumulation of adjectives. Every passage seems to be written to show off how crazy and careless he and Zelda are during the trip. The more interesting aspect of the book are the lyrically suggestive descriptions of the landscape.

It63.   Andreani, Alberto. "In viaggio sul '*Rottame Vagante*'" [Travelling in the 'Rolling Junk']. Rev. of *La crociera del Rottame Vagante* [*The Cruise of the Rolling Junk*], by F. Scott Fitzgerald. *Le piccolo* 24 Aug., 1985: n.p.

Fitzgerald shows a late-romantic outlook on life and art: in him there is a tragic contradiction between the exaltation of modern life with its opportunities and the fierce critique against modern commercialism. In their trip to Alabama, Scott and Zelda try to recapture the lost innocence of the countryside, but they are unable to do so, because they are too self-absorbed. Fitzgerald experiments here for the first time with the American theme of travel and the symbolic aura of the automobile.

It64.   Cancellieri, Gianni. "Quel Romantico 'Rottame'" [That Romantic 'Junk']. Rev. of *La crociera del Rottame Vagante* [*The Cruise of the Rolling Junk*], by F. Scott Fitzgerald. *Auto* 17 Apr. 1986: n.p.

In *The Cruise of the Rolling Junk* the automobile is used as a symbol of freedom and purity and becomes the propulsive power of the narration, the cause of countless anecdotes, beautiful landscapes, and reflections on the illusion of the American Dream.

It65.   Cortellazzo, S. Rev. of *Festa da ballo* [*The Dance*], by F. Scott Fitzgerald. *L'indice*, 85 (6 Sep.1985): n. p.

The story is a fine example of the use of rhythm and the narrative ability of Fitzgerald. It is surprising that the writer did not include this thriller in any of his collections. With great success he recreates the environment of a small town in the South, with its secrets, scandals, submerged passions.

It66.   Curuz, M. Bernardelli. "Quel lungo viaggio di Scott Fitzgerald" [The Long Voyage of Scott Fitzgerald]. Rev. of *La crociera del Rottame Vagante* [*The Cruise of the Rolling Junk*], by F. Scott Fitzgerald. *Giornale di Brescia* 21 Sept., 1985: n.p.

The book, written explicitly in hopes of earning easy money, does not show Fitzgerald at his best: it is mechanically written and with no particular inspiration. The story is more valuable as a sociological document of the status of concepts like the road, travel, the automobile in American society of the time. Scott and Zelda, while trying to escape the stiff social conventions of the city, still retain a snobbish sense of superiority towards all aspects of rural life.

It67. Lilli, Laura. "Con Zelda sul Rottame" [With Zelda in the Junk]. Rev. of *La crociera del Rottame Vagante* [*The Cruise of the Rolling Junk*] and *Festa da ballo* [*The Dance*], by F. Scott Fitzgerald. *Le Repubblica* 18 Sept. 1985: n.p.

The Cruise of the Rolling Junk is "one of the first prose poems on the automobile to be written in the United States." It starts a long tradition of personification of the car, while at the same time undercutting the myth of the object with irony. Fitzgerald's style is highly entertaining and the dialogues are exhilarating. *The Dance* shows the other side of the writer, the anxiety and discomfort under the glittering surface.

It68. Marcoaldi, Franco. "In viaggio con il grande Gatsby" [Travelling with the Great Gatsby]. Rev. of *La crociera del Rottame Vagante* [*The Cruise of the Rolling Junk*], by F. Scott Fitzgerald. *Monitor libri* 21 Aug., 1985: 19.

Scott and Zelda's trip represents the utopian attempt to go back to a genuine and uncontaminated dimension, embodied by the immobile and eternal South. Travel is not valued in itself, as later in Kerouac, but as yet another expression of the drive towards the remote object of one's dreams. Since such a dream is by its nature unattainable, the style that Fitzgerald successfully adopts is full of bitter irony and controlled lyricism.

It69. Marrocu, Luciano. "Con Scott Fitzgerald nella crociera del rottame vagante" [With Scott Fitzgerald in the Cruise of the Rolling Junk]. Rev. of *La crociera del Rottame Vagante* [*The Cruise of the Rolling Junk*], by F. Scott Fitzgerald. *L'uniche Stampa* 29 Nov., 1985: n.p.

Fitzgerald catches the fascination of the automobile in its transitional phase: not any more a luxury item for a very few chosen, but not yet a mass commodity. The story is thus suffused both with a romantic attachment to the car, and with irony for its precarious condition as 'junk.'

It70. Morpurgo, Lisa. "In viaggio con Francis e Zelda" [Travelling With Francis and Zelda]. Rev. of *La crociera del Rottame Vagante* [*The Cruise of the Rolling Junk*], by F. Scott Fitzgerald. *Uomo* Nov./Dec., 1985: n.p.

The tone of the long story is picaresque and light-hearted; there are already all the elements that will make up *Tender Is the Night* and *The Great Gatsby*, although not yet developed to their potential. Only at the end does a melancholic mood set in as Fitzgerald observes the house of Zelda's parents, which is symbolically empty.

It71.   Nugnes, Barbara. "Le nostalgie del grande Gatsby" [The Nostalgias of the Great Gatsby]. *Il nostro tempo* 46.5 (3 Feb. 1991): 5.

In *The Great Gatsby* Fitzgerald reveals himself as not only a keen observer of contemporary society, but above all one of the greatest artists of Modernism. The novel is perfectly orchestrated, every page and every detail necessary for the overall construction of the mythical paradigm. Yet, unlike Hemingway's style which is based on understatement, Fitzgerald's does not fear lyrical and more exalted moments: the author is endowed of a "double vision" that gives him an extremely lucid sense of observation, while at the same time retaining the capacity to dream, and to believe in his dreams. Fitzgerald becomes thus the best interpreter of America, suspended itself between the original purity of its ideals and the empty materialism of its reality.

It72.   Orengo, Nico. "La motocicletta corre per le strade della letteratura" [The Motorcycle Rides on the Streets of Literature]. Rev. of *La crociera del Rottame Vagante* [*The Cruise of the Rolling Junk*], by F. Scott Fitzgerald. *La Stampa* [*The Press*] 31 Aug., 1985: n.p.

This article is written on the one hundredth anniversary of the invention of the motorcycle. The motorcycle has not been used often in literature and in the arts. With the exception of Musil, artists from the Italian Futurists to Proust have preferred the automobile. Also for the Americans Fitzgerald, Kerouac, and Miller, the automobile has been the privileged symbol of freedom and speed.

It73.   Perosa, Sergio. "A Quarant'anni Dalla Morte di Francis Scott Fitzgerald: Hemingway, Dov'e'il Tuo Cuore Puro" [Forty Years After the Death of Francis Scott Fitzgerald: Hemingway, Where Is Your Pure Heart?]. *Corriere Della Sera* 15 Dec., 1980: n.p.

It74.   Perosa, Sergio. Rev. of *Fitzgerald's Craft of Short Fiction*, by Alice Hall Petry. *Studies in American Fiction* 18 (Autumn 1991): 244-45.

Petry's study is on the whole convincing although the biographical material intrudes too much on her analysis of early stories here as well as in *Taps at Reveille*, in which Fitzgerald actually achieved objectification.

It75.   Pignata, Piero. "Scott Fitzgerald: Il suo rapporto con Hollywood" [Scott
        Fitzgerald: His Relationship with Hollywood]. *Il nostro tempo* 46.5 (3
        Feb. 1991): 5.

Fitzgerald's relationship with Hollywood is a mutual attraction, which never
becomes 'love'; the writer had always been fascinated by the incarnation of the
American Dream represented by the movie industry, but he could also see very
clearly its limits and contradictions. As it is the case with Chandler, Faulkner, or
Nathanael West, Fitzgerald's career as a screenwriter in Hollywood is not a
success, given also his problems with alcohol, which made it extremely difficult
for him to work in a team. Although some of Fitzgerald's screenplays can be
considered positively, his experience can be characterized as a failure; on the
other hand, the film versions of Fitzgerald's works have also been generally
modest, with the exception of Kazan's "The Last Tycoon," which is a very good
movie, although it gives only a partial reading of the novel. The best result of
Fitzgerald's work in Hollywood are thus his stories of the period and especially
The Last Tycoon, which is together with *Day of the Locust* the most
accomplished novel about Hollywood, its dreams, and their failure.

It76.   Pignata, Piero. "Scott Fitzgerald: una luce verde sulla rivaopposta" [Scott
        Fitzgerald: A Green Light on the Opposite Shore]. *Il nostro tempo* 46.5
        (3 Feb. 1991): 5.

At the fiftieth anniversary of Fitzgerald's death it may do to summarize the
events that lead to the writer's crisis after his early success and to his being
abandoned and forgotten by almost everybody in his last years. With *Tender Is
the Night* Fitzgerald is not anymore in accord with the spirit of the time, which
tends toward explicit social engagement. Yet his style and his narrative ability
mature and his later novels are not inferior to *The Great Gatsby*. *The Last
Tycoon* would have been his masterpiece if he had finished it. In it Fitzgerald
profits from his acute observations of Hollywood and its social dynamics. The
writer's relationship to the entertainment industry is contradictory: he admires
the possibilities offered by the new medium, but he is also well aware of the
risks of superficiality and falsity.

It77.   Scaraffia, Giuseppe. Rev. of *La crociera del Rottame Vagante* [*The
        Cruise of the Rolling Junk*], by F. Scott Fitzgerald. *Automobile Classico*.
        May-June 1986: n.p.

This review gives a very brief summary of the story and comments on the fine
pictures of Scott and Zelda that are included in the Italian edition.

It78.   Tomasi, Liliam. "*La crociera del Rottame Vagante* di Francis Scott

Fitzgerald." Rev. of *La crociera del Rottame Vagante* [*The Cruise of the Rolling Junk*], by F. Scott Fitzgerald. *Confidenzi* [*Confidences*] 4 Apr. 1986: n.p.

Fitzgerald embarks on the trip South because of a sense of guilt that the reckless life in the city generates; he and Zelda search for the lost innocence of origins, but when they arrive in Montgomery, the people are a disappointment and Zelda's parents are absent. The tone of the story is mostly melancholic, with moments of deep irony and brilliant descriptions.

It79.   Zorzi, Rosella Mamoli. "Generazione dell'angoscia" [Generation of Anguish]. Rev. of *La crociera del Rottame Vagante* [*The Cruise of the Rolling Junk*], by F. Scott Fitzgerald. *Il Garrellino* 21 Dec., 1990: n.p.

On the occasion of the fiftieth anniversary of Fitzgerald's death, one should point out that his lasting success proves that his reputation was not superficially based on the fashion of the roaring Twenties, but on real artistic greatness. In *The Pat Hobby Stories*, recently published in Italian translation, the writer presents a character/narrator who is a Hollywood screenwriter struggling to survive in an environment in which falsity, deception and envy are the rule. Through him Fitzgerald presents his deep insight into the world of cinema as he experienced it in his last years.

DISSERTATIONS

It80.   Balsamo, Silvia Lucia. "The 'postwar temps' nei romanzi di F. Scott Fitzgerald" [The 'Post War Times' in the Novels of F. Scott Fitzgerald]. Instituto Universitario di Lingui Moderne [University Institute of Modern Languages], 1990/91.

It81.   Locatelli, Silvia. *"The Great Gatsby*: dal romanzo di F. Scott Fitzgerald ai testi felmici" [*The Great Gatsby*: from F. Scott Fitzgerald's Novel to Its Witnesses]. Test di lourea, Instituto Universitario di Bergamo, 1989-90.

TEACHER/STUDENT GUIDES AND EDITIONS

It82. Fitzgerald, F. Scott. *Il diamante grosso come l'Hotel Ritz* [*The Diamond as Big as the Ritz*]. Trans. Bruno Oddera. Preface by Linda Conetti. Milan: Emme, 1974. Milan: Mondadori, 1993.

It83. Fitzgerald, F. Scott. *The Great Gatsby. Teacher's Guide.* Ed. G. Moech D'Agostino. Turin: Loescher, 1994.

It84. Fitzgerald, F. Scott. *The Great Gatsby.* Ed. Winifred Farrant. Bevilacqua. Reading Classics. Genoa: Cideb, 1994. ix-lxvii. 208.

Germany

In the five decades after the first German translation of *The Great Gatsby* appeared in 1928, Fitzgerald's reputation in Germany passed through three stages similar to those observed of his reception in other European countries during the same years: little interest before the post-war period, some post-war recognition, and greater attention after 1960. The optimism that his reputation in Germany would continue to grow was guarded; "The size of his following in Germany is small, however, and there are few signs that it will expand. Considerably fewer German than French and British scholars are writing about Fitzgerald, although those German critics who have taken an interest in him have a deeper admiration for his work than many of their British counterparts" (Stanley, 1980, 135). One critic, Helmut Papajewski, believed that Fitzgerald was "a formative element in the spiritual orientation of post-war Germany with its two main streams: the specifically religious and the literary-secular" (Papajewski, 1965, 77). Indeed, Hans-Jürgen Heise commented that "literary connoisseurs" predicted he will one day be popular in Germany (Heise, 1963, n. pag.).

Since 1980, the cautious optimism has been supported as 30 monographs and articles have been written about Fitzgerald as opposed to 20 in the preceding 50 years. With the rights to Fitzgerald's work in translation going to the Swiss-based publishing house of Diogenes in 1974, practically everything that Fitzgerald wrote has been translated and published in German. Diogenes has had translated seven collections of Fitzgerald's short stories since 1978, and subsequently, seven essays have been written on his stories. The translation of *This Side of Paradise* in 1988 coincided with a dissertation on the novel that became both a book and an article by Udo Hebel (G23, G87). Only *The Beautiful and Damned* remains to be translated.

As well as additional translations of Fitzgerald's work, new theoretical approaches to the study of literature have produced more scholarship on the writer. Horst Kruse, the pre-eminent Fitzgerald scholar in Germany, credits the advent of American Studies programs in German universities for the increase in scholarly interest (Kruse, 13 Aug. 1995), while Udo Hebel believes that the new textual studies approach is also responsible for the growing body of scholarship (Hebel, 2 Sept. 1995). Other factors include continuing interest in the Jack Clayton film of *The Great Gatsby*, occasioned by German scholars' involvement in film studies and also the influence of Jacques Lacan's psychoanalytic theory.

In addition to the translation of *This Side of Paradise* by Arche (Zürich) in 1988, eight Diogenes translations of Fitzgerald's short stories, and the translation of the "Crack-Up" essay by Merve in 1984, Fitzgerald's stories appeared in translation in at least six anthologies. Horst Kruse notes that while "it took the publisher all of twenty years—until 1974—to sell the 8000 copies of *The Great Gatsby*" (G57), several subsequent editions of *This Side of Paradise* appeared between 1988 and 1991. All of the Diogenes editions of stories also have gone into a subsequent edition. Six English-language editions of *The Great Gatsby* compete for the school market accompanied by student study guides and often teacher guides as well. Moreover, several short story collections also appeared in school editions.

Current German scholarly work on Fitzgerald falls into several categories, reflecting both traditional approaches and new trends in literary criticism: five biographical studies, six primarily new critical works, two influence studies, two myth analyses, four studies in the *geistesgeschichte* mode, three thematic approaches, nine studies from an American Studies point of view either on consumer culture or popular culture. A textual study on *This Side of Paradise* citing the influence of Derrida, Barthes, Foucault, Kristeva, Pfister and Genette (G23, G87) and another on *The Great Gatsby* developing a Lacanian point of view (G44) indicate the influence of post-structural theory, narratology, and new historicism.

The biographical studies include the fairly traditional such as Jürg Federspiel's linkage of Monroe Stahr's numbered days in the Hollywood "dream factory" to Fitzgerald's own numbered days and ultimate death (G36). Gerda Marko includes Zelda and Scott in a 12-volume study of writer couples: the question she poses is "How does one manage closeness and writer's isolation?" (G66). Taking a similar approach, Elisabeth Schnack quotes Fitzgerald "Everyone is alone. An artist must be alone" in her book *Must the Artist Be Alone?* in which she discusses, among other authors, Fitzgerald's life and work (G71 19). *Zelda and F. Scott Fitzgerald: An American Dream,* a fairly traditional biography written by Kyra Stromberg (and translated into Italian), presents the couple as "two irreconcilable souls, whose bond never dissolved" (G29).

Other traditional scholarship includes two influence studies: Joachim Gerke sees as possible influences on *The Great Gatsby* Horatio Alger's *Ragged Dick,* T. S. Arthur's 1851 popular story "Where There's a Will, There's a Way," and Cotton Mather's *A Christian at His Calling; Two Brief Discourses* (G39). Klaus

Lubbers describes Benjamin Franklin's *Autobiography*, clearly an influence on the young James Gatz, as a "bourgeois book advocating wealth as its own justification" (G63).

Studies in the New Critical vein include Udo Hebel's "The Moon That Never Rose" in which he analyzes the final passage in *The Great Gatsby* (G42) and Horst Kruse's close reading of the opening and closing three paragraphs of *Tender Is the Night* (G60). In his monograph, Eugen Huonder investigates the function of setting in Fitzgerald's novels (G26), and Eckhard Grabe portrays Fitzgerald's technique in *The Last Tycoon* as a combination of both filmic and literary styles (G40). In a structural study, Klaus Lubbers reveals the two beginnings in "Babylon Revisited" (G64), and in a study of the narrators in *This Side of Paradise* and *The Great Gatsby*, Dieter Meindl looks at the two "I" novels as self-projections of the author (G67).

Of the thematic approaches, two are myth studies: in *Arthurian Matter and the Theme of the Grail in the Modern American Novel*, Gabriele Krämer sees Jay Gatsby as fatherless like the knight of the Grail but, unlike him, having a less substantial vocation as Quester (G28). Cathy Waegner, in *The Devil in the American Dream: Toward the Faust Tradition in the New World*, claims that a Faustian bargain describes the driving power of American civilization, with Wolfsheim as a Mephisto figure and Gatsby as Faust in his attempt to overcome time (G74).

Other thematic studies focus on conflicting or sequential strands in United States culture. Armin Staats perceives a relationship played out in the country's history between the "genteel tradition" and the "liberal imagination" (G73). In one book chapter, Gerhard Hoffmann says Fitzgerald opposed the American Dream to reality in order to radicalize the grotesque (G47) and in two others Hoffman wrote in the same volume he argues that the "civilization grotesque" gives way to the "existential grotesque" (G48, G49). In his article on "Babylon Revisited" Horst Kruse asserts that the story is the dramatization between two powerful ideologies: strict puritanism and materialistic hedonism (G58). Finally, in his "What is 'American' About American Literature: The Case of *The Great Gatsby*," Luther Luedtke interprets the United States as moving successively in its image of itself from Republican ideals, to those of Nature, Time, the Hero, and Pluralism (G65).

In the German *geistesgeschichte* thematic tradition are Bettina Friedl's "Tracing History: F. Scott Fitzgerald's 'Bernice Bobs Her Hair' and the Panorama of Social Change" (G37); Heinz Ickstadt's two studies "F. Scott Fitzgerald: 'May Day'" and "New York and the 'City Novel' of American Modernism," both on the empty future of the city and the lost agrarian past (G51, G52); and Walter Schürenberg's "Preface" to *The Great Gatsby* (1974) in which he sees the novel as "regardless of styles, fads and filmings, the most exacting and lasting witness of the American twenties" (G72).

The relatively recent American Studies approach in Germany has influenced the writing of five essays and two monographs that focus on either consumer or popular culture. In his book, *F. Scott Fitzgerald: Die Philosophie des Jazz Age,* Tilman Höss describes *The Great Gatsby* as a parable of the American Dream in the consumer society that was developing in response to the egotism with which Americans reacted to the chaos of the war (G25). In each of Fitzgerald's novels, Karl Keiner sees space, time, and characters as marked by the new wealth (G27). Günther Klotz, in two articles on *The Great Gatsby* and *The Last Tycoon* respectively, analyzes the American Dream ideal as a paradise of signs lacking real meanings and yet containing a still vital transcendental energy of will (G54, G55).

Jens Peter Becker wrote three articles and book chapters on American popular culture in the 1920s. In "The Automobile in American Prose Fiction: Fitzgerald's Yellow Rolls Royce," Becker claims that Americans' uneasy relationship to nature led to the culture's dependence on the automobile (G33). Becker's other two essays are on Jack Clayton's 1974 film of *The Great Gatsby:* in "Hollywood Between Art and Business," he writes that Hollywood was out of touch with the state of American culture in the 1970s and that therefore Clayton's film ignored the rags to riches story which, according to Max Weber, ties capitalism and religion together (G35). "Echoes from the Jazz Age" repeats the out-of-touch theme and suggests that neither the director nor producer had ever read the novel (G34). Finally, Bettina Friedl asserts that, while Fitzgerald, like Nathanael West and Budd Shulberg, believed film encouraged viewers to live vicariously and left them little room to resist, he also admired the impressive results of film's "architectural planning" (G38).

The final three German studies borrow from other recent critical developments: textual studies (considered by some a sub-set of American Studies) and Lacan's psychoanalytic theory. In his dissertation and monograph on *This Side of Paradise,* Udo Hebel discusses the intertextuality, metatextuality, and cotextuality of the novel, borrowing from Derrida, Barthes, Foucault, Kristeva, Pfister, and Genette for a theoretical foundation for his "Intertextual Allusion Paradigms" (G23, G87). Finally, Bernd Herzogenrath draws on Lacan's notion of "object a" to interpret Gatsby's desire for Daisy as an enchanted object (G44).

Of Hebel's dissertation/monograph, Peter Wagner comments in his review, "This dissertation proves Foucault's Utopia, unbelievable in 1969, that endless dimensions will open, if the discourse and not its author become the object of investigation" (G85). Among the 30 scholarly works to appear on Fitzgerald in Germany in the last two decades of the twentieth century, Hebel's work does attempt to present something new in Fitzgerald scholarship.

Always cautious, Horst Kruse pointed out of Fitzgerald's current reputation in Germany that "if we go by the sheer number of critical studies published he would continue to be surpassed by Hemingway and Faulkner among his contemporaries." He further commented that Germany did not show much interest in Fitzgerald's Centennial in 1996, citing two articles in the *Frankfurter Allgemeine Zeitung* and a program by Gerd Schäfer sponsored by the Radio

Station of the Saar-land (G57). Articles also appeared in other German-speaking countries, including in Zurich and Vienna, including an article by Andrea Seiler for the *Neue Züricher Zeitung,* that reaffirms the depth if not the breadth of appreciation for Fitzgerald in German-speaking countries when she writes that Fitzgerald "develops new, more sensitive organs which perceive the colored reflexes of demonic realities and reproduce them in words. His prismatic style— conscious coloring, conscious painting in sounds—is an instrument of a refined narrative realism. This is Fitzgerald's historic deed. . ." (G83). Despite his caution, Kruse concluded his presentation on Fitzgerald's reputation in Germany at the Princeton Centennial Conference by being willing to assert that "In scholarly and critical work, therefore, Fitzgerald has definitely come into his own in Germany" (G57).

As for his popular reputation, Kruse commented at Princeton that the writer's "inimitable, evocative, and highly individual style . . . is immensely difficult if not impossible to render in another language, and those readers who read his work in German translation have not been impressed. However, Fitzgerald's novels and short stories in the original English are widely taught in German schools. Of literature in English, only some plays of Shakespeare are taught more than *The Great Gatsby.* . . . as far as the reading and the appreciation of *The Great Gatsby* in the original are concerned, the German reading public, as of 1996, has indeed taken Fitzgerald to its heart at last" (G57).

REFERENCES

Hebel, Udo. Letter to the author. 2 Sept. 1995.

Heise, Hans-Jürgen. "Hollywood, das Geld, der Glanz." Review of *Der letzte Taikun. Deutsche Zeitung und Wirtshaftszeitung* (Köln) 3 Feb. 1963. n pag.

Kruse, Horst. Letter to the author. 13 Aug. 1995.

Papajewski, Helmut. "The Critical Reception of Hemingway's Works in Germany Since 1920." *The Literary Reputation of Hemingway in Europe.* Ed. Roger Asselineau. New York: New York University Press, 1965.

Stanley, Linda C. *The Foreign Critical Reputation of F. Scott Fitzgerald: An Analysis and Annotated Bibliography.* Westport, CT: Greenwood Press, 1980.

Parenthetical citations to entry numbers refer to annotated references in this chapter.

TRANSLATIONS/EDITIONS

G1. Fitzgerald, F. Scott. *Der grosse Gatsby* [*The Great Gatsby*]. Trans.
     Maria Lazar. Berlin: Knaur, 1928. 255. Reprinted 1932; Trans. Walter
     Schürenberg. Berlin: Blanvalet, 1953; Frankfurt: Büchergilde Gutenberg,
     1958; Berlin and Weimar: Aufbau-Verlag, 1968; Zürich: Diogenes, 1974,
     1994, 1997 (Revised Edition). 192.

G2. Fitzgerald, F. Scott. *Zärtlich ist die Nacht* [*Tender Is the Night*]. Trans.
     Grete Rambach. Berlin: Blanvalet, 1952, 1968; Aufbau-Verlag, 1976.
     424; Trans. Walter E. Richartz and Hanna Neves. Preface Malcolm
     Cowley. New edition. Zürich: Diogenes, 1986. 400.

G3. Fitzgerald, F. Scott. *Die besten Stories* [*The Best Stories*]. Trans. Walter
     Schürenberg. Berlin: Blanvalet, 1954. 264.

G4. Fitzgerald, F. Scott. *Der letzte Taikun* [*The Last Tycoon*]. Trans. Walter
     Schürenberg. Bibliothek Suhrkamp 91. Frankfurt/Main: Suhrkamp, 1962,
     1968, 1975; Zürich: Diogenes, 1977, 1990, 1998. 224.

G5. Fitzgerald, F. Scott. *Aus den tollen zwanziger Jahren* [*Out of the Roaring
     Twenties*]. Trans. Theo Schumacher. Ebenhausen b. München:
     Langewiesche-Brandt, 1963. Reprinted 1973.

G6. Fitzgerald, F. Scott. *Darf ich um den Walzer bitten?* [*May I Have This
     Waltz?*]. Trans. Elizabeth Schnack. Olten: Walter-Verlag, 1972.

G7. Fitzgerald, F. Scott. *Ein Diamant, so gross wie das Ritz* [*The Diamond as
     Big as the Ritz*]. Trans. Elga Abramowitz and Walter Schürenberg.
     Berlin: Aufbau-Verlag, 1972; *Ein Diamant—so gross wie das Ritz:
     Erzählungen 1922-1926*. Zürich: Diogenes, 1980, 1990, 1998. 304.

G8. Fitzgerald, F. Scott. *Pat Hobby's Hollywood-Stories*. Trans. Harry
     Rowohlt. Zürich: Diogenes Verlag, 1978; *Pat Hobby's Hollywood
     Stories: Erzählungen*. Ed. and Trans. Harry Rowohlt. New edition.
     Zürich: Diogenes, 1989. 224.

G9.   Fitzgerald, F. Scott. *Der gefangene Schatten: Erzählungen* [*The Captured Shadow: Stories*]. Zürich: Diogenes, 1980, 1991. 272.

G10. Fitzgerald, F. Scott. *Die letzte Schöne des Südens: Erzählungen* [*The Last of the Belles: Stories*]. Trans. Walter Schürenberg, Elga Abramowitz, Walter E. Richartz. Zürich: Diogenes, 1980. New edition, 1989. 240.

G11. Fitzgerald, F. Scott. *Der Rest von Glück: Erzählungen* [*The Lees of Happiness: Stories*]. Trans. Walter Schürenberg. Zürich: Diogenes, 1980. New edition, 1989. 272.

G12. Fitzgerald, F. Scott. *Wiedersehen mit Babylon: Erzählungen* [*Babylon Revisited and Other Stories*]. Trans. Walter Schürenberg and Walter E. Richartz. New edition. Zürich: Diogenes, 1980, 1991. 240; Ed. and trans. K. D. Sommer. Leipzig: Insel Verlag, 1981.

G13. Fitzgerald, F. Scott, and Gilles Deleuze. *Der Knacks: Porzellan und Vulkan* [*The Crack-Up: Porcelain and Volcanos*]. Trans. Walter Schürenberg (from Eng.) and Michaela Ott (from French). Internationaler Merve Diskurs 118. Merve, 1984. 64.

G14. Fitzgerald, F. Scott. *Der ungedeckte Scheck: Erzählungen* [*The Rubber Check and Other Tales*]. Trans. Alexander Schmitz. Zürich: Diogenes, 1985. 256.

G15. Fitzgerald, F. Scott. "Dice, Brass Knuckles and Guitar." *Roaring Twenties: Geschichten der Wilden Zwanziger Jahre* [*Stories of the Roaring Twenties*]. Ed. Manfred Kluge. München: Heyne, 1985.

G16. Fitzgerald, F. Scott. Story in *Familiengeschichten. Von W. Somerset Maugham bis F. Scott Fitzgerald* [*Family Stories. From W. Somerset Maugham to F. Scott Fitzgerald*]. Ed. Mary Höttinger. New edition. Zürich: Diogenes, 1987. 352.

G17. Fitzgerald, F. Scott. *Meistererzählungen* [*Great Stories*]. Trans. Walter Schürenberg, Anna von Cramer-Klett, Elga Abramowitz and

Walter E. Richartz, ed. Elisabeth Schnack. New Edition. Zürich: Diogenes, 1988, 2002. 368.

G18. Fitzgerald, F. Scott. *Diesseits vom Paradies* [*This Side of Paradise*]. Trans. Martina Tichy and Bettina Blumenberg. Zürich: Arche, 1988, 1993. 373; Neuwied: Luchterhand, 1991; München: Deutscher Taschenbuch Verlag, 1991.

G19. Fitzgerald, F. Scott. *Das Liebesschiff: Erzählungen* [*The Love Boat: Stories*]. Trans. Christa Hotz and Alexander Schmitz. New edition. Zürich: Diogenes, 1991, 1999. 240.

G20. Fitzgerald, F. Scott. *Amerikanische Erzähler. Von F. Scott Fitzgerald bis William Goyen* [*American Storytellers: From F. Scott Fitzgerald to William Goyen*]. Ed. Elisabeth Schnack. Zürich: Manesse, 1991. 624.

G21. Fitzgerald, F. Scott. *Manhattan, Baltimore, Paris: Erzählungen aus den zwanziger und dreissiger Jahren* [*Manhattan, Baltimore, Paris: Stories from the Twenties and Thirties*]. Trans. Bettina Abarbanell. Frankfurt: Deutscher Taschenbuch Verlag, 1993. 184.

G22. Fitzgerald, F. Scott. "The Baby Party." *Einladungen: Kleine und grosse Feste in der Weltliteratur* [*Invitations: Parties Small and Large in World Literature*]. Zürich: Manesse Verlag, 1997.

BOOKS: FULL-LENGTH STUDIES AND COLLECTIONS

G23. Hebel, Udo J. *Romaninterpretation als Textarchäologie: Untersuchungen zur Intertextualität am Beispiel von F. Scott Fitzgeralds* This Side of Paradise [*Interpreting the Novel as Textual Archeology: An Intertextual Analysis of F. Scott Fitzgerald's* This Side of Paradise]. Mainzer Studien zur Amerikanistik 23. Frankfurt/Main; NY; Paris; Bern: Lang, 1989. xiii, 640.

The author reveals 447 intertextual references in *This Side of Paradise*. He asserts that, with a strong tendency toward self-reflexivity, the novel positively represents naturalism, aestheticism, and social criticism, and casts sentimental popular culture and classical literature in a negative light. The book is a protest against tradition, Victorianism, and conventionality. In revisiting studies of intertextuality—standard works by Pfister, Broich, Lachmann, studies by Bakhtin, Kristeva, Genette—Hebel adapts notions of the text as *lieu de jouissance*, *chambre d'echos*, and palimpsest. He concludes that the novel fulfills the classified categories of density ("Dichte") and variability ("Streubreite"). Allusary paradigms serve as illustrations for settings or as characterizations, allowing the reader to draw further philosophical, ethical and religious conclusions. The 300-page appendices include a detailed list of all references by category, a bibliography of the intertextual references including musical scores and magazines, and an extensive reference bibliography of over 1,000 titles.

G24. Hofmann, Eva. *Decadence Revisited: F. Scott Fitzgerald und das europäische Fin de siécle* [*F. Scott Fitzgerald and the European Fin de siecle*]. Frankfurt am Main: Peter Lang, 2000.

In the first chapter—"(Not) a 'very unamerican American'"—Hofmann lists among Fitzgerald's influences—and Amory's wide reading in *This Side of Paradise*—particularly Oscar Wilde; the English aesthetes; Rupert Brooke; writers directly associated with the French decadent movement, such as Huysmans, and European writers contemporary with Fitzgerald whom she considers decadent, such as Thomas Mann. Hofmann sees the loss of meaning, anomie, and alienation of the First World War contributing to Fitzgerald's life-long receptivitiy to the themes and motifs of European *fin de siècle* literature. Hofmann's second chapter—"Décadence"—traces the convergence and variation in meanings of terms like 'decadence,' 'symbolism,' and 'aesthete' across Europe, emphasizing the persistence of its ideas—the dark Romanticism of flaunting forbidden experiences and its insistence on the superiority of artifice to nature—into the 1920s as precision of labels fell away. The third and core chapter—"Toeing the Decadent Line in the Work of F. Scott Fitzgerald"—is broken down into six subcategories addressing: (1) the vision of the "unutterable," (2) Fitzgerald's beautiful, self-obsessed, female characters, (3) "the romantic egoist as decadent dandy," (4) the abandonment of the search for wholeness in favor of the lost dream of it, (5) "mask and spectacle," and (6) Fitzgerald's "artful" depiction of nature. Chapter four—"Sympathy with the Abyss: the difficult conquest of Décadence"—deals with the existential struggles Hofmann sees imbedded in early 20th-century "decadents," coming out of the nihilism she associates with the Schopenhauer-Nietzsche tradition, particularly in *The Crack-Up*.

G25. Höss, Tilman. *F. Scott Fitzgerald: Die Philosophie des Jazz Age* [*F. Scott Fitzgerald: The Philosophy of the Jazz Age*]. European University Studies 14. Frankfurt/Main: Peter Lang, 1994. 148.

Fitzgerald's central theme is the parable of the American Dream in a consumer society, which evolved after WWI in opposition to the "society of the masses." The shock of the war resulted in angst, in disturbed relations between society and the individual, who realized his unimportance and concentrated on his own well-being. Egotism becomes a sign of integrity and independence, salvation is found in spending money. Fitzgerald's protagonist's search for happiness in this society is a failure. Fitzgerald's heroes hope for political renewal and a release from the pressures of the old society, but following the disappointment of the war, a new order quickly re-consolidates society. Youth, another important factor in the Jazz Age, is connected to the American Dream, as it holds the hope for a better world. But there is no promise for youth or America in a consumer society that does not mature. The contradiction of the American Dream is shown in Fitzgerald in the connection between hero and opponent, idealism and materialism, in the sexual revolution and emancipation of women, in the breakdown of family, and with it, values and social structure.

G26. Huonder, Eugen. *The Functional Significance of Setting in the Novels of Francis Scott Fitzgerald.* Bern: Herbert Lang; Frankfurt/Main: Peter Lang, 1974. 128. (European University Papers, Series XIV, Vol. 20).

Fitzgerald uses setting as a means of creating atmosphere, character, meaning, and symbol. He uses it to increase the verisimilitude and thus the credibility of action. Domestic settings reflect the social standing of characters and are in keeping with their owner's characters; conversely characters outgrow characteristic settings. Protagonists sometimes characterize themselves by their reactions to settings and settings function as expressions of the heroes' moods, often dramatizing their existential situation. Settings also function as commentaries on the protagonists' emotional instabilities, imparting satirical and ironic attacks on persons or situations. Fitzgerald's style, whose forcefulness resides primarily in its appeal to the senses, and of which setting is a major mode of expression, is not fully realized in his first two novels. In *The Great Gatsby* and *Tender Is the Night* Fitzgerald succeeds in depicting an external world that is not only entirely in harmony with the mind, but, at the same time, functions as thematic determinant.

G27. Keiner, Karl E. *Die Funktion des Reichtums im Erzählwerk von F. Scott Fitzgerald mit besonderer Berücksichtigung seiner Romane* [*The Function of Wealth in the Narratives of F. Scott Fitzgerald with Special Consideration of His Novels*]. Frankfurt/Main: Lang, 1985.

Fitzgerald's three essays "My Lost City," "How to Live on $36.000 a Year," and "The Crack-Up" show how clouded his view of the leisure class was. *This Side of Paradise* follows the wealthy of Minneapolis, Princeton, and New York through the various equations of wealth with education, social appearances, power, and language. In *The Beautiful and Damned* wealth consists no longer of real estate but of investments, the beginning, middle, and end of the novel marked by the protagonist couple's relationship with the inheritance they expect. *The Great Gatsby* offers a different configuration of wealth based on distinctions of West and East, New and Old, merchants and plantation owners, and honest and dishonest ways of making money. Bridging the transition to *Tender Is the Night* are the short stories "The Rich Boy," "A Rough Crossing," and "One Trip Abroad." *Tender Is the Night* continues the use of Fitzgerald's many water metaphors in a study of the break-up of a marriage because of the unequal economic standing of the partners. "Magnetism" and "Crazy Sunday" are the short precursors to *The Last Tycoon*, a novel which depicts the economic cycles of prosperity, crisis, and reorientation in the film industry.

G28. Krämer, Gabriele. *Artusstoff und Gralsthematik im modernen amerikanischen Roman: Eine exemplarische Darstellung an Werken von F. Scott Fitzgerald, Ernest Hemingway, Truman Capote, Jerome D. Salinger sowie Bernard Malamud [Arthurian Matter and Grail Themes in the Modern American Novel: Examples in the Works of F. Scott Fitzgerald, Ernest Hemingway, Truman Capote, Jerome D. Salinger, and Bernard Malamud].* Giessen: Hoffman, 1985. 290.

Novels such as *The Great Gatsby*, *Absalom, Absalom!*, and *The Sun Also Rises*, which originate from the epic of King Arthur, do not show obvious allusions. Compared to *The Natural*, references to the Grail in *Gatsby* are discrete; even Gatsby's remark that he had "committed himself to the following of a grail," does not receive much support from the rest of the text. The comparison of the Grail with Daisy, repeatedly offered by critics, reduces the quest metaphor to "*cherchez la femme*." Gatsby becomes insubstantial in his real vocation as quester and is eventually destroyed.

G29. Stromberg, Kyra. *Zelda und F. Scott Fitzgerald: Ein amerikanischer Traum [Zelda and F. Scott Fitzgerald: An American Dream]*. Berlin: Rowohlt, 1997. 159. Reinbek bei Hamburg: : Rowohlt Taschenbuch Verlag, 1998. 191.

With *This Side of Paradise* Fitzgerald establishes himself as the spokesman and one of the finest interpreters of the postwar lost generation; financially, the novel gives him the possibility of fulfilling his rash dream of marrying Zelda. Already, the publication of *The Beautiful and Damned* marks the first problems for the couple: the glamour is gone for them after two years of reckless life in New York and the birth of their daughter Scottie. The frequent trips to Europe seem to provide a momentary but evident relief: Scott finds the necessary serenity to work on *The Great Gatsby* and finish it by 1925, while Zelda shows more and more signs of recklessness. Scott begins to work on *Tender Is the*

Night, which will take several years of particularly tormented elaboration; the situation precipitates in 1930, with Zelda's first crisis and commitment to a mental institution. With the encouragement of the only female doctor she encounters, Zelda is able to finish her novel, *Save Me the Waltz*; after the usual strict supervision over her creativity, Scott encourages the publication in 1932. Her crises become more frequent and serious and for the first time in their married life, the couple, so united even in the bad periods, separate physically for a long time. As he works on his last novel, *The Last Tycoon*, he looks back on his life with Zelda and reflects on the reasons for their failure. Until Scott's sudden death in 1940, the two keep corresponding frequently and show an emotional closeness that is made possible by their physical separation, the sign of the strong complex relationship between two irreconcilable souls, whose bond never dissolved.

German Editions of American Studies and Collections

G30.   Graham, Sheilah, and Gerold Frank. *F. Scott Fitzgerald: Meine grosse Liebe: Furchtlose Memoiren* [*F. Scott Fitzgerald: Beloved Infidel: Fearless Memoirs*]. Frankfurt/Main: Ullstein, 1992.

G31.   Turnbull, Andrew. *F. Scott Fitzgerald: Das Genie der Wilden zwanziger Jahre* [*F. Scott Fitzgerald: The Genius of the Roaring Twenties*]. München: Heyne, 1986.

ESSAYS/CHAPTERS/NOTES/CONFERENCE PAPERS

G32.   Ahrends, Günter. "F. Scott Fitzgerald und Ernest Hemingway." *Die amerikanische Kurzgeschichte: Theorie und Entwicklung* [*The American Short Story: Theory and Development*]. Stuttgart: Kohlhammer, 1980: 143-9.

One must differentiate between Fitzgerald's style of living and his literary analysis, because he can distance himself from his personal experience. His criticism turns against hypocritical morality, the thoughtlessness and irresponsibility which destroy the relations between people, against the materialism which corrupts character and smothers the ability to love, and against the degradation of the American Dream. Using analytical narrative, Fitzgerald reveals the corruption of his protagonist and the decadence of the post-war generation in "Babylon Revisited." The antithetical structure of "May

Day" is a vision of the coming collapse, comparing decadence to sordid street life. Both stories, while appearing different, are two contrasting depictions of a doomed world.

G33.   Becker, Jens Peter.   Introduction and "Das Automobil in der amerikanischen Erzählliteratur: Fitzgeralds gelber Rolls-Royce [The Automobile in American Prose Fiction: Fitzgerald's Yellow Rolls Royce]." *Das Automobil und die amerikanische Kultur [The Automobile and American Culture]*. Ed. David Galloway, Crossroads Studies in American Culture, Trier: WVT, 1989. 93-142.

An uneasiness with nature is the reason for America's automobile-centered culture. Woven throughout the chapter are details from automobile history, advertisements contemporary to Fitzgerald, discussions of the more symbolic meaning of the development of automotive culture and social structure (the "valley of ashes" and methodological asides about popular culture studies). Becker's interpretation of *The Great Gatsby* can be summarized into a few themes: all automobiles in the novel are symbolic representations of the people who drive them; cinematically described drives are an ideal means to represent restlessness of character; cars are central to the action of the novel.

G34.   Becker, Jens Peter.   "Echoes from the Jazz Age: *The Great Gatsby*." *Literaturverfilmungen [Films from Literature]*. Eds. Franz-Josef Albersmeier and Volker Roloff. Frankfurt/Main: Suhrkamp, 1989. 324-46.

Gatsby was performed on Broadway in 1926, and appeared as a movie in 1926, 1949, and 1974. The last time it was meant to be a vehicle for Ali McGraw. Much publicity and marketing preceded the release of the film. The screenplay boasted much original dialog from the novel, and great attention to the details of the '20s. An original Francis Ford Coppola script was shortened by 30 pages. Jack Clayton was chosen—inexplicably—as director. The film never takes advantage of the visual potential in the actual book—some critics have called *Gatsby* pure movie-writing. It attempts to establish Nick as a central character, but only half-heartedly. Love scenes dominate the film. But the novel is too complex and its characters too symbolic to be reduced to mere advertisement. Still, there is some genuine film narrative which stands in welcome contrast to the long-winded narcissism of the film. This most literal of the three films made of *Gatsby* fails because of a false compromise between studio, director, and screenwriter.

G35.   Becker, Jens Peter.   "Hollywood zwischen Kunst und Kommerz: Die

Verfilmung von *The Great Gatsby* [Hollywood Between Art and
Business: The Screening of *The Great Gatsby*]." *Filmphilologie: Studien
zur englischsprachigen Literatur und Kultur in Buch und Film* [*Film
Philology: Studies in English-Language Literature and Culture in Book
and Film*]. Eds. Paul G. Buchloh, Jens Peter Becker, Ralf J. Schröder.
Kiel: Kieler Verlag Wissenschaft Bildung, 1982. 117-34.

In 1926, again in 1949 (with Alan Ladd), and again in 1974, Hollywood
produced the nostalgia blockbuster, *The Great Gatsby*. When the 1974 film
appeared, all previously existing copies of the film disappeared. *Gatsby* can be
compared to *The French Lieutenant's Woman*, as both novels are subtle, with a
complicated narrative structure that cannot be translated to film. The '74 *Gatsby*
was a financial success, but a flop artistically. There were quarrels about leading
roles, choice of director, and the script. Jack Clayton reworked it with special
regard to keeping as much original dialog as possible, including sex and bed
scenes to heighten the romance between Gatsby and Daisy, and making all the
characters sympathetic.

G36.   Federspiel, Jürg. "Tod in der Traumfabrik: Zum Werk von Francis Scott
        Fitzgerald [Death in the Dream Factory: On Francis Scott Fitzgerald's
        Work]." *Träume aus Plastic: Aufsätze zu Literatur, Kunst und Film*
        [*Dreams of Plastic: Essays on Literature, Art and Film*]. Zürich:
        Benziger, 1972. 103-123.

The dizzying rise of Fitzgerald to stardom, his attainment of Zelda, and his
wealth, are seen in the context of America's wild spin from wealth to
bankruptcy and back again. Fitzgerald is compared to Gatsby, and America:
their lack of scruples and childish longing for paradise create tension.
Fitzgerald's spiritual and creative bankruptcy parallels America's. Monroe
Stahr's numbered days as ruler of the "dream factory" are linked to Fitzgerald's
untimely death.

G37.   Friedl, Bettina. "Tracing History: F. Scott Fitzgerald's 'Bernice Bobs
        Her Hair' and the Panorama of Social Change." *Literatur in
        Wissenschaft und Unterricht* [*Literature in Scholarship and Teaching*] 24
        (1991): 225-240.

Written in 1928, as a new society is emerging, this short story marks the end of
the Victorian traditions regarding the behavior of women. "Through an elaborate
comparison between Bernice and Marie Antoinette on her way to the guillotine,
between the loss of one's hair and the loss of one's head, Fitzgerald dramatizes
the revolutionary quality of the haircut as an incision between historical
periods." Like Jane Austen's novels, the story is a comedy of manners.

G38. Friedl, Bettina. "'Vicarious Participation': Hollywood in American
       Fiction." *Film und Literatur in Amerika [Film and Literature in
       America]*. Eds. Alfred Weber and Bettina Friedl. Darmstadt:
       Wissenschaftliche Buchgesellschaft, 1988. 189-212.

The few novels, novellas and short story cycles which appeared around 1940,
and which Leslie Fiedler classified as anti-Hollywood fiction or more recently
as post-Hollywood fiction, now form the body of literature which is generally
said to be Hollywood fiction: Nathaniel West's *The Day of the Locust* (1939),
Fitzgerald's fragmentary *The Last Tycoon* (published posthumously 1941), the
seventeen stories collected later under the title *The Pat Hobby Stories* which
Fitzgerald had written between 1938 and his death in 1940, and finally Budd
Schulberg's novel *What Makes Sammy Run?* (1941). A consequence of the
acceptance of film as an art form is that Hollywood is no longer blamed for
having caused the end of literary culture by inviting audiences to a mindless
visual form of vicarious experience.

G39. Gerke, H. Joachim. "'A Man in a Boat, Rowing for Heaven': Literary
       and Religious Allusions in F. Scott Fitzgerald's *The Great Gatsby*."
       *Literatur in Wissenschaft und Unterricht [Literature in Scholarship and
       Teaching]* 25.4 (1992): 307-13.

How closely Fitzgerald follows and parodies the genre of the success story
becomes readily apparent by a comparison of the scene describing Gatsby's
meeting with Dan Cody to the last chapters of Horatio Alger's 1867 novel
Ragged Dick and to Cotton Mather's *A Christian at His Calling* (1701).
Fitzgerald very carefully establishes a context that is obviously intended to
evoke specific religious connotations and traditions. It is striking how perfectly
Gatsby's efforts in the matter serve a higher purpose or ideal answer to Mather's
description of the accomplished fusion of one's "Personal" and "General"
calling. Fitzgerald effectively evokes the "Puritan business ethic" by a pattern of
allusions to Protestantism and to Mather's work.

G40. Grabe, Eckhard. "'The Whole Equation of Pictures': F. Scott Fitzgerald,
       The Last Tycoon." *Cinematologie und Poetologie: Kunstbetrachtung im
       Hollywood-Roman [Cinematology and Poetology: Reflections on the Arts
       in the Hollywood Novel]*. Würzburg: Königshausen und Neumann, 1992.
       Chapter V, 107-141. (Epistemata: Reihe Literaturwissenschaft, Band 91).
       294.

With Monroe Stahr as his hero in *The Last Tycoon*, Fitzgerald is the first author
to develop cinematology using the studio system as the center of a novel. The
film industry was not a new theme to Fitzgerald—he was fascinated with it since
his first visit to Hollywood in 1927. The style he used in his film scripts

influenced his last three novels. *Tycoon* is visually conceived, as demonstrated by its episodical structure. Fitzgerald aimed to connect film and literary technique.

G41. Hebel, Udo. "Fitzgerald in Germany." First International F. Scott Fitzgerald Conference. Hofstra University, 24 Sept. 1992.

See Chapter Introduction.

G42. Hebel, Udo J. "'The Moon That Never Rose': The Final Passage of F. Scott Fitzgerald's *The Great Gatsby* Revisited." *Literatur in Wissenschaft und Unterricht* [*Literature in Scholarship and Teaching*] 18.3 (Sept. 1985): 237-257.

It is crucial to a complete understanding of the novel that we realize that this portion of the conclusion was composed early in the writing process. The novel's conclusion is not Fitzgerald's culminating insight into Gatsby's representative quality; it is the origin and core of Fitzgerald's concept of Gatsby as the archetypal American dreamer. At the same time, deleting the reference to "America" contributed to the passage's sense of a larger, more universal experience, without, however, renouncing its specifically American implications. For those readers who are still torn between their admiration and affirmation of the "Gatsbyian qualities" of faith and dedication and their insight into the hopelessness and defeat of Gatsby's struggle, Baker's sense of a "nostalgic mood" in the face of loss and frustration can serve as a possible compromise. Possibly the most important hint at the fundamental insincerity of the relationship between the American Dream and its object is the image of the trees that "had once pandered in whispers to the last and greatest of all human dreams."

G43. Hebel, Udo J. "'Platitudes and Prejudices and Sentimentalisms': F. Scott Fitzgerald's *This Side of Paradise* and Sentimental Popular Culture." *Sentimentality in Modern Literature and Popular Culture.* Ed. Winfried Herget. Tübingen: Narr, 1991. 139-153.

This Side of Paradise bears early evidence of Fitzgerald's ambivalent, though finally disparaging attitude towards popular culture in general and sentimentality in particular. *The Great Gatsby* is totally devoid of sentimental passages. At the same time, however, Fitzgerald vigorously attacked the sentimental literature that the American reading public had cherished so ardently since the late nineteenth century. Nevertheless, Fitzgerald engages sentimental popular culture metatextually by means of intertextual allusions. *This Side of Paradise* manifests yet another intertextual variation of modernism's alleged antisentimental bias and of the struggle against sentimentality so closely identified with the modern period.

G44. Herzogenrath, Bernd. "From the Lost Generation to Generation X: *The Great Gatsby* vs. Kurt Cobain." *Near Encounters: Festschrift for Richard Martin*. Frankfurt: Lang, 1995. 121-140.

Freud noticed a climate of faithlessness and disillusionment which was partly due to the decline of religion and that conversely devout religious believers are safeguarded in a high degree against the risk of certain neurotic illnesses. The nostalgia of the Lost Generation, its feeling of loss and anxiety in the absence of a stable reference point, is illustrated and focused on in Gatsby's quest for the lost love, the lost time, his preoccupation with beginnings. The problem with the past is that it only exists as a dream. The connection of Gatsby to rock singer Kurt Cobain is provided by Fitzgerald's remark that "all good writing is swimming under water and holding your breath."

G45. Hoffmann, Gerhard. "Situationalism—Culture, Society, Individual." *Der zeitgenössische amerikanische Roman: Von der Moderne zur Postmoderne* [*The Contemporary American Novel: From Modern to Postmodern*]. Volume 1: Elements and Perspectives: München: Fink, 1988: 120.

Hoffman discusses Jasper's "border situation" (Grenzsituation)—a quality in a situation which challenges the limits of human experience—as the core element in the works of Melville, Crane, Sherwood Anderson, Fitzgerald, Hemingway, and Faulkner.

G46. Hoffmann, Gerhard. "Satire." *Der zeitgenössische amerikanische Roman: Von der Moderne zur Postmoderne* [*The Contemporary American Novel: From Modern to Postmodern*]. Volume 1: Elements and Perspectives: München: Fink, 1988: 232-248.

The satirical perspective rests on the contrast between a deformed society and its critic, who reacts to its threat to legitimate values. The relationship between novel and satire became central and problematic in the '20s. The work of Fitzgerald shows it was possible to use the myth of the American Dream to oppose a concrete societal reality; this was an important object of analysis for the author. The final consequence of such a satirical view of the world is not represented by the fate of a single social group, as in *Gatsby*, but by the anonymous masses and their frustration, on the one hand, and the decline of "I" on the other.

G47. Hoffman, Gerhard. "The Grotesque Space." *Raum, Situation, erzählte Wirklichkeit: Poetologische und historische Studien zum englischen und amerikanischen Roman [Space, Situation, Narrated Reality: Poetological and Historical Studies in the English and American Novel].* J.B. Mertzlersche Verlagsbuchhandlung, Stuttgart, 1978: 137.

A type of grotesque space—space designed as grotesque civilization—is represented by *The Great Gatsby*, as well as by Conrad's *Heart of Darkness*, West's *The Day of the Locust*, and Hawkes' *The Cannibal*.

G48. Hoffman, Gerhard. "F. Scott Fitzgerald, *The Great Gatsby*." *Raum, Situation, erzählte Wirklichkeit: Poetologische und historische Studien zum englischen und amerikanischen Roman [Space, Situation, Narrated Reality: Poetological and Historical Studies in the English and American Novel].* J.B. Mertzlersche Verlagsbuchhandlung, Stuttgart, 1978: 139-141.

Influenced by the "magical suggestiveness" of Conrad and T.S. Eliot, the grotesque location shifts from the edge of Western civilization to the middle, evidenced by *Gatsby*. The "waste land" between West Egg and New York is probably a reference to Eliot, and as a grotesque space it describes the irony of American history in the corruption of the American Dream. Through the relation between deformity and disorientation—between the grotesqueness of civilization and existential grotesqueness—Gatsby and Nick change at the end of the novel, the latter from an objective, critical observer into a complementary figure who stands with Gatsby against other corrupt characters. The expression of the grotesque rests in the traumatic repetition of experiencing the space.

G49. Hoffman, Gerhard. "Types of Situation." *Raum, Situation, erzählte Wirklichkeit: Poetologische und historische Studien zum englischen und amerikanischen Roman [Space, Situation, Narrated Reality: Poetological and Historical Studies in the English and American Novel].* J.B. Mertzlersche Verlagsbuchhandlung, Stuttgart, 1978: 562-565.

In *Gatsby*, an interior/exterior relationship is replaced by references to temporal nearness and distance. The description of Gatsby's murder suggests an association with an interior death that precedes the real one. A traditional novel such as *Gatsby* has manifold techniques at its disposal, from the subjective (the experience of "I") to the objective (designed to communicate with the reader).

G50. Höss, Tilman. "Kunst als Recycling: *The Great Gatsby*, *Casablanca* und das moderne Erzählen [Art as Recycling: *The Great Gatsby*, *Casablanca* and Modern Storytelling]." *Anglistik: Mitteilungen des*

Deutschen Anglistenverbandes [*Study of English Language and
Literature: Report from the German English Association*] 11.2 (Sept.
2000): 55-73.

Höss takes his cue from those critics of *The Great Gatsby* who blame the author
for his "strategy of vagueness" which is reflected in the characterization of the
protagonist, the surprising lack of specific information about the Twenties and
the allegedly inconsistent handling of point of view. Adequate appreciation of
the novel, he claims, presupposes better understanding of its method, whose
salient points emerge more clearly when it is compared to that of *Casablanca*, a
"cult" movie. As Umberto Eco has shown, the extraordinary success of
Casablanca (as of cult movies in general) is due to its use of archetypes in a
kind of intertextual collage. However incompatible such archetypal elements
may be from the point of view of psychological credibility, their presence in the
movie guarantees its immediate appeal. *The Great Gatsby* follows the same
method of collage in that in both the portrayal of the protagonist and the
development of plot elements Fitzgerald resorts to archetypes. Höss suggests the
use of the Barthean term "mythologeme" to indicate that these archetypes
possess or acquire specific mythic meanings. He argues that many of these
mythologemes were too new to be readily understood when the novel was first
published (which accounts for its initial failure as a book), but that they have
since become nodes in the interrelatedness of literary texts, films, commercials,
and images in the media. Höss's preliminary list of mythologemes combined in
The Great Gatsby includes the automobile, the gas station, the West, the self-
made man, the gangster, the swimming pool, the golden girl, the rich bitch, the
billboard and the showdown. Fitzgerald's lack of success in following Mencken
as a commentator upon the contemporary scene as well as in taking naturalistic
writers as models was compensated for by his turning to the mythopoetic
tradition of America and to the mythopoetic potential of his times and thus
presenting his commentary through mythologemes. Höss concludes his
investigation by pointing out that the procedure of recycling mythologemes has
become a dominant mode of narration in the novel as well as in movies. It is the
rise of this mode of narration that accounts for the eventual success of *The Great
Gatsby* and also gives it a prominent place in the history of modernism.

G51. Ickstadt, Heinz. "F. Scott Fitzgerald: 'May Day.'" *Die englische und
     amerikanische Kurzgeschichte* [*The English and American Short Story*].
     Ed. Klaus Lubbers. Darmstadt: WBG, 1990. 255-64.

"May Day" is the Fitzgerald story least "marred" by the author's adjustments to
the formulas of popular magazines. It is a "fictional probing" into the author's
own life and culture. The story's "spatial and temporal unity is strictly
maintained." The activities of its protagonists are foreshadowed in order for
Fitzgerald to "create a tight network of social interaction and interrelatedness."

All the characters can be grouped by "overlapping semantic oppositions." Contrast and opposition are the story's main organizing principles and overall, it is an "exercise in realism and irony." Obviously experimental, "May Day" "displays Fitzgerald's new commitment to naturalism rather vauntingly but uses its conventions superficially. . . ." In the stereotypes of the story we can "recognize the bare outline of a vision that Fitzgerald developed much more fully in his later work."

G52.   Ickstadt, Heinz. "New York und der Stadtroman der amerikanischen Moderne [New York and the City Novel of American Modernism]." *Medium Metropole: Berlin, Paris, New York.* Eds. Friedrich Knilli and Michael Nerlich. Heidelberg: Winter, 1986. 111-124.

The Great Gatsby and Dos Passos's *Manhattan Transfer* are the most brilliant depictions of '20s New York, in which the city is no longer a natural force of anarchic freedom, but a thoroughly artificial world. The character of Gatsby sets up a "hierarchy of vital wishes": at the top, objects of desire who do not themselves desire; then, those who are real only through the power of their desires, like Gatsby; and finally, those who inhabit the shadow world of disappointed longings. Gatsby's knowledge of the "empty future" of the city and the lost agrarian past creates an insurmountable ideological emptiness.

G53.   Klotz, Günther. "Francis Scott Fitzgerald: Die Autorität des Scheiterns [Francis Scott Fitzgerald: The Authority of Failure]." *Der nordamerikanische Roman 1880-1940: Repräsentation und Autorisation in der Moderne [The North American Novel 1880-1940: Representation and Authorization in the Modern Period].* Ed. Robert Weimann. Berlin: Aufbau-Verlag, 1989. 324-363.

"An almost trivial melodrama plot" in *The Great Gatsby* is transformed by Nick's narration into a strategy of productive tension between illusion and reality. The tension inherent in Fitzgerald's work—called by him "the authority of failure"—parallels an unbridgeable gap in America between the dream of endless possibilities and the reality of depression and collapse. Tracing Fitzgerald's critique of illusion/delusion in the "dream factory" in *The Last Tycoon*, Klotz maintains that Fitzgerald's work in general is best understood from within the metaphor of film: film as symbol of seductive illusion; figures who make spectacles into personal rituals. Art creates illusions of life which in turn influence life to become like the art, thus sealing the power relation between image-creation and individual consumer. While Monroe Stahr and Gatsby think they are individuals exerting the power of their own dream-illusions over millions, they are in reality only products of the larger monopoly of dream-interests (big business, advertising, politics). Fitzgerald tells the story of the end of the personal control of dreams.

G54. Klotz, Günther. "Macht und Gemachtsein des massenwirksamen Diskurses in Francis Scott Fitzgeralds *The Last Tycoon* [Power and Fabrication of Popular Discourse in Francis Scott Fitzgerald's *The Last Tycoon*]." *Zeitschrift für Anglistik und Amerikanistik [Journal for English and American Studies]* 36.3 (1988): 205-216.

An earlier working of the second part of an essay ("Francis Scott Fitzgerald: Die Autorität des Scheiterns") appearing in Robert Weimann's *Der nordamerikanische Roman 1880-1940* in 1989. Klotz traces Fitzgerald's critique of illusion/delusion in the "dream factory" of *The Last Tycoon*, concluding that Fitzgerald tells the story of the end of the personal control of dreams.

G55. Klotz, Günther. "Spannungen zwischen Erzähltem und Erzählen in Francis Scott Fitzgeralds *The Great Gatsby*." *Zeitschrift für Anglistik und Amerikanistik* 36.2 (1988): 112-23.

(This article is a version of the first part of the essay "Francis Scott Fitzgerald: Die Autorität des Scheiterns" appearing in Robert Weimann's *Die nordamerikanische Roman 1880-1940*.) The tension inherent in Fitzgerald's work parallels an unbridgeable gap in America between the dream of endless possibilities and the reality of depression and collapse.

G56. Klotz, Günther. "Critical Realism and the Study of the American Novel Between the Wars." *Zeitschrift für Anglistik and Amerikanistik* 33.2 (1985): 133-144.

After the Second World War members of the thirties movement characterized by the founding of *Partisan Review* distanced themselves from American materialism and disrupted the democratic and critical tradition in American literature. Fitzgerald, Dos Passos and Hemingway were shocked by the degeneration of modernity and by the war. They sought a new narrative continuum based on consciousness and they disdained in their works the glib slogans of the American Dream. They were courageous because the reading public still preferred to believe in the harmony of nations. In their "leaning away" from the official spectacle of bourgeois affirmation they inherently kept up attitudes of dissent arising from early critical realism and naturalism.

G57. Kruse, Horst H. "F. Scott Fitzgerald's Reputation in Germany." Paper delivered at F. Scott Fitzgerald Centennial Conference, Princeton Univ., 21 September 1996.

See Introduction to Chapter.

G58. Kruse, Horst H. "Fitzgerald: 'Babylon Revisited.'" *Die amerikanische Kurzgeschichte* [*The American Short Story*]. Eds. Karl Heinz Göller and Gerhard Hoffmann. Düsseldorf: Bagel, 1972. 225-234.

Kruse summarizes the story to establish an overriding thematic which has relevance, not only to the limited field of Fitzgerald studies, but also within an historical-sociological context. The relatively simple plot of the story is supplemented by inner significance. The action calls up memories from the protagonist's past, forcing him to come to terms with past mistakes. The process of self-knowledge raises questions of determinism and man's potential to change or rearrange his fate. Kruse concludes that the story is a dramatization of the conflict between two powerful ideologies in American society, both of which Fitzgerald experienced as threats to the American Dream: strict Puritanism and materialistic hedonism.

G59. Kruse, Horst H. "The Long Shadows of Hemingway and Fitzgerald: Intertextuality and Its Function in Joan Didion's *Democracy*." *Literatur in Wissenschaft und Unterricht* [*Literature in Scholarship and Teaching*] 25 (1992): 261-68.

In having her narrator call *Democracy* a "novel of fitful glimpses" Didion references *The Great Gatsby*. Rumors emerge about Lovett's past and dealing, as they do regarding *Gatsby*. Narrators in both novels are ready to grant their protagonists special status, turning them into mythic figures. In *Democracy* as in *Gatsby*, it is the idea of love that counts, rather than "its actual consummation." The most obvious parallels between Didion's novel and those of Fitzgerald and Hemingway occur toward the end of the narrative in a procedure of "delayed intertextual referentiality." *Democracy* asks to be considered "in terms of the tradition represented by these authors as serious and responsible fiction."

G60. Kruse, Horst. "Teaching Fitzgerald's *Tender Is the Night*: The Opening and Closing Chapters of a Great Novel." *Literatur in Wissenschaft und Unterricht* [*Literature in Scholarship and Teaching*] 31.3 (1998): 251-67.

To do Fitzgerald justice, *Tender Is the Night* must be studied. Reading and interpreting the opening and closing chapters should show Fitzgerald's "dexterity as a writer" and make students eager to read the novel in its entirety. The opening paragraph is, in George Garrett's words, "a series of sensory-affective details." The second paragraph "contributes an auditory element;" Kruse draws a parallel between this text and Auden's interpretation of the painting "The Fall of Icarus" in the poem "Musée des Beaux Arts." The two paragraphs together (Garrett again) hint at the novel's central theme: change and loss. In the third paragraph, as pointed out by Matthew Bruccoli, a large number of time words "reinforces the theme of mutability and deterioration." Three sources are helpful in interpreting the novel's ending: Joseph Conrad; an argument with Hemingway about the ending for *A Farewell to Arms*; and Garrett's *Lady Into Fox*. Fitzgerald's narrative strategy "will induce the reader to examine and reject the deficient story" told in the conclusion, and attempt to reconstruct it using his own inference and "incomplete evidence." The final chapter is, above all, a moralizing.

G61. Kruse, Horst H. "Zelda and Scott in Recent German-Language Publications." *F. Scott Fitzgerald Society Newsletter* 8 (1998): 26.

Mention of Gerda Marko's (G66) and Kyra Stromberg's (G29) studies of the Fitzgeralds as having been occasioned by interest in Zelda as much as, if not more than, by interest in Fitzgerald himself. Also mention of the inclusion of "The Baby Party" in a volume of the "prestigious" Manesse Bibliothek der Weltliteratur (Manesse Library of World Literature). (See Translations and Editions, G22).

G62. Link, Franz H. "F. Scott Fitzgerald, 1896-1940." *Geschichte der amerikanischen Erzählkunst 1900-1950* [*History of American Narrative Literature 1900-1950*]. Stuttgart: Kohlhammer, 1983. 99-113.

Fitzgerald's primary concern is that segment of society which, by virtue of its wealth, attempts to establish the reality of its dream world. Fitzgerald became a spokesman for those without means who, because they felt helpless in a world grown meaningless, sought temporary pleasures. The rest of Link's discussion is a basic summary of Fitzgerald's life and some of his works: *This Side of Paradise*, "May Day," "A Diamond as Big as The Ritz," *The Great Gatsby*, *Tender Is the Night*, and *The Last Tycoon*.

G63. Lubbers, Klaus. "Die 'Lost Generation' [The 'Lost Generation']." *New York in der zeitgenössischen amerikanischen Erzählliteratur* [*New York in Contemporary American Narrative Literature*], ed. Eberhard Kreutzer. Heidelberg: Winter, 1985. 104-138.

Fitzgerald embodied decisive attitudes of the Jazz Age and turned them into artistic creations. *The Great Gatsby* is more complex than Fitzgerald's other novels by virtue of its plot and its carefully chosen perspective—of distance—which he learned from Conrad. *Gatsby* is an analytical novel whose chronological progress, presented by the drama's last act, is interrupted by glances back to what happened in the past. The American Dream, maintains Lubbers, is a romantic enlarging of the possibilities of imagining life on a level where the material and spiritual mix. Fitzgerald launched a double attack in *Gatsby*, against the moneyed class on the one hand, and the degradation of the American Dream into the American Success Story on the other. The novel thematicizes the evils of capitalism from a bourgeois point of view. The "dream," overestimated sometime in the past, will always be betrayed by the desolate reality of the present.

G64. Lubbers, Klaus. *Typologie der Short Story* [*Typology of the Short Story*]. Darmstadt: WBG, 1977. 99, 146, passim.

A form of build-up in a short story is when two or more simultaneous beginnings from different starting points are brought together. Fitzgerald's "The Baby Party" illustrates at least one feature—introducing a husband come to fetch his wife and daughter from a party next door, then backing up to show how the party became a fiasco—which points it in this direction. Extension of time is shown in Fitzgerald's Basil Duke Lee Stories, which deal with episodes from the life of the protagonist from when he is 14 to his freshman year at college.

G65. Luedtke, Luther S. "'What is 'American' About American Literature: The Case of *The Great Gatsby*." *Understanding the USA: A Cross-Cultural Perspective*. Ed. Peter Funke. Tübingen: Narr, 1989. 177-199.

Luedtke proposes a "paradigm for analysis that can help in the practical task of discussing individual works of literature," using "five strata" that have marked the growth of American literature: Republicanism (a commitment to glory and memory), Nature (the "romance of the moving frontier"), Time (commitment to the future), the Hero ("the rage for . . . cultural rebirth"), and Pluralism. After defining and exploring them, he applies them to *The Great Gatsby*. Republicanism: Struggles of "peasants and republicans" provide a "socio-ideological context for the novel's jeremiad on the lost mission of America." Nature: Fitzgerald "depicts an originally beautiful . . . nature polluted by the march of history." Time: Gatsby displays a fierce resistance to time, supported by symbols of "defunct clocks." The hero: Gatsby is a myth in his own time. Pluralism: "Threatening and unstabilizing both Eggs . . . are the ethnic communities and melting pot of New York City." Few works of American literature are "so self-consciously nationalistic" as *Gatsby*.

G66. Marko, Gerda. "Auslöschung: Francis Scott and Zelda Fitzgerald [Extinction: Francis Scott and Zelda Fitzgerald]." *Schreibende Paare: Liebe, Freundschaft, Konkurrenz* [*Writing Couples: Love, Friendship, Rivalry*]. Zürich/Düsseldorf: Artemis und Winkler, 1995. Rpt. Stuttgart: Suhrkamp Taschenbuch Verlag, 1998. 211-228.

Zelda "ached" because everyone recognizes her as the female protagonist of her husband's stories. "Lacking patience" and interest, she was unable to create decent working conditions for Fitzgerald, leaving him no choice but to constantly "fill himself up." Unable to compete with Fitzgerald's writing, Zelda showed a humility that was her protection from his criticism and rejection. Nevertheless, she has her own method of expression. She can create bold, lean sentences of "magical sadness." Eventually, Zelda claimed the substance of her life as her rightful property—not Fitzgerald's. Criticism of her novel hit her hard—a pubic rejection of her claim that she was an unusual human being. Fitzgerald told friends he could not endure her as a writing competitor. When Zelda surrendered to his superiority, he immediately took on the role of instructor, a pattern which worked until shortly before his death.

G67. Meindl, Dieter. *Der amerikanische Roman zwischen Naturalismus und Postmoderne, 1930-1960: Eine Entwicklungsstudie auf diskurstheoretischer Grundlage* [*The American Novel Between Naturalism and Postmodernism, 1930-1960: A Study of Its Development on a Discourse Theory Basis*]. München: Fink, 1983. In passim.

Nick Carraway is an example of the use of a dramatized narrator, for which one must make the distinction between mere observers and "narrator-agents." *The Great Gatsby* is part of a flowering of "I" novels in the 1920s, as are *The Sun Also Rises* and *A Farewell to Arms*.

G68. Morton, Bruce. "Macomber and Fitzgerald: Hemingway Gets Even in 'The Short Happy Life of Francis Macomber.'" *Zeitschrift für Anglistik und Amerikanistik: A Quarterly of Language, Literature and Culture* [*Journal for English and American Studies: A Quarterly of Language, Literature and Culture*] 30 (1982): 157-160.

As Matthew Bruccoli suggests, Francis Macomber was a reference to Francis Scott Fitzgerald. The story was written at a time when Hemingway was "appalled" by Fitzgerald's confessional *Esquire* articles and additionally, saw him as a man dominated by his wife. Both Macombers are a "parody of the rich whom Fitzgerald held in awe." Hemingway's knowledge of Zelda's affair with a French naval aviator "suggests a prototype for the allusion to Margot's ... unspecified affair." The two marriages, real and fictional, are too similar to be anything but a conscious effort on the part of Hemingway.

G69. Nischik, Reingard M. "Leidenschaften und Besitz: F. Scott Fitzgerald. *The Great Gatsby*. Ed. Reingard M. Nischik. *Leidenschaften literarisch*. Texte zur Weltliteratur 1 (Konstanz: UVK, 1998): 253-269.

Not available for annotation.

G70. Schirmer, Walter Franz, and Arno Esch. *Kurze Geschichte der englischen und amerikanischen Literatur* [*A Short History of English and American Literature*]. Tübingen: Niemeyer, 1977. 378.

Fitzgerald never outgrew the problems of the Lost Generation. *The Great Gatsby*, his most famous novel, is more than just a document of the Jazz Age; the character of Gatsby is brilliantly and artfully styled and constructed to make his symbolic function clear: the American Dream is hollow and hopeless. Schirmer makes very brief mention, also, of *Tender Is the Night* and *The Last Tycoon*.

G71. Schnack, Elisabeth. *Müssen Künstler einsam sein? Leben und Werk von Scott Fitzgerald, Sean O'Faolain, Liam O'Flaherty, Francis Stuart, Katherine Mansfield, Frank O'Connor, George Moore* [*Must the Artist Be Alone? Life and Works of Scott Fitzgerald, Sean O'Faolain, Liam O'Flaherty, Francis Stuart, Katherine Mansfield, Frank O'Connor, George Moore*]. Zürich: Pendo, 1991. 19-27.

"Everyone is alone. An artist must be alone," declared Fitzgerald. Since he had no resistance to alcohol and his bored, vain, envious wife encouraged long drinking bouts, he developed a life-threatening alcoholism and the sad realization that an artist had to be alone if he didn't want to destroy himself, his marriage, and his friendships. More than a chronicler of the rich, Fitzgerald deals with themes of Seeming and Being in his work. His origins (outlined in some detail by Schnack) and fatal marriage drove him to a deplorable end. His life story is even more dramatic and tragic than what he describes in his narratives.

G72. Schürenberg, Walter. Preface. *Der Grosse Gatsby* [*The Great Gatsby*]. Zürich: Diogenes, 1974.

A depicting of the "Gatsby-world": demi-monde, playboys, champagne. Gatsby's reputation, as parvenu, gangster, war hero, is the American Dream and nightmare in one. Gatsby's fate is the essence of the glitter and illusion of the American '20s. Fitzgerald, more than any other writer, depicted people who were driven, "the elegant anarchy and despair of the age that was both painful and comfortable at once." Despite fads and filmings, *The Great Gatsby* remains a lasting witness to the American '20s.

G73. Staats, Armin. "'Genteel Tradition' und 'Liberal Imagination.'" *Mythos und Aufklärung in der amerikanischen Literatur: Zu Ehren von Hans-Joachim Lang* [*Myth and Enlightenment in American Literature: In Honor of Hans-Joachim Lang*]. Intro. & ed. Dieter Meindl, bibliography

Friedrich W. Horlacher, foreword Martin Christadler. Erlangen: Universitätsbund Erlangen-Nürnberg, 1985. 353-373. (EFG 38).

Both *The Great Gatsby* and W.D. Howells's *A Modern Instance* circle around the problem of values in an open society within the context of horizontal and vertical mobility. Staats posits a change of emphasis from the "genteel tradition" (maintaining time-honored values above the needs of the individual) to the "liberal imagination" (a progression toward romantic individualism) by way of a shift toward the individual in the constant dialectic: an individual's needs/society's needs. Nick Carraway is an observer of romantic individualism who comes from a "genteel tradition." Gatsby is the "symbolic imagination," the Utopian promise of individual fulfillment within society as a result of a sublimated, but conscious, dialectic between disciplined consciousness and romantic longing. The novel's final image is like Trilling's concept of the dialectical struggle between the individual and society. The "liberal imagination" functions within this struggle for the pursuit of individual happiness within a social construct.

G74.   Waegner, Cathy. "Der Teufel im American Dream: Zur Faust-Tradition in der Neuen Welt [The Devil in the American Dream: On the Faust Tradition in the New World]." *Zeitschrift für Literaturwissenschaft und Linguistik [Journal of Literary Studies and Linguistics]* 17.66 (1987): 61-84.

The Faustian figure of Western civilization becomes the victim of his own economic success. The New World above all, with its unlimited possibilities for expansion and immense resources, is particularly susceptible to this fate. The little observed Faust tradition in American life and literature is comparable to the driving power of American civilization. A variation of the Faust bargain is the Horatio Alger story of a virtuous rise from rags to riches; behind it is the equation of happiness (America's birthright) with money. A man may gain the world, but may also lose his soul and money. Gatsby is in part a version of the Alger mentality of grasping opportunity. His attempt to overcome time can be paralleled to the Faust theme. His connection to the Mephisto-like Wolfsheim seduces him to use nefarious means to get rich and realize his dream. Nick's romanticism ennobles Gatsby's dream; but Gatsby's attachment to the "foul dust" of the corrupted American Dream leads him into the realism of empty materialism and superficiality.

G75.   Wagner, Peter. *A Short History of English and American Literature.* Stuttgart: Klett, 1988. 257-59, 283.

Fitzgerald "wrote many excellent short stories and dealt with the frenetic and frivolous youth of the post-war years (*This Side of Paradise*), disillusionment

(*Tender Is the Night*), and the American Dream (*The Last Tycoon*). *The Great Gatsby* is his masterpiece."

G76.   Weimann, Robert, ed. Introduction. "Gesellschaft, Autorisation and Repräsentation im modernen amerikanischen Roman." *Der nordamerikanische Roman 1880-1940*. Aufbau-Verlag, 1989. 5-7.

The Great Gatsby, Absalom, Absalom!, and *The Grapes of Wrath* are modern novels written under the sustained impression of the defeat of liberal bourgeois civilization during WWI and subsequent world economic/industrial collapse. The modern American novel is a mixture of strategies, from Realism to Modernism, which separate it from the ruling discourse on politics and economics in order to create a new sort of authorization of writing and reading.

BOOK REVIEWS/NEWS ARTICLES/RADIO PROGRAMS

G77.   Janik, Georg. "Künstliches Paradies und reale Hölle als eine Parzelle [Artificial Paradise and Real Hell on One Piece of Earth]." *Bücherschau* [*Books in Review*] (Vienna) 3 (1996): 9-16.

A portrait of Fitzgerald, on the occasion of his 100th birthday. There is hardly another author whose life and work form such a tangled web. In his own time, he was too often considered a successful, fashionable proponent of the greedy "lost" generation, even though his writing was its ironic opponent.

G78.   Kleeberg, Michael. "Ein Darling der zwanziger Jahre: Francis Scott Fitzgerald—der Dichter der Unschuld Amerikas [A Darling of the Twenties: Francis Scott Fitzgerald—the Poet of American Innocence]." *Süddeutsche Zeitung* (München) 22/23 Dec. 1990.

F. Scott Fitzgerald's story is that of an American epoch and how its image changed from glory to decay. Fitzgerald's generation established cultural references for a young, "uncivilized" America. Ten years after his death, Fitzgerald's "resurrection" began. An America which reached adulthood recognized that the great writer's epic grandeur lies in his accepting defeat while keeping faith with the bitter truth.

G79.   Kruse, Horst. Rev. of *The Functional Significance of Setting in the Novels of F. Scott Fitzgerald*, by Eugen Huonder. *Jahrbuch für Amerikastudien* [*Yearbook for American Studies*] 23 (1978): 368-69.

Huonder offers an initial definition of what setting is—"a place of action"—but decides against a systemic approach to Fitzgerald. Instead, he devotes a chapter to each of the four novels, in chronological order, and discusses them under sub-headings arranged by place names, thereby allowing convenience to get the better of clarity. For the chapter on *Gatsby*, he analyzes houses as "extensions" of their occupants. Discussing *Tender Is the Night*, the author testifies to Fitzgerald's "dexterity in exploiting setting." Huonder should impress on the reader how vital settings in Fitzgerald are to clarifying his work, but ultimately he does not "establish the analysis of setting as a unique and indispensable tool of literary criticism." Still, he demonstrates that Fitzgerald not only knew how to deal with setting but purposefully kept it "subservient to . . . more essential concerns."

G80.   Leppmann, Wolfgang. "Das süsse Leben Amerikas: Francis Scott
        Fitzgerald und sein Debüt *Diesseits vom Paradies* [The Sweet American
        Life: Francis Scott Fitzgerald and His Debut: *This Side of Paradise*]."
        Rev. of *Diesseits vom Paradies*, by F. Scott Fitzgerald. *Frankfurter
        Allgemeine Zeitung* 211 (10 Sep. 1988): 28.

Wilson was correct in his seemingly paradoxical remark about the "uncultured book of worth." For those unfamiliar with the America of Fitzgerald's era, the "worth" of *This Side of Paradise* rests on Fitzgerald's unconcern, the freshness of his descriptions of a young Amory Blaine bursting to reveal himself.

G81.   Schäfer, Gerd. "Anlässlich des 100. Geburtstages von F. Scott
        Fitzgerald [On the Occasion of the 100th Birthday of Francis Scott
        Fitzgerald (1896-1940)]." *Saarländischer Rundfunk* [*Radio Station of the
        Saarland*] 21 Sept. 1996.

Summaries of Fitzgerald's life and work. In his writing, "Fitzgerald tries to catch up with transmitted comparisons in order to save them, since the world of traditional images (also that of dreams) continuously loses value because of industrialization, so that in the end there is only an ever-present disillusion," a diagnosis of which appears in "Babylon Revisited."

G82.   Schürenberg, Walter. "Francis Scott Fitzgerald: Chronist der Roaring
        Twenties [Francis Scott Fitzgerald: Chronicler of the Roaring Twenties]."
        Zeit Magazin 23 Nov. 1979. N. pag.

More than any of his contemporaries, Fitzgerald represented the so-called "lost generation." *This Side of Paradise* is not only the prototype for the lost generation novel but, by describing the hollowness of the Jazz Age, it begins a theme which recurs in Fitzgerald's stories and, above all, in *Gatsby*. The realization that "the rich are different" occupies Fitzgerald again and again, as does the realization that ascent into their circle is always closed to the "little man."

G83.   Seiler, Andrea. "Ein amerikanischer Märchenprinz: Zum 100. Geburtstag von Francis Scott Fitzgerald [An American Fairy Tale Prince: On the 100th Birthday of Francis Scott Fitzgerald]." *Neue Zürcher Zeitung* 24 Sept. 1996: n. p.

With Fitzgerald, the schematic split between Romanticism and Realism has lost its meaning. He is a narrator who neither merely portrays events nor puts himself beyond them. He develops new, more sensitive "organs" to perceive the colored reflexes of demonic realities and to reproduce them in words. His prismatic style is the instrument of a refined narrative realism. Achieving this is Fitzgerald's historic deed, not his chronicling of the frivolous Jazz Age.

G84.   Vormweg, Heinrich. Review of Short Story Collections. *Tages-Anzeiger* 22 Nov. 1980.

Diogenes Pocket Books has published five volumes of stories written by Fitzgerald between 1920 and 1940. Each of the stories is not only worth reading, but is immediately gripping, moving, charming, disturbing.

G85.   Wagner, Peter. Rev. of *Romaninterpretation als Textarchäologie: Untersuchungen zur Intertextualität am Beispiel von F. Scott Fitzgeralds* This Side of Paradise [*Interpreting the Novel as Textual Archaeology: An Intertextual Analysis of F. Scott Fitzgerald's* This Side of Paradise], by Udo J. Hebel. *Amerikastudien* 37.4 (1992): 685-7.

In 1969, before the birth of Intertextuality, Michel Foucault wrote: "One can imagine a culture in which discourse would be accepted without the function 'author' ever being mentioned." In addition to a critical viewing of intertextuality, Hebel is concerned with the analysis of the explicit potential of allusions in *This Side of Paradise* according to "intertextual allusional paradigms." The exploitation of the allusion paradigm as a text is noteworthy. Hebel shows proof of the language-art dimension of *Paradise*, and how some of its parts are metatextual documents of the so-called cultural revolution of the '20s. Analysis of *Paradise* as a text-archaeological guide takes Hebel 260 pages, which gives an idea of how extensive an analysis would be of the allusion potentials that are not marked. Hebel proves Foucault's Utopia, that endless dimensions will open up if discourse, not its author, is the object of investigation.

DISSERTATIONS

G86. Grabe, Eckhard. "Cinematologie und Poetologie: Kunstbetrachtung im Hollywood-Roman." Münster, 1991.

G87. Hebel, Udo J. "Romaninterpretation als Textarchäologie: Untersuchungen zur Intertextualität am Beispiel von F. Scott Fitzgeralds *This Side of Paradise*." Mainz, 1988.

G88. Hoenisch, Michael. "Untersuchungen zum Formwandel im Werk F. Scott Fitzgeralds [Examples of Form Change in the Work of F. Scott Fitzgerald]." Berlin, 1969.

G89. Keiner, Karl E. "Die Funktion des Reichtums im Erzählwerk von F. Scott Fitzgerald mit besonderer Berücksichtigung seiner Romane." Mainz, 1984.

G90. Krämer, Gabriele. "Artusstoff und Gralsthematik im modernen amerikanischen Roman: Eine exemplarische Darstellung an Werken von F. Scott Fitzgerald, Ernest Hemingway, Truman Capote, Jerome D. Salinger sowie Bernard Malamud." Giessen, 1985.

G91. Krehayn, Joachim. "Weltliteratur als Massstab: Zur Rezeption der Belletristik Grossbritanniens und der USA in der Deutschen Demokratischen Republik [World Literature as Standard: On the Reception of British and American Literature in the German Democratic Republic]." Diss. Greifswald, 1973.

G92. Lumer, Helga. "Zur Rezeption der Literatur der USA in der deutschen kommunistischen Presse (1918-1933) [On the Reception of American Literature in the German Communist Press (1918-1933)]." Diss. Berlin, 1978.

G93. Misgin, Marianne. "Die Rezeption der Literatur der USA in der deutschen sozialdemokratischen Presse (1890-1933)" [The Reception of American Literature in the German Social Democratic Press (1890-1933)]. Diss. Berlin, 1975.

G94. Möllers, Hildegard. "A Paradise Populated with Lost Souls":
    Literarische Auseinandersetzungen mit Los Angeles. Diss. Paderborn,
    1998.

G95. Muster, Ludwig. "Probleme der amerikanischen Jugend in den Werken
    Fitzgeralds, Wolfes and Farrells [The Problem of American Youth in the
    Work of Fitzgerald, Wolfe, and Farrell]." Graz, 1955.

G96. Richter, Bernd. "Gesellschaftliche Bedingungen und literarische
    Kommunikation in den USA der 20er Jahre: Werte und Wertungen der
    Romane F. Scott Fitzgeralds [Social Conditions and Literary
    Communication in the USA in the 1920s: Values and Evaluations of the
    Novels of F. Scott Fitzgerald]." Potsdam, 1982.

TEACHER/STUDENT GUIDES AND EDITIONS

G97. Abbott, Anthony S., ed. *Lektürehilfen F. Scott Fitzgerald* The Great
    Gatsby [*Reading Guide to F. Scott Fitzgerald's* The Great Gatsby].
    Stuttgart: Klett, 1990; 1994; 1995. 102.

G98. Bischoff, Peter. "F. Scott Fitzgerald: *The Great Gatsby* (1925)." *Der
    Roman im Englischunterricht der Sekundarstufe II: Theorie und Praxis*
    [*The Novel in English Instruction, Advanced Level: Theory and Pratice*].
    Eds. Peter Freese and Liesel Hermes. Paderborn: Schöningh, 1977. 131-
    153. Revised edition, 1981.

G99. Esseln, Hans-Joachim, ed. *The Great Gatsby*, by F. Scott Fitzgerald:
    Vokabularien zum Penguin-Taschenbuch [*Word Explanations for the
    Penguin Paperback*]. (Aschendorffs Vokabularien zu fremdsprachigen
    Taschenbüchern) Münster: Aschendorff, 1982; 1986. 135. New ed.,
    1991. 143.

G100. Fitzgerald, F. Scott. *The Baby Party and Other Stories.* Paderborn:
    Schöningh, n.d. 80.

G101. Fitzgerald, F. Scott. *The Diamond as Big as the Ritz and Other Stories.*

Bielefeld: Cornelsen, n.d.

G102. Fitzgerald, F. Scott. *The Great Gatsby.* Berlin; München: Langenscheidt-Longman, n.d. 208.

G103. Fitzgerald, F. Scott. *The Great Gatsby.* Frankfurt/Main: Diesterweg, n.d. 165.

G104. Fitzgerald, F. Scott. *The Great Gatsby* (abridged). Stuttgart: Klett, n.d.

G105. Fitzgerald, F. Scott. *The Great Gatsby.* Stuttgart: Klett, n.d.

G106. Fitzgerald, F. Scott. *The Great Gatsby: Interpretationshilfe* [*The Great Gatsby: Interpretation Guide*]. Berlin; München: Langenscheidt-Longman, n.d. 71

G107. Fitzgerald, F. Scott. *The Great Gatsby. Lehrerheft* [*The Great Gatsby: Teacher's Book*]. Stuttgart: Klett, n.d.

G108. Freese, Peter. *The American Short Story I: Initiation—Interpretations and Suggestions for Teaching.* Paderborn: Schöningh, 1986.

G109. Gerber, Hans H., ed. *The Great Gatsby,* by F. Scott Fitzgerald, Berlin: Cornelsen, 1994. 164.

G110. Gerber, Hans H., ed. *The Great Gatsby.* Cornelsen Senior English Library. Berlin: Cornelsen, 1994. 72.

G111. Jens, Walter, ed. *Kindlers Neues Literatur Lexikon* [*Kindler's New Literary Lexicon*]. München: Kindler, 1989. 5: 581-591.

G112. Lenz, Susanne, ed. *The Great Gatsby,* by F. Scott Fitzgerald. Stuttgart: Philipp Reclam Jr., n.d.

G113. Pohlenz, Dagmar, and Richard Martin, eds. *The Great Gatsby: Student's Book.* Paderborn: Schöningh, 1984. 140.

G114. Pohlenz, Dagmar, and Richard Martin, eds. *The Great Gatsby: Interpretations and Suggestions for Teaching/Teacher's Book.* Paderborn: Schöningh, 1986, 1994. 238. (Texts for English and American Studies 14)

G115. Tracy, Brian, and Erwin Helms. *American Dreams—American Nightmares.* Paderborn: Schöningh, 1981 (Students' Book); 1982 (Teacher's Book).

G116. Wolpers, Theodor, ed. "Babylon Revisited," by F. Scott Fitzgerald. *American Short Stories, Vol. VI: Isolated People in the Modern World..* Paderborn: Schöningh, n.d.

Denmark

As in most European countries, Fitzgerald's reputation in Denmark did not begin to grow until after the Second World War. In 1948, the first translation of *The Great Gatsby* appeared, followed in 1954 by a translation of *Tender Is the Night. Gatsby* has been reprinted four times and *Tender* three, but Fitzgerald's novels have never become bestsellers in Denmark, although the Jack Clayton film version of 1974 increased the sales of the former considerably. Three of his novels, *This Side of Paradise, The Beautiful and Damned,* and *The Last Tycoon* have not yet been translated into Danish. Translations of two collections of short stories were published in 1966 and 1967 (D7, D9) and the best stories from the two-volume version were republished in one volume in 1998 (D15). *The Pat Hobby Stories* were translated and published in 1988 (D12). While translation of Fitzgerald's work clearly has been sluggish, still it has persisted.

The assessment of Fitzgerald's work in Danish literary histories reflects the pattern elsewhere in Europe in which he was ignored or dismissed in the twenties and thirties but rediscovered in the more non-ideological and existentialist postwar years. As Claus Secher discovered in his research for his paper on Fitzgerald's reputation in Denmark at the Fifth International Fitzgerald Conference in Nice in 2000 (D30), Fitzgerald figures in two older American literary histories by Danish scholars. Frederik Schyberg in his *Modern American Literature 1900-30* (Schyberg) focuses on the revolt in American literature against the New England Puritan tradition. Along with most scholars of the period, his heroes are the more socially conscious Upton Sinclair, Theodore Dreiser, Sinclair Lewis, Sherwood Anderson, Carl Sandburg and the early Eugene O'Neill. Schyberg regards the literature of the 1920s as a moral and sexual revolt against the creed of the prewar generation, and he emphasizes the nihilism of the younger generation of writers, especially Hemingway (Schyberg 1930). Secher asserts that Schyberg skewed Fitzgerald's biography, probably from a misreading of *This Side of Paradise,* because he describes him as a desperate man returned from the war. Although he praises Fitzgerald's good intelligence and clear thinking, he only mentions the title of *The Great Gatsby,* and one doubts whether he has read much of his work (D30).

Sven Møller Kristensen, an undogmatic Marxist, in *American Literature 1920-47* (Kristensen, 1948), has, according to Secher, a better grasp of the qualities of Fitzgerald's writings. He classifies his work as the most typical representation in America of the generational novel. He mentions Fitzgerald's ambivalence about rich people, and he praises *The Great Gatsby* and the short stories (D30).

As Secher assessed, in two newer Danish literary histories, Politiken's from 1974 (Lindtner 1974) and Gyldendal's from 1992 (Pedersen 1992), Fitzgerald is treated with fairness and respect, as almost of the same quality as Faulkner and Hemingway. Not only *Gatsby* but also *Tender Is the Night* and his best short stories are dealt with as major works in modern American literature. *This Side of Paradise* is mainly regarded as a bestseller and as a typical even trivial expression of its time, which may account for its not being translated into Danish, although the novel did inspire a famous Danish novel from 1931, Knud Sønderby's *In the Middle of a Jazz Age* (D30).

When the translation of *The Great Gatsby* finally came out in 1948, the reviews in the Danish newspapers were mixed. In *Berlingske Aftenavis,* Hans Brix, a professor at the University of Copenhagen, expresses disdain for the novel and for anything coming from the USA, where in his opinion everything is outdated from the day it is born, *The Great Gatsby* having arrived 23 years late (Brix 1948). In *Politiken* the most influential critic of his time, Tom Kristensen, himself a great poet and novelist, is admiring of the novel's mixture of realism and romanticism, but also finds that the translation was too delayed (Kristensen 1948). Jens Kruuse, in *Jyllands-Posten,* respects the book and its portrayal of the jazz age, but he mentions that while Fitzgerald is very intelligent, he may not be wise. In comparison with Hemingway's novels, *The Great Gatsby* is not as deeply tragic. It is in Kruuse's words "a soap bubble that bursts without leaving any stain" [Kruuse 1948] (30).

Secher pointed out that it has been Fitzgerald's fate in Denmark as elsewhere in Europe to be compared with Hemingway, to live in his shadow, but Niels Kaas Johansen in *Information* enthusiastically prefers Fitzgerald to Hemingway (Johansen 1948), and the earlier mentioned Sven Møller Kristensen, also a critic at the Danish communist newspaper *Land og Folk,* wrote a very positive review. *The Great Gatsby,* he writes, "is at the same time an ironic picture of its time, a romantic love story, and as well plotted as dramatic in its tragic feeling, a forerunner of the hardboiled outlook, but much finer in spirit" [Kristensen 1948] (D30).

The reviews of *Tender Is the Night* from 1954 in Denmark show the same diversity in the evaluation of Fitzgerald, according to Secher. The most negative critic Jens Kistrup, argues in *Berlingske Tidende* that this novel is too close to Fitzgerald's own life. The style is too sentimental, and he compares it unfavorably to *The Sun Also Rises*. He also talks about Fitzgerald's "sentimental neurotic smartness, his unhappy urge to private exhibitionism" (Kistrup 1954). Hans Brix (*Berlingske Aftenavis*) thinks that there are too many characters and episodes in the novel, that Nicole should be the protagonist instead of Dick Diver, and that while there are lovely passages, there is no structure. "Scott Fitzgerald is a writer, not a poet; he may be talented, but he is not a genius" (Brix 1954 n.p.). Jacob Paludan in *Nationaltidende* misses the lion's claw of Hemingway (Paludan 1954). Mogens Knudsen in *Information*, writes very precisely about *Tender Is the Night:* "It is not a very profound book, for Fitzgerald's capacity for intellectual reasoning was small, but it is pervaded by a naked pain, which, couched in a moving and colorful style, makes the reading not only an artistic pleasure, but also a human experience" (Knudsen 1954). Henrik Neiiendam in *Ekstrabladet* found that its real relevant subject was the story of a man who sells his soul for money, beauty and comfort, and he saw a striking parallel in the modem Danish Welfare State, where Danes sell their souls to get jobs and pensions [Neiiendam 1954] (D30).

When the short stories came out in 1966 and 1967, the critics' response, however, was unanimously positive. While the first collection, *Babylon Revisited,* contained three major stories, the two volume-collection of 1967 translated by Hans Hertel was composed in such a way that the first consisted of short stories from the Jazz Age, the 1920s, while the second reflected the hangovers and the depression of the 1930s. All reviewers agreed that Fitzgerald was a very gifted short story writer, and that he incarnated the feelings and sensations of those two decades (D36, D49, D54). *The Pat Hobby Stories,* which were translated in 1988, were on the other hand considered humorous in their satire, but not as belonging to the important body of Fitzgerald's work [D35, D50] (D30).

Moving to the more substantial and modern criticism, Secher asserted that two important points must be made. No important academic scholarship on Fitzgerald's work has been accomplished yet in Denmark. One 1989 academic article by Helle Porsdam, "The Inheritance from Henry James: the International Theme in Ernest Hemingway and F. Scott Fitzgerald," in the academic review *Passage* 6, discusses both the influence of James and the revolt against him in Hemingway's and Fitzgerald's writings and focuses on the international theme and gender roles in their fiction. It has some interesting points on the masculinity of Hemingway and femininity of Fitzgerald and the extent to which these aspects of their personalities affected their assessments of James [D25] (D30).

The second point Secher stressed is that the best material on Fitzgerald in Denmark has been written by other writers, poets, and novelists who, like Tom Kristensen, have at the same time been literary critics at the bigger Copenhagen newspapers. In Denmark, Fitzgerald is a writer's writer. Klaus Rifbjerg, both a fiction writer and a poet who is one of the most famous Danish modernists from the 1960s and is still active, wrote two famous articles on Fitzgerald in

Politiken, which in 1967 were collected in a book, *Rif*. Rifbjerg's articles focus on Fitzgerald's biography which he claims is impossible to separate from his work. "His life was one great romantic, tragic novel." The evolution of Fitzgerald from the status of king of the youth in the early twenties to the crisis, dissolution and oblivion in the 1930s, and finally to the reappraisal after the war gives his story a mythological resonance. Gatsby's lonely funeral was a prediction of his own. Rifbjerg also makes the interesting observation that Fitzgerald to a much greater degree than Hemingway represented something specifically American, which may explain why his works have not been so well accepted in Denmark and the rest of Europe [D26, D27] (D30).

According to Secher, an essay of Danish fiction-writer Anders Bodelsen that appeared in *Foreign Writers in the 20th Century* (1968) is the best that has been written on Fitzgerald in Denmark. Bodelsen makes many intelligent observations such as "Success not money is the key to all Fitzgerald's writing." He enlarges on the theme: "As the need for success is taken for granted, the worthlessness of success or at least disillusion, is taken for granted." Bodelsen also comments on the mythological geography of Fitzgerald. To him, the East means success and the West, failure. The South is success in love, while the North, failure. South and East (including the Riviera of France) mean the realization of the dreams of both love and success. Fitzgerald, however, ended in Hollywood (the far West) as an underpaid script writer. Bodelsen sums up his portrait of the writer: "All his writing is about the one way to keep one's self-respect: to remain open and pay what it costs. To lesser poets, this has meant an escape into innocence and permanent puberty. To Fitzgerald it was a way to become adult" [(D18])D30).

Bo Green Jensen's article in *Afstandens indsigt* in 1982 is actually a review of Matthew J. Bruccoli's *Some Sort of Epic Grandeur*. His second and much longer article in *Ind i det amerikanske*, a book on American culture appearing in 1992, is a biographical essay and also a long review on the occasion of the 1987 reprinting of *Tender Is the Night*, entitled "Poor Butterfly: F. Scott Fitzgerald and *Tender Is the Night."* A writer of fiction and a poet himself, Bo Green Jensen agrees with many other Danish critics that Fitzgerald was not an intellectual writer but rather wrote from intuition, feeling and instinct. He praises the novel for the total honesty of its self-portrait. And for the author's not giving in to the temptation to turn Dick Diver into a martyr. Secher asserts that Jensen, an enthusiastic critic of American literature, film, and rock music, is often driven by his own rhetoric. On the final page he writes, " Fitzgerald did without doubt best in the short form. He was a sprinter, where Hemingway was a long distance runner, but *Tender Is the Night* stands as his only long text written without the temptation to seize himself, his generation, and his century by the throat. . . . No other American novel is so rich, so cruel and so generous as *Tender Is the Night*" [D22, D23, D43] (D30).

Secher concludes that Fitzgerald may not yet be loved by the masses in

Denmark, but he was and is loved by many writers, critics, teachers, and ordinary readers because he so intensely incarnates their ambiguous love of America (D30).

REFERENCES

Brix, Hans. "Dollargraad," Review of *Den store Gatsby [The Great Gatsby]. Berlingske Aften* (13 Sept. 1948).

---. "Hans eget Meldrama [His Own Melodrama]," Review of *Natten er blid [Tender Is the Night]*, *Berlingske Aftenavis* (10 Mar. 1954).

Johansen, Niels Kaas. "Jazztidens Digter [Poet of the Jazz Age]." Review of *Den store Gatsby [The Great Gatsby]*, *Information* (1948).

Kistrup, Jens. "Gravmæle over en Generation [Sepulchral Monument of a Generation]," Review of *Natten er blid [Tender Is the Night]*. *Berlingske Tidende* (30 Mar.1954).

Knudsen, Mogens. Review of *Natten er blid [Tender Is the Night]*. *Information* (26 July 1954).

Kristensen, Sven Møller. *Amerikansk Litteratur: 1920-1940*. Copenhagen: Athenæum, 1942.

Kristensen, Sven Møller. "En moderne amerikansk klassiker [A Modern American Classic]." Review of *Den store Gatsby [The Great Gatsby)*. *Land og Folk* (27 Sept. 1948).

Kristensen, Tom. Review of *Den store Gatsby [The Great Gatsby*. *Politiken* (6 October 1948).

Kruuse, Jens. "De Nye Bøger [The New Books]," Review of *Den store Gatsby [The Great Gatsby]*. *Jyllands Posten* (1948).

Lindtner, Chr. Niels. "Scott Fitzgerald: Jazz-Alderen [Scott Fitzgerald: The Jazz Age"]. *Verdenslitteraturhistorie: 1920-1945 Mellemkrigstiden [History of World Literature: 1920-1945 Between the Wars]*, Vol. 11. Politikens Forlag, 1974.

Neiiendam, Henrik. Review of *Natten er blid [Tender Is the Night]*. *Ekstrabladet* (30 Apr. 1954).

Paludan, Jacob. "Jazztidens litterære Fyrste [The Jazz Age's Literary Prince]," Review of *Tender Is the Night*. *Nationaltidende* (14 Mar. 1954).

Pedersen, Viggo Hjørnager. "Der fortabte generation [The Lost Generation]," *Verdenslitteraturhistorie [History of World Literature]* Vol. 6. Copenhagen: Gyldendal, 1992.

Schyberg, Frederik. *Moderne Amerikansk Litteratur: 1900-1930.* Copenhagen: Gyldendalske Boghandel-Nordisk Forlag, 1993.

Parenthetical citations to entry numbers refer to annotated references in this chapter.

TRANSLATIONS/EDITIONS

D1.   Fitzgerald, F. Scott. *Den store Gatsby [The Great Gatsby].* Trans. Ove Brusendorff. Copenhagen: Thaning and Appel, 1948; Gyldendal, 1960, 1971 (wrappers); Gyldendals Bogklub, 1971 (cloth), 1974, 1984, 1992, 1997; Søren Gyldendals klassikere, 1998. 176

D2.   Fitzgerald, F. Scott. *Natten er blid [Tender Is the Night].* Trans. by Helga Vang Lauridsen and Elsa Gress. Copenhagen: Wangel, 1954; Skrifola, 1961; Gyldendal, 1971, 1975, 1987 (4th ed.).

D3.   Fitzgerald, F. Scott. "Den rige dreng [The Rich Boy]." Trans. Henri Lassen. *Udenfor sæsonen og andre amerikanske noveller [Outside the Season and Other American Short Stories].* Ed. Sven Møller Kristensen. Copenhagen: Carit Andersens Forlag, 1956. 7-48.

D4.   Fitzgerald, F. Scott. "Babylon Revisited." *American Literature-4 Themes.* Copenhagen: Gyldendal, 1966, 1972. 215-238.

D5.   Fitzgerald, F. Scott. *Tilbage til Babylon [Babylon Revisited].* Trans. Bendix Bech-Thostrup and Elise Norsbo. Copenhagen: Carit Andersens, 1966. 152

D6.   Fitzgerald, F. Scott. "Bernice bli'r bobbet [Bernice Bobs Her Hair]." Trans. Hans Hertel. *Noveller fra USA [Stories from the USA].* Copenhagen: Gyldendals Tranebøger, 1967. 24-53.

D7. Fitzgerald, F. Scott. *En forfatters eftermiddag og andre noveller* [*Afternoon of an Author and Other Stories*]. Trans. & Intro. by Hans Hertel. Copenhagen: Steen Hasselbalchs Forlag, 1967.

D8. Fitzgerald, F. Scott. "En forrykt søndag [Crazy Sunday]." Trans. Karen Meldsted. *Filmens Verden Berømte danske og udenlandske forfattere fortæller* [*The World of the Film as Described by Famous Danish and Foreign Writers*], selected by Erik Ulrichsen. Copenhagen: Carit Andersens Forlag, 1967. 62-84; Copenhagen: Aschehoug, 1998.

D9. Fitzgerald, F. Scott. *Historier fra jazztiden.* [Tales of the Jazz Age]. Trans., intro., and edited by Hans Hertel. Copenhagen: Steen Hasselbalchs Forlag, 1967. 224

D10. Fitzgerald, F. Scott. "Outside the Cabinet-Maker's." *In Full Swing.* Ed. Aage Salling and Erik Hvid. Copenhagen: Grafisk Forlag A/S, 1976. 14-18.

D11. Fitzgerald, F. Scott. "The Night Before Chancellorsville." *Nineteen Humorous Stories.* Ed. Paul Monrad. Copenhagen: Det Schønbergske Forlag, 1979. 68-73.

D12. Fitzgerald, F. Scott. *Pat Hobby, Hollywood.* Trans. and foreword by Jørgen Stegelman. Copenhagen: Nyt Nordisk Forlag Arnold Busck A/S, 1988.

D13. Fitzgerald, F. Scott. "Gretchen's Forty Winks." *New York City: The Making of the Urban Individual,* ed. René Bühlmann. Forlaget Systime A/S, 1993. 32-50.

D14. Fitzgerald, F. Scott. "Bernice bli'r bobbet [Bernice Bobs Her Hair]." Trans. Hans Hertel. *Søndag i August og andre noveller/Sunday in August and Other Stories.* Ed. Ellinor Carit Andersen. Copenhagen: Carit Andersens Forlag, n. d.: 5-39.

D15. Fitzgerald, F. Scott. *Historier fra jazztiden: udvalgte noveller 1920-40* [*Tales of the Jazz Age and Other Stories*]. Trans. and Ed. Hans Hertel. Copenhagen: Aschehoug, 1998. 240.

D16. Fitzgerald, F. Scott. "Ti år ud af kalenderen [The Lost Decade]."
     Euroman 2 (Feb. 2000): 74-75.

American Scholarship in Translation

D17. Aldridge, James. *Et sidste glimt [The Last Glimpse]*. Trans. Anna Marie
     Nielsen. Copenhagen: Schultz Forlag, 1977.

ESSAYS/CHAPTERS/NOTES/CONFERENCE PAPERS

D18. Bodelsen, Anders. "F. Scott Fitzgerald." *Foreign Writers in the 20th
     Century*, Vol. II. Ed. Sven Møller Kristensen. Copenhagen: G. E. C.
     Glads Forlag, 1968: 447-459.

"Begin with an individual and before you know it, you have created a type;
begin with a type and you find you have created nothing," said Fitzgerald in the
introduction to one of his best short stories, "The Rich Boy" (1926). In *This Side
of Paradise*, he began with an individual and discovered that he had created a
type. For the next ten years, people thanked him for helping them discover
themselves, but he would die largely poor and unread. His five novels and about
160 short stories make him one of the century's most industrious writers. The
critics were severe with *This Side of Paradise*, but the public loved Amory, the
disillusioned youth. Fitzgerald had created a type. He felt split between literature
and economic success, unnecessarily so, as his most popular stories, in *The
Saturday Evening Post*, were his best. The signals of his downfall were already
given in "The Rough Crossing"(1929) and "One Trip Abroad"(1930). The 1929
crash was his crash—Zelda's breakdown and his own decline in popularity.

D19. Hertel, Hans. Indledning [Introduction]. *En Forfatters Eftermiddag og
     andre noveller [Afternoon of an Author and Other Stories]*, by F. Scott
     Fitzgerald. Copenhagen: Steen Hasselbalchs Forlag, 1967: 7-10.

It is a myth that Fitzgerald lost his literary talent, for he continued to write
excellent and increasingly personal short stories. He dealt with female
psychology, marriage and divorce in his Josephine stories of 1930-31, his
European stories, and in "Babylon Revisited." After his breakdown, he turned to
the past in "News from Paris—15 Years Ago." He wrote of the pain of
emotional bankruptcy and also of the pleasure in a world of poetic possibilities
in "Afternoon of an Author," and "The Lost Decade." The seventeen satirical

Pat Hobby stories about the seedy scriptwriter deal with brutality, opportunism and frustrated ambition. A similar theme appears in his last novel, *The Last Tycoon* (1941), which shows a new artistic competence and is considered his comeback. The stories of this period show him as more professional, objective, and ironic. The narrative is written in the third person and the stories, less experimental than earlier, are quieter and clearer. Restlessness and disillusionment appear in "Winter Dreams" and the loss of feeling in "The Rich Boy." His development was America's development, yet he never lost faith in himself. He is a moralist who pointed out the differences between appearances and reality in America. He knew alienation and the passing nature of all things.

D20. Hertel, Hans. Indledning [Introduction]. *Historier fra jazztiden [Tales of the Jazz Age]*. Copenhagen: Steen Hasselbalchs Forlag, 1967: 7-11.

Although much attention has been given to *This Side of Paradise, The Beautiful and Damned,* and Fitzgerald's masterpiece, *The Great Gatsby,* it was in his short stories that he most clearly expressed his period and formed its style. This can be seen from the titles of the collections: *Flappers and Philosophers* (1921), *Tales of the Jazz Age* (1922), and *All the Sad Young Men* (1926). However, now in Denmark only five of his stories have been translated. A re-evaluation of his skill as a short story writer started in 1951 with Malcolm Bradbury and later with Arthur Mizener's discovery of stories from the 20's and 30's in *The Smart Set, Vanity Fair* and the *Saturday Evening Post,* reprinted in two volumes, from which these seventeen stories are taken. Stories in which Scott and Zelda plunged into the world of the Charleston and wild parties, first in New York and then the Riviera. Scott said he didn't know if they existed or were people in his novels. He made more money than he ever dreamed of, and watched the drama that goes on in youth's changeable, cruel world. Fitzgerald idolized the rich, but was often repelled by them, an ambivalence which he never denied, and which is seen in "A Diamond as Big as the Ritz" and "The Rich Boy."

D21. Hjørnager Pedersen, Viggo. "Der fortabte generation [The Lost Generation]." *Verdenslitteraturhistorie [History of World Literature]*. Vol. 6. Copenhagen: Gyldendal, 1992: 174-176.

Fitzgerald and his heroes are desperately looking for new values as the old ones dissipate.

D22. Jensen, Bo Green. "Francis Af Encino." *Den Samme Flod to Gange [The Same Flood Twice]*. Copenhagen: Borgen, 1990: 12-15.

A version in verse of Fitzgerald's life.

D23. Jensen, Bo Green. "Stakkels sommerfugl: F. Scott Fitzgerald og *Natten er Blid* [Poor Butterfly: F. Scott Fitzgerald and *Tender Is the Night*]." *Ind i det Amerikanske: en bog om Amerikansk kultur: 99 stykker Americana 1982-1992* [*Into the American: a Book about American Culture: 99 pieces of Americana*]. Copenhagen: Borgen, 1992: 355-375.

Hemingway was disappointed with *Tender Is the Night* (1934), feeling that Fitzgerald had not only analyzed his own tragedy, but also abused the confidence of friends. The book was dedicated to Sara and Gerald Murphy, wealthy patrons of the arts, who had started an American colony at Cap d'Antibes in the 1920's. However, Dick Diver and Nicole Warren in the book have much more in common with the Fitzgeralds than the Murphys, as the latter admitted. Fitzgerald's first novel, *This Side of Paradise* made him an instant success and his short stories were successful and lucrative, but in the 30's things were not going well. He felt overwhelmed by Hemingway's success and arrogance. In Denmark Fitzgerald has never been taken as seriously as Hemingway, Faulkner or Thomas Wolfe, partly because of editing difficulties. T.S. Eliot said *Gatsby* entertained him more than any other new novel. Fitzgerald saw himself as a metaphor for the century; their rise and fall coincided. *Tender Is the Night* is his only novel that doesn't grab one by the throat. It seeks the moment when change happens.

D24. Jensen, Jesper Uhrup. "Kongen af Jazztiden: F. Scott Fitzgerald, en amerikansk drøm og tragedie [King of the Jazz Age: F. Scott Fitzgerald, an American Dream and Tragedy]." *Euroman 2* (Feb. 2000): 70-72.

Fitzgerald was the American dream and nightmare in one person. His best stories have lasted as surgically precise literary snapshots of people in a time in which hope was often subordinate to disappointment.

D25. Porsdam, Helle. "Arven Fra Henry James: Det 'internationale tema' hos Ernest Hemingway og F. Scott Fitzgerald [The Heritage from Henry James: The International Theme in Hemingway and Fitzgerald]." *Theme: The Novel. Passage 6.* Institute for Literary History, University of Aarhus, 1989: 105-118.

Henry James played a role for both Fitzgerald and Hemingway. Fitzgerald admitted that there is a feminine side to his nature and that all his characters, male and female, are reflections of himself. However he denied James's influence on *The Great Gatsby*, saying that it had been influenced more by the masculine tone of *The Brothers Karamazov* than the feminine one of *Portrait of a Lady*. Hemingway depicted Fitzgerald in *A Moveable Feast* (1964) as a weak hypochondriac. Hemingway characterized James as "a weak, delicate snob" and Fitzgerald as "a damned bloody romanticist." His blatant masculinity had little patience for their feminine sides. Fitzgerald felt that his own feminine decadence, as he considered it, was a reflection of America's weakness. In *Gatsby* and *The Last Tycoon*, there is a feeling that there is no longer room in America for the romantic and visionary. James, in turning from America to Europe, expressed the same feeling. James, Hemingway and Fitzgerald became more American in Europe, using distance to elucidate America.

D26. Rifbjerg, Klaus. "Den arme djaevel [The Poor Devil]." *R.I.F.* Copenhagen: Gyldendal, 1967.

Fitzgerald's novel *The Great Gatsby* deals with disappointment in American dreams of success, the story of a little man from the midwest who tries to move into the upper reaches of society. As usual, Fitzgerald wrote his own story, but this time he appears in two characters with Nick telling Gatsby's story and Gatsby the archetype of American cultural history. The book succeeds in making the little man a tragic figure. In his helpless vulgarity he takes on a symbolic dimension which represents the entire nation. Gatsby has a large villa and gives parties for crowds of guests. No one knows or cares who he is or the source of his money, but all ends in disillusion and tragedy. As a depiction of the times, *Gatsby* ranks with Dos Passos' *USA*, Sherwood Anderson's *Winesburg, Ohio*, Masters' *Spoon River Anthology* and Hemingway's best novels.

D27. Rifbjerg, Klaus. "Geniets saert vidunderlige gestalt: F. Scott Fitzgerald [The Strange and Wonderful Manifestations of Genius: F. Scott Fitzgerald]." *R.I.F.* Copenhagen: Gyldendal, 1967.

Because he was an exceptional writer, one must attempt to separate his private life from his writings, the man from the myth. It is difficult because his life was a romantic, tragic novel. Today we are attracted to the 20's, but at his death in 1940, Fitzgerald had been dead already in the public mind. Ten years earlier he had been a foremost writer and the only renewer of the American novel since Henry James. But to understand Fitzgerald one must realize that, more than Hemingway, he represented something specifically American. Dreiser's *An American Tragedy* is also Fitzgerald's both in life and art.

D28. Schepelern, Peter. "Den amerikanske drøm i softfocus [The American Dream in Soft Focus]." *Kosmorama* Vol. 20. No. 123/124 (1974-75): 328-332.

The first two film versions of *The Great Gatsby* had each presented the novel as a sensational story of romance and murder. However, the third version is faithful to the book on the insistence of Fitzgerald's daughter. It is pleasant, but has problems connected with Nick's telling the story in the first person. Since

Fitzgerald gave no account of the feeling between Gatsby and Daisy from their reunion to the catastrophe, the director, Jack Clayton, had to flesh out the romance in the film. The other characters are recognizable types, but Gatsby, an enigma, remains an idea. Gatsby's and Daisy's tête-à-tête, in soft focus, seems a little infantile and the effect is diminished. Clayton, a strong craftsman but without artistic wings, has arranged everything with great competence with all details accurate, but in vain, for the film is lifeless and artificial. Scenes in which main characters meet are good because Fitzgerald wrote them well and the players are good: Bruce Dern, Sam Waterston, Lois Chiles, Scott Wilson and Karen Black, but Robert Redford and Mia Farrow are problematic.

D29.   Secher, Claus. "American Literature in Denmark." *Images of America in Scandanavia*. Eds. Poul Houe and Sven Hakon Rossel. Amsterdam; Atlanta: Rodopi, 1998. 24-37.

Literary and theater critic Frederik Schyberg, in his *Modern American Literature 1900-1930* refers to *Gatsby* as a mere "youth novel." Nor does Sven Møller Kristensen (*American Literature 1920-1947*) greatly esteem Fitzgerald, calling him "average." *Gatsby* was not translated into Danish until 1948, by which time critic Emil Frederiksen found it obsolete, if well-written. The book was never a financial success.

D30.   Secher, Claus. "F. Scott Fitzgerald's Reputation in Denmark." Paper delivered at F. Scott Fitzgerald Centennial Conference, Princeton U, Sept. 1996; Fifth International Fitzgerald Conference, Nice, June, 2000.

See Chapter Introduction.

D31.   Stegelmann, Jørgen. Forard [Foreword]. *Pat Hobby, Hollywood*. Copenhagen: Nyt Nordisk Forlag Arnold Busck A/S, 1988: 4-6.

Fitzgerald wrote the story of Pat Hobby at a point when he himself had Hollywood behind him and a very uncertain future before him. He wrote partly to make money and partly to free himself from the suspicion that he himself was a Pat Hobby. He tried to become influential in Hollywood and was moderately successful. In Tom Dardis's "Sometimes in the Sun," one reads that five authors managed as scriptwriters in Hollywood: Huxley, West, Agee, Faulkner and Fitzgerald, but it is not right to conceal the fact that it was most difficult for the last man. Fitzgerald went to Hollywood in 1938 at the advice of his agent to try film. He had some trouble with Joseph Mankiewicz, but the real trouble was drink. Like Hobby, he tried to stay away from it without success and was fired. He then wrote the Hobby stories for *Esquire* which paid him well. Both humble and impudent, Hobby is a grotesque portrait of a talentless man who trusts that in Hollywood is to be found life's most beautiful meaning.

D32. Terp, Knud. "Generationskronikører [Chronicler of a Generation]."
      Vaegtlos i Tiden [*Weightless in Time*]. Copenhagen: Attika, 1975: 147-
      154.

Every generation in our century has had a narcissistic desire to be reflected in
the literature of its youth, tending to seek life's meaning outside our cultural
circle, such as in Fitzgerald and Salinger. Fitzgerald exposed the Jazz Age as a
neurotic epoch with an ambivalent attitude toward the success-fiasco complex
which he manifested as an artist and citizen. He was in many ways a naïve,
romantic writer whose life and art were interwoven. Fitzgerald became the same
type as Amory Blaine and was the model for a generation who regarded him as a
romantic victim of disillusionment. The result was he wasted his talent in order
to wear a mask, becoming not an artist, but a public idol. *This Side of Paradise*
made him instantly famous and fulfilled his and Armory Blaine's dream of
success. He eventually realized that the cost of success was too great, a shock he
never got over. In the widest sense, *The Great Gatsby* is America's energetic
and disappointing attempt to realize its dream.

D33. Terp, Knud. "Hollywood som Amerikansk Symbol [Hollywood as an
      American Symbol]." *Vaegtlos i Tiden* [*Weightless in Time*].
      Copenhagen: Attika, 1975: 101-106.

Hollywood deals with the use of make-up to cover reality. It says American
reality is unreality and self-deception. Compromise and double standards have
kissed each other in Hollywood's Technicolor creations. Fitzgerald's feelings
about Hollywood's illusion were ambiguous, for in a way he loved glamour and
illusion. Perhaps it is in the tension between fascination and disillusionment that
his art finds its surest form, but in life this tension destroyed him. Fitzgerald
cannot really be considered a moralist, yet his beautiful and illusion-filled novels
which punched holes in illusionism are highly moral. His work is central to
understanding America in this century. His 1930s Pat Hobby Stories, like
Hollywood, worship social status, money and success. Hobby is only an
unimportant wheel in an inhuman machine, although he denies it. Although
Fitzgerald died before finishing his other book on Hollywood, *The Last Tycoon*
it is one of the best novels on Hollywood for in it, Fitzgerald created a tragic
figure and dissected himself with clinical objectivity and lyrical sensitivity. *The
Last Tycoon* is a stylistic and moral achievement.

D34. Terp, Knud. "Tilbage til Tyverne [Back to the Twenties]." *Vaegtlos i
      Tiden* [*Weightless in Time*]. Copenhagen: Attika, 1975: 160-164.

In the 1920s, Hemingway and Fitzgerald discussed how to depict the young
generation. Fitzgerald suggested romantic but bittersweet disillusionment.
Hemingway added a hard-boiled edge to disguise injured innocence. The new

was praised because it was new. Never before had the spirit of the times been felt by so many. Like the new electrical communication, everything happened immediately, but people were cynical and nihilistic. The artists of the '20s were in harmony with the spirit of the age, not because they depicted the time's glamorous picture of themselves, but because they unmasked these pictures. Fitzgerald did it with irony, seeing the emptiness behind the display. *The Great Gatsby*, a most American novel, has become the national conception of the American dream, or Gatsby's interpretation of it. One sets one's standards and realizes oneself through money. The tragic ending is inevitable. Gatsby wants to live in the past; the book shows that man cannot. In the 20's, for the first time people began to feel global uncertainty, but also a sense of global possibilities. The decade is interesting for the future, but it is nothing to be nostalgic about.

BOOK REVIEWS/NEWS ARTICLES/RADIO PROGRAMS

D35. Blædel, Michael. "Forfatterbums i Hollywood [Bum Writer in Hollywood]." Rev. of *Pat Hobby, Hollywood*. *Berlingske Tidende* 22 Nov., 1988: n.p.

The stories are full of (black) humor, but they are also funny precisely at the point where the slapstick comedy and generosity meet. This is where a man like Pat Hobby, in spite of his mediocrity, can survive.

D36. Bodelsen, Anders. "Vent lidt [Wait Awhile]". Review of *Tilbage til Babylon [Babylon Revisited]*, by F. Scott Fitzgerald. Trans. Bendix Bech-Thostrup and Elise Norbo. Information (24 Nov. 1966).

It is a mystery that Fitzgerald never had a breakthrough in Denmark. Now it might happen. But the impatient are recommended to wait a little while. The three short stories Carit Andersen has published under the title *Tilbage til Babylon*, will be published next year in a two-volume edition of Fitzgerald's short stories. "May Day" (the only new translation) is an early story dealing with social conflict, and is uncharacteristic of this phase in his career. "The Rich Boy" contains the theme of *The Great Gatsby* in a concentrated form. "Babylon Revisited," maybe Fitzgerald's best short story, is from the time when the party was over and the hangovers set in: America during The Depression, Fitzgerald personally in decline.

D37. Bredsdorff, Thomas. "Det forpassede øjeblik [The Lost Moment]." Rev. of *Historier fra Jazztiden [Tales of the Jazz Age]*. *Politiken* 18 July 1998: n.p.

Bredsdorff discusses Fitzgerald's short stories particularly "May Day" which he thinks is the best. Fitzgerald is good at keeping a distance from his characters who have a hard exterior while still maintaining a softer side. The distance Fitzgerald has from his characters makes them clear to the reader.

D38. Frederiksen, Nils. "Forfatter frem i lyset [Revival of a Writer]." *Land Og Folk [Country and People]*. 29 Dec. 1976: n.p.

For a long time, Fitzgerald's literary production eluded an "objective," critical valuation, because there was a tendency to judge the authorship, solely in the light of his own destiny, which was as colorful and dramatic as one of the characters in his stories and novels. During the last dozen years, however, his writing has become the subject of a continuously growing interest, and he is today considered a classic, one of modern American literature's central writers, and greatest writers of prose. Fitzgerald was in many ways a sensitive and naïve romantic, but at the same time he was an extremely sharp and precise observer of his time, and his books contain a clear-sighted exposure of a civilization that destroys human values like helpfulness, goodness, faithfulness and honesty, qualities that Fitzgerald himself possessed in large scale. Fitzgerald wrote a brilliant, fluent and unforced prose. His books are still fresh and worth reading.

D39. Hellmann, Helle. "Bliv ikke til mandag . . . [Don't Stay Until Morning]." Rev. of *Invented Lives*, by James R. Mellow. *Politiken* 15 Sep. 1985: 8.

Zelda and Scott are portrayed as charming, crazy and appalling especially Fitzgerald, who always staggered around drunk. These two people kept each other as hostages and once this was realized it was too late. Fitzgerald's characters' lives are analogous to his and Zelda's own lives.

D40. Henriksen, Michael Bach. "Gatsbys grønne lys [Gatsby's Green Light]." *Kristeligt Dagblad [The Christian Newspaper]* 31 May 1996: n.p.

There is probably no better novel to start off the promises of summer with than Fitzgerald's 1925 classic *The Great Gatsby*: the story of millionaire Jay Gatsby's impossible love for Daisy, his early love, set in the American roaring '20s is still matchless and moving. The novel is clear in its form and general in its content. Its fine poetic language catches the atmosphere and intensity of an era and at the same time points far ahead. *The Great Gatsby* is one of this century's greatest American love stories.

D41. Holbek, Michael. "Champagnebrus [Sparkling Champagne]." Rev. of *Historier fra Jazztiden [Tales of the Jazz Age]* by F.S. Fitzgerald. Ed.

and trans. by Hans Hertel (Aschehoug, 1998). Ekstrabladet (24 June 1998).

The unsurpassed feature writer of the Jazz Age was far better than Hemingway, who undeservedly overshadowed him. This collection contains the best stories from two previously published editions of short stories and covers Fitzgerald's rise in the '20s and fall in the '30s. His short stories are both antiquated and modern at the same time. The environments and characters belong to a world that is gone, but their moral dilemmas are still absolutely relevant.

D42.   Jaurnow, Leon. "Scotts bekendelser [Scott's Confessions]." *Politiken* 15 Sep. 1996: 4-5.

In 1935, Fitzgerald was 39 years old, he was an alcoholic, financially ruined, with not insignificant psychiatric problems. In a small hotel room in North Carolina he took stock of his life, resulting in the essays known as "The Crack-Up," published in *Esquire* in the spring of 1936. Hemingway thought that Fitzgerald needed to be hurt to be able to write, and there is no doubt that Fitzgerald was severely hurt. As Hemingway also thought, however, Fitzgerald is only able to contemplate and play with his wounds in his "Crack-Up" essays. He confesses the details of his breakdown, but the deeper reasons remain undisclosed. His alcoholism, his sense of guilt towards Zelda, the dissolution of his family, are not mentioned. It might therefore be more correct to claim that Fitzgerald's confessions in "The Crack-Up" consist mainly in what he does not confess. He was so deeply rooted in his past success, that he could not free himself from it, no matter how necessary it might be for his well-being. It would have meant a total destruction of his identity; therefore he could not confess anything.

D43.   Jensen, Bo Green. "En form for episk storhed. Om F. Scott Fitzgerald. [Rev. of Some Sort of Epic Grandeur: About F. Scott Fitzgerald.]" *Afstandens indsigt. Essays om litteratur 1980-1984. Portraetter og praesentationer. [The Insight of Distance. Portraits and Presentations, Essays About Literature, 1980-84.]* Copenhagen: Borgen, 1985: 94-96.

In *Some Sort of Epic Grandeur*, Matthew J. Bruccoli sums up 30 years of Fitzgerald research, his own and others—including the two most recent biographies: Arthur Mizener's *The Far Side of Paradise* (1951), and Andrew Turnbull's *Scott Fitzgerald* (1962)—in a well-written and well-documented book of 600 pages. There has been a deluge of Fitzgerald materials in recent years: memoirs, photo albums, letters, notebooks. In any book about that period Fitzgerald's name is almost always mentioned. Bruccoli has immersed himself in Fitzgerald anecdotes and half-truths, particularly *Scott and Ernest* (1978), about the relationship between Hemingway and Fitzgerald and a good addition to the tower of books about Fitzgerald. Here Bruccoli deals with nothing new, but gathers together so much of the known material that this biography must be considered definitive. The last 100 pages contain an appendix, notes, bibliography, and brilliant gloss of Bruccoli's own writings on Fitzgerald. Bruccoli destroys many of the myths about Fitzgerald, showing that Fitzgerald is a legend despite everything.

D44. Jensen, Jesper Uhrup. "Tyvernes største Tømmermænd [The Biggest Hangovers of the Twenties]." Rev. of *Historier fra Jazztiden* [*Tales of the Jazz Age*] by F.S. Fitzgerald. Ed. and trans. by Hans Hertel (Aschehoug, 1998). *Euroman* (Sep. 1998): n.p.

While Fitzgerald was never able to repeat his early success, he is emblematic of the 1920s and *Tender Is the Night* is the best example of this. Like his friend and colleague Hemingway, Fitzgerald's strength lay in the short form.

D45. Kjølbye, Marie-Louise. "*Stemmen fra jazztiden* [*The Voice from the Jazz Age*]." Review of *Historier fra jazztiden* [*Tales of the Jazz Age*], by F. Scott Fitzgerald. *Information* 15 July 1998: n.p.

Stories like these later short stories show what can come out of a comet-like fiery life—that is, recognition.

D46. Levine, Paul. "Scott Fitzgerald: Som et møl flagrede han om de riges lys . . . Stakkels fyr [Scott Fitzgerald—As a Moth He Fluttered Around the Light (or Candle) of Rich People . . . Poor Guy]." Rev. of *Scott Fitzgerald*, by Jeffrey Meyers. *Weekendavisen* 25 July, 1997: n.p.

Scott's relationship to money is perpetuated through his relationship to Zelda after she breaks off her engagement with him, as it doesn't look like her expectations of him becoming rich will be realized. Although this problem is perpetuated through their relationship, the roots of this insecurity, the reader later finds out, run much deeper. "The goal of all biographies of Fitzgerald have been to separate the myth from the real man. . . . What can Meyers add to our understanding of the author who personified and brought about myths about the twenties?" Meyers's explanation of Scott and Zelda's attraction to each other is convincing. Meyers paints a darker picture of Fitzgerald's life than previous authors have done. He emphasizes Fitzgerald's drinking, Zelda's madness, the problems in their sex life and Scott's love affair before Zelda's madness. "The outcome is a character with less magic than Jay Gatsby and more doomed to failure than Edgar Allan Poe." Meyers makes a direct analogy between Fitzgerald's and Poe's hypoglycemia and their addiction to alcohol. Fitzgerald's and Hemingway's relationship he treats as a binary. That is, when Fitzgerald is up, then Hemingway is down and vice versa. The review ends with a quote from Hemingway that Scott was a better author at the end of his life in spite of his drinking problem.

D47. Michaëlis, Bo Tao. "Hollywoods rekviem: Vellykket filmatisering af F. Scott Fitzgeralds roman *The Last Tycoon* [Hollywood Requiem: Successful Screen Version of F. Scott Fitzgerald's Novel *The Last Tycoon*]." *Politiken* 19 Apr., 1998: n.p.

When Fitzgerald came to Hollywood in the middle of the 30's as a poor divorced alcoholic, he came to work his way out of an enormous debt, so that he could afford to keep his insane wife Zelda in an expensive mental hospital. He was not successful as a script writer, but his meeting with Irving Thalberg in Hollywood during the Depression inspired him to write his splendid novel, which unfortunately was unfinished because Fitzgerald died in 1940 of the damages caused by a long life of drinking. Kazan made his masterly movie in 1976, a film that both captures all of Fitzgerald's elegiac aura of wasted chances and at the same time is a disillusioned portrait of what later has been called the golden age of Hollywood. Typically for Fitzgerald and Kazan, the naïve American dream became a realistic nightmare long ago. The film is a masterpiece, one of the best adaptations for the screen made from an American literary masterpiece.

D48. Michaëlis, Bo Tao. "F. Scott Fitzgeralds bedste bog listede ud på markedet [F. Scott Fitzgerald's Greatest Novel Emerges on the Market]." Sommerlæsning [Summerreading]. Litterært ukorrekt [Literary Incorrect]. *Politiken* 3 July 1996: 4.

Fitzgerald is internationally famous for his 1925 novel *The Great Gatsby,* which has secured him a place in literary history. However, *Gatsby* is not nearly as good a book as his following novel, *Tender Is the Night,* which snuck into the book market ten years later. Fitzgerald's life had taken a dramatic turn since the '20s: too many drinks, and too many empty short stories to pay for bar bills and his wife Zelda's hospitalization. Many found the book disappointing because it showed no sign of political involvement or social realism. *Tender Is the Night* is a well-written, melancholy, and labyrinthine love story concerning the willing spirit and the weak flesh. *Tender Is the Night* is written by a mature Fitzgerald whose poetic-realistic tone is unique. It is one of the best novels of the 30's.

D49. Mohn, Bent. "Dansen der blev afbrudt [The Interrupted Dance]." Review of *Historier fra Jazztiden* [*Tales of the Jazz Age*] and *En forfatters eftermiddag* [*Afternoon of an Author*], by F. Scott Fitzgerald.

Trans. Hans Hertel. *Politiken* 25 Nov. 1967: n.p.

Fitzgerald's books from the '20s contain a mixture of romance, sharp cool wit and an atmosphere of disaster. There is a lot of drinking to keep reality away. The dream is to stay young in an everlasting dance. Fitzgerald was a great observer and artist, but especially unsurpassed when it comes to combining tenderness and humor, sadness and gaiety. When his art is best it can remind you of the art of Mozart. The abundance, the sweetness and the purity, and behind all this, immense awareness of the deepest and heaviest sorrow in the world. This large selection of stories is a real event. It contains minor things, but it is first of all exciting, cheerful and moving reading. The dance of life was interrupted, but Fitzgerald remained a great writer to the end.

D50. Monty, Ib. "Hidtil uoversatte noveller af Francis Scott Fitzgerald [Short Stories of Francis Scott Fitzgerald Translated Thus Far]." Rev. of *Pat Hobby, Hollywood*. *Jyllandsposten* 25 Oct. 1988: n.p.

The short stories should be read in separate sittings as it becomes monotonous to read that many stories about a guy who does everything wrong in one sitting.

D51. Petersen, Niels V. "Den Amerikanske Drøm [The American Dream]." Rev. of *Historier fra Jazztiden* [*Tales of the Jazz Age*] by F.S. Fitzgerald. Ed. and trans. by Hans Hertel. Aschehoug, 1998. *Vendsyssel Tidende* (4 July 1998): n.p.

It is ironic that the stories of Fitzgerald's short life and his impressive oeuvre are both stories of the fulfillment of the American dream and of its collapse. *This Side of Paradise* made the young middleclass midwesterner a wealthy literary star. However, contemporaneous with the social and economic depression of the 1930s, Fitzgerald became involved in scandals and was unable to write. In spite of elements indicative of the time, Fitzgerald's work still seems immune to fashionable literary ideas.

D52. Ruppert, Holger. "Klassikere frem i lyset [Reappearance of Classics]." Rev. of *Den store Gatsby* [*The Great Gatsby*] by F.S. Fitzgerald, trans. by Ove Brusendorff (Gyldendal, 1998), and *Historier fra Jazztiden* [*Tales of the Jazz Age*] by F.S. Fitzgerald, ed. and trans. by Hans Hertel (Aschehoug, 1998). *B.T.* (28 June 1998).

The renewed interest in Raymond Chandler and F.S. Fitzgerald in Denmark is due to new reissues of their work. *Tales of the Jazz Age* gives one an even better impression of the scope of Fitzgerald's writing than *The Great Gatsby*.

D53.   Sveistrup, Søren. "Et stormfuldt venskab [A Stormy Friendship]."
       Samvirke March 1996: 96-99. Rpt from *Scott og Ernest. Kristeligt
       Dagblad [The Christian Newspaper]* (5 July 1995).

The most famous friendship in American literary history is that between
Fitzgerald and Hemingway, and it is at the same time the story of the American
dream. As modern writers, both helped lift the US out of the shadow of
European literature, but their personal relationship has attracted almost as much
interest as their books. Both wrote bestselling novels, several of which later
became classic movies. When they met in Paris in 1925, Fitzgerald was the star
of American literature. Fitzgerald was proofreading Hemingway's first novel,
The Sun Also Rises, and admired his work. Ten years later their contact ceased
almost completely at a time when Fitzgerald was in personal and artistic decline,
while Hemingway was at the peak of his popularity. In 1940 Fitzgerald died,
completely forgotten, while working on *The Last Tycoon*, which should have
been his comeback. At the same time he witnessed Hemingway's biggest
success so far, *For Whom the Bell Tolls*, which sold 270,000 copies in one year.
The total sale of Fitzgerald's books this year was 21 copies.

D54.   Winding, Thomas. Review of *Tilbage til Babylon [Babylon Revisited]*,
       by F. Scott Fitzgerald. Bendix Bech-Thostrup and Elise Norsbo. *Aktuelt*
       23 Dec. 1966: n.p.

Fitzgerald's renaissance in the United States has not been easy to trace in
Denmark. *The Great Gatsby* is available in paperback and now three of
Fitzgerald's short stories have been published. Fitzgerald has returned because
he, with all of his style and all of his grace, was a knowledgeable man, who was
talented and precisely described something he knew. He lost his illusions early
and first acted like a spoiled child who doesn't get what it wants, but later fought
to accept life as it is. There is something heroic in this attitude, but it also
expresses his view that life is decided by destiny. Considering the amount of
uninteresting literature that is translated and published, you wonder why so
many of Fitzgerald's short stories haven't been translated.

TEACHER/STUDENT GUIDES AND EDITIONS

D55.   Fitzgerald, F. Scott. *The Great Gatsby*. Ed. Hanne Bitsche Hansen.
       Copenhagen: Grafisk Forlag, 1992. "Graduated reading exercises for
       students of English"

D56. Fitzgerald, F. Scott. *Babylon Revisited and Other Stories*. Copenhagen:
       Munksgaard, 1965.

Russia, Ukraine and Other Countries of the Former USSR

In the former Soviet Union as in other European countries, Fitzgerald was more or less unknown until 1957 when *Literaturnaya Gazyeta* published an article by the American writer James Aldridge in which he broods over the fate of young people in the West. In his article, Aldridge mentioned Fitzgerald's name for the first time in the USSR mass media in the context of expressing his sorrow in connection with the untimely deaths of some other prominent writers, Jack Kerouac and Vladimir Mayakovskiy. Aldridge's point was that a whole generation had been lost. "Their youth is obliterated by the severe demands put upon them by the epoch, and maturity preposterously eludes them in the struggle for existence, while instead they should be experiencing all the joys of artistic perception and the creation of life" (Ru27).

A year later, in 1958, the first translation of a Fitzgerald story occurred when "May Day" appeared in *Amerikanskaya Novella* (*American Short Stories*), translated by T. Ozyorskaya and published in Moscow by Hudozhestvennaya Literatura. As Svetlana Voitiuk, an Americanist at the University of L'viv, in Kiev, Ukraine, commented at the First International Fitzgerald Conference at Hofstra University in 1992, "The choice was quite justified for it is one of the most socially pragmatic stories by Fitzgerald, beginning from its very title, as for years May 1 was one of the greatest holidays in the USSR, celebrating the solidarity and fraternity of the working people all over the world" (Ru61).

Despite the publication of "May Day" and a thoughtful article on Fitzgerald in *Voprosy literatury* in 1956 by M. Mendelson, who concentrates on Fitzgerald's double values in both admiring the wealthy and criticizing bourgeois society (Ru48), Russian critics early classified Fitzgerald as a "bourgeois aesthete" who was "unworthy of Soviet attention" (Deming Brown, 1962, 31). Ernest Hemingway, on the other hand, as in the rest of Europe, was widely received along with, understandably, the more proletarian American writers.

In the 1960s and early 1970s, Fitzgerald's reputation in the USSR began to improve. In 1960, *Voprosy Literatury* published "The Tragedy of an American Writer," by Michael Landor, a major USSR critic, in which he reviews Fitzgerald's literary career and activities in the context of the 'lost generation' period in American literature (Ru46). Writing five years later in 1965, Landor comments on the growing interest of critics, translators, and readers in Fitzgerald's work (Ru44) and discusses Dostoevsky as Fitzgerald's greatest role model (Ru45).

In 1965, the same year as Landor wrote his articles, Hudozhestvennaya Literatura presented readers in the USSR with Evgenia Kalashnikova's translation of *The Great Gatsby* and six years later, in 1971, Kalashnikova's translation of *Tender Is the Night.* Landor offers a glowing commentary on Kalashnikova's work: "(Her) translation conveys the many levels of style . . . — from parody of the society pages to dark visions in the spirit of el Greco. The Russian text preserves the novel's poetry, and this required inventiveness as well as imagination and great sensitivity to words" (Ru45 xiv-xv). As Carl Proffer confirms, "In Russia translating was an extremely well-regarded and highly-paid profession, with many Russian writers and poets doing the translating, and Evgenia Kalashnikova is a major Russian translator" (Proffer,1972, xiv).

Landor's work was soon followed by a number of other articles between 1965 and 1974, including those by A. N. Gorbunov, I. N. Zasurskiy, and A. I. Startsev, all of whom reflect the Communist view of American society but are sympathetic to Fitzgerald's work. In his 1974 book, *The Novels of F. Scott Fitzgerald*, which is basically an introduction to Fitzgerald's life and works, Gorbunov declares that the writer was not a capitalist despite his ambivalence about the rich (Ru33), a theme that Startsev pursues in his articles "Fitzgerald's Bitter Fate" (Ru54) and "Scott Fitzgerald and the 'Very Rich'" (Ru56, Ru57). Startsev's work appeared in *Inostrannaia literatura* or *Foreign Literature,* which, according to Proffer, was "the most important periodical for the publication of all non-Russian literature in the Soviet Union" (Proffer, 1972, xv). Zasurskiy, like Gorbunov and Startsev, stresses Fitzgerald's reading of Marx whose influence he sees evident in "May Day" and "A Diamond as Big as the Ritz" and in the novels (Ru63).

Fitzgerald's reputation in the USSR was solidified in 1977 when *Inostrannaya Literatura* published *The Last Tycoon,* translated by O. Soroka, and Hudozhestvennaya Literatura published *Francis Scott Fitzgerald. Selected Works in Three Volumes,* by various Russian translators, including Kalashnikova. Volume I includes *This Side of Paradise* and *The Great Gatsby;* Volume II, *Tender Is the Night* and *The Last Tycoon*; and short stories and essays are collected in Volume III. Of Fitzgerald's novels, only *The Beautiful and Damned* remains to be translated; while Kolesnikova quotes in Russian from the novel in her "F. Scott Fitzgerald's Novel *The Beautiful and Damned,*" no bibliography lists her as actually having translated the entire novel (Voitiuk e-mail to author 1998). In addition to "May Day" other short stories included those in *The Price Was High:* "Return to Babylon," "The Family in the Wind," "Outside the Cabinet Maker's," "Presumption," "Myra Meets His Family, and "The Rich Boy." In 1984, *The Vegetable* appeared.

Also, in the late 1970s and 1980s, several additional scholarly works were published on Fitzgerald by N. B. Kolesnikova, N. A. Anastasiev, and A. Zverev. In "The 'American Tragedy' of the Talented and Intelligent in the USA," Kolesnikova writes that young talent is often destroyed by the powerful in America and that *Tender Is the Night* addresses this problem (Ru35). Anastasiev believes Fitzgerald's views on society often seem mutually exclusive and describes him as a romantic humanist (Ru29). In his Introduction to the three-volume Hudozhestvennaya Literatura collection of Fitzgerald's work, Zverev repeats the point of view that he expresses in several other articles which is that Fitzgerald was intricately linked to his age and that his tragedy and that of his characters was therefore inevitable (Ru65). Two of the latest pieces of literary criticism of Fitzgerald's prose is Zverev's introduction to the 1989 Pravda edition of *The Great Gatsby* (Ru67) and his afterword to the 1990 Pravda translation of *The Last Tycoon* (Ru68).

Several theses and dissertations on his work appeared between 1971 and 1983: Belchuk's and Kolegayeva's theses for the *kandidat nauk* in philology and Kolesnikova's, Kuhalashvili's, Lidskii's dissertations for the *doctor nauk*. As Voitiuk explains, "*Kandidat nauk* is an academic degree hierarchically corresponding to your Ph.D. but in this country one can still defend after it a dissertation for *doktor nauk*, which in translation means Ph.D" (Voitiuk, 9 Sept. 1999).

The first translation of F. Scott Fitzgerald's novels into Ukrainian appeared in 1975 when M. Pinchevskiy translated *Tender Is the Night* for Dnipro in Kiev. Seven years later, Pinchevskiy also translated *The Great Gatsby*. Beginning in 1989, just a few years after Mikhail Gorbachev declared *glasnost* in 1986 and continuing after the collapse of the Soviet Union in 1991, various publishers in the former Soviet states, including Ukraine, began publishing collections of Fitzgerald's work, for the most part using the translations of the three-volume Russian edition. As Voitiuk said, "Based on the bibliographical data of the L'viv State University Scientific Library, the republication of Fitzgerald's prose in Russian translations (irrespective of publishing company) falls in the years 1989-1990, and we can make the modest assumption that the number of Fitzgerald's novels and short stories published in these years stands to prove his popularity among readers" (Ru61).

Voitiuk claimed that when it comes to Fitzgerald's Russian or Ukrainian reputation, one cannot speak of translation only, for the publication of his works in the original English was always quite an event for the scholars of the English language and American literature. She asserted that "In my mind's eye, I see my fellow students and myself back in 1979 when in the fifth year of studies in the

English Department of the L'viv State University Foreign Language Faculty, we were reading Fitzgerald's short stories, which had just been published, for our classes in homereading and enjoying the psychologically-elaborated coloring of his narrative style" (Ru61).

Contrary to the pattern in other countries, Russian scholarship on Fitzgerald appears to wane if not actually to cease after 1992, the year Mochnachiova wrote an article on "Transformation of the Canon of the Keenly Plotted Short Story in the Works by F. Scott Fitzgerald" for *Literaturniy Protsess* (Ru49). While the title suggests increasing sophistication in Russian literary criticism, the early 1990s also mark the beginning of what Gayatri Spivak terms the "new postcoloniality" of the states of the former USSR (Spivak, 2003, 84). As a result of this need to recreate economic and social structures, the mid 1990s saw a dramatic increase in American Studies programs in the universities of the former states as scholars sought models for or reflections of their new societies. While the founders of American Studies in America were mostly historians, sociologists, and political scientists, the attempt to institutionalize the study of the United States in Europe has been most successful in the area of literature. Yet, the countries of the former Soviet bloc have been most interested in American social and economic systems. Svetlana Voitiuk concurs that the citizens of these countries, including literary scholars, have turned from literary concerns to national and economic problems in the last decade (Voitiuk, 9 Sept. 1999). As Tatiana Zemba, of Moldova's American Studies Center, explains in an article on "American Studies as a Global Academic Enterprise,"

> A survey of international dimensions of American studies, or Amerikanistik as it is termed also, will help us to define the place and tasks of our country. . . . In our attempts to study America and to teach the younger generation we have to know about experience and achievements in other countries, which have understood long ago that increased knowledge and understanding is an essential ingredient for successful relations among people and nations. By examining each others' cultures, American studies scholars and their students outside the U. S. see their own countries anew. For as we study another culture, we are also looking at ourselves" (IATP 6/22/2000).

Zemba also addresses the issue of American literary scholarship focusing narrowly "on something, on a theme" as opposed to the current broad sweep of literary criticism in the former Russian states, further emphasizing why the production of literary scholarship in the states of the former USSR has taken a different turn:

> We can't allow ourselves such leisure. Time and circumstances have forced us to become 'universal.' So we try to study and teach something on everything. All of us are preoccupied with the idea of making our work more effective, to widen spheres of application of American experience in Moldova and possibilities of utilizing it for improving education and the general situation in our country (Zemba, 22 June 2000, 7).

Currently, literary work is being conducted in three areas: "Ethnic cultures and literatures of the USA," "Woman in American Culture" and fantasy and science fiction as evidenced in the literary and artistic journal *Sverhnovaya* [*Fantasy & Science Fiction*] (Zemba, 4, 6). The role of the first two approaches to literature in the former states of the USSR faced with the need to create a new society can be fairly well established. How the study of Fitzgerald might play a part in their future culture can perhaps be seen in the fact of a recent Fulbright application seeking to study Fitzgerald's insights on how youth can survive in a rapidly changing society (Voitiuk, Sept. 2000).

Dana Heller, of Old Dominion University, based on a recent experience teaching at Moscow State University, writes that "comprehending the place of American Studies programs in such a rapidly changing context requires critical tools sensitive to Bourdieu's notion of the relative autonomy of cultural forms and capable of insisting upon an expansion of that notion that would take up, in all respects, questions of convertibility and translatability of symbolic capital across boundaries of nation states" (Heller, 25 May 2003, 5). Heller anticipates that the Amerikanistiks of these former Soviet states may heed the call by Jane C. Desmond and Virginia R. Dominguez for a "resituation" of American Studies as an academic site that "truly decenters U. S. scholarship while challenging it with new formulations, new questions, and new critiques" (Desmond and Domingues, Sept. 1996, 485).

That the reading of Fitzgerald from an American Studies approach, singly or in conjunction with other writers, might in the crucible of the societies of the former USSR result in a decentering of American scholarship is a possible outcome greatly to be anticipated.

REFERENCES

Baghirov, Husein. "Rethinking Education: The Birth of Western University." *Azerbaijan International 9.4* (Winter 2001), Online posting, 24 May 2003 <http://www.azer.com/aiweb/categories/magazine/94_folder/94_articles/94 _husein_baghirov.html5/24/03.

Brown, Deming. *Soviet Attitudes Toward American Writing*. Princeton: Princeton UP, 1962.

Desmond, Jane C., and Virginia R. Dominguez. "Resituating American Studies in a Critical Internationalism." *American Quarterly* 48.3 (Sept. 1996): 485.

Heller, Dana. "From *Dr. Zhivago* to the *Barber of Siberia*: Or, How I Stopped Worrying and Learned to Love Internationalization." *Towards an Internationalization of American Studies—The State of American Studies in*

Post-Cold War Europe, Online posting, 23 May 2003
http://epsilon3.georgetown.edu/~coventrm/asa2000/panel2/heller.html.

Proffer, Carl R. ed. *Soviet Criticism of American Literature in the Sixties.* Ann
Arbor: Ardis, 1972.

Spivak, Gayatri Chakravorty. *Death of a Discipline.* NY: Columbia UP, 2003.

Voitiuk, Svetlana. E-mail to the author. 9 Sept. 1999.

---. Fullbright application, Sept. 2000.

Zemba, Tatiana. *American Studies as a Global Academic Enterprise.* Online
posting, 22 June 2000. http://www.iatp. . . . /Tatiana_Zemba-
American_Studies_as_a_ Global_Academic_Enterprise. html.

Parenthetical citations to entry numbers refer to annotated references in this
chapter.

TRANSLATIONS/EDITIONS

Russia

Ru1.   Fitzgerald, F. Scott. "Pervoye Maya [May Day]." *Amerikanskaya
        Novella [American Short Stories]* . Vol. 2. Trans. T. Ozyorskaya.
        Moscow: Hudozhestvennaya Literatura, 1958. 256-307.

Ru2.   Fitzgerald, F. Scott. *Velikiy Getsbi [The Great Gatsby].* Trans. E.
        Kalashnikova. Moscow: Hudozhestvennaya Literatura, 1965, 1966. 180.

Ru3.   Fitzgerald, F. Scott. *Vozvrashcheniye v Vavilon, Rasskazy [Return to
        Babylon and Other Stories].* Trans. Ekaterina Vasilieva. Moscow:
        Pravda, 1969. 48.

Ru4.   Fitzgerald, F. Scott. *Notch Niezhna [Tender Is the Night].* Trans. E.
        Kalashnikova. Moscow: Hudozhestvennaya Literatura, 1971. 384;
        Moscow: Raduga, 1983. 395; Leningrad: Lenizdat, 1983. 334;

Leningrad: Otd., 1989. 237; Leningrad: Iskusstvo, 1989. 288.

Ru5.   F. Scott Fitzgerald. *Izbranniye Proizvedeniya v 3-h Tomah* [*Francis Scott Fitzgerald: Selected Works in Three Volumes*]. Ed. A. Zverev. Moscow: Hudozhestvennaya Literatura, 1977, 1984.

Ru6.   Fitzgerald, F. Scott. *Po Tu Storonu Raya, Velikij Getsbi* [*This Side of Paradise, The Great Gatsby*] *Izbranniye Proizvedeniya v 3-h Tomah* [*Francis Scott Fitzgerald. Selected Works in Three Volumes*]. Vol. 1. Trans. M. Loriye and E. Kalashnikova. Ed. A. Zverev. Moscow: Hudozestvennaya Literatura, 1977. 439; 1984. 445. Irkutsk: Vostochno-Sibirskoye Krizhnoye Izdatelstvo, 1987. 384.

Ru7.   Fitzgerald, F. Scott. *Notch Niezhna, Posledniy Tayfoon* [*Tender Is the Night, The Last Tycoon*]. *Izbranniye Proizvedeniya v 3-h Tomah* [*Francis Scott Fitzgerald: Selected Works in Three Volumes*]. Vol. 2. Trans. E. Kalashnikova and O. Soroka. Ed. A. Zverev. Moscow: Hudozhestvennaya Literatura, 1977. 487; 1984. 493.

Ru8.   Fitzgerald, F. Scott. *Novelly, Esse* [*Short Stories, Essays*]. *Izbranniye Proizvedeniya v 3-h Tomah* [*Francis Scott Fitzgerald: Selected Works in Three Volumes*]. Vol. 3. Ed. A. Zverev. Moscow: Hudozestvennaya Literatura, 1977. 431; 1984. 461.

Ru9.   Fitzgerald, F. Scott. *Selected Short Stories*. Moscow: Progress, 1979. 357.

Ru10. Fitzgerald, F. Scott. *The Great Gatsby*. Moscow: Vissaya Shkola, 1984. 144.

Ru11. Fitzgerald, F. Scott. *Portret v Dokumentah* [*A Portrait in Prose*]. Trans. A Zverev. Moscow: Progress, 1984. 344.

Ru12. Fitzgerald, F. Scott. *Razmaznya* [*The Vegetable*]. Trans. V. Kharitonov and R. Cherny. *Teatr* 9 (1984): 163-91.

Ru13. Fitzgerald, F. Scott. *Tender Is the Night*. Magadan, 1984. 364.

Ru14. Fitzgerald, F. Scott. *Velikij Getsbi, Notch Nyezhna, Rasskazy* [*The Great Gatsby, Tender Is the Night, Short Stories*]. Trans. E. Kalashnikova. Moscow: Hudozhestvennaya Literatura, 1985. 703; Moscow: Izdatelstvo Pravda, 1989. 509; Tomsk: Isdatelstvo Tomskogo Universiteta, 1990. 491; Moskva: Sovetskiy Pisatel, 1992. 445.

Ru15. Fitzgerald, F. Scott. *Velikij Getsbi, Rasskazy* [*The Great Gatsby, Short Stories*]. Trans. E.Kalashnikova. Moscow: Hudozhestvennaya Literatura, 1990. 333.

Ru16. Fitzgerald, F. Scott. *Velikij Getsbi* [*The Great Gatsby*], *Posledniy Tayfoon* [*The Last Tycoon*], *Short Stories*. Trans. E.Kalashnikova and O. Soroka. Moscow: Hudozhestvennaya Literatura, 1990. 335.

Ru17. Fitzgerald, F. Scott. *Posledniy Magnat, Rasskazy, Esse* [*The Last Tycoon, Short Stories, Essays*]. Trans. O. Soroka., A. Zverev, and others. Moscow: Pravda, 1990, 1991. 511.

Armenia

Ru18. Fitzgerald, F. Scott. *Velikiy Getsbi, Posledniy Magnat, Novelly* [*The Great Gatsby, The Last Tycoon, Short Stories*]. Trans. E. Kalashnikova, O. Soroka, and others. Yerevan: Iuys, 1990. 415.

Belarus

Ru19. Fitzgerald, F. Scott. *Velikiy Gatsgy, Notch Niezhna Rasskazy* [*The Great Gatsby, Tender Is the Night, Short Stories*]. Trans. E. Kalashnikova. Minsk: Mastats. Lit., 1989. 687.

Dagestan

Ru20. Fitzgerald, F. Scott. *Velikiy Getsbi. Notch Niezhna. Rasskazy* [*The Great Gatsby, Tender Is the Night, Short Stories*]. Trans.E. Kalashnikova. Mahachkala: Dagestan Knizhnoye Izdatelstvo, 1990. 670.

Kyrghystan

Ru21. Fitzgerald, F. Scott. *Veloikiy Getsbi. Notch Niezhna. Rasskazy* [*The Great Gatsby, Tender Is the Night, Short Stories*]. Trans. E. Kalashnikova and others. Frunze: Adabiyat, 1989. 668.

Republic of Moldova

Ru22. Fitzgerald, F. Scott. *Velikij Getsbi, Notch Nyezhna,* [*The Great Gatsby, Tender Is the Night, Short Stories, Essays*]. Trans. E. Kalashnikova and others. Kishinev: Literatura Artistike, 1981. 655.

Ukraine

Ru23. Fitzgerald, F. Scott. *Neetch Lahidna* [*Tender Is the Night*]. Trans. M. Pinchevskiy. Kiev: Vyd-vo 'Dnipro,' 1971, 1975, 1982. 335.

Ru24. Fitzgerald, F. Scott. *Velikiy Getsbi, Neetch Lahidna* [*The Great Gatsby, Tender Is the Night*]. Trans. M. Pinchevskiy. Kiev: Vyd-vo Dnipro, 1982. 472; Kiev: Vishcha Shkola, 1990. 495.

BOOKS: FULL-LENGTH STUDIES AND COLLECTIONS

Ru25. Gorbunov, Andrei Nikolaevich. *Romany Frensisa Skotta Fitsdzheralda* [*The Novels of Francis Scott Fitzgerald*]. Moscow: Nauka, 1974, 151 pp. Trans. Margarita Vulikh.

In a basically introductory work, Gorbunov describes Fitzgerald as one of the most important American writers of his time, along with Faulkner, Wolfe, Anderson, Dreiser, and Sinclair Lewis. Fitzgerald was an intelligent person, an important personality, a good writer, and a great judge of human behavior. Gorbunov gives a detailed biography and plot summaries of his novels. He develops his analyses from the perspective that Fitzgerald is describing himself and his own life in all his works. While Fitzgerald was ambivalent about the rich, he was not a "nasty capitalist" but rather a "great humanitarian educated in the democratic tradition of the United States with its love for wealth and money." Fitzgerald even tried to sympathize with Marx but in the end was unable to understand him.

Russian Editions of American Studies and Collections

Ru26. Turnbull, Andrew. *Scott Fitzgerald*. Trans. E. and G. Loginova. Moscow: Molodaya Gvardiya, 1981.

ESSAYS/CHAPTERS/NOTES/CONFERENCE PAPERS

Ru27. Aldridge, James. "Razdumja o Sud'bah Molodiozhy na Zapadie [Meditation on Youthful Fortune Ensnared]." *Literaturnaya Gazeta* [*Literary Gazette*]. Organ Pravlenija Soyuza Pisatelej [Editoral Board, Writer's Union, SSSR]. 16 May 1957: 4.

Fitzgerald, like Jack London and Vladimir Mayakovsky, passed away in the prime of his career, embodying the tragic fate of young people in the West. The American writers of the 1920s were indeed the "lost generation," subject to tragedies that are characteristic of all artistic personalities.

Ru28. Anastasiev, N. A. "Gibel Miechty, ili Uroki Skotta Fitzgeral'da [The Failure of a Dream or the Lessons of Scott Fitzgerald]." *Literaturnaya Gazeta* [*Literary Gazette*]. Organ Pravlenija Soyuza Pisatelej, SSSR [Editoral Board, Writer's Union, SSSR]. 13 Dec 1978: 15.

Fitzgerald's creative work is of great importance for the development of American and world literature.

Ru29. Anastasiev, N. A. Introduction. "Po Obie Storony Raya [This Side of Paradise]." *Notch Nyezhna* [*Tender Is the Night*]. Moscow: Raduga, 1983. 7-28.

Fitzgerald is a romantic humanist. In his work, his viewpoints on American society often seem mutually exclusive. He both seemingly admired the upper classes but also dwelt on the decay of personality among them, on their tragic loss of the most important human traits of character.

Ru30. Baturin, S. Introduction. "Fransis Scott Fitzgerald." *Velikij Getsbi, Notch Nyezhna, Rasskazy.* [*The Great Gatsby, Tender Is the Night, Short*

Stories]. Moscow: Hudozhestvennaya Literatura, 1985. 3-20; Minsk: Mastatskaya Lit, 1989.

Fitzgerald is the singer of the jazz age. He is a classic twentieth-century writer of American literature, a talented novelist who opened up for the reader many side of life in America during this period.

Ru31. Davidova, E. D. Afterword. "F. S. Fitzgeral'd i Kino [F.S. Fitzgerald and Cinema]." *Notch Niezhna [Tender Is the Night]*, by F. Scott Fitzgerald. E. Kalashnikova, trans. Leningrad: Iskusstvo, 1989. 287-288.

Tender Is the Night is Fitzgerald's masterpiece. Genuine fame came to Fitzgerald after his death, when the film of the novel was released. This edition will undoubtedly bring more readers into the already numerous circle of his true fans. The text is printed according to the "Izbranniye Proizvedeniya v 3-h tomax [Selected Works in 3 Volumes]" edition, Vol. 2, Moskva [Moscow], 1977.

Ru32. Denisova, T. N. "Estrangement According to Fitzgerald." *Existentialism and the Contemporary American Novel.* Kiev, 1985. 245.

Text unavailable for annotation.

Ru33. Gorbunov, Andrei Nikolaevich. "Romany Skotta Fitsdzheralda 20-X godov [Scott Fitzgerald's Novels of the Twenties]." *Vestnik Moskovskogo Universiteta* (Serija VII, filologija, Zurnalistika), XX, 2 (1965). 21-32.

This is a shorter, earlier version of Gorbunov's book on Fitzgerald.

Ru34. Iskhakov, V. "Fransis Scott Fitzgerald: Tsena Byla Vysoka Ural [Francis Scott Fitzgerald: The Price Was High] *Jezhemiesyachniy literaturno-hudozhestvenniy i publitsisticheskiy journal [Ural Monthly Literary-Artistic and Journalistic Magazine]* 6 (1993): 241-243. Ekaterinburg [Yekaterinburg].

These stories, here translated for the first time into Russian, were unknown to readers in the former Soviet Union. Fitzgerald paid a high price for his writings—he gave his own life.

Ru35. Kolesnikova, N. B. "'Amerikanskaya Tragediya' Talantivogo Intelligenta v SShA: 'Silniye Mira Sego' v Romanie F. Scotta Fitzgerl"da *Notch Niezhna* [The 'American Tragedy' of the Talented and Intelligent

in the U.S.A.: 'Their Powerful World' in F. Scott Fitzgerald's novel
Tender Is the Night]." *K Probleme Romantizma i Realizma v
Zarubezhnoy Literature Kontsa XIX-Nachala XX Vekov: Vyp.2* [*Problems
in Romanticism and Realism in 19ᵗʰ⁻ and Early 20ᵗʰ-Century Foreign
Literature*] Vol. 2. Moskva: Moskovskiy Gosudarstvenniy
Pedagogicheskiy Institut [Moscow: Moscow State Pedagogical Institute]:
1975. 150-160

The tragic death of an intelligent young person in the United States is a common
problem. Such talents are usually destroyed by "the powerful" who, controlling
wealth, destroy morality and the collective soul. *Tender Is the Night* is a
masterpiece that confronts this problem.

Ru36. Kolesnikova, N. B. "Nachalo Tvorcheskogo Puti F. Scotta Fitzgeralda
[The Beginning of F. Scott Fitzgerald's Literary Career]." Uchioniye
Zapiski Moskovskogo Oblastnogo Pedagogicheskogo Instituta imeni
N.K. Krupskoy [Teaching Notebooks of the N.K. Krupskoy Moscow
Regional Pedagogical Institute]. 175, 10 (1967): 175-194.

Tender Is the Night is Fitzgerald's masterpiece.

Ru37. Kolesnikova, N.B. "Roman F. Skotta Fitzgeral'da *'Prekrasniye i
Proklatiye'* [F. Scott Fitzgerald's Novel *The Beautiful and Damned*]."
Uchioniye Zapiski Moskovskogo Oblastnogo Pedagogicheskogo Instituta
Imeni N.K. Krupskoy [Teaching Notebooks of the N.K. Krupskoy
Moscow Regional Pedagogical Institute]. 175, 10 (1967): 205-218.

The Beautiful and Damned is a masterpiece.

Ru38. Kolesnikova, N. B. "Roman F. Scotta Fitzgeral'da 'Velikiy Gatsby' [F.
Scott Fitzgerald's Novel *The Great Gatsby*]." Uchionye Zapiski
Moskovskogo Oblastnogo Pedagogicheskogo Instituta imeni N.K.
Krupskoy [Teaching Notebooks of the N.K. Krupskoy Moscow Regional
Pedagogical Institute]. 220, 11 (1968): 139-51. Moskva [Moscow].

The plot, character development, and narrative style of *The Great Gatsby* are
unique.

Ru39. Koreneva, M. Foreword. "F. Scott Fitzgeral'da. Chekovek, Pisatel',
Sud'ba [F. Scott Fitzgerald: Man, Personality, Fate]." In *Scott
Fitzgerald*, by Andrew Turnbull. Trans. E. and G. Loginova. Moscow:
Molodaya Gvardiya [Moscow: Young Guard], 1981. 5-12.

Fitzgerald's personality determined his fate.

Ru40. Koreneva, M. "Predisloviye [Foreword]." *Selected Short Stories*, by F. Scott Fitzgerald. Moscow: Progress, 1979. 3-25.

The narrative style of Fitzgerald's short stories is peculiar.

Ru41. Kovalev, Yu. V. Afterword. "Fransis Scott Fitzgerald I ego roman *Notch Niezhna* [F. Scott Fitzgerald and His Novel *Tender Is the Night*]." *Notch Niezhna* [*Tender Is the Night*]. Leningrad: Lenizdat, 1983. 334. Leningrad Otd., 1989. 316-333.

This edition is published according to the "Izbranniye Proizvedeniya v 3-h tomah" [*Selected Works in 3 Volumes*]. Tom [Volum] 2. Moskva [Moscow]: Hudozhestvennaya Literatura [Belles-Lettres], 1977. Fitzgerald has made a bridge from the tradition of Romanticism and Humanism to the realistic achievements of contemporary prose.

Ru42. Kuhalashvili, V. Afterword. "F. Scott Fitzgerald ta Yoho Roman *Neetch Lahidna* [F. Scott Fitzgerald and His Novel *Tender Is the Night*]." Trans. M. Pinchevskiy. Kiev: Vyd-vo 'Dnipro,' 1971, 1975, 1982. 329-335.

This novel is Fitzgerald's masterpiece in which he showed the contradiction between the character of the artist and his dreams.

Ru43. Kuhalashvili, Volodymyr. "Romany F. S. Fitzgeral'da [The Novels of F. Scott Fitzgerald]." *Velikiy Getsbee, Neetch Laheedna* [*The Great Gatsby, Tender Is the Night*]. Kiev: Vyd-vo Dnipro, 1982. 465-471.

Fitzgerald's personal problems and those of his characters reflect the problems of America in the 1920s and 1930s.

Ru44. Landor, M. "F. Scott Fitzgerald Vozdelai Svoy Sobstvenniy Sad [F. Scott Fitzgerald Cultivated His Own Garden]." *Voprosy Literatury* [*Questions of Literature*], 2 (1965), 182-88.

Critics, translators and readers have been very interested in Ftizgerald's literary heritage.

Ru45. Landor, M. "Gift of Hope." *Novyi Mir* 10 (1965): 244-47. In Carl R. Proffer, ed. and trans., *Soviet Criticism of American Literature in the Sixties*. Ann Arbor: Ardis, 1972. 111-15.

"The story of the lonely and doomed dreamer turns into a novelistic plot quite naturally. . . . In the same figure we see national self-criticism and the poetry of the national character. . . . For all the freshness of Fitzgerald's gift, one senses his high literary culture; beyond the narrator-moralist's tone, one catches hints that the French and English have been read carefully. But Fitzgerald gave preference to the great Russian writer: I always liked Dostoevsky with his great appeal more than any other European, he wrote Hemingway. . . . And defending *The Great Gatsby* against the charge of being anecdotal, Fitzgerald observed that one could reduce *The Brothers Karamazov* to an anecdote too but it was important to keep a second level in mind."

Ru46. Landor, M. "Tragediia amerikanskogo pisatelia [The Tragedy of an American Writer]." *Voprosy Literatury* [*Questions of Literature*], 10 (1960): 224-30.

Fitzgerald was popular with the war-afflicted youth of the 1940s and '50s because, in Hemingway's words, he had "confused growing up with getting older." Arthur Mizener's biography *The Far Side of Paradise* draws a pessimistic picture, showing Fitzgerald's fate as a representative of Western man, although it does provide hitherto forgotten book reviews and unpublished memories. Fitzgerald's greatest role model was Dostoevsky. It is an irony of fate that after virtually none of Fitzgerald's works were published in the 1940s, the '50s saw a new rise in interest, and that now his late works are more appreciated than his early writing.

Ru47. Lidskiyi, Yu. Ya. "Frensis Skott Fitsdzherald." *Ocherki ob amerikanskikh pisateliakh XX veka* [*Essays on Twentieth Century American Writers*]. Kiev, 1968. 79-115.

This book contains some biography but mainly a detailed analysis of each novel. *The Great Gatsby* is one of the best American novels of the century because Fitzgerald's critical realism is at its height in this work in which he points out the terrible sides of the bourgeois world. Lidskii quotes from Turnbull that Fitzgerald wanted to do two incompatible things: become a good writer and make a lot of money. His desire for wealth weakened much of his writing. In his best work, he satirized the rich, but his ambivalence about them often caused him to soften his critical realism and ignore social problems.

Ru48. Mendelson, M. "'Vtoroe zrenie' Skotta Fitsdzheral'da [The 'Second Sight' of Scott Fitzgerald]." *Voprosy literatury* 3 (1956): 102-25.

This article concentrates on Fitzgerald's double values: wanting to be rich and influential like most Americans but at the same time, as a liberal, understanding his own mistakes. Fitzgerald's weakest works were written when he was describing his first side: his admiration for wealth. His strongest works reflect his other side: a critical attitude toward the bourgeois society. Fitzgerald even called himself "in essence a Marxist." Although he was not a Marxist, he showed sympathy with the left in many of his writings. His works sometimes lack truth, but nevertheless he is a remarkable social realist. He compares with Faulkner, Anderson, and Wolfe.

Ru49. Mochnachiova, O. V. "Transformation of the Canon of the Keenly Plotted Short Story in the Works by F. Scott Fitzgerald." *Literaturniy Protsess: Traditsii i Novatorstvo* 1992: 139-149.

Text not available for annotation.

Ru50. Mulyarchik, A. S. Foreword. "Novella v Literature SShA XX veka [The Short Story in Twentieth-Century American Literature]." *Amerikanskaya Novella XX Veka [The American Short Story in the Twentieth Century]*. Moskva [Moscow]: Hudozhestvennaya Literatura [Belles-Lettres]: 1976. 5-26.

This is the foreword to a collection of translated short stories by twentieth-century American short story writers. Fitzgerald's stories "Molodoy Bogach [The Rich Boy]" and "Opyat' Vavilon [Babylon Revisited]" are included.

Ru51. Mulyarchik, A. S. "Pisatel' i Sovremennaya Amerika [Writing and Contemporary America]." *Amerikanskaya Litertura i Obshchestvenno-Politicheskaya Bor'ba [American Literature and the Public Political Fight]*. Moskva [Moscow]: Nauka [Study], 1977. 6-41.

Rich people who become talented writers create writing to their order.

Ru52. Petruhina, M. Foreword. "*Velikij Gatsby* i Mir Fransisa Scotta Fitzgeral'da [*The Great Gatsby* and the World of Francis Scott Fitzgerald]." *The Great Gatsby*. English Ed. Moscow: Vissaya Shkola, 1984. 3-13.

Critics must concentrate on the connections between the writing of the novel and Fitzgerald's spiritual world, his fortune and misfortune.

Ru53. Shvidkoy, M. "Dramaturgicheskiy Experiment Fitzgeral'da [The Fitzgerald Dramaturgical Experiment]." *Journal Dramaturgii i Teatra [Dramaturgy and Theater Magazine]*, 9 (1984): 160-61. Organ Soyuza

Pisateley SSSR i Ministerstva Kultury SSSR [Writer's Union and Minister of Culture].

This first Russian translation of Fitzgerald's play *The Vegetable* is intended to illustrate that the play is written by a person who keenly and masterfully feels life and the theater and who manages to deeply penetrate into the secrets of the American social system. In this play, Fitzgerald opens up his pain and concern about the future of his native country.

Ru54. Startsev, A. "Gor'kaya Sud'ha Fitzgeralda [Fitzgerald's Bitter Fate]." *Inostrannaya Literatura [Foreign Literature]* 2 (1965): 172-180. In Carl R. Proffer, ed. and trans. *Soviet Criticism of American Literature in the Sixties.* Ardis: Ann Arbor, 1972. 97-109. (In English).

Fitzgerald's case "draws the attention of thinking people all over the world to the vices of American capitalistic culture and the 'American way of life' with its stony coldness to the fates of men. . . . For many personal reasons Fitzgerald did not take part in the social campaign of American writers . . . which typified the thirties." But Marxist influence is evident in "May Day," "The Diamond as Big as the Ritz," and his novels. His letters to his daughter indicate that he read Marx and *Ten Days That Shook the World* by John Reed. *The Great Gatsby* is similar to Alain Fournier's *Le Grand Meaulnes* of which Aragon said, "it is a terrible condemnation of society." So is *The Great Gatsby*. "Fitzgerald's bitter fate and his works are an inseparable part of the basic rejection of the capitalistic world by the twentieth-century masters of Western culture.

Ru55. Startsev, A. Predisloviye [Foreword]. *Notch Niezhna [Tender Is the Night]*. Moskva [Moscow]: Hudoszhestvennaya Literatura [Belles-Lettres], 1971. 5-22.

Fitzgerald is a bright and prominent figure in the development of the "social novel."

Ru56. Startsev, A. "Skotta Fitsdgeralda i 'Ochen Bogatiye Lyudi' [Scott Fitzgerald and the 'Very Rich People']." *Ot Uitmena do Kheminguèya [From Whitman to Hemingway]*. Moscow: Sovetskii pisatel', 1971. 407; 1981. 374.

Writers such as Fitzgerald, Faulkner, and Hemingway represent a historic process in which the arts "fight to free the social and aesthetic consciousness of the people from the enslavement of bourgeois ideology." There is a close link between corruption and amorality as prevailing characteristics of society. Fitzgerald shows an ambiguous position towards society while being sympathetic to Marxist and communist ideas. Fitzgerald's early success lead him to believe that the artist has a right to a life free of sorrows and is therefore entitled to "invest his artistic wealth." Fitzgerald's stories for the *Saturday Evening Post*, which earned him $4,000 each, are indicative of the entanglement of the financial and artistic aspects of his life. For Fitzgerald, rich people are the key figures of a self-destructive society. The author's articles in *Esquire* are "one of the most tragic documents of new American literature, albeit too late to save Fitzgerald personally." While Fitzgerald was deeply affected by reading Marx's *Capital*, he took no active part in the class struggle for "many personal reasons." *The Great Gatsby* is one of the great achievements of the American social novel in the twentieth-century.

Ru57. Startsev, A. "Skotta Fitsdgeralda i 'Ochen Bogatiye Lyudi' [Scott
    Fitzgerald and the 'Very Rich People']." *Inostrannaya Literatura* 5
    (1971): 225-33.

As Hemingway noted, Fitzgerald had a "romantic fascination" with the rich, however Fitzgerald made a distinction between "foreign" rich people and the majority of the people he depicted. He displays a serious social consciousness on a high level of social reality. *Tender Is the Night* is somewhat experimental in the idealistic and political issues the author raises by attempting to construct the image of a "communist-idealist-moralist"—a goal he did not achieve in the novel's published version. However, *Tender Is the Night* is Fitzgerald's best work whose impact lies in his demonstration that the rich do not set the right moral and social standards, and that every man has the task to serve mankind.

Ru58. Tieliegina, N. I. "Symvolika v novelistytsi F. Scott Fitsdzheralda [The
    Symbolism in the Novels of F. Scott Fitzgerald]." *Radikal
    Literaturoznavstvo [Radical Literary Connection]: Naukovo-Teoretychnyi
    Zhurnal* 2.314 (February 1987): 53-59.

On the division in modernist literature between realism and symbolism, Fitzgerald can be grouped together with Proust, Kafka, Eliot, and Valéry, writers who feature "romantic symbolism" in their work. Fitzgerald employs symbolism to create characters and plots that allow him to undertake serious social analysis. He develops a characteristic method that achieves a level of realism through its use of symbolism.

Ru59. Tolmachev, V. M. "Kompozitsionnoye svoyeobraziye *Velikogo Getsbi* F.
    Scott Fitsdzheral'da: Funktsiia povestvovatelia [Compositional
    Peculiarities in F. Scott Fitzgerald's *The Great Gatsby*]." *Vestnik
    Moskovskogo Universiteta [Moscow University Bulletin]*. Seriya 9,
    Filologiya 4 (July-Aug. 1982): 28-35.

The narrator of *The Great Gatsby* is a participant in the events narrated, such as in the work of Christopher Marlowe or Joseph Conrad.

Ru60. Tolmachev, V. M. "The Metaphor of History in the Work of F. Scott Fitzgerald." *Russian Eyes on American Literature*. Eds. Sergei Chakovsky (intro.) and Inge M. Thomas (preface). Jackson: UP of Mississippi, 1992. xiv, 310.

Fitzgerald's historicism is naïve and melodramatic, but is one of the most important and unique aspects of his world-view. While it has been well-noted that his sense of time is primarily biographical, his historical method remains to be fully described. He is post-Flaubertian in his goal of capturing the exact feel of a moment in time and space, but is too fascinated by wealth and its emotions to be a positivist Flaubertian. Rather, he is interested in the experience of the fragile, magnetic beauty of wealth as a metaphor for the newest creative energy, a "heroism of sorts" of the American myth, the model of contemporary tragedy. The historical conflict in his prose is the irony of beauty revealed in the unsolvable contradiction between illusion and reality. His hero takes in against his will something larger than himself and grows into the image of his generation. The experience of tragedy, however, takes Fitzgerald's writing beyond positivistic conceptions and makes him into a historian. His attitude toward history is in the tradition of critical or historical understanding as moral precept. Like Dostoevsky, he chose the ideal of the Christian theodicy, the possibilities of creative redemption through suffering. His relationship to history is double-edged: the desire to say as well as possible what only he knows seems to have devoured him, to have shortened his life.

Ru61. Voitiuk, Svetlana. "F. Scott Fitzgerald's Reputation in Ukraine and the Former Soviet Union." Paper delivered at the First International F. Scott Fitzgerald Conference, Hofstra University, Sep. 1992.

Ru62. Vorobiova, O. P. and T. V. Lik'ianova. "Do problemy analizu lohitnoho aspekty khudochn'oho tekstu [On the problem of the linguistic aspects of an artistic text]." *Movoznavstvo: Naukovo Teoretychnyi Zhurnal Viddilennia Literatury, Movy i Mystetstvoznavstva Akademii Nauk Ukr* 2.134 (Mar-Apr. 1989) 64-67.

A short passage chosen randomly from Fitzgerald's "The Diamond as Big as the Ritz" can be broken down in order to understand how sentence structure defines meaning: "And now, for a certain time, he was to be away from home. That respect for a New England education is a bane of all provincial places that drains them yearly of their most promising young men, had seized upon his parents. Nothing would suit them but that he should go to St. Midas' School near Boston.

Hades was too small to hold their darling and gifted son." By dividing this passage into sentences with subordinate clauses, shorter sentences without subordinate clauses, and other shorter syntactical combinations, the reader finds that the order of the sentence's parts establishes a certain hierarchy in meaning and thus defines which part of the sentence holds the strongest emphasis.

Ru63. Zasurskiy, Ya. N. "Poteriannoe pokolenie, Frencis Skott Fidzherald i 'poeziia otritsatel'nykh velichin' [The Lost Generation, Francis Scott Fitzgerald and 'Negative Value Poetry']." *Amerikanskaia literatura XX. veka. Nekotorye aspekty literaturnogo protsessa [Twentieth-Century American Literature: Some Aspects of the Literary Process]*. Moskva [Moscow]: Izdatel'stvo Moskovskogo Universiteta [Moscow U. Press] 1966, 1984. 158-191.

Fitzgerald's relation to prosperity as a societal and personal problem makes his work part of 'lost generation' literature. The group's works are characterized as contradictory and unique in the way they focus on the fate of post-WWI youth in destructive bourgeois America. Fitzgerald's problematic relationship with 'rich people' is reflected in his critical stance toward mass media versus "realistic literature, close to the real world." The tendencies to pessimism and cynicism are traced through his works, emphasizing that being rich presents certain moral and ethical dilemma. Fitzgerald did attempt to find new values in Marxist socialist ideas, although this is not reflected in his work.

Ru64. Zverev, A. "From the letters." *Voprosy literatury [Questions of Literature]* 2 (1971): 158-191.

Turnbull's *Letters of F. Scott Fitzgerald* (Scribner's, 1963) should be of significant interest to academics and readers, providing answers to critics who had for a long time critiqued Fitzgerald for not having an organized system of work or a clear-cut conception of the role of the artist and for representing a period of realism in American literature. Fitzgerald was a victim of the "public image," although he was forced by necessity to produce saleable stories, which in some instances lead to a parody of his own artistic achievements. *Tender Is the Night* signifies Fitzgerald's turn toward analytic, psychologically rich prose.

Ru65. Zverev, A. Introduction. *F. Scott Fitzgerald. Izbranniye Proizvedeniya v 3-h Tomah [Francis Scott Fitzgerald. Selected Works in 3 Volumes]*. Ed. A. Zverev. Moscow: Hudozhestvennaya Literatura Vol. I (1977, 1984): 5-26.

Fitzgerald is inseparably linked with his epoch, and his tragedy, together with the tragedy of his protagonists, was inevitable.

Ru66. Zverev, A. "Fitzgerald: Legenda i Istina [Fitzgerald: Legend and Truth]."
Portret v Dokumentah [Portrait in Prose]. Moscow: Progress, 1984. 7-
23.

Fitzgerald himself was the hero of a tragedy who responded to the contradiction
of his age. Through his autobiographical prose we can see the drama of the lost
generation.

Ru67. Zverev, A. Introduction. "Podziemniye Tolchki [Underground Shocks]."
Velikiy Getsbi [The Great Gatsby]. Moscow: Pravda [Truth], 1989.

Fitzgerald belongs to the group of writers who are able to feel very keenly the
atmosphere of their time. Through his artistic ear, he felt the underground
shocks of history and they echoed in his literary masterpieces. He opened up the
"jazz age" in literature and revealed everything his contemporaries lived
through.

Ru68. Zverev, A. Afterword. "Poslie Shedevrov [After the Masterpiece]."
Posledniey Magnat, Rasskazy, Esse [The Last Tycoon, Stories, Essays].
Moscow: Izdatel'stvo Pravda [Truth Publishers], 1990. 502-510.

In this book we meet a Fitzgerald less known, yet these pieces are as masterfully
plotted and written as is the rest of his work. The heroic spiritual deed of
Fitzgerald is that he showed that a person will achieve character only after
having done away with his illusions.

DISSERTATIONS

Ru69. Belchuk, V. I. "Traditsii I Novatorstvo v Tvorchestve F.S. Fizgerald'da
[Traditions and Innovation in the Work of F.S. Fitzgerald]." Avtoref.
diss. kand. filol. nauk [Diss]. Moskva [Moscow]: Moskovskiy
Gosudarstvenniy Pedagogicheskiy Institut [Moscow State Pedagogical
Institute], 1981. 20.

Fitzgerald's masterfully styled plots are highly evaluative. He is one of the most
talented figures in early-20th-century American literature.

Ru70. Kolegayeva, I. M. *Yazik Romanov F. Scott Fitzgeral'da [The Language
of F. Scott Fitzgerald's Novels]*. Avtoref. diss. kand. filol. nauk [Diss].
Odessa, 1977.

The language of Fitzgerald's novels needs unveiling.

Ru71. Kolesnikova, N. B. "Tvorcheskiy Put' Fransisa Scotta Fitzgeral'da [The Creative Career of Francis Scott Fitzgerald]." Avtoref. diss. kand. filol. nauk [Diss]. Moskva: Moskovskiy Gosudarstvenniy Pedagogicheskiy Institut [Moscow: Moscow State Pedagogical Institute]. 1971. 20.

The most important periods in Fitzgerald's private life are connected with the creative work that constitutes his literary career.

Ru72. Kuhalashvili, V. K. F. S. Fitzgerald I Amerikanskiy Literaturniy Protsess 20-30 godov XX Veka [The Place of F. S. Fitzgerald in the American Literature of the 20s and 30s of the Twentieth Century]. Institut Literatury A N Ukr.SSR., 1981; Kiev: Naukova Dumka. Kiev: 1983. 230.

Fitzgerald's writing method is highly evaluated and deserves the special attention of scholars.

Ru73. Lidskiyi, Yu. Ya. *Scott Fitzgerald. Tvorchestvo.* [*Scott Fitzgerald: Creative Work*]. *Naukova Dumka* [*Meditative Study*]. Kiev, 1982. 367.

Fitzgerald is a classic of American literature whose unique style deserves a place in American cultural heritage and in the further development of world literature.

Romania   *with Virgil Mihaiu*

It is difficult for anyone who did not live under its rigors to comprehend the nature of the censorship on the arts imposed during communism. The idea was to do away with artists altogether, in order to create a "homogeneous working people." A peculiar feature of the Ceausescu-brand autarchy was that, unlike in the Soviet Union, where censorship was directed mainly at the printed word, in Romania attention was focused primarily on what could be seen directly, rather than on literature or music, explaining the decay of film, photography and of plastic art exhibitions, but the relative survival of literature, including theatre—which apparently bored the semi-literate presidential couple. Choreography—fundamentally a most sensuous art—was doomed to almost complete extinction, and dozens of talented dancers were lost, or chose exile. Visual arts followed suit. The more direct the perceived impact, the more censorship was applied.

Music was the only art able to develop relatively normally in the given situation, the sound world being the most difficult to control. Besides, the high ranking officials in charge of ideological matters had too little time for symphony or jazz concerts. Their chief concern in this respect was to destroy the material basis of music, especially at the school level. Despite the hostile environment, musicians were able to preserve a remarkable level of independence in their options, protected by the non-explicit character of their art. Remaining in contact with the world's new musical trends, composers contributed to the education of their listeners. The respect for culture inherent in the tradition of East European peoples is a feature that greatly helped jazz become a "serious art form" in this area. In Romania, jazz has acquired cultural significance in order to merit the many sacrifices required to promote and protect it. Jazz fans, employing all kinds of strategies and tactics, succeeded in building up a network of clubs, festivals, concerts and radio broadcasts that might have seemed impossible for any other art.

The historical conjuncture which permitted Fitzgerald's introduction to the Romanian literary consciousness occurred after April 1964. At that moment a so-called "Declaration of Independence" of the Romanian Communist Party was issued, asserting its right to pursue its own line, unimposed upon by Moscow and Beijing. This translated into a considerable relaxation of the ideological grip. Romania's intelligentsia grasped this opportunity, in order to retrieve the country's own past values. An atmosphere of cultural effervescence and social hope replaced the terror that had accompanied the dictatorship of the proletariat. Romania was on the threshold of seven good years, which were terminated abruptly by Ceausescu's visit to North Korea and China in 1971.

So, there is no wonder that the first important translation of Fitzgerald into Romanian appeared in 1967, in the midst of that most "liberal" period of the totalitarian decades. It comprised *The Great Gatsby,* translated by Mircea Ivănescu, plus "The Diamond as Big as the Ritz" and "May Day," both translated by Liana Dobrescu. This volume is still a valuable reference for Romanian scholars. Its preface was written by the translator who has meanwhile become one of the leading Romanian poets, as well as the personality thanks to whom readers became acquainted with masterpieces by Joyce, Musil, and other great writers. This is one of the most comprehensive studies on Fitzgerald published in Romania under the communist regime (Ro33).

The almost automatic association between the name "Scott Fitzgerald" and the magic word "jazz" influenced the writer's reception in Romanian intellectual circles. Rather than a superficial link, jazz carried a symbolic load. By 1965, jazz had finally emerged from the catacombs to which it had been confined during Stalinism. Moreover, it bore the aureola of martyrdom, the symbolism of underground resistance against totalitarianism. Passing the test of harsh persecutions, jazz was hailed as an almost providential way of becoming free to assert one's individuality, in an epoch of forcibly achieved collectivization. Thus, the simple mentioning of Fitzgerald's name in any publication that was allowed to reach the Romanian public had a considerable weight.

In the spring of 1969, Romania's major literary weekly, *România literară*, had reached such a degree of freedom that it could venture to publish, for instance, an essay of Daniel Aaron, professor of literature at the University of Massachusetts, entitled "The American Writer and the Academic Environment." That text appeared under the significant heading *"Ferestre"* or "Windows," which suggested intellectuals' thirst for a re-opening towards the world. It should be noted that almost every time Fitzgerald's name is mentioned, it happens in a context intimating the idea of normality. It is a paradox that, from the angle of a repressed society, the most typical representative of *les années folles* appeared to be an epitome of normal, unconstrained behavior (Ro17).

On the other hand, such glimpses of "normality" were also combined—in the subconscious of the average Romanian reader—with a secret admiration for the glamorous aspects of a forbidden life style. *Sinteza*, an illustrated magazine containing American scientific and cultural news, published in Romania by the

U.S. Embassy in Bucharest, was a much sought-after item. Martin Kasindorf's 1975 mention of Fitzgerald is employed to add some past charm to more recent occurrences in the film industry (Ro35). Glick writes in *Dialogue SUA* that Fitzgerald is the Jazz Age representative in literature (Ro30). Nevertheless, there were other more specialized American references to Fitzgerald translated into Romanian such as Marcus Cunliffe's *Literature of the United States*, which enjoyed instant success (Ro15). At the same time, Romania's "socialist liberalization" reached its apex, and Richard Nixon was enthusiastically greeted by Bucharest's inhabitants when he arrived there in July 1969.

The most convincing study about Fitzgerald written in Romanian during the 1960s belonged to Dan Grigorescu, and was included in his volume *13 American Writers*. Sometimes Fitzgerald's critical undertones directed against the ruthlessness of a society governed by the money-myth are emphasized by the Romanian exegete, in order to prove loyalty to Marxist "aesthetic principles." Nevertheless, "Scott Fitzgerald si visul romantic" remains a valid document for the manner in which the Americanists' attitude was becoming ever more flexible at the end of the decade (Ro31). Furthermore, after having the good fortune of spending some years in New York as manager of the Romanian Library there, Grigorescu published an impressive *Chronological Dictionary of American Literature* in which the publication dates of Fitzgerald's novels are mentioned as well as the date of his death (Grigorescu 1977).

The second important editorial event concerning Fitzgerald in Romania happened in 1974 when Mircea Ivănescu managed to publish his translation of *Tender Is the Night*. The cultural atmosphere of the 1970s was rapidly deteriorating. After years of being alternately impressed with the political styles of Tito and DeGaulle, Dubcek and Willy Brandt, Gomulka and Nixon, Ceausescu once and for all discovered an approach to governing that appealed to him: visiting Kim II Sung in North Korea in 1971 he realized that a people can be put totally under the control of an autocratic will, humiliated, reduced to silence and fear, spiritually annihilated. His implementing such a regime had terrible consequences for the Romanian intelligentsia, which was thus placed under a state of siege for almost two decades, until December 1989.

In this political context, any mention in the Romanian media of the life and work of a liberal symbol like Fitzgerald was a moral victory against the primitivism of the political regime. The yearly almanacs issued by Romanian magazines provided an opportunity to slip in translations of foreign literatures. In the 1973 *Flacara Almanah 13*, Fitzgerald's "A Man in the Way," the second of the Pat Hobby Stories, appeared in Iulia Scutaru's translation, under the title *Subiect pentru un film (Subject for a Movie)* (Ro5). In 1976 Virgil Mihaiu's translation of the same story appeared in the *Tribuna Almanah 1976* (Ro5).

In 1974, a photograph from the Jack Clayton film of *The Great Gatsby* appeared in the "foreign affairs" column of the *Cinema* monthly, written by Radu Cosasu (Cosasu 1974). A year later, in November 1975, the film was shown in Romania's movie theaters. Mircea Alexandrescu promptly reviewed it for *Cinema* (Ro51). The most detailed review of the film appeared in *România literară* written by the "dean" of Romania's film critics, D. I. Suchianu, whose regular column for this weekly of the Writers' Union enjoyed great respect from readers (Ro54).

Thanks to journalist Felicia Antip, writing several articles in *România literară*, Romanian readers also came to know the biographies of both Fitzgeralds, but primarily Zelda (Ro19, Ro20, Ro22). In 1975 the cultural weekly *Tribuna* of Cluj tackled the Zelda issue with S. Damian's article "The Sun Also Sets." Belonging to the happy few Romanian intellectuals allowed to work in Western countries during the communist regime, S. Damian summarizes a *Frankfurter Allgemeine Zeitung* article by Kyra Stromberg about Nancy Milford's book on Zelda (Ro29).

As Romania was heading towards an autarchic state during the second half of the 1970s, the teaching of foreign languages was drastically reduced. The intellectual elite seemed doomed to extinction. Strong, uncompromising cultural magazines like the *Echinox* in Cluj became necessary and were even permitted to appear under the guise of a quasi-close-circuit university press. In a similar way, two of Fitzgerald's stories became accessible to English speaking students: "Babylon Revisited" in a collection of texts edited by the Department of English at the Germanic Languages Faculty of Bucharest University (Ro7) and "Pat Hobby and Orson Welles," included in *Twentieth Century Short Stories of the English Speaking World: An Anthology* (Ro8). A highly interesting study concerning "The Play with Colors" in *The Great Gatsby* was published by Sanda Cernea in *Studia Universitatis Babeş-Bolyai* in 1979 (Ro26). In the same year, Virgil Mihaiu reviewed *The Letters of F. Scott Fitzgerald*, edited by Andrew Turnbull, for *România literară*. Because this was the first discussion of his letters, the publication devoted two pages to the review (Ro38).

During the 1980s, the general atmosphere of Romania's totalitarian society continued to deteriorate. In spite of that, Fitzgerald did not sink into oblivion. The decade's greatest achievement related to him was the translation by Ruxandra Soroiu of André Le Vot's biography in 1983. As the book was first published by Julliard in Paris in 1979 (F40), its appearance in Romania four years later signified a feat (Ro16). Comparatively, it received a very pale response from the literary press. Irina Burlui's review in the *Cronica* is symptomatic (Ro52).

Other scholarly contributions should be mentioned, all originating from the English Studies Department of the University in Iasi: Irina Burlui's "F. Scott Fitzgerald—The Loss of a Dream" and Sorin Parvu's "*The Great Gatsby*: the Showdown Title." They were published in a volume entitled *American Fiction: A Contextual Approach* under the auspices of the Al..I. Cuza University in Iasi, not long before the fall of Ceausescu's dictatorship. Such "texts for connoisseurs" were more or less hidden from the public eye (Ro25, Ro46).

Other contributors to the Fitzgerald phenomenon include the young prose writer Cristian Teodorescu who published a brief record of F. Scott Fitzgerald's life and work in *Contemporanul* in 1985, ironically when the publication, founded in 1881, was being used by Ceausescu as a primitive propagandizing tool in the hands of the so-called council of Socialist Culture and Education (Ro50). During that same autumn, the brilliant man of letters Marian Papahagi, co-founder of *Echinox* cultural magazine, wrote a detailed review about Mihaiu's volume of essays on jazz, *The Resonance Box*, which had just appeared at Bucharest's Albatros publishing house. Inevitably, F. Scott Fitzgerald tops the list of writers who registered jazz in its complete novelty and suggestiveness from its first stages of development (Ro45).

When Ceausescu's Orwellian regime was finally overthrown in a desperate general upheaval at the end of 1989, many insiders spoke about the event as Romania's late hour emergence from the Second World War. The main characteristic of the post-totalitarian years has been confusion on all planes. Fortunately, there has been one great achievement of the 1989 revolt which has prevailed ever since: freedom of expression. Be they audio-visual or written, the media have reached an unprecedented multiformity, plurality of opinions and an impressive number of institutionalized forms. While having one of the poorest economies in Europe, Romania still boasts a surprisingly rich cultural life. An outcome has been an uncontrollable multiplication of publishing houses, as well as of cultural magazines, which try hard to survive under the precarious conditions of an over-saturated market. With very little left over from the national budget, libraries have lost their monetary status as far as the autochtonous book production is concerned. Worse than that, the distribution of printed matter inside the country is haphazard at best, if not downright chaotic. These are only some explanations for the hardships one has to face when trying to keep track of the latest developments in Fitzgerald's Romanian reputation.

Soon after 1989, it became clear that Romanian editors were trying to make up for the many wasted decades. Yet now that virtually everything could appear in print, many valuable *oeuvres* passed almost unnoticed. It was, however, the duty of those concerned to preserve them, and thus, Mircea Ivănescu re-issued his translation of *The Great Gatsby* at three different publishing houses: Excelsior and Noua Europa (1991) and Sophia (1994). The same translator's version of *Tender Is the Night* appeared in Chisinau with Hyperion in 1991 and with Bucharest's Simrom-Europartner in 1994. Georgete Padreleanu's translation of *The Beautiful and Damned* was printed in the well-known "Romanul secolului XX" series of the Univers publishing house in 1991. Liviu Papuc published a selection of 14 stories (*Winter Dreams and Other Stories*) at Editura Moldova in 1992. The following year *The Last Tycoon* was translated by Alla Verbetchi for Editura Arania. *This Side of Paradise*, translated by Ionel Buruiana, appeared at Noema in 1995. Another editorial event was the publication of *The Crack-Up* essays at Editura Marineasa in 1994, translated by Hortensia Parlog. Mircea Mihaies, the literary critic from Timisoara, contributed a lengthy Afterword (Ro36).

References to Fitzgerald in Romania's countless cultural magazines of today are rather hard to track down. And sometimes they can be quite deceptive. Thus, the prestigious *România literară* displayed a two-page article entitled "From Heinrich the Green to *The Great Gatsby*." The expectations raised by the article's alluring title remained unfulfilled however as it was a bombastic review of Peter Handke's novel *Short Letter for a Long Parting*. Fitzgerald is merely given credit for influencing Handke.

Luckily, the regained freedom of speech has not produced only void or vague by-lines in relation to Fitzgerald. Felicia Antip chose four of Fitzgerald's less known "confessions," grouped them under the title *Craft of the Writer* and accompanied them with some pertinent comments, in the excellent Romanian edition of the *Lettre Internationale* magazine (Ro21). In 1997, Sorin Parvu published a technical study based largely on Norman Friedman's work in *Poetics of the Novel* (1955) and *Point of View in Fiction* (1955) (Ro47).

Virgil Stanciu's sophisticated study, *The Cognitive Dimension of Narrative Discourse in F. Scott Fitzgerald's* The Great Gatsby, represented a genuine celebration of Fitzgerald's centennial. This essay opens a volume of *Studia Universitatis Babeş-Bolyai* written by members of the English Department of Cluj University, in which Anglo-American fictional works are tackled through the conceptual framework of narratology or critical theory. The theoretical contribution that has prompted Professor Stanciu's research belongs to the French school of semiology by Greimas and Courtes: *The Cognitive Dimension of Narrative Discourse* (published in New Literary History, Vol. VII, No. 3, 1976). *Gatsby* is seen in Greimas's terms as a complex narrative in which the distribution of knowledge becomes an important organizing principle (Ro49).

Mihaiu also took advantage of the 1996 Fitzgerald anniversary in order to bring out two essays in magazines of the Romania's Writers' Union. The first appeared just in time for the September celebration in *România literară :* "Spokesman of the Jazz Age" (Ro39). A more "musical" though less extended commemoration of the centennial appeared in *Steaua*, in the Jazz Context monthly section of which Mihaiu has been editor since 1990: "The Writer was Thinking the Way Monk Would Play" (Ro44). The thesis here is that Fitzgerald's work seems to assimilate themes, rhythms, harmonies and dissonances suspended in the air of his time. Mihaiu concludes that Fitzgerald and Monk are two inverted anarchists sacrificing themselves for the sake of our sacred right to error and pleasure.

Fitzgerald's reputation in Romania is in tune with the tormented *spiritus loci*. The American writer's imprint upon the Romanian literary and cultural consciousness could be summarized as rather partial, sporadic, fragmentary, unsystematic. In a culture whose own classical writers have hardly enjoyed complete publication of their works, the amount of extant documents concerning Fitzgerald may be considered more or less satisfactory. One commendable feature of these texts is their variety. Still, quite a few of them were fortuitous, or tried to supply basic knowledge about an author too easily pigeonholed into preconceived meta-literary role-playing. That is why it is hard to imagine a Fitzgerald-counterpart to the monumental Faulkner monograph produced by Sorin Alexandrescu in 1969.

More than a decade after the fall of the Berlin wall, Romania's cultural atmosphere, though vivacious, is still ailing. The ideological repression has been replaced by economic restraints. The glorious "resistance through culture" against the dictatorship has been almost forgotten. Highbrow forms of art, literature in particular, are confronted with a worldwide sub-cultural aggression. Nowadays, a writing about Fitzgerald in Romania is allowed to be as honest as possible, yet it will certainly have a more restricted impact than previous to December 1989.

After years of registering Romanian reactions to F. Scott Fitzgerald, Mihaiu says, "I have ascertained that he is one of the most sympathized with American writers hereabouts. Practically, I haven't come across any symptom of clear-cut rejection towards this author among our readers or critics. Maybe such a benevolent attitude should also be sustained through some ampler, less derivative critical investigation into this fascinating subject."

REFERENCES

Grigorescu, Dan. *Dictionar cronologic*. Literatura americana. Bucharest: Editura stiintifica si Enciclopedica, 1977.

Cosasu, Radu. *Alti doi ani pe un bloc de gheata [Two More Years on an Iceberg]*. Bucharest: Editura Eminescu, 1974.

TRANSLATIONS/EDITIONS

Ro1. Fitzgerald, F. S. "Afară, in faţa atelierului de tâmplarie [Outside the Cabinet-Maker's]." Trans. Antoaneta Ralian. *Secolul 20. Magazine for World Literature* 7.6 (1967): 8-11.

Ro2. Fitzgerald, F. Scott. *Marele Gatsby [The Great Gatsby]*. Trans. and Preface Mircea Ivănescu. Bucharest: Editura de stat pentru literatură universala, 1967. 272; Timişoara: Editura Excelsior, 1991. 222; Craiova: Editura Noua Europa, 1991. 144.

Ro3. Fitzgerald, F. Scott. "Un diamant mare cât hotelul Ritz [A Diamond as Big as the Ritz]." In *Marele Gatsby*. Trans. Liana Dobrescu. Bucharest: Editura de stat pentru literatura universala, 1967. 272. Timisoara: Editura Excelsior, 1991. 222; Craiova: Editura Noua Europa, 1991. 144.

Ro4. Fitzgerald, F. Scott. "Îtâi Mai [May Day]." *Marele Gatsby*. Trans. Liana Dobrescu. Bucharest: Editura de stat pentru literatura universala, 1967. 272. Timisoara: Editura Excelsior, 1991. 222; Craiova: Editura Noua Europa, 1991. 144.

Ro5. Fitzgerald, F. Scott. "Subject pentru un film [Subject for a Movie (*The Pat Hobby Stories I*)]." Trans. Iulia Scutaru. *Flacara Almanah* 1973. 295-297; "Un incurca lume [A Man in the Way (*The Pat Hobby Stories II*)]." Trans. Virgil Mihaiu. *Almanah Tribuna*, Cluj-Napoca 1976: 254-56.

Ro6. Fitzgerald, F. Scott. *Blândeţea nopţii [Tender Is the Night]*. Trans. Mircea Ivǎnescu. Colectia romanului de dragoste [The Love-Novel Collection]. Bucharest: Editura Eminescu, 1974. 360; Chişinǎu (Republic of Moldavia): Editura Hyperion, 1991. 336; Bucharest: Simrom-Europartner, 1994. 304.

Ro7. Fitzgerald, F. Scott. "Babylon Revisited." *Texts for the Special Course in 20th Century American Literature*. Ed. Christopher Givan. Department of English at the Germanic Languages Faculty of Bucharest University. Bucharest (1977): 25-45.

Ro8. Fitzgerald, F. Scott. "Pat Hobby and Orson Welles." *Twentieth Century Short Stories of the English Speaking World: An Anthology*. Eds. Hertha Perez, Irina Burlui, Dumitru Dorobat. Bucharest: Editura Didactica si Pedagogica, 1979: 123-129.

Ro9. Fitzgerald, F. Scott. *Cei frumosi si blestemati [The Beautiful and Damned]*. Trans. Georgeta Padureleanu. Romanul secolului XX [Novels of the Twentieth Century]. Bucharest: Editura Univers, 1991. 416.

Ro10. Fitzgerald, F. Scott. *Visuri de iarnǎ si alte povestiri [Winter Dreams and*

Other Stories]. Trans. Liviu Papuc. Iaşi: Editura Moldova, 1992.

Ro11. Fitzgerald, F. Scott. *Ultimul magnat [The Last Tycoon]*. Trans. Alla
Verbetchi. Brasov: Editura Arania, 1993. 240.

This also contains a brief biographical bibliographical note on Fitzgerald.
Besides *The Last Tycoon*, this edition also contains a Romanian variant of "May
Day."

Ro12. Fitzgerald, F. Scott. "Meseria de scriitor [Craft of the Writer]." Trans.
Felicia Antip. *Lettre Internationale [Ediţia romana]* 8 (Winter 1993-
1994): 83-84.

Ro13. Fitzgerald, F. Scott. *Ecouri din epoca jazzului [Echoes of the Jazz Age
(The Crack-Up)]* . Trans. Hortensia Pârlog, Afterword by Mircea
Mihăies. Timişoara: Editura Marineasa, 1994. 140.

Ro14. Fitzgerald, F. Scott. *Dincoace de paradis [This Side of Paradise]*. Trans.
Ionel Buruiana. Piatra Neamţ: Editura Noema, 1995.

Foreign Scholarship in Translation

Ro15. Cunliffe, Marcus. "Proza dupa Primul Razboi Mondial [Prose After the
Second World War]." *Literatura Statelor Unite [Literature of the United
States]*. Trans. Rodica Timis. Bucharest: Editura pentru Literatura
Uuniversala, 1969: 303-307.

Ro16. Le Vot, André. *F. Scott Fitzgerald*. Trans. Ruxandra Soroiu. Bucharest:
Editura Eminescu, 1983. 590.

ESSAYS/CHAPTERS/NOTES/CONFERENCE PAPERS

Ro17. Aaron, Daniel. "Scriitorul american si mediul academic [The American
Writer and the Academic Environment]." *România literară* 2 (30).18 (1
May, 1969): 20.

The contrast between the daily lives and preoccupations of American writers in

1939 and in 1969 is a contrast that may correspond to socio-cultural changes that have deeply reformed the standards of existence for the American writer.

Ro18. Alexandrescu, Mircea. "Marele Gatsby." *Cinema*, 13 (155). 11, November 1975, pp. 14.

A review of Jack Clayton's movie version of *The Great Gatsby*. The film was shown in Romania in 1975, and Alexandrescu states that *Gatsby* would become a "symbol of the American way of writing." Clayton's film reconstitutes "the mad years," with their fashionable outbreaks. This vast social picture, for which Francis Ford Coppola wrote the scenario, deals primarily with the surface of the novel, but nevertheless evinces a desire to surpass the nostalgia about this era which ended in an economic crash.

Ro19. Antip, Felicia. "Destinul Zeldei Fitzgerald [Zelda Fitzgerald's Destiny]." *România literară* 6.5 (Feb. 1973): 30.

Zelda's entire life was an attempt to emulate her husband, to attain triumphs that would rival his. While Scott was heading towards nothingness, leaving behind diamonds bigger than the Ritz, Zelda left only traces of her ambitions uncovered by creative talent. Scott was angered by Zelda's imitation of the rhythm and subject of *Tender Is the Night,* which he had published after several drafts in 1934. Conversely, *Save Me the Waltz* was completed by Zelda in only six weeks' time. Nancy Milford's book about Zelda records the latter's repeatedly failed efforts to equal her husband. Her adventure with Jozan was perhaps also an attempt to emancipate herself from the domination of a husband whose genius surpassed hers on all accounts. Zelda's novel offers at least two essential testimonies about its authoress: an inability to understand her husband, who irritated and puzzled her, combined with the lack of spiritual communication between them, and a second—involuntary—testimony to her pathetic endeavors to achieve personal triumph, a glory to be compared to that of the man whose success was killing her.

Ro20. Antip, Felicia. "Era charlestonului [The Charleston Era]." *România literară* 8.21 (5 June 1975): 22.

The Charleston Era was the 1920s, when fervent modern literature was being produced in Paris, New York, London, Berlin. Artists like Modigliani, Henry Miller, Cocteau, championed a bohemian life-style working to achieve aesthetic excellence. As an antidote to Fitzgerald's playboy image, the spoiled child of American literature, one should go directly to the source: *The Great Gatsby*'s facsimile, recently published by Matthew Bruccoli. Budd Schulberg in his review of it in *The New York Times Book Review* emphasizes Fitzgerald's infinite labor to obtain the final form of his masterpiece.

Ro21. Antip, Felicia. Footnote. "Meseria de scriitor [Craft of the Writer]," by
F. Scott Fitzgerald. Trans. Felicia Antip. *Lettre Internationale* [*Editia
Romana*] 8 (Winter 1993-1994): 83-84.

Fitzgerald continuously rewrote himself. During his short 20-year literary
career, he kept a sort of fragmented diary of short stories and essays, not
published in book-form during his lifetime. These four texts chosen for the
Romanian version of *Lettre Internationale* magazine are proof of his fiery
endeavor to remain not only an artist, but also a writing professional throughout
his lifetime. The Romanian translations are published in the following order:
"Cine este cineva—si de ce [Who's Who—and Why]," originally published in
the *Saturday Evening Post* (1920); "Dupa-amiaza unui scriitor [Afternoon of an
Author]," published by *Esquire* (1930); "Cum sa irosesti materialul: Insemnare
despre generatia mea" [How to Waste Material: A Note on My Generation], first
published in *The Bookman* magazine (1926).

Ro22. Antip, Felicia. "Iubiri atipice [Atypical Loves]." *România literară* 6.47
(13 Sept. 1973): 30.

Nancy Milford used documents and memories provided by Sheilah Graham in
order to write her monograph of Zelda. Conscious of the resemblance between
Zelda and Sheila, Fitzgerald seems to have been attracted by the delusion that he
might find in the latter a double for his life's love: one having a more balanced
personality, yet as beautiful and exuberant as his initial model of what he had
dubbed "the century's encounter": the golden Southern beauty and the brilliant
Northern success. Although by 1938 the Jazz Age dreams were quite shattered,
Fitzgerald's female ideal remained the embodiment of the '20s, the flippant
irresponsible queen of her generation: Zelda. Theirs was a tragedy caused by
selfishness disguised in tenderness and tenderness undermined by selfishness, by
a combination of self-destructive elements. Every love is different, theirs was
damned. It obliged them to do each other the greatest evil by wishing to do each
other all the best in the world.

Ro23. Antip, Felicia. "O poveste de iubire nebună, nebună, nebună [A Mad,
Mad, Mad Story of Love]." *Lumea din ziare* [*The World in Newspapers*].
Cartea românească& Porto-Franco, 1991: 252-259.

This chapter of Antip's book is composed of her previously published articles
dealing with the Zelda-Scott relationship (see summarized versions of "Zelda
Fitzgerald's Destiny", "Atypical Loves" and "The Charleston Era"). It is a
portrayal of the Fitzgeralds' relationship based on Nancy Milford's biography of
Zelda, Scott's portrayal in *Tender Is the Night*, Zelda's in *Save Me the Waltz*, an
interview of Sheilah Graham in *The London Times*, the film based on Graham's
book, and William Shirer's memories of the couple.

Ro24. Boeriu, Doina, Cristina Corciovescu, Rodica Pop-Vulcanescu, Bujor T. Ripeanu, Ioana Creanga, eds. *Secolul cinematografului: Mica enciclopedie a cinematografiei universale* "Cinema Century: Short Encyclopedia of Universal Cinematography". Editura stiintifica si enciclopedica: Bucharest, 1989. 605.

After his novel *The Great Gatsby* had been adapted for the screen by Director Herbert Brenon in 1926, Fitzgerald became one of Hollywood's writers. Discontent with servitude to the film studios, he repeatedly abandoned and resumed this activity. This phenomenon was characteristic for other writers as well who were recruited by the producers immediately after the invention of the talking movies, such as Dorothy Parker, William Faulkner, J. S. Perelman, John O'Hara, Nathanael West, William Saroyan, and Robert Benchley. As soon as they got tied to the conveyor belt of the great studios, none of these gifted writers managed to produce any valuable work for the screen.

Ro25. Burlui, Irina. "F. S. F.—the Loss of the Dream." *American Fiction: A Contextual Approach.* Eds. Irina Burlui and Sorin Parvu. Iasi: Iasi Al. I. Cuza University Press, 1983.

A scholarly contribution of note, originating from the English Studies Department of the University at Iasi, not long before the fall of Ceausescu's dictatorship. This was essentially a 'text for connoisseurs,' and as with others like it, more or less hidden from the public eye. Text not available for annotation.

Ro26. Cernea, Sanda. "Jocul culorilor la F. Scott Fitzgerald: *Marele Gatsby* [Play With Colors in *The Great Gatsby*]." *Studia Universitatis Babeş-Bolyai. Series Philologia* 24.2 (1979): 15-19.

The narrative of *The Great Gatsby* develops by means of symbols both material and complex. The former are deeply rooted in reality, such as Gatsby's mansion, West Egg, or Dr. Eckleberg's eyes. The latter refer to death and resurrection, as in contrasts such as light/darkness. This essay is limited to parallels between colors and situations or states of mind. The narrative develops by sliding the warm colors into cold ones up to their depersonalization and disintegration into grey. Chapters 1, 3, 4, and 5 are characterized by an intensification of warm colors, while chapter II is dominated by cold. In Fitzgerald's vision, one and the same color can have multiple meanings, sometimes totally different from the traditional ones. Most often white is associated with opulence, and suggests the discrepancy between the apparent purity of a desired world and its actual corruption. Green is used only twice, symmetrically, in Chapters 1 and 8, associated with the light at the end of Daisy's jetty. Green results from mixing the symbols suggested by blue (the color of dreams) and yellow (the symbol of brutal material reality).

Ro27. Chiru, Ileana. "F. S. Fitzgerald and the Great Jazzby." *Revista de studii britanice si americane [British and American Studies]* 6 (2000): Hestia Publishing House, Timisoara—Romania, 2000. 52-57.

An attack upon American materialism, *The Great Gatsby* is about the foreclosure of the American dream. Fitzgerald makes room for characters who are 'shortcuts from nothing to nothing,' disfigured in some way as human beings, incapable of wholeness or deeply spiritual experience. Both Nick and Gatsby himself come out of the middle-class imagination. The latter is nowhere with his dream because he understands wealth only mythically and there is no fate he can embrace except estrangement and death. While the rest of the novel's characters are all alike in their dim aspiration and baseless pretensions, Gatsby's stature is augmented by their limitations, for he alone in the novel has been given the capacity for transcendence. The continental changes of address and shiftings about imply the restless, unsettled, mobile nature of their society, further emphasized by the attention paid to vehicles throughout the novel. The novel has the features of mythic literature, using the mythic mode which exemplifies profound truths of man's universal experience. An embodiment of the American dream, divided between power and dream, Gatsby comes to tragically stand for America itself. In this novel, Fitzgerald moves to a vision of disorder that prepares the way to the Postmodern novel of an existentially senseless world.

Ro28. Constantinescu, Romanita. "De la Heinrich cel Verde la *Marele Gatsby* [From Heinrich the Green to *The Great Gatsby*]." *România literară* 29 (July 1998): 20-21.

A lately hard-to-find reference to Fitzgerald in Romania, covering a bombastic review about the Romanian translation of Peter Handeke's novel *Short Letter for a Long Parting/Scurta scrisoare pentru o lunga despartire* (1972, translated into Romanian in 1998 by Mariana Lazarescu, Univers, Bucharest). The expectations raised by the article's alluring title are unfulfilled. Handeke's American travelogue becomes a pretext for a parade of void neologistic terms, an ostentatious display of the reviewer's infatuation with her "learnedness." The only instance where *Gatsby* is mentioned contrasts the European spirit of Gottfried Keller's Bildungsroman *Heinrich the Green* and the Austrian author's attempt to adjust himself to the American mentality. The opposite pole of this juxtaposition is represented by *Gatsby*, with which, states Contantinescu, Handeke "practices the reading of identification: *The Great Gatsby* inspires him with an appetite for transforming aesthetic into life for life's sake."

Ro29. Damian, S. "Şi soarele apune totuşi [The Sun Also Sets]." *Tribuna* 9.47 (20 Nov.1975): 4.

In a *Frankfurter Allgemeine Zeitung* article by Kyra Stromberg about Nancy Milford's book, Zelda, who seems to be naggingly despotic, is in fact the victim in the couple's drama. Zelda found it difficult to be one who aspires to live according to her own laws and yet longing to be loved and protected. This conflict was a sign of the approaching illness, which has its origin in the puritan fear of excess and intemperance. Paradoxically, the fear was also felt by someone determined to push all her experiences to the extreme. All of Fitzgerald's female characters are embodiments of Zelda. Despite the doctors' terrible diagnosis, Zelda's letters to Scott sent from various sanatoriums are astonishingly lucid. Milford points out the sufferings of both spouses in a world in which art depends on money. When Scott died in 1940, Zelda returned to the protective South. Whenever her excesses returned, she docilely got herself admitted to a hospital, dying in a 1948 fire. The tragedy of the decay of a gifted young woman teaches us a lesson about the meandering implied by jocular euphoria and delusions of glory.

Ro30. Glick, Nathan. "Frecventand cinematografele-Radacinile sociale ale filmului american [Frequenting the Cinema Halls—the Social Roots of American Film]." *Dialog SUA* 9.1 (1980): 28-41.

The defining characteristics of the Jazz Age were individualism and experimentation, even more spectacular as they co-existed with the decency and the puritanism of American life. The representative of the Jazz Age in literature is Fitzgerald whose short stories and novels reflect the living disposition of a coffeeshop world where richness and talent intermingled.

Ro31. Grigorescu, Dan. "Scott Fitzgerald şi visul romantic [Scott Fitzgerald and the Romantic Dream]." *13 scriitori americani: De la romantici la "generatia pierduta" [13 American Writers: From the Romanticists to the "Lost Generation"]*. Bucharest: Editura pentru literaturăuniversală, 1968. 102-119.

The effort to separate illusion from reality characterizes 20th-century American literature. Gatsby is a romantic who rejects vulgar reality by replacing it with fetishes. Between the Gatsby-Daisy love episode and Hollywood's spectacular but void clichés, the characters lose their substance and are transformed into allegories. This is Fitzgerald's way of suggesting their moral emptiness. The tragedy of Gatsby and Daisy is the tragedy of Jazz-Age society. In *The Last Tycoon* the dream has become conventional and false, not exempt from corruption and immorality. Cinematography is, in itself, an illusion, and the face projected on screen is only a shadow of reality. Stahr looks for real values here, whereas the American dream has become a universal convention in which no one trusts any longer. One might say that, among the lost-generation authors, Fitzgerald was most tragically linked to contemporary society.

Ro32. Irimia, Mihaela Anghelescu. Afterword: "Blanda noapte racoroasa [The Cool Tender Night]." *Blândetea noptii [Tender Is the Night]* by F. Scott Fitzgerald. Trans. Mircea Ivănescu. Iasi: Editura Polirom, 2001: 433-449.

Fitzgerald shares with Hemingway—another provincial midwesterner of tremendous ambition—the epithet of "living myth" of the 1920s, the latter, however, being a source of envy for the former. Playing first *homme manqué*, then *homme épuisé*, Fitzgerald launched himself into exorbitant adventures with Zelda, whom Hemingway would eventually pronounce stark mad in *A Moveable Feast*, a portrait of Scott and his wife to which Irimia gives much credit. Fitzgerald's entire artistic and existential trajectory was motivated by a desire to surpass his subordinate condition as son of a modest family of Irish descent. One finds in Fitzgerald's behavior and work the romantic pose alongside the moralizing tone characteristic of the frontiers' tradition and of the Celtic familial fund, the chimerical artistic projects of an idealist's mind and the bohemian pleasure to shock, the exquisite narrator and the Hollywood hack, the decadent stylist and the on-the-spot commentator. T.S. Eliot appreciated Fitzgerald's genius as residing in his transmutation of the existential into the aesthetic, of fact into fiction, doubled by a sterling handling of style.

French sources such as Jamin & Williams see jazz as the multiple signal of modernity as discontinuity, asymmetry, and surprise. Fitzgerald embodies these qualities by compromising between the referential that claims to be document and the romantic through the use of a unique narrator who is usually a secondary character who is at once actor and spectator of the plot. The narrative technique of *Tender Is the Night*—the "subjective mediation" of the implied observer—confirms the divided perspective: the naked facts on one hand and emotionally charged impression on the other.

Ro33. Ivănescu, Mircea. Introduction. *Marele Gatsby [The Great Gatsby]*, by F. Scott Fitzgerald. Trans. Mircea Ivănescu. Bucharest: Editura de stat pentru literatura si arta, 1967. 272. Timisoara: Editura Excelsior,1991. 222. Craiova: Editura Noua Europa, 1991. 144.

This translation in 1967, during a liberal period between totalitarian regimes, was the first important one to appear of Fitzgerald's work. It comprised *The Great Gatsby*, translated by Ivănescu, "The Diamond as Big as The Ritz," and "May Day," both translated by Liana Dobrescu. The preface was also written by Ivă nescu, who ascertains that major American novels are permeated by

Romantic visions. Writers of the Lost Generation represented a moral reaction to Prohibition and gangsterism, and Fitzgerald expressed this period in convincing artistic terms. *This Side of Paradise* suffers from lack of artistic maturity, but the book as a whole embodies a sincerity that is characteristic of Fitzgerald's work. *The Beautiful and Damned* is limited in scope. Gatsby is found to be a "complex symbol...trying to make other values hold out against the brutally distorting action of his time." "In spite of all hardships, a relentless affirmation of human consciousness, with all its responsibilities and implications, remained active inside Fitzgerald." Nowadays, Fitzgerald reemerges as a "significant representation of the American epic tradition."

Ro34. Kapp, Isa. "New York, oras al diversitatii si vitalitatii—Scriitorul si orasul [New York, City of Diversity and Vitality—the Writer and the City]." *Sinteza* 47 (1981): 25-30.

Fitzgerald's attitude towards New York was as a city where anything can happen unexpectedly, "probably reminding himself of his own triumph and failure".

Ro35. Kasindorf, Martin. "Incotro se îndreaptămaşina de vise a Hollywood-ului? [Where Does the Hollywood Machine of Creating Dreams Lead?]" *Sinteza* 18 (1975): 57.

In contrast to Francis Coppola's unconventional life and working style, young movie maker Peter Bogdanovich is so attached to Hollywood's tradition that he chooses to live like a character from Fitzgerald's novel *The Last Tycoon*. He inhabits a Spanish villa in Bel-Air and is married to actress Cybill Shepherd whom he "discovered" himself. In one of the vast rooms he watches films by Hollywood's classicists, like John Ford and Howard Hawks, after having completed a monograph on Orson Welles.

Ro36. Mihaies, Mircea. Afterword. *Ecouri din epoca jazzului [Echoes of the Jazz Age (The Crack-Up)]*, by F. Scott Fitzgerald. Trans. Hortensia Parlog. Timisoara: Editure Marineasa, 1994: 123-138.

Fitzgerald was an embodiment of that seductive chimera that bore the name of "American Dream." Coming from his provincial Minnesota to conquer New York City, he managed to add his own eccentric mark to the excesses of the megalopolis. He seemed to have inherited the predispositions towards originality, excess and defiance characteristic of his Irish ancestors. Very early, he proved to have a taste for adventure and an extraordinary talent at dissipating into countless useless activities. At Princeton the provincial rebel finally discovered a world worthy of his dreams. Here Fitzgerald met some of his best friends: Sigourney Fay, John Peale Bishop, Edmund Wilson. His marriage with

Zelda turned daydreaming into a way of life. An analysis of the roaring twenties' phenomenon should take into consideration another oddity: the propelling forces of the Jazz Age came only from within itself. Frightened that they might become contaminated by such notions as respectability, tradition, morality, the youth formed some sort of surrealist colony which desperately tried to elaborate its own laws. Everything was possible, a moveable feast, as Hemingway, one of its protagonists, would name it. "My Lost City" is one of Fitzgerald's most beautiful autobiographical texts. The supreme product of this society was the transformation of illusion into an ultimate reality. The Jazz Age could also be called the Age of Confusion. The game, the mask become now more important than the substance, no connection whatsoever to reality. Tradition has lost its exemplary character. Nevertheless, the writer does not lose his lucidity. Behind the improvised stage awaits—as usual—solitude, the other side of the coin. Aggressive histrionics on the one hand, anguished solitude on the other. Playing the main role becomes more and more difficult. The star position is hard to keep, under the impact of changing times. During the writing of *The Great Gatsby* a reciprocal exchange of faculties took place as the novelist gradually confounded himself with his character. Edmund Wilson compared Francis Scott Fitzgerald to an old woman presented with a diamond who doesn't quite know what to do with it.

Ro37. Mihaiu, Virgil. "Când fitzgeraldienii se intâlnesc la Nisa [When Fitzgeraldians Meet in Nice]." *România literară* 32 (15-22 August 2000): 22.

The second of two articles (the first being "The F. Scott Fitzgerald Congress at Nice" for *Curentul*) written by Mihaiu after the Summer 2000 conference. This one, published in the prestigious weekly of the Writers' Union of Romania, explains how Mihaiu first communicated with Linda Stanley and was ultimately invited by her to present his paper, "Fitzgerald's Romanian Reputation." Mihaiu discusses the choice of setting for the conference, its keynote address by Allan Gurganus, and various panels.

Ro38. Mihaiu, Virgil. "F. Scott Fitzgerald—epistolar [F. Scott Fitzgerald—in Letters]." *România literară*, Bucharest 13.37 (Sep. 1979): 20-21.

A comprehensive study of *The Letters of F. Scott Fitzgerald*, edited by Andrew Turnbull (Penguin Books, first published in the U.S.A. 1963). The first part refers to epistles sent to his daughter, Frances Scott Fitzgerald. Some of them contain frank opinions about life in general, the arts, politics, etc. The most consistent selection of letters results from the writer's relationship to his editor, Maxwell Perkins. Under all circumstances, a unique great obsession: writing. Fitzgerald's opinions surpass the limits of his age, and sound very much related to our mentality. The final part of the study broaches Fitzgerald's rapport with his fellow-writers, his literary memories, the way he used his own prestige in order to promote young talents. He evinces a constant openness towards genuine novelty in prose writing (Joyce, Kafka, Dos Passos, Hemingway, Malraux, etc.), and keeps in touch with Edmund Wilson, John Peale Bishop, Christian Gauss, Sherwood Anderson, Gertrude Stein, H.L. Mencken, Thomas Wolfe, John O'Hara, etc. Everywhere in Fitzgerald's letters one can detect an absolute sincerity suffused with benign irony, as if to remind us of the artist's Celtic roots.

Ro39. Mihaiu, Virgil. "Fitzgerald's Romanian Reputation." Fifth International F. Scott Fitzgerald Conference, Nice, June 29, 2000.

See Chapter Introduction.

Ro40. Mihaiu, Virgil. "Fitzgerald's Romanian Reputation, I." *Transylvanian Review* 9.1 (Spring 2000): 122-136.

Part I of a two-part article, this covers "Romanians on Fitzgerald During the Totalitarian Decades" (ending in 1989). Fitzgerald was permitted introduction into the Romanian literary consciousness after April 1964, when the Communist Party declared independence from the party line of Moscow and Beijing. Seven years of "cultural effervescence" followed. In 1967, a volume comprised of biography and translations of *The Great Gatsby*, "The Diamond as Big as The Ritz," and "May Day" appeared. The translation of the novel (by poet Mircea Ivănescu) was the first entire presentation of *Gatsby*; in a preface, Ivănescu avers that the novel does not answer a fundamental question posed by earlier Fitzgerald writings: "how one can live in such a delirious age . . . without giving up human values. . . ." "Jazz was synonymous with "Fitzgerald" among intellectual circles, a seemingly superficial link until the symbolism of music forbidden under totalitarian regimes is considered. By Romanian readers, Fitzgerald's world was considered at once "normal" and "glamorous." Essays by American and Romanian scholars about Fitzgerald and his work appeared in print (notably in *România litarara* and *Tribuna*) in the '60s. Ivănescu managed to publish his translation of *Tender Is the Night* in 1974, as the cultural atmosphere in Romania was rapidly deteriorating; states Mihaiu, "a liberal symbol like Fitzgerald brought joy to the connoisseurs among the oppressed." The movie version of *Gatsby* was screened and reviewed, and was called a "symbol of the American way of writing." A translation of "Babylon Revisited" appeared in 1977, "Pat Hobby and Orson Welles" in 1979.

Ro41. Mihaiu, Virgil. "Fitzgerald's Romanian Reputation II" *Transylvanian Review* 9.2 (Summer 2000): 146-158.

As a student, Mihaiu wrote a paper on *The Great Gatsby* that in 1973 appeared in *Steaua*, contrasting the novel to Rilke's *Dingdedichte* and finding that the people/object relationship had changed to one in which people had become "easily manageable through the sheer effect of money." Articles in *Tribuna* (1975), *Studia Universitatis Babes-Bolyai* and *România literară* (both 1979) by Mihaiu and others covered Zelda, the use of color in *Gatsby*, and a review of Turnbull's *The Letters of F. Scott Fitzgerald*. In the '80s, despite a surge in totalitarianism, Fitzgerald continued to receive critical attention and publication in Romania: a translation of Le Vot's biography, a teacher's guide, articles, and other "texts for connoisseurs." After the overthrow of Ceausescu, editors attempted to "make up for so many wasted decades." Ivănescu's translation of *Gatsby* was re-issued at three houses; translations of other Fitzgerald work, most notably *The Crack-Up*, appeared. Essays in cultural magazines in the late '90s deemed *Gatsby* a "literary text of well thought-out perfection" (Virgil Stanciu) and " a complex narrative" (A.J. Greimas). In 1996, Mihaiu published two centennial articles on Fitzgerald concerning the symbolic reflection of Jazz in the human condition. Today, Fitzgerald's reflection on Romanian literary consciousness is "partial, sporadic, fragmentary, unsystematic." Writing about the author today can be as "honest as possible, yet it will certainly have a more restricted impact that previous to December 1989."

Ro42. Mihaiu, Virgil. *"Marele Gatsby* şi disoluţia miturilor [T*he Great Gatsby* and the Dissolution of Myths]." *Steaua* 24.24 (Dec. 1973): 24.

Almost 50 years after its publication, *The Great Gatsby* continues to stir up a greater interest than most other American novels of this century. It represents not only the quintessence of the Jazz Age, but also that of Fitzgerald's prose itself. The realistic and symbolic elements are fused in a masterful work of art. In Fitzgerald's vision, symbols appear connected to the American myths, which throughout the novel, are being desacralized. The romantic past of the American West is counterpoised to the unromantic Eastern present. A world in which everything is subjugated by money makes true ideals impossible: the dream is corrupted into myth, and ends up in destroying the dreamer. Analysis of the symbolic significance of the "Wasteland" (where the only encounter of all the main characters takes place), the parties given at Gatsby's mansion, various "effigies" (Jordan Baker's chin, the drunken intruder into Gatsby's library, the wardrobe show-off meant to impress Daisy, etc.). Sometimes nature and objects are treated in a personifying manner, while people undergo a paradoxical mortification. The people/objects relationship is no longer the same as in Rilke's *Dinggedichte*. There, man had the liberty and the power to determine the fate of surrounding objects, whereas in Fitzgerald's novel people become easily manageable through the sheer effect of money. The fundamental myth, generating individual and social disasters, underlying all actions in the novel, is money. Even the central feminine character, with her "voice full of money", represents in itself a myth, as vain as the others. Fitzgerald finds a perfect stylistic equivalent to an environment from which nature is gradually disappearing, giving room to the oppressive chaos of an epoch dominated by exactitude.

Ro43. Mihaiu, Virgil. "Purtatorul de cuvant al (epocii) jazzului [Spokesman of (the) Jazz (Age)]." *România literară* 29.36 (Sep. 1996): 21.

The marking of Fitzgerald's one hundredth birthday coincided with the centennial jubilee of two new art forms: cinematography and jazz. Retrospectively, the date of September 24, 1996 (when the conceiver of the term "Jazz Age" was born) might be a source of speculations concerning the interweaving of Fitzgerald's destiny with the arts of filming and improvised music during their first decades of existence. Musically, ragtime had not exhausted its vogue, and the victory of jazz wasn't yet too obvious, when Fitzgerald published *Flappers and Philosophers*. Nevertheless, in *The Offshore Pirate* jazz already acquired the function of a reference point in Fitzgerald's prose. As usual, Fitzgerald creates a supple epic texture, abundantly fed with poetic connotations. These are often engendered by amalgamating jazz with the temptations of dancing. They serve as a foil to idealized love, which became possible under such circumstances. Jazz music's inherent potential to symbolically reflect the human condition was grasped from its very beginning, and made use of, for the first time in great literature, by F. Scott Fitzgerald. Soon after WWI, he had already managed to capture the intensity of the new life style. Love affairs seem to have been contaminated by the agitation of music which, after centuries of academic taming, reveals its latent rhythms. Everything is controlled by elusive change, by an unprecedented propensity towards playfulness. If Europe begins sublimating its anarchies through Dadaism, in the U.S. "the game of love and chance" takes place against the musical background provided by the Afro-American synthesis. The outburst of ludic sense, stimulated by jazz, dancing, and cinema, caused the usual stirring and resentment among the "moral majority" of its time. At a closer look one can notice that, by assuming his age, Fitzgerald becomes a convincing Apologist of Adolescence. He fully relishes the jubilations of the foreplay, postponing as much as possible maturity's "fulfillments", inescapably accompanied by disillusionment. The intoxication of promised love, of effusive music and dancing, of youthful dreaming, translates into the illusion of liberty, a goddess worth sacrificing for. To some extent, Fitzgerald's career as a writer had to suffer the consequences of his frank literary indulgence in the whirlwind of a "frivolous" age.

Ro44. Mihaiu, Virgil. "Scriitorul gândea precum va cânta Monk [The Writer
Was Thinking the Way Monk Would Play]." *Steaua*, Cluj-Napoca.
47.11-12 (1996): 85.

Fitzgerald's work assimilates (like a musician taking part in a jam session)
various themes, rhythms, chords and discords floating in the air of his time. His
craftsmanship can suggest, to a lecturer who is aware of subsequent jazz
developments, comparisons with unsurpassed stylists who would later on
illustrate this musical genre. Here is a possible literary/jazz parallel, over the
decades, between F.S.F. and Thelonious Monk. Both of them are inventors of
plots whose delights lie in the details, in the surprising twists and turns of
phrases and ideas. Both detest faultless but void technique—of language, of the
keyboard more exactly: the abuse in vain virtuosity, the pompous and sterile
academism. Both are masters at playing with volumes, structuring contents and
emptiness, sound and silence, creative frenzy and seasonable moments of
respite. Fitzgerald was blamed by purists for his sloppy use of orthography, and
Monk was repeatedly accused by impotent "aesthetes" to have allegedly scorned
the laws of pianistics. Yet both have created their own systems of harmony and
counterpoint, their unique timbres. They are immediately identifiable after the
first phrases of their (prose or musical) pieces. Fitzgerald and Monk are two
introspective anarchists sacrificing themselves for our right to error and . . .
pleasure.

Ro45. Papahagi, Marian. "Cronica literara-Unora le place jazz-ul [Literary
Column: Some like the Jazz]." *Tribuna* 45 (7 Nov.1985): 4.

A detailed review of Virgil Mihaiu's volume *The Resonance Box—Essays on
Jazz from Today's Cultural Perspective.* (Editura Albatros/Publishing House,
Bucharest, 1985). F. Scott Fitzgerald is on top of the list of the writers who
registered jazz in its complete novelty and suggestiveness from its first stages of
development. Virgil Mihaiu also recalls Jean Cocteau, Boris Vian, Julio
Cortazar, John Osborne, Alejo Carpentier, Malcolm Lowry, while Marian
Papahagi adds Hermann Hesse's novel *Steppenwolf,* as well as Romanian poets
Ion Vines and Ion Barbu. This first Romanian book dedicated to the connections
between jazz and the contemporary arts contains a special chapter entitled
Poetical Jazz/Jazzified Poetry, which brings together jazz-related poets from
Romania, the U.S.A., Brazil, Russia, Poland, Italy, Germany, etc.

Ro46. Parvu, Sorin. *"The Great Gatsby*: the show down title." *American
Fiction: A Contextual Approach.* Eds. Irina Burlui and Sorin Parvu. Iasi:
Iasi Al. I. Cuza University Press, 1983.

A noteworthy "text for connoisseurs" emanating from the English Studies Department at the University in Iasi before the fall of Ceausescu. Text not available for annotation.

Ro47. Parvu, Sorin. *Poetics of the Novel.* Iasi: Editura Junimea, 1997.

Norman Friedman's taxonomy as outlined in his 1955 *Forms of the Plot* includes 14 types of plot. *Tender Is the Night* is an example of the degeneration plot, in which the once sympathetic and ambitious protagonist gives up his goals and ambitions. *The Great Gatsby* exemplifies the disillusionment plot in that the hero starts out believing in his ideals but is subjected to some kind of loss, threat, or trial, and loses that faith entirely. In his 1955 *Point of View in Fiction*, Friedman classifies point of view. *The Great Gatsby* is an example of the "I" as Witness point of view, in that the author surrenders his omniscience and allows his witness to tell the reader only what he as observer may legitimately discover.

Ro48. Stanciu, Virgil. "The Cognitive Dimension of Narrative Discourse in F. Scott Fitzgerald's *The Great Gatsby*." *Studia Universitatis Babes-Bolyai/Philogia* 41.3-4 (1996): 2-11.

The Great Gatsby is a masterpiece precisely because Fitzgerald found the natural, organic structuring of his communication process that his story demanded. He knew how to make deft use of the elements of "generic stories": the American success story, the detective thriller, the love romance. Such elements belonging to well-established narrative sub-species yielded a new fictional product: a complex, intriguing story, as rich in suggestions and ambiguities as it seems deceptively simple in a first reading. The "I" of the text seems to be the same as the "I" of what A. J. Greimas and J. Courtes in *The Cognitive Dimension of Narrative Discourse (1976)* call the true enunciation (*enunciation proprement dite*) but we soon realize that they are actually different, as the producer of the true enunciation is the author while the producer of the uttered enunciation (*enunciation enoncée*) is one of the characters, Nick Carraway. By taking into consideration the opposition between being and appearing, Greimas and Courtes show that the knowledge of the enunciator, being projected into the discourse, can bring into view four different cognitive positions from which the characters' doing and being are observed. While Nick and Jordan's positions are mostly true in that their being coincides with their appearing, the positions of other informers—Wolfsheim, Henry C. Gatz—are either false (being is different from appearing) or delusive (not being and appearing). Gatsby's position is secret (being and not appearing). As Nick uncovers more and more significant details about Gatsby's real life, the object of knowing moves closer to becoming true (appearing for what it is)—even though the essential mystery of Gatsby remains untouched. *The Great Gatsby* is, in Greimas's words, a "complex narrative" in which the distribution of knowledge becomes an important organizing principle. "The seamless web of observation and experience creates an osmosis which we accept as artistically perfect, due to the convincing impression of a life seen through layers of observation which are masterfully handled in order to convey a feeling of genuine experience."

Ro49. Tăranu, Dana. "Scott Fitzgerald şi mirajul banului [Scott Fitzgerald and the Mirage of Money]." *Tribuna* 1 (Jan. 1969): 8.

A synthetical, informative presentation of Fitzgerald's life and work. Opinions expressed by Arthur Mizener, Dos Passos, Hemingway and Malcolm Cowley are blended into a no-nonsense portrait of the author, whose masterpiece had been published into Romanian just a year earlier. Gatsby appears as a reflection of the writer's own biography. This hymn to pure love, finally killed by a mercantile world, avoids any melodramatic accents. After three decades, the perspective of this article is still relevant.

Ro50. Teodorescu, Cristian. "Scott Fitzgerald." *Contemporanul* 37 (13 Sep. 1985): 15.

Before becoming a real writer, Fitzgerald had been for the average American reader yet another myth, all the more fascinating as it met the standards of the Jazz Age: an unknown youngster who starts writing, and achieves full success with his very first book. Nevertheless, all his successes proved to be insignificant palliatives for the traumas and complexes inherited from adolescence. Fitzgerald lived through the obsessions of his time in *This Side of Paradise, The Beautiful and Damned, A Diamond as Big as the Ritz, The Rich Boy, Tender Is the Night*. In *Gatsby*, there is a special romanticism, incompatible with the rich men's world in which this character tries to make room for himself. Gatsby considers wealth a way of retrieving the love of his earlier years, but Daisy is in reality a superficial woman causing the hero's tragic failure.

BOOK REVIEWS/NEWS ARTICLES/RADIO PROGRAMS

Ro51. Alexandrescu, Mircea. *"Marele Gatsby [The Great Gatsby]."* *Cinema* 11 (Nov. 1975): 14.

Jack Clayton's movie version of *The Great Gatsby* was shown in Romania in 1975. *Gatsby* would become a "symbol of the American way of writing." Clayton's film reconstitutes "the mad years," with their fashionable outbreaks. This vast social picture, for which Francis Ford Coppola wrote the scenario, deals primarily with the surface of the novel, but nevertheless evinces a desire to surpass the nostalgia about this era which ended in an economic crash.

Ro52. Burlui, Irina. "Scott Fitzgerald şi destinul unei generaţii [Scott Fitzgerald
and the Destiny of a Generation]." *Cronica* 2 (13 Jan.1984): 7.

A review of André Le Vot's monograph *F. Scott Fitzgerald*, translated by
Ruxandra Soroiu (Editura Eminescu, Bucharest, 1983. 590.). This monograph
offers an objective, impartial image of F.S.F., the incurable romantic.
Fitzgerald's prose would be hard to understand without a proper knowledge of
its author's personality. André Le Vot makes use of various sources—Edmund
Wilson, Hemingway, Gertrude Stein, and Fitzgerald's own confessions (*The
Crack-Up*). The time lapses between the important novels were filled up with
rather commercial short-story productions. Le Vot's monograph insists upon
Fitzgerald's destiny as a novelist: why did he suddenly lose his popularity in
comparison to Hemingway's ascension? The answer should be sought not only
in his romantic predispositions, but also in his aesthetic compromises. Anyway,
Fitzgerald is *the* author of the twenties, of those excessive years for which he
found a suitable prose vehicle. For him, the novel was not the place of
sophisticated technical exercises but a supple medium of conveying thought and
emotion from one human being to another.

Ro53. Mihaiu, Virgil. "Congresul F. Scott Fitzgerald de la Nisa [The 5th
International F. Scott Fitzgerald Conference]." *Curentul* (8 August
2000): 6.

This article, which appeared in one of Romania's most credible national, daily
newspapers, gives a concise account of the Nice conference's main events.
Mihaiu wrote a second article about the event, which was published in the
prestigious Romanian weekly, put out by the Writers' Union of Romania,
România literară.

Ro54. Suchianu, D. I. "*Marele Gatsby* [*The Great Gatsby*]." *România literară*
8.47 (20 Nov. 1975): 20.

Jack Clayton's movie based on Francis Ford Coppola's screenplay is superior to
the 1949 filming of the same subject by American director Elliot Nugent. The
romantic, sentimental, brave, proud and disillusioned hero has only one aim: to
find his lost beloved and marry her. He acts with angelic purity and with the
steadfastness of a conquistador—"two souls inhabit the same heart", as Goethe
would have put it. A psychic alchemy marvelously portrayed by that great actor,
Robert Redford. His feminine counterpoint is subtly played by Mia Farrow,
another Faustian character, torn between a Romeo-Juliet love and the prejudices
of her clannishness. Gatsby's legend is similar to that of a Don Quijote dressed
up in the garments of Wall Street jackals. "A touching film; full of charms; a
somewhat sinister charm, yet charming."

DISSERTATIONS

Ro55. Peterhansel-Antonescu, Andrea. "The Romanian Translation of F. S. Fitzgerald's *The Great Gatsby*: A Stylistic Approach." Paris IV Sorbonne, June 1996. 40.

Mircea Ivănescu's translation is in nine chapters like the English original, but differs in division of paragraphs, the necessity of additional word-forms which explain a particular mood or attitude of the narrator towards the other characters and their behavior, and characters' particularities of speech. Incoherencies leading to error occur in the translation of American measurement and the different use of tenses in Romanian. Choices in dealing with proper nouns do not always capture the idea behind Fitzgerald's nicknames, while the metaphorical use of colors is consistent and Ivănescu is sensitive to Fitzgerald's delicate use of symbolic verbs, although he lacks the author's fluidity. Through literal translation, the elements that compose a syntagm often lead to misinterpretations and confusion as in the case of geographical places. This also occurs through the use of loan translations and borrowings. Concerning dramatic action and the key passages in the book, those passages where the density of life is compressed into energetic actions, the translator is at the height of his task. But the Romanian reader is at a loss from a stylistic point of view—a text like *The Great Gatsby*, full of symbols, needs a closer approach.

Ro56. Mihaiu, Virgil. *A Writer of Our Time: F. Scott Fitzgerald.* Babeş-Bolyai University Cluj-Napoca, 2002. 30.

Postmodernism both accepts "the lesser risks of the lowest common denominator" and is a "saving grace for theoreticians in their search to achieve (an actually improbable) consensus." Fitzgerald understood this "cultural polytheism" due to his clairvoyant sensibility, which appears in his major novels and the Pat Hobby stories. *Gatsby* is an "all embracing ecumenism of postmodern aesthetics" in the novel's variety of thematic angles and its interweaving of historical facts and illusions with the grand narratives that also permeate it, including the grail myth and the American Dream. In her androgyny and ambiguity, Fitzgerald sees Jordan Baker as a forerunner of the postmodern woman. Primarily, because of his own interest and knowledge of jazz, he concentrates on the intertextuality in the novel of music and words, a theme that has been explored before, but not with the intimate familiarity and both creative and scholarly comprehension that Mihaiu, a poet and jazz musician, brings to both words and jazz. Mihaiu contends that *Tender Is the Night*, unlike *Gatsby*, is not a novel for the late 20th century. Its "apocalyptic typology . . . is reinforced and qualified by echoes of Spengler" while "postmodernism has taught us to live evil." The cultural decay that Fitzgerald perceived he attached to the United States alone, but the decay has subsequently been globalized. Nonetheless, Fitzgerald was still clairvoyant, particularly in the battle of the sexes which has also become globalized. Mihaiu most astutely sees that the contribution of *Tender Is the Night* to the postmodern aesthetic lies in the technical difficulties Fitzgerald experienced with the plot and "his hesitations about the right structuring of the novel" as a result of the tension between the conservative and experimental dimensions of his aesthetic. *The Last Tycoon* "represents the last of the novelist's fictional testament about the death of his own craft. . . . In Stahr's world (books) exist only as manipulative pretexts for a manipulative art."

TEACHER/STUDENT GUIDES AND EDITIONS

Ro57. Christopher, Givan, ed. "Babylon Revisited," by F. Scott Fitzgerald. *Texts for the Special Course in 20th Century American Literature.* Universitatea din Bucuresti, Facultatea de limbi germanice, Catedra de limba engleza: Bucharest, 1977: 25-45.

Ro58. "F. S. F. and the Lost Generation." *A Guide to American Literature for Teacher Training and Refresher Courses.* Eds. Hertha Perez, Stefan Avadanei, Dumitru Dorobat. U. of Iasi: Iasi, 1981. 202-245.

Lecturer on Jazz at the Cluj Music Academy, Virgil Mihaiu has published *Between the Jazz Age and Postmodernism: F. Scott Fitzgerald* (Timisoara: Editura Universitatii de Vest, 2003).

India

Up until thirty to forty years ago, syllabi for courses on literature in English in Indian universities included only British writers. In recent decades, the study of American literature has become more prevalent for various reasons. Several Nobel Prizes have been won by American writers, the American Studies Research Center has been established in Hyderabad, India, and serves as the largest resource library on the United States in Asia, and the various USIS libraries in the major metropolitan areas have provided scholars with easy access to books. American authors are now included in university study, both undergraduate and graduate. According to Somdatta Mandal, of Visva-Bharati University, Santiniketan, in a presentation on the Indian reception of Fitzgerald at the Fitzgerald Centennial Conference at Princeton University in 1996, *The Great Gatsby* has become one of the most representative texts featured in university syllabi (In30).

Many articles and collections of articles have been written about Fitzgerald in India since the late 1970s. Between 1975 and 1980, three books and four articles were published and two dissertations were written. While in the next decade, only one book and one article appeared, six dissertations were written. In the decade from 1990-2000, in response to the 1996 Fitzgerald Centennial celebrations, three books, including two collections, 42 articles (most from the collections), and six additional dissertations appeared.

At the Princeton conference, Mandal asserted that "good and scholarly" works have appeared on Fitzgerald in India. The approaches to his novels and short stories are, for the most part, representative of approaches elsewhere in Europe and the United States. Thematic studies still prevail: Tirthankar Chattopadhyay (In3) and A. K. Sethi (In51) both see *The Great Gatsby* as a Modernist text influenced by T. S. Eliot's wasteland imagery. Subhash Chandra (In15, In16) and Brajesh Sawhney (In48) emphasize the influence of materialism on the characters and their society; P. G. Rama Rao (In46), Manasi

Sinha (In8), Satyam Moorty (In36), R. Raja Govindasamy (In21), and Pradip Kumar Dey (In18) look at both the historically idealistic and current materialistic aspects of the American Dream as portrayed in Fitzgerald's novels. The 1920s as a historical period are studied by M. Sivaramkrishna (In9), Sanjukta Dasgupta (In17), Somdatta Mandal (In32), Isaac Sequeira (In49), Gulfishaan Moin (In35), and Pratima Agnihotri (In10). Sukrita Paul Kumar (In27), Mary Magdalene Dorairaj (In20), Rajyasree Khushu-Lahiri (In26) and K. B. Razdan (In47) examine gender roles from a traditional perspective. Other writers, Rama Nair (In40, In41) and Sourin Guha (In22), emphasize the romantic strains in his work.. Gautam Kundu (In28), Somdatta Mandal (In29), Soumyajit Mandal (In33) and Tutun Mukherjee (In37) look at the influence of Hollywood on Fitzgerald's life and writings.

Feminist theory, narratology studies, and post-structural work also influence current Indian literary criticism. Current feminist theory informs the work of Vijay Sharma and Sherine Upot. In her "Woman as Object: Feminism vs. Fitzgerald's Romantic Egotism," Sharma claims that the women in Fitzgerald's novels are seen as "commodified objects of desire and possession" (In52). In "She-Centering *The Great Gatsby*: Fitzgerald, Barthelme and the Gender Question," Upot claims that Fitzgerald's novel is male-centered and that narrative realism reinforces the patriarchal order and marginalizes women, whereas in Barthelme's *Snow White*, patriarchal assumptions are contested through deconstruction of language and questioning the mechanisms of the creation of meaning (In55).

Prasenjit Biswas and V. C. Harris use French theorists to frame and support their perspectives. In "Lover's Discourse in *The Great Gatsby*: A Barthesian Conspectus," Biswas reads Fitzgerald's novel in light of Barthes's *A Lover's Discourse*, with Gatsby as the typical Lover with "signs" that set him apart from other characters and entrap him in his own discourse in reference to the object of his own desire (In13). In "*Tender Is the Night*: Rape, Racism and Romance," Harris sees shocking reality transformed into the traditional structures of romance, while Dick's racist comments are a Derridian "invention of the other" on whom to project his frustration and impotence (In23).

Mandal also stressed the difference in the Indian perspective on studying American literature from that of the West. The American Dream of unlimited growth is in direct opposition to the Indian belief in "karma" or that what you are is correlated to your earlier rebirths. Fitzgerald, then, is seen as a writer who tries to redo his own map of reality and fails. The Indian response to his excesses and failings both as a writer attempting to cope with his society and as a man coping with his life is that he should have instituted a series of checks and balances. Two articles, Rama Nair's "Sense(s) and Sensibility in *The Great Gatsby*" and M. Sivaramkrishna's "Some Indic Pathways to Fitzgerald's

'Paradise'" see Fitzgerald's characters in the context of their excessive attachment to "artha" (wealth) and "kama" (desire), rather than "dharma" (ethics) and "moksha" (freedom). According to Sivaramkrishna, Dick Diver cannot dissociate "dharma" from "kama" and "artha" (In54). Likewise, Rama Nair believes that Gatsby should have balanced the four aspects of life, and not concentrated on "artha" (In39). According to Mandal, R. K. Narayan's novel, *The Financial Expert*, "is a good illustration of why it is necessary for a person to maintain money-oriented checks and balances" (In30). (Also see Chandra's "Fair Means for a Fair End! Fitzgerald's *The Great Gatsby*" and Narayan's "*The Financial Expert* in the Light of Gandhian Thought" [In15]).

Fitzgerald is often compared to Indian poet Michael Madhusudan Dutt, a fruit of the nineteenth century Bengal renaissance, who wrote in English. Both writers experienced marital discord, both were distressed by acute financial problems despite earning significant royalties, and both took to drinking and wasted their productive years, and both died a premature death. Neither writer applied checks and balances and, as Mandal contended, neither fulfilled the obsessive need of the Indian scholar to place the writer in a particular ideological mold, a practical as well as a scholastic need. As literature can be a powerful social force, the Indian scholar wants to make the writer work for a specific political goal.

Despite cultural and religious judgments about the value of Western literature, Mandal claimed Indian people "are open to other cultures and peoples. We are trying to assimilate the experience of all mankind and accept other people's methods. For us, American culture occupies a great place in the process of recovering our own heritage. . . . It would therefore not be overemphasizing if we say that a writer like F. Scott Fitzgerald enables scholars like us to explore avenues for a true cultural synthesis" (In30).

TRANSLATIONS/EDITIONS

In1.   Fitzgerald, F. Scott. *Lalasa [The Great Gatsby]*. Trans. Ajeya. Delhi: Rajpal, 1969.

In2.   Fitzgerald, F. Scott. *The Great Gatsby. American Literature Texts.* Intro., Notes and Bibliography by M. Sivaramkrishna. Delhi: Oxford Univ. Press, 1981; 1992. 156.

BOOKS: FULL-LENGTH STUDIES AND COLLECTIONS

In3.   Chattopadhyay, Tirthankar. *The Artist and the City.* West Bengal:
        University of Kalyani Press, 1978. 59.

In their novels, Scott Fitzgerald, Thomas Wolfe, and Nathanael West combine
the modernist characteristics of introspective self-analysis and "metamorphic
impetus" through their fusions of the themes of the artist and the city.
Fitzgerald's heroes, unlike those of Wolfe, are incapable of growth, betraying
Fitzgerald's inability to transform experience into art. In their symbolic
treatment of New York City, both Wolfe and Fitzgerald see the city as a
romantic symbol of the possibility of contemporary society, while at the same
time portray it as a waste land. For West, the city is seen in greater relief as
"both a victim and an attacker." "Comprehensive realism" is what all three
authors are striving for, a realism that fuses both artistic introspection and the
background metaphor of the city. Where Wolfe seeks to preserve "the Golden
City," despite its failures, and West "attacks the unreal values but cannot
establish any real ones," Fitzgerald fails in "reconstructing the image of the city
on more objective lines."

In4.   Kumar, Sukrita Paul. *Man, Woman and Androgyny: A Study of the
        Novels of Theodore Dreiser, Scott Fitzgerald, and Ernest Hemingway.*
        New Delhi: Indus, 1989.

Fitzgerald's works reflect the "shifting sex roles" of the period; the writer
believes in the "equality principle" between genders in his amoral vision of sex
and romance, and wants to correct the falsity of the "sexless individuals" that
populated traditional American fiction. In his celebrated Flapper, Fitzgerald
conflates "the dark lady and the fair damsel," revealing his puritanical
attachment to the illusion of innocence, while at the same time absorbing the
lessons of Freud and D. H. Lawrence and their inquiries into the male-female
polarity. As early as in his first stories, his female characters are informed by
such shifting of the traditional roles; Amory Blaine shows all the insecurity
derived from such instability and struggles to achieve a relationship with
Eleanor, in whose mind femininity and masculinity are equally mixed. Anthony
Patch, yet another "adolescent drunk on youth, beauty, and purity," is a
narcissistic character who ends up being manipulated by the *femme fatale*, in a
typical inversion of roles. In *The Great Gatsby*, which is a critique of self-
sufficiency that precludes "love and tenderness," sex is pursued by Gatsby as a
symbol of incarnation, of the androgynous union of man and woman, but his
narcissism and the objectification of Daisy doom the experience to failure. With
Tender Is the Night, Fitzgerald is able to give the first full portrait of femininity.
In Nicole's recovery and Dick's self-destruction, the writer expresses "the
unconscious belief that the female dominates"; she achieves sanity and an

uninhibited expression of her sexual desire through the traditional maleness of Tommy Barban, contrasted with Dick's conflation of gender roles.

In5.   Mandal, Somdatta, ed. *F. Scott Fitzgerald: A Centennial Tribute.* 2 vols. New Delhi: Prestige, 1997.

Collection of essays annotated here. Writers include Subhas Chandra ("What Price Riches!"), Sanjukta Dasgupta, Sourin Guha, Judy Hen, Gautam Kundu, Somdatta Mandal ("Introduction" and "The Glitter and the Glory"), Soumyajit Mandal, Jerome Mandel, Satyam Moorty, Tutun Mukherjee ("The Other Side of Paradise"), Rama Nir ("Deconstructing Fitzgerald's Romanticism"), Murari Prasad, Qing Qian, and P. G. Rama Rao ("Foreword").

In6.   Ramanan, Mohan, ed. *F. Scott Fitzgerald: Centenary Essays from India.* New Delhi: Prestige, 1998. 204.

Collection of essays annotated here. Writers include Pratima Agnihotri, Suman Balan, Prasenjit Biswas, B. R. Burg ("Preface"), Subhash Chandra ("Fair Means for a Fair End!"), Pradip Kumar Dey, R. K. Dhawan, Mary Magdalene Dorairaj, R. Raja Govindasamy, V. C. Harris, A. Noel Joseph Irudayaraj, Rajyashree Khushu-Lahiri, Somdatta Mandal ("The Twenties"), Gulfishaan Moin, Tutun Mukherjee ("The Last Tycoon, Citizen Kane and the American Dream"), Nirmala Rita Nair, Rama Nair ("Tragedy Without Transcendence"), Pramod K. Nayar, Mohan Ramanan ("Introduction"), Brajesh Sawhney, Isaac Sequeira, A. K. Sethi ("T. S. Eliot's 'The Waste Land' and the Novels of Scott Fitzgerald"), Vijay K. Sharma, M. Sivaramkrishna ("Some Indic Pathways"), and Sherine Upot.

In7.   Rao, B. Ramchandra. *The American Fictional Hero: An Analysis of the Work of Fitzgerald, Wolfe, Farrell, Dos Passos and Steinbeck.* English Language and Literature 4. Chandigarh: Bahri, 1979.

These roughly contemporary writers treat the figure of the American hero caught between the needs of society and those of the individual. Despite the crisis of values of the Twenties and the technical innovations of Modernism, the Lost Generation represents the culmination of a longer period of change and growth in American fiction. The discovery and definition of selfhood has long been a distinctive trait of the American novel, which toward the end of the 19th century begins to show a particular interest in the education of the hero through the acquisition of experience. All of Fitzgerald's main characters, in one way or another, embody the figure of the post-WWI disenchanted hero embarked on a quest for meaning; for them making experience means relinquishing the illusions of youth, which leads to "self-knowledge without self-realization." Thus they all fail, some by accepting reality, some more tragically. In *The Great*

Gatsby Fitzgerald expands this romantic and tragic vision to a national dimension, showing how the innocence of the American Dream is "defeated by the forces of evil."

In8.   Sinha, Manasi. *Journey from Innocence to Experience: Writings of F. Scott Fitzgerald*. New Delhi: Decent Books, 1998. 173.

Although the biography cannot be used as a direct explanation for the novels, the fact that Fitzgerald saw his own life as a fictional creation allows one to see how the writer, as well as his characters, is embarked on a "journey from innocence to experience." The pole of innocence can be traced back to the concept of the American Dream, which shows a remarkable ability to persist and influence American society; such persistence reaches one of its peaks with the Jazz Age and its celebration of youth, expansion, and energy. Nonetheless, the more perceptive minds, such as Fitzgerald's, can already foresee the sense of impending doom and moral exhaustion amidst the festive climate of the era. With *The Great Gatsby*, Fitzgerald's tragic vision of the conflict between dreams and reality matures, and in Gatsby he portrays the idealist who fails to realize the futility of the object of his dreams, as well as the fundamental corruption of the social environment he desperately wants to be a part of. In *Tender Is the Night* Fitzgerald brings his critique of the American dream one step further, showing how it carries within itself "the seeds of its own corruption." While Gatsby remained romantically attached to his impossible dreams and was destroyed by their failure, Dick Diver shows the degeneration of idealism and the willingness to abandon one's own dreams in hopes of gaining wealth and social respect. The long journey started in the early novels ends on a pessimistic note in *The Last Tycoon* with a more general vision of the "decline of moral and spiritual values"; nonetheless, Fitzgerald never abandons his admiration for the original "purity of the dream" and the possible, albeit improbable, return of innocence within a cyclical scheme of human experience.

In9.   Sivaramkrishna, M. *Icarus of the Jazz Age: A Study of the Novels of F. Scott Fitzgerald*. Hyderabad: Osmania University, 1978. 169.

Fitzgerald's main accomplishment was the understanding of the disillusionment and the tragic sense of life hidden beneath the glossy surface of 1920s America. Fitzgerald can be rightly inserted within the long American tradition of the quest for identity and the "pressure on the individual" to achieve his goals; within the mutated social context of the 1920s, such dynamics result in his characters' discovery of the meaninglessness of modern life. In his more mature works the protagonists present a lucid tragic outlook on life, while still preserving their dedication to the original ideal. In *The Crack-Up*, the autobiographical elements of Fitzgerald's writing show a pattern of promising idealism followed by the realization of the illusory nature of reality. In *This Side of Paradise* it is thanks to such a paradigm that the novel can be appreciated as more than a youthful and autobiographical debut. With *The Beautiful and Damned* Fitzgerald moves into the field of adulthood and in Anthony Patch he presents a protagonist who reveals the absurdity of life and human endeavors when confronted with the limits of time and history. Gatsby is Fitzgerald's first mature creation, as shown in the novel's controlled structure and successful style; the character is here fully developed to represent the purity of the romantic impulse, which is nonetheless directed at the wrong object. With *Tender Is the Night*, Fitzgerald gives a mature portrayal of his "disturbing vision of life"; Dick Diver invests all his hopes in his medical profession and the superficial object of his romantic and idealistic interest, Nicole. His flaw is the inability to separate these two aspects of his personality, which results in his attempt to perform an impossible "miracle of transference," leading to failure and isolation. In *The Last Tycoon*, Fitzgerald successfully detaches himself from the protagonist through a canny use of the point of view technique. Monroe Stahr embodies a universal "longing for innocence" which is confronted with the futility of success and the falsity of one's public image. Stahr's ethos, dedication, and true belief in a dream are in stark contrast with the reality of Hollywood, seen as a reflection of contemporary American society and its lack of solid values.

ESSAYS/CHAPTERS/NOTES/CONFERENCE PAPERS

In10. Agnihotri, Pratima. "This 'Other' Side of *The Great Gatsby*." *F. Scott Fitzgerald: Centenary Essays from India*, ed. Mohan Ramanan. New Delhi: Prestige, 1998. 125-132.

Jay Gatsby is "the Tantalus of the modern age" who strives to achieve a dream that constantly recedes from him and remains ultimately unattainable. Gatsby embarks in a path of self definition, which is examined in the tradition of the "Emersonian, Whitmanian American self" looking to achieve his dream. The establishing of a self through the opposition to what is perceived as 'alien' is active on a racial, religious, economical and social level; yet its main occurrence is within the gender issue, which sees Gatsby's self definition through the quintessentially 'other', the woman. Gatsby shapes his own identity based on an ideal concept of Daisy, who fails to live up to his expectations; this causes him to be tantalized into desiring what is not worth his effort. Such entrapment is not present only on a personal level, but it is transferred to the American dream itself, showing that Emerson's and Whitman's dream of the triumph of the self is shattered by the social and economical consumerism of the Twenties.

In11. Arora, V. N. "*The Great Gatsby*: The Predicament of the Dual Vision."
       Indian Journal of American Studies 8.1 (Jan. 1978): 1-9.

The Great Gatsby is mainly the story of Nick and the transformation of his point of view from a traditionally strict midwestern morality to a more mature comprehension and sympathy for the actions of others. Gatsby is a projection of one of the sides of Nick's personality: Nick is endowed with a double vision, which lets him clearly realize that Gatsby's inner dream is an illusion and yet consider it as a virtue against the corruption of the cynical rich. Thus at the end, Gatsby's death is an "aesthetic necessity" because his acceptance of reality would have resulted in the perversion of his vision and his entering the world of the Buchanans. In the closing pages of the novel, Gatsby's name dissolves into a collective 'we' that universalizes the story and hints at Nick's problematic balance between "heart" and "head."

In12. Bala, Suman. "Point of View: A Comparative Study of Scott Fitzgerald's
       Nick and Joseph Conrad's Marlow." *F. Scott Fitzgerald: Centenary
       Essays from India.* Ed. Mohan Ramanan. New Delhi: Prestige, 1998.
       143-50.

The figure of Marlow in four of Conrad's books is an important antecedent for the character of Nick in *The Great Gatsby*; both are point of view characters and both are used as first person narrators in the texts. By doing so, Fitzgerald and Conrad introduce a narrating voice that gives immediacy and authenticity to the story, as the narrator is the direct witness of the events narrated. At the same time, both Marlow and Nick distance themselves from their story, by placing it in the past and looking back at things after they have happened. The reader experiences the characters and the events in the same way as the narrator is experiencing them. Yet both Nick and Marlow manipulate their narration, mainly by disrupting the chronological order and by expressing their own sympathies and judgement about other characters. Even when their vision is most lucid and disenchanted, they manage to express a deep fascination with some of the main characters of the books.

In13. Biswas, Prasenjit, "Lover's Discourse in *The Great Gatsby*: A Barthesian
       Conspectus." *F. Scott Fitzgerald: Centenary Essays from India*, ed.
       Mohan Ramanan. New Delhi: Prestige, 1998. 78-84.

Seen from the perspective of Roland Barthes' *A Lover's Discourse*, the character of Gatsby assumes all the traits of the typical Lover, those 'signs' that set him apart from the rest of the characters and entrap him in his own discourse. In mystifying the object of his own desire, the Lover mystifies himself and his position in the world; he thus objectifies the other and makes it unapproachable, which in turn propels his need to know the other and causes his use of more lover's discourse. Gatsby fits perfectly into this pattern as he not only desires Daisy, but projects on her his own desire because he needs to create a fantasy in which she desires him. In doing so, he definitely separates himself from reality in the eyes of the other characters, who can clearly see that he is acting out a dream constructed by himself and not supported by any objectivity. By the end of the novel, his entrapment in his own dream causes his total failure, as he in incapable of completing that return of the subject to himself, which is the ultimate goal of the Lover's desire.

In14. Burg, B. R. Preface. *F. Scott Fitzgerald: Centenary Essays from India.* Ed. Mohan Ramanan. New Delhi: Prestige, 1998. 9-10.

These essays were written for the seminar organized by the American Studies Research Centre in the occasion of Fitzgerald's centenary. The essays reflect the overall approach of the seminar, which called for the application of contemporary theory to the reading of Fitzgerald's works, resulting especially in comparative and interdisciplinary contributions to the study of the writer.

In15. Chandra, Subhash. "Fair Means for a Fair End! Fitzgerald's *The Great Gatsby* and Narayan's *The Financial Expert* in the Light of Gandhian Thought." In *F. Scott Fitzgerald: Centenary Essays from India*, ed. Mohan Ramanan. New Delhi: Prestige, 1998. 116-124.

Both Fitzgerald and R. K. Narayan appear as moralists who condemn their protagonists to failure because of their inability to pursue their legitimate goal through appropriate means. In his pursuit of Daisy, Gatsby is overwhelmed by the moral and material corruption of the Twenties and becomes obsessed with material wealth and its ostentatious display in extravagant parties. By showing Gatsby's downfall, Fitzgerald remains faithful to his Catholic heritage and the values of his upbringing, which make him disdain the same material success and fame he is attracted to and fascinated by. The same happens to Narayan's protagonist, who forgets his moral values and Gandhi's idea of fair means in his excessive attachment to financial success and the attempt to achieve it.

In16. Chandra, Subhash. "What Price Riches!: A Study of 'The Diamond as Big as the Ritz.'" *F. Scott Fitzgerald: A Centennial Tribute* Vol. I. Ed. Somdatta Mandal. New Delhi: Prestige, 1997. 65-70.

This short story should be read in light of the theme of wealth and corruption as it is present throughout Fitzgerald's production. This is a reflection of the social environment of the American 1920s, with their booming economy and the unprecedented corruption and crime. Fitzgerald displays an ongoing love-hate relationship with the rich, whom he envies and despises. In the story this is clear from the criminal actions and arrogant behavior of the possessor of the huge diamond, who in the end makes a grotesque attempt to bribe even God, and finally destroys himself and his own wealth to prevent its sharing with the world.

In17. Dasgupta, Sanjukta. *"The Crack-Up*: Scott Fitzgerald, Ernest
Hemingway and the Lost Generation." *F. Scott Fitzgerald: A Centennial Tribute* Vol. I. Ed. Somdatta Mandal. New Delhi: Prestige, 1997. 30-38.

All the previous certainties of the past are questioned and shattered in the works of these two writers, and the new generations find themselves in an unprecedented way free but disoriented. All of Fitzgerald's works can be read as a portrayal of these frustrations and difficult times; this will be suggested by the writer himself, when he writes *The Crack-Up* as a poetic assessment of the exhaustion underlying the seemingly carefree 1920s. Such tragic vision of the age is a common feature of many writers of the time. The close friendship between Fitzgerald and Hemingway came to an end because it became strained mostly due to the difference in personality and in the two writers' relationship to their audience. While Hemingway builds a permanent bridge to his readership, thanks to his accessible style and his ability to harmonize the critics and the wider public, Fitzgerald becomes progressively estranged from the readers of the time and suffers greatly for his commercial and critical failure. Scott's psychic problems made things worse and distanced him further from Hemingway's vitality and success. In a final irony, it is Hemingway's own 'crack-up' and suicide that ideally bring the two back together as the two best and most tragic representatives of the Lost Generation.

In18. Dey, Pradip Kumar. "The End of the American Dream: *The Great Gatsby*." *F. Scott Fitzgerald: Centenary Essays from India*, ed. Mohan Ramanan. New Delhi: Prestige, 1998. 133-37.

Unlike Sinclair Lewis, Fitzgerald presents in *The Great Gatsby* an "unsatirical view of post-war modernity," in which the protagonist represents the self-made man who hopelessly struggles to succeed in a society in which success and fame have become the absolute property of the higher classes. The dream of social mobility and self-fulfillment for the individual has been destroyed by the moral cynicism of the Twenties, but Gatsby stubbornly pursues his indefinite goal of reversing time and changing reality, ultimately destined to fail. In doing so, he strives to achieve material success, but unlike in the traditional American ideal of the self-made man, this does not come with "ethical and spiritual values." Through the tragic destiny of Gatsby, Fitzgerald presents his critique of modernity and his hatred for the materialism and relativism of the Twenties, thus making his character into a victim both of his own high expectations and the hypocrisy of the surrounding characters.

In19. Dhawan, R. K. "The Permanent Realitites of Existence: A Comparative
       Study of Fitzgerald's *The Great Gatsby* and Joseph Conrad's *Heart of
       Darkness.*" *F. Scott Fitzgerald: Centenary Essays from India*, ed. Mohan
       Ramanan. New Delhi: Prestige, 1998. 151-59.

Both Gatsby and Kurtz are self-centered and stubborn pursuers of an impossible
dream, which ultimately fails leaving them defeated and causing their death.
Although Kurtz has become an incarnation of pure evil with animal traits by the
time we see him, he started off as an idealist of colonialism, just as Gatsby
represents the American dream of endless possibilities. Both are corrupted by
the accumulation of material riches, even though Kurtz seems to be more
greedily focused on wealth for its own sake, while Gatsby always uses it as a
means to win Daisy's love. Both characters are self-made men, who have a
mysterious past and remain to a certain extent an enigma for the reader; this is
reflected in the difficulty that the other characters experience in trying to
understand them, resulting in different and contradictory opinions about them.
By the end of the novels, their romantic idealism has been shattered and they
remain in total isolation from the rest of the world; only the narrators, Nick and
Marlow, show some sympathy for them and are the only ones who stand by
them at the moment of their death.

In20. Dorairaj, Mary Magdalene. "A Portrait of the Ladies: A Contrastive
       Study of the Women in the Novels of Henry James and F. Scott
       Fitzgerald." *F. Scott Fitzgerald: Centenary Essays from India*, ed.
       Mohan Ramanan. New Delhi: Prestige, 1998. 98-104.

James's female characters represent morality and innocence in their
confrontation with adverse social conditions and ruthless individuals who cause
the women's defeat. Their goal is generally marriage which is seen in a romantic
light, but which finally becomes a prison for them, although not without a
"masochistic touch." On the contrary, Fitzgerald's women, modeled on Zelda
and her contemporaries, are the reflection of the flappers of the Twenties; they
are independent, strong and domineering. Their sexual and social behavior is
extremely free, and in their self-centeredness they think of marriage and love
only in terms of money and power. They are often presented as 'vampires' who
exploit men and leave them disenchanted and humiliated.

In21. Govindasamy, R. Raja. "The Dream as Nightmare in Fitzgerald's *The
       Great Gatsby* and Dreiser's *An American Tragedy.*" *F. Scott Fitzgerald:
       Centenary Essays from India*, ed. Mohan Ramanan. New Delhi: Prestige,
       1998. 90-97.

Despite the many differences in style and approach, the two works share a
similar situation and the two main characters, Gatsby and Clyde Griffiths, both

embody the prototype of the hero pursuing a particular form of the quest, which is the American dream of the success of the talented against all odds. Yet in both cases the dream in its 'rags to riches' version leads to a tragic ending, as the original idealism has been turned into the pursuit of material riches and the superficial 'pretty girl.' The materialism of the American dream is thus exposed, and the two characters are revealed as variations on the 'boy' figure, so common in American literature, for they have failed to realize the futility of their dreams as they become adults; they are prisoners of their attempt to change, or repeat, the past, against any realistic chance. The main difference, apart from Dreiser's realism and Fitzgerald's 'impressionism', is that Dreiser presents his protagonist as the common man, the victim of a typical American tragedy, whereas Fitzgerald's stresses Gatsby's exceptional greatness, certainly with a dose of irony, but also with admiration.

In22. Guha, Sourin. "Anguish and Despair in Fitzgerald's Letters." *F. Scott Fitzgerald: A Centennial Tribute* Vol. I. Ed. Somdatta Mandal. New Delhi: Prestige, 1997. 39-50.

Fitzgerald's letters address very different matters, as they were written to different people and for different purposes. If to the daughter Scottie the author writes mostly about her scholastic career and how important it is that she works hard to avoid her parents' mistakes, in the letters to Zelda he expresses his unconditional love for her, even in the most difficult moments. With friends and colleagues like Maxwell Perkins, Edmund Wilson, or Hemingway, more literary topics emerge, such as Scott's judgments on his own novels, his ideas, his financial problems and the inability to establish a lasting success. Fitzgerald's letters, although not presenting a coherent and complete theory of literature, are nonetheless "warm, human and touching," establishing him as a great letter writer, in the tradition of Byron, Shelley, Keats, and others.

In23. Harris, V. C. "Rape, Racism and Romance: A Reading of *Tender Is the Night*." *F. Scott Fitzgerald: Centenary Essays from India.* Ed. Mohan Ramanan. New Delhi: Prestige, 1998. 160-67.

There is a parallel between Dick Diver's doomed fate in *Tender Is the Night* and the difficult history of the writing and publication of the novel, which was by most considered a failure. Both the character and the book suggest the concept of dissipation of talent through decadence from the initial great promise. This is why Fitzgerald frames the novel within the perspective of the Romance, a genre that by its nature suggests decadence; at the same time, though, the Romance ambience is also used to gloss over certain problematic themes at the center of the story. In the first place, Nicole's incestuous rape, which is presented by her father as a romantic attachment that goes too far, is later symbolically reenacted by Dick in his relationship with Rosemary, the "Daddy's girl." Thus what could potentially be a destructive and shocking reality is transformed into the traditional structures of Romance; the same happens on another level with Dick's propensity for racist comments and intolerance towards other races. In doing this, Dick is engaged in a Derridian "invention of the other" on whom to project his frustration and impotence.

In24. Hen, Judy. "'Never a Burglar': Melodrama in Juvenalia by Fitzgerald and Hemingway." *F. Scott Fitzgerald: A Centennial Tribute* Vol. I. Ed. Somdatta Mandal. New Delhi: Prestige, 1997.

Fitzgerald's comedy "The Captured Shadow" and Hemingway's short story "Judgement of Manitou" both display significant elements of a melodramatic imagination. A favorite of both writers while growing up were the books of Horatio Alger, in addition to other authors occasionally prone to melodrama, such as Poe, Byron, Robert Louis Stevenson, and Kipling. These influences are evident in the comedy and the short story, which contain standardized characters, a stereotyped and excessively contrived plot, and sentimental effects.

In25. Irudayaraj, A. Noel Joseph. "The Faces of Romantic Egoism in Fitzgerald's Short Stories." *F. Scott Fitzgerald: Centenary Essays from India*, ed. Mohan Ramanan. Preface, B. R. Burg. New Delhi: Prestige, 1998. 59-63.

Many intersecting socio-cultural paradigms can help read the behavior of many characters in Fitzgerald's short stories. The framing idea is that of an 'American transcendence' in its three manifestations: theistic transcendence (the Puritans and Transcendentalists), altruistic transcendence (Whitman), and egoistic transcendence (represented by, among others, Poe, Melville, Benjamin Franklin, Fitzgerald). The characters in Fitzgerald's short fiction mostly fall within the last category and show the typical excesses and self-absorption of the Romantic ego. In all fields, from sexual customs to world-view, from moral values to narcissism, they display a consistent behavioral pattern and they clash with other characters who have a different point of view, such as a more deterministic idea of the world, or a stricter position on sexual conduct or a more moralistic vision of beauty.

In26. Khushu-Lahiri, Rajyashree. "Sexual Politics in Life and Fiction: A Study of *Tender Is the Night*." *F. Scott Fitzgerald: Centenary Essays from India*. Ed. Mohan Ramanan. New Delhi: Prestige, 1998. 168-77.

Tender Is the Night focuses on the 'sexual politics' that characterize the interaction between Scott and Zelda as a couple. Although Scott is fascinated with Zelda's independence and eccentricity, he is also constantly reminding her that he is the one in charge, despite his being the weaker one in personality. This becomes particularly dramatic in light of Zelda's attempt at self-expression through creativity; never supportive of her aspirations as a dancer, Scott reacts aggressively when she steps into his domain by publishing her novel. Such ambiguous interaction is reflected in the novel in the marriage of the Divers: Dick first objectifies Nicole's beauty, and then imposes on her the same logic of her paternal abuse, while pretending to cure and protect her, thus imprisoning her in the patriarchal structure that has caused her schizophrenia. At the end of the novel, Nicole's sudden recovery may be seen as the expression and exorcism of Scott's persistent and oppressive sense of guilt for causing Zelda's breakdown.

In27. Kumar, Sukrita Paul. "Towards the New Woman: The Shifting of Sex Roles in Dreiser, Fitzgerald and Hemingway." *Indian Journal of American Studies* 17.1/2 (Winter & Summer 1987): 65-73.

Against the theory of Leslie Fiedler, who reads much of the American novel in terms of homoeroticism and its cultural dynamics, it is necessary to investigate above all the gender differences in American literature and how the fiction of the early 20th century reflects a shift in the position and social perception of women. After being mostly ignored by American fiction, or reduced to the Puritanical opposition of good and evil, the woman as autonomous subject starts to play a role in the novels of Henry James and in Kate Chopin's *The Awakening*. It is in Dreiser, though, that female sexual instincts are first recognized as a social force, directing the destiny of characters in a rather deterministic way; Fitzgerald, based partly on the idealization of his own desire for Zelda, popularizes the 'flapper,' further developing the need for emancipation typical of the age, and later adds the Freudian vocabulary (especially in *Tender Is the Night*), which overcomes the mere determinism of desire; Hemingway continues on this line and invests his characters, both male and female, with an urgency to find real connection through sexual encounters, something which will finally degenerate in the neurosis of Henry Miller's novels.

In28. Kundu, Gautam. "Fitzgerald's 'Camera Eye': Visual Imagination in the Major Novels." *F. Scott Fitzgerald: A Centennial Tribute*, Vol II. Ed. Somdatta Mandal. New Delhi: Prestige, 1997. 9-33.

The cinematic quality of Fitzgerald's style has always been commented on. Fitzgerald uses sentences as a director uses "the lens of his camera to select, to highlight, to distort, and to enhance." Beginning with *This Side of Paradise*, the author shows an eminently visual imagination and style, not merely in a general pictorial or photographic way, but clearly in a moving cinematic context. The technique becomes even more pervasive in *The Great Gatsby*, where most of the introductory scenes are constructed as cinematic 'establishing shots,' with the written equivalent of a long shot that progressively focuses more and more on the single characters, until it reaches a close-up quality. The center of such technique is of course the 'point of view' character Nick, who expresses the conflict between the need for objectivity and the limitation of the subjective gaze, which remains one of the main cruxes of the 'camera eye.' With *Tender Is the Night* there is a further multiplication and distortion of the points of view, which suggest the impossibility of a single unifying vision. In addition to mimicking the extreme angles of the camera (low, 'Dutch', pan shots, etc.), Fitzgerald parallels the slow motion and the freeze frame, which represent the attempt to stop time and control reality. Finally, with *The Last Tycoon*, the cinematic qualities invest not just single passages or descriptions, but the overall structure of the novel, which is extremely episodic and scenic. The reader, as the spectator at the movies, is asked to complement the fragmentary structure and to bring to life the figures, who are often only suggested on the page with brief evocative sentences.

In29. Mandal, Somdatta. "The Glitter and the Glory: Hollywood and the
       Cinematic Imagination of F. Scott Fitzgerald." *F. Scott Fitzgerald: A
       Centennial Tribute* Vol. II. Ed. Somdatta Mandal. New Delhi: Prestige,
       1997. 34-52.

Hollywood proves important both as real place and as an idea throughout Fitzgerald's career. The writer's fascination with the film industry begins early on, with the presence of movie people as characters in novels and short stories. Fitzgerald uses cinematic references to suggest the confusion between reality and imagination. In this early phase, Fitzgerald, although he is already aware of the drawbacks of Hollywood, presents it as an ideal world of dreams. In *Tender Is the Night* Rosemary embodies such ambiguity, as she displays both the vitality of youth and the signs of corruption given by stardom: she sees reality as a movie scenario. In the later part of his career Fitzgerald develops a more cynical and disillusioned vision of Hollywood, due to his own failed experience as screenwriter. He never stops admiring the glitter of the cinematic world and its communicative potential, but he clearly sees the destructive effect of this environment. This is the context of the Pat Hobby stories, which show an unprecedented bitterness and hatred for the hypocrisy and falsity of Hollywood. Finally, with *The Last Tycoon*, Fitzgerald projects a comprehensive assessment of the movie industry, which shows how Hollywood represents the embodiment of the American Dream in its more explicit and complete formulation, which ultimately leads to its betrayal.

In30. Mandal, Somdatta. "The Indian Critical Response to F. Scott Fitzgerald."
       Paper delivered at the F. Scott Fitzgerald Centennial Conference,
       Princeton U. Sep. 1996.

See Chapter Introduction.

In31. Mandal, Somdatta. Introduction. *F. Scott Fitzgerald: A Centennial Tribute.* New Delhi: Prestige Books, 1997. 11-23.

After being considered for too long a mere chronicler of his own age, Fitzgerald has now reached the full critical attention that he deserves as a great American novelist: he is "one of the 'Big Three' American authors of the first half of the twentieth century," together with Hemingway and Faulkner. Many activities were organized to celebrate the Fitzgerald centennial in 1996, both in India and in the rest of the world. Books, seminars, videos, a film festival, even a statue in St. Paul, all testimony to the renewed interest for the writer as a major figure in American culture. The commemorative stamp released by the U.S. Postal Service is a "belated honor for an American icon."

In32. Mandal, Somdatta. "The Twenties." *F. Scott Fitzgerald: Centenary Essays from India,* ed. Mohan Ramanan. Preface, B. R. Burg. New Delhi: Prestige, 1998. 15-26.

The social and economic conditions of the postwar period shape the mood of the nation and the behavior of the masses. It is an era of booming economy, urban development and mindless entertainment, which Fitzgerald best interprets by capturing both its enthusiastic energy and its sense of impending doom. On a social level, the decade was characterized by a revolution of sexual habits, the increasing independence of women, the ubiquity of alcohol, Jazz music and dancing, which overshadowed more serious political issues. Paris played a vital role for an entire generation of intellectual expatriates as a symbol of pleasure, sophistication and openness to the world.

In33. Mandal, Soumyajit. "Hollywood and *The Great Gatsby.*" *F. Scott Fitzgerald: A Centennial Tribute* Vol. I. Ed. Somdatta Mandal. New Delhi: Prestige, 1997. 156-59.

The third film adaptation of *The Great Gatsby,* released in 1974 with a huge advertising campaign and starring Robert Redford and Mia Farrow in the leading roles, is usually considered a flop, both commercially and artistically. Despite the presence in the novel of many cinematic elements and techniques, the production remains a superficial exercise in faithful calligraphy, an 'embalming', as it has been defined, while failing to embody the very aura of Gatsby's dream and the finer psychological and symbolic aspects of the text. Its main achievement lies in promoting the figure of Fitzgerald among the wider public.

In34. Mandel, Jerome. "The Grotesque Rose: Medieval Romance and *The Great Gatsby.*" *F. Scott Fitzgerald: A Centennial Tribute* Vol. I. Ed. Somdatta Mandal. New Delhi: Prestige, 1997.

There are many themes and symbols taken from Medieval romance in *The Great Gatsby*, which is partly motivated by Fitzgerald's interest and fascination for the genre. Apart from the explicit mention and use of the quest structure and the grail theme, what is striking is the extent to which the characters of the novel and their actions are modeled on Medieval examples. Places also pay tribute to Medieval tradition: Tom's and Gatsby's clans embody the idea of the two rival courts, one of which (Tom's) represents the 'evil' court, where intrigue and deception rule. But the clearest example is the theme of the 'garden of love', which is the favorite environment for Medieval lovers: it is a world apart that allows the lovers privacy and intimacy. Seen as a Medieval knight, Gatsby is able to overcome all the obstacles, except for the ultimate one, which is time: he cannot conquer this dimension, and his dream of love (symbolized in Medieval terms by the rose) is destined to wither away. Thus we can claim that up to a certain point Fitzgerald meant the novel to be "the myth of America retold as medieval romance."

In35. Moin, Gulfishaan. "The Twenties in Black and White: A Comparative Study of Fitzgerald's *The Great Gatsby* and Wright's *Black Boy* and *American Hunger.*" *F. Scott Fitzgerald: Centenary Essays from India*, ed. Mohan Ramanan. New Delhi: Prestige, 1998. 110-115.

Despite the obvious differences, Richard Wright and Gatsby embody a similar figure in the social environment of the Twenties. Both are isolated characters, constantly struggling to succeed within an adverse society: Gatsby identifies his fulfillment with his love for Daisy and the desperate attempt to be accepted by the higher classes she belongs to; for Wright, the dream is that of abandoning the native South and moving to the North, only to discover that his sense of alienation does not end there. Unlike Gatsby, Wright lacks the clear vision of one defined goal, but also realizes that he is not the only one to suffer, thus creating a sort of class and race consciousness, which is absent in Gatsby, who always remains extremely self-centered.

In36. Moorty, Satyam S. "F. Scott Fitzgerald's 'The Swimmers': A Study in Cross-Cultural Conflict." *F. Scott Fitzgerald: A Centennial Tribute* Vol. I. Ed. Somdatta Mandal. New Delhi: Prestige, 1997. 58-64.

The short story "The Swimmers" has been defined by Fitzgerald himself as "the hardest story I ever wrote." Such difficulty is motivated by the fact that behind the personal story of the main characters and their divorce lies a much more complicated intent: to portray the historical and social opposition between America and Europe. The French woman and her husband from Virginia represent the respective nations and cultures. The conflict is resolved by Fitzgerald in favor of American energy and authenticity against the French sophistication and moral exhaustion. Swimming becomes the metaphor for the American character's learning how to cope with and escape from the European wasteland thanks to his vitality and integrity.

In37. Mukherjee, Tutun. *"The Last Tycoon, Citizen Kane* and the American Dream." *F. Scott Fitzgerald: Centenary Essays from India.* Ed. Mohan Ramanan. New Delhi: Prestige, 1998. 195-202.

The two main characters, Charles Foster Kane and Monroe Stahr, are both portrayals of the self-made man (based respectively on William Randolph Hearst and Irving Thalberg) who pursues his dream with ruthlessness and absolute dedication and becomes a tyrannical media mogul, materially successful but isolated and abandoned by others. Each lacks love and satisfaction in his life and offers a disenchanted outlook on how the American Dream proves futile in the contemporary world of opportunism ad hypocrisy. Kazan sees in Stahr almost exclusively the romantic side of Fitzgerald's character, and he presents him sympathetically as an innocent idealist caught within the Hollywood environment of falsity. The director does so by casting a charming de Niro and using such stylistic devices as frequent close-ups and soft focus. Welles's style is more expressionistic: Kane is presented as the sum of several people's perceptions of him, suggesting the impossibility of framing him in a coherent way. He is shot through extreme camera angles, which underline his isolation from others and his entrapment in his own dream and its corruption. More than a condemnation of the two individuals, the films are rather a general denunciation of the utopia of the American Dream.

In38. Mukherjee, Tutun. "The Other Side of Paradise: The Subtext of *Tender Is the Night* and *Save Me the Waltz.*" *F. Scott Fitzgerald: A Centennial Tribute* Vol. I. Ed. Somdatta Mandal. New Delhi: Prestige, 1997. 114-22.

Scott's and Zelda's novels are contrasting narratives sharing the same subtext, i.e., the couple's own biographical events around the 1930s. Both texts are clearly inspired by real life events, Zelda's since its first conception, and Scott's more and more with each new revision. The competing quality of the two texts is easily revealed also in Scott's many attempts to assert his superiority as a writer and his right of prime ownership on the 'material' which becomes the inspiration for the two novels. Zelda's more experimental and poetic style represents a contrast with Scott's treatment of the same subject matter, which is more psychological and sociological. Thus, the two novels benefit from a parallel reading, as they reveal a common narrative subtext, which is the couple's life, itself conceived and presented as a text, and offered for public display.

In39. Nair, Nirmala Rita. "Sense(s) and Sensibility in *The Great Gatsby.*" *F. Scott Fitzgerald: Centenary Essays from India*, ed. Mohan Ramanan. New Delhi: Prestige, 1998. 85-89.

Despite the portrayal of moral emptiness and insincerity that is contained in *The Great Gatsby*, "the novel is not dark, gloomy, or pessimistic." Nick, with his sense of morality and humanity provides a redeeming balance against the other characters' behavior. On a more stylistic level, the pessimism is balanced by the presence of color and sound, which evoke images of beauty. The paradoxical coexistence of the most lucid disillusionment with an almost innocent talent for hope, which Fitzgerald later advocated in *The Crack-Up*, is what explains the presence of such redeeming qualities in a novel that is otherwise a strong condemnation of superficiality and cruelty. The more optimistic side is expressed through the appeal to the senses, with pictorial descriptions of beauty in its colorful aspects; in the same way, beautiful sounds or a regenerative silence counterbalance the discordant noises of modernity and society. It is such a vital presence of natural beauty that preserves for the reader the "enduring freshness" of the novel, despite its bleak ending.

In40. Nair, Rama. "Deconstructing Fitzgerald's Romanticism: The Case of *The Beautiful and Damned.*" *F. Scott Fitzgerald: A Centennial Tribute* Vol. I. Ed. Somdatta Mandal. New Delhi: Prestige, 1997. 77-82.

Anthony, the protagonist of the novel, shows a dissociation of reason and imagination, which fails to achieve the ideal union of them advocated by the Romantics. He is the synthesis of the two most typical figures of Romanticism, the sufferer and the rebel, but he does not reach redemption because he is unable to ultimately harmonize spirit and matter. In this he shows a peculiarly Western limit, whereas Indian philosophy has always stressed the necessity to bring together the spiritual and the material.

In41. Nair, Rama. "Tragedy without Transcendence: An Indian Reading of *The Great Gatsby.*" In *F. Scott Fitzgerald: Centenary Essays from India*, ed. Mohan Ramanan. New Delhi: Prestige, 1998. 138-42.

In *The Great Gatsby* Fitzgerald delineates the passage in American society from idealism to mere materialism; Gatsby's endeavor can be read through the lens of the four principles of Indian philosophy: *artha* (wealth), *Kama* (desire), *dharma* (ethics), and *moksha* (liberation). An appropriate balance of all these four aspects is required to achieve real spiritual transcendence. Gatsby appears thus obsessively and unilaterally concentrated on wealth and material desire, and he does not stop to think that these should only be goals to achieve with appropriate means. Instead, he cancels from his perspective any preoccupation for ethics or real individual freedom, thus condemning himself to fail in his pursuit of self-realization. Despite the vitality of his dream, its lack of a solid foundation on universal principles does not lead him to any kind of redemption.

In42.   Nayar, Pramod K. "Lineaments: The Line Motif in *The Last Tycoon.*" In *F. Scott Fitzgerald: Centenary Essays from India.* Ed. Mohan Ramanan. New Delhi: Prestige, 1998. 186-94.

The story itself, left unfinished by the author, has been given different possible linear developments based on the outline left by the writer for the unwritten parts. But throughout the text, the very concept of linear progression of cause and effect is contested in favor of a more open structure. In addition, there is a particular attention to the activity of writing in which various characters are engaged, and the characters themselves are presented as a series of signs, starting from the very lineaments of their faces that must be interpreted by others. Thus the idea of the self as a coherent unity is replaced by the multiple accumulations and repetitions of layers, and the characters so created interact according to horizontal and vertical intersecting relationships. All this uncertainty about the self relates naturally to the basic ambiguity of the world of movie making, i.e. the distinction between reality and illusion, which are indeed separated by a very fine line.

In43.   Prasad, Murari. "F. Scott Fitzgerald and Michael Madhusudan Dutt: 'Mediocre Caretakers of Talent.'" *F. Scott Fitzgerald: A Centennial Tribute* Vol. I. Ed. Somdatta Mandal. New Delhi: Prestige, 1997. 123-31.

The short lives of Fitzgerald and Madhusudan, an important Bengali poet and dramatist of the mid-nineteenth century, present several analogues, more in their attitude towards their art and person, than in the texts that they left. Both possess a clearly self-destructive side, which eventually infects their talent and their own life, as they both die young. Whereas Fitzgerald, after his early success, fails to cultivate his talent and audience, Madhusudan lives in a very different cultural context, and his formal pre-modernist innovation fails to break through the unfavorable cultural context of the India of his time. Both writers share the same kind of fate, as they end their life in failure, whereas their posthumous reputation has grown ever since among the critics and the audience, giving them a canonical position in the respective literatures.

In44. Qian, Qing. "The Lacuna at the Centre: A Rereading of 'Babylon Revisited.'" *F. Scott Fitzgerald: A Centennial Tribute* Vol. I. Ed. Somdatta Mandal. New Delhi: Prestige, 1997. 71-76.

While feeling guilty for his wife's death, Charlie Wales constantly tries to blame her for their marital problems and for the tragic outcome. In his gendered perspective, he fails to see his own faults; yet this is not only due to his personal attitude, but it is a social product of the male chauvinism of the time. In a way, the male-centered point of view is shared by Fitzgerald himself, who enacted in his relationship with Zelda some of the same dynamics that are inscribed in the text.

In45. Ramanan, Mohan. Introduction. *F. Scott Fitzgerald: Centenary Essays from India.* Ed. Mohan Ramanan. New Delhi: Prestige, 1998. 11-14.

Fitzgerald's best accomplishment is his "balance of exuberance and restraint," which allows him to speak with grace, wit and irony even of the harshest mental distress. He is a "minor classic of our times."

In46. Rama Rao, P. G. Foreword. *F. Scott Fitzgerald: A Centenary Tribute.* Ed. Somdatta Mandal. 2 vols. New Delhi: Prestige Books, 1997. 9.

Fitzgerald's critical reputation is now fully established, so that his readers can think of the many other great novels Fitzgerald "might have written had he lived longer."

In47. Razdan, K. B. "Marital Dichotomy and Psychic Disorientation: Man-Woman Relationship in Scott Fitzgerald's *Tender Is the Night* and Anita Desai's *Cry, The Peacock.*" Presented at "F. Scott Fitzgerald Centenary Seminar," American Studies Research Centre, Hyderabad, 23-24 Sep., 1996.

Both the Divers in *Tender Is the Night* and the couple in Anita Desai's 1963 novel *Cry, the Peacock* (Maya and Gautama) present a bleak image of marriage, in which the spouses after an initial attraction end up torturing each other emotionally and physically. Nicole is an opportunistic, shallow, and immature woman who corrupts Dick's talent with her money and imprisons him in a destructive relationship, ignoring his desire for love and beauty. There is also a lack of intimacy and communication between Maya and Gautama, but the blame is here put on the husband, who fails to respond to Maya's need for expression and closeness. The two things that Maya shares with Nicole are instead the very problematic father complex, and the schizophrenia developed from it and from the difficulties of married life, which finally drives her to murder her husband and then to commit suicide.

In48. Sawhney, Brajesh. "Social Change in the Fiction of F. Scott Fitzgerald."
       F. Scott Fitzgerald: Centenary Essays from India, ed. Mohan Ramanan.
       Preface, B. R. Burg. New Delhi: Prestige, 1998. 39-50.

Fitzgerald is a keen observer of the social changes of his time, and portrays them in his novels through his characters' behavior and ideals. In *This Side of Paradise* and *The Beautiful and Damned* Fitzgerald presents characters whose initial romantic idealism is shattered by the ruthless world of Postwar America, which leaves them completely disenchanted. In *The Great Gatsby*, through the presentation of the typical Jazz Age environment of parties, the author exposes the moral futility and corruption of the time, which finds its more tragic and bleak embodiment in the 'valley of ashes.' Finally, in *Tender Is the Night*, Fitzgerald creates a protagonist whose ideals are destroyed by the materialism of the society he lives in; he yields to the lure of money, sex and moral indifference, revealing thus the overwhelming corruption and violence of the social context.

In49. Sequeira, Isaac. "The Jazz Age." *F. Scott Fitzgerald: Centenary Essays
       from India*, ed. Mohan Ramanan. Preface, B. R. Burg. New Delhi:
       Prestige, 1998. 27-32.

Jazz music had a great influence on both artists and the wider public in the Twenties, which have also been aptly nicknamed 'the Jazz Age.' It was then that jazz began for the first time to spread out of the Southern African American community, where it had originated. Jazz became popular, not only among white musicians, but also among writers and poets, who used its key concepts of rhythm and improvisation in their works. The Jazz Age is thus an era of dramatic contrasts: it saw the rise of Hollywood, the Harlem Renaissance, a flowering in literature and painting, and the affirmation of women's rights. On the other hand, partly as a reaction to these changes, it was also a period of renewed bigotry, racism, organized crime and political repression.

In50. Sethi, A. K. "Hollywood Novels of F. Scott Fitzgerald and Nathanael
       West." *Indian Journal of American Studies* 28.1-2 (Winter & Summer
       1998): 7-14.

Fitzgerald regarded himself as one of the first to recognize Nathanael West's talent, and West credited Fitzgerald's "kindness" in the preface to the Modern Library edition of *The Great Gatsby*, as giving him "a great life just at a time when I needed one badly, if I was to go on writing." While there are marked differences between *Gatsby* and *The Day of the Locust*, similarities abound: the themes of dissolution, the corruption of language and the breakdown of love, recurrent confusions of identity, motifs of facade and deception, and confusion between reality and illusion. Although the correspondence between the two men is "not available," parallels between the two novels show how each writer influenced the other. The symbolic image in West's novel is the studio's central dumping ground of sets, flats, and props which was anticipated in *Tender Is the Night* when Rosemary visits the studio and saw "the bizarre debris of some recent picture. . . ." Harry's funeral scene in which West concentrated all the sham and distortion of Hollywood is likewise a prototype for the funeral scene Fitzgerald planned for Monroe Stahr. In both novels, the dreams of the characters are affected by Hollywood films, but Hollywood itself made fulfillment impossible. Both novelists reveal themselves to be moralists through their extreme sensitivity to the impact of the movie on society and on the writer.

In51. Sethi, A. K. "T. S. Eliot's 'The Waste Land' and the Novels of Scott
       Fitzgerald and Nathanael West." *F. Scott Fitzgerald: Centenary Essays
       from India*, ed. Mohan Ramanan. Preface, B. R. Burg. New Delhi:
       Prestige, 1998. 64-77.

The waste land theme is a significant presence both in *The Great Gatsby* and in *Miss Lonelyhearts*. In Fitzgerald's novel, the most obvious reference is the 'valley of ashes', which is explicitly described as a waste land representing the moral emptiness and material corruption of contemporary society. The figure of Gatsby alludes to another fundamental theme of *The Waste Land*, the quest of the grail and the wound of the Fisher King. In West's novel, the description of a dry and desolate garden near the office of Miss Lonelyhearts evokes the image of the waste land, which is also extended on a more symbolic and spiritual level to the actions of the characters and the words of the people who write to Miss Lonelyhearts for advice. The protagonists fail to find transcendence in either religion or sex, as they both prove vain attempts to escape the desolation of the modern world. Thus Fitzgerald and West appear to be far more pessimistic than Eliot, as their characters are unable to find even the slightest hope of redemption, which is suggested in the poet's use of images of regeneration.

In52. Sharma, Vijay K. "Woman as Object: Feminism vs. Fitzgerald's
       Romantic Egotism." *F. Scott Fitzgerald: Centenary Essays from India*.
       Ed. Mohan Ramanan. Preface, B. R. Burg. New Delhi: Prestige, 1998.
       51-58.

Fitzgerald's treatment of women in his novels resonates with the traditional conceptual superiority of soul (male) over body (female), of spirit over matter. The writer presents women as commodified objects of desire and possession, inspired by his experiences with Ginevra King, Zelda, and Sheilah Graham, and by the condemnation of sex typical of his Catholic upbringing. Daisy, as well as all the other women in *The Great Gatsby*, fits into such a stereotype and is presented as a shallow and irritating character, desired and manipulated by the men in the book. The only relationship that seems to escape this pattern is the one between Nick and Jordan Baker, who act more as equals; nonetheless, their affair ends in miscommunication and regret.

In53. Sivaramkrishna, M. Introduction. *The Great Gatsby*. American
       Literature Texts. Delhi: Oxford University Press, 1981; 1992. vii-lvii.

Some of the general traits of American literature are a strong idealism coupled, sometimes problematically, with individualism and the myth of personal success. Amidst the great social changes of the 1920s, is the fundamental struggle between pragmatism and Puritanical moral absolutism, or between realism and romance, which leads to the writer's deep disillusionment in public values and dedication to the myth of self accomplishment. Fitzgerald is the perfect representative of his era; the critic sees the midwestern familial background and the Catholic upbringing as some of the lasting influences on the author's conflicting oscillation between mundane pleasures and a moralistic vision. *The Great Gatsby* is Fitzgerald's first mature accomplishment, whose main theme is the individual's romantic quest for meaning and success. On a more universal and modernist level, Gatsby's tragedy is his failure to accomplish his desired "redemption of time" and his inability to reconcile myth and history. Despite such a grand thematic paradigm, Fitzgerald is also able to work on the minute details of characterization, which contributes to the creation of a believable image of the Twenties. Technically, Fitzgerald reaches a successful balance between Wells's 'Saturation' and James's 'Selection' techniques, excluding any direct authorial intervention, but investing Nick of a "double vision" which allows the expression of sympathy and detachment at the same time. Fitzgerald's style, which can be romantically overstated and abundant in adjectives, is successfully controlled in *The Great Gatsby*, presenting poignant and evocative sentences, but also a sobriety that is somehow unusual for the author.

In54. Sivaramkrishna, M. "Some Indic Pathways to Fitzgerald's 'Paradise.'"
       F. Scott Fitzgerald: A Centennial Tribute Vol. I. Ed. Somdatta Mandal.
       New Delhi: Prestige, 1997. 24-29.Also in *F. Scott Fitzgerald: Centenary
       Essays from India*. Ed. Mohan Ramanan. New Delhi: Prestige. 33-38.

Many of Fitzgerald's characters show an excessive attachment to the most superficial goals of material life, *artha* and *kama*, i.e. wealth and desire. This is not only a personal characteristic of Fitzgerald, but also a common thread in American culture. On the other hand, the opposite values of *dharma* and *moksha* (ethics and freedom) are also present in Fitzgerald's books, as the characters make decisions, while knowing the futility of doing so. Such tragic double vision could correspond to the Indian dialectics of *maya* (the world as illusion) and *leela* (the labyrinth), imprisoning the heroes in a dream of which they know the impossibility and the vanity. Thus *Tender Is the Night* is the most accomplished of the writer's novels, in which Dick is "unable to dissociate the dharma of a healer from the compulsive urges of *kama* and *artha* as a person."

In55.   Upot, Sherine. "She-Centering *The Great Gatsby*: Fitzgerald, Barthelme and the Gender Question." *F. Scott Fitzgerald: Centenary Essays from India*, ed. Mohan Ramanan. New Delhi: Prestige, 1998. 105-109.

In *The Great Gatsby* the 'gender issue' is best exemplified in the figure of Daisy, whose depiction is always subordinate to the construction of Gatsby's greatness. She is characterized as shallow, insignificant and capricious. The few moments that suggest her intelligence are usually overlooked, except sometimes by Nick, who is the only one who seems to treat her as an independent person. Such an attitude is typical of narrative realism, a technique that reinforces the patriarchal order and marginalizes women. Therefore, the novel is undoubtedly a "male-centered text." On the contrary, in texts like Barthelme's *Snow White*, even when the author's intention is not explicitly anti-patriarchal, such assumptions can be contested through the deconstruction of language and the questioning of the mechanisms of the creation of meaning.

BOOK REVIEWS/NEWS ARTICLES/RADIO PROGRAMS

In56.   Rao, Raghavendra. Rev. of *The Artist and the City: Two Themes in the Novels of F. Scott Fitzgerald, Thomas Wolfe and Nathanael West,* by Tirthankar Chattopadhyay. *Indian Journal of American Studies* 11.1 (1981): 90-3.

Chattopadhyay's book clearly and concisely examines the "perennial artist-city theme" as it appears in Fitzgerald, Thomas Wolfe, and Nathanael West. Despite the important differences, all three writers share a "distaste for the committed writers of the thirties," choosing instead to present the city through a combination of metaphor and introspection, which constitutes a "Modernist realism." Such a contradictory category results in the unresolved oscillation of the city image between the ideal "Golden City" and the decadent waste land.

DISSERTATIONS

In57. Arun, Prabha. "F. Scott Fitzgerald and the Jazz Age." Allahabad: Aligarh Univ., 1982.

In58. Chengapa, Cauvery. "F. Scott Fitzgerald and the Celebration of Wealth." Mysore, 1989.

In59. Guha, Sourin. "F. Scott Fitzgerald: His World and Sensibility." Calcutta: Rabindra Bharati University, 1993.

In60. Jindal, Vandana. "Treatment of Women in the Novels of F. Scott Fitzgerald." Kurukshetra, 1994.

In61. Kumar, Sukrita Paul. "Man-Woman Relationships in the Fiction of F. Scott Fitzgerald, Ernest Hemingway and Theodore Dreiser." Aurangabad: Marathawada University, 1975.

In62. Mandal, Somdatta. "Magnificent Obsession: The Cinema and Scott Fitzgerald's Fiction." M Phil. Dissertation. Calcutta: Jadavpur University, 1985.

In63. Mandal, Somdatta. "Interrelations: Film and Fiction: Cinematic Themes and Techniques in the Fiction of William Faulkner, F. Scott Fitzgerald and Ernest Hemingway." Ph. D. dissertation. Jadavpur University, Calcutta, 2000.

In64. Michael, Subhasini. "Tragic Sense of Fitzgerald." Kanpur, 1978.

In65. Raju, G. Chandrasekhara. "The Apocalyptic Vision of the Lost Generation with Special Reference to F. Scott Fitzgerald and Hemingway." Tiruchirapalli, 1993.

In66. Sarkar, Seema. "F. Scott Fitzgerald: The Man and His Novels." Rewa: Awadesh Pratap Singh University, 1992.

In67. Sethi, Ashwini Kumar. "Social Criticism in the Novels of F. Scott Fitzgerald and Nathanael West." Jaipur, 1987.

In68. Shiv Kumar, P. "Valley of Ashes: Theme of Failure in the Novels of F. Scott Fitzgerald." Hyderabad, 1967.

In69. Sivaramkrishna, M. "Fitzgerald Hero: Anatomy of *The Crack-Up* Being a Study of the Theme of Deterioration." Hyderabad, 1968.

In70. Vithal, A. P. "Dream and Disillusionment in the Novels of F. Scott Fitzgerald." Aurangabad: Marathwada University, 1981.

In71. Waheeduddin, Syeda Jeelani. "Time and Myth in the Novels of F. Scott Fitzgerald." Hyderabad: Osmania University, 1982.

Japan

The Fitzgerald Bibliographical Center in Japan is a unique feature of that country's approach to Fitzgerald Studies. Proposed on October 15, 1978, by Kiyohiko Tsuboi of Okayama University at the 17th Annual Meeting of the American Literature Society of Japan, the Center was established in the office of Sadao Nagaoka at Yamanashi University. Because most scholarly publications in Japan, as in much of Europe, are published within universities and not distributed throughout the country, the major aim of the Center is to collect publications about Fitzgerald in Japan and to make them available to anyone engaged in the study of the author and his work.

In an article on the establishment of the Center that Sadao Nagaoka wrote for the *Fitzgerald/Hemingway Annual* of 1979, he indicates that "about 28 (treatises and articles) were published between 1950 and 1960, about 68 between 1960 and 1970, and about 106 between 1970 and 1979" (Nagaoka, 1979, 145-46). Thus, it is immediately apparent from the number of publications submitted to the Center that Fitzgerald's reputation in Japan has followed a trajectory similar to that of the European countries and the United States: virtually no scholarly attention before 1950, attention beginning to grow in the next decade, and increasing consistently from the late 1960s to 1980. Furthermore, between 1975 and 1995, 350 additional items were collected, indicating that Fitzgerald's reputation in Japan has continued to expand (Nagaoka, 1995).

The 1980 edition of *The Foreign Critical Reputation of F. Scott Fitzgerald* was sent to press about the time of the announcement of the Center's establishment. Because the National Diet Library did not have a substantial holding of work by Japanese scholars on Fitzgerald, the introduction to the earlier volume traced Japanese scholarship on Fitzgerald from only 1955 to 1969. This introduction will amplify the 1980 introduction, based on material from the Bibliographical Center. As Sadao Nagaoka has determined, the first translation into Japanese of a work of Fitzgerald's dates back to 1930 when "The Bridal Party" appeared in December, just five months after it appeared in the *Saturday Evening Post*. "At Your Age" was translated and published in February 1933, four years after its *Post* publication (Nagaoka, Bib Center 1979). However, as the 1980 Introduction to the Japanese chapter indicates, "Before World War II, the Japanese were more interested in Russian and French literature than in American" (Stanley, 1980, 195). Furthermore, they thought of literature from the United States merely as a subset of British literature. By the middle 1950s, however, largely due to American Studies programs thriving in Japanese universities, translations of Fitzgerald's novels and stories began to appear, to be followed shortly by publications by scholars (Miner in Stanley, 1980). Sadao Nagaoka also credits the 1954 release of the movie *The Last Time I Saw Paris* based on "Babylon Revisited" as at least in part responsible for the "new fervor for this author in Japan" (J167).

For the past century, English has been required of junior high school students, and since World War II, a junior high school education has been compulsory. Many Japanese can read English; university students can both read and write it. In fact, the teaching of English consists of exercises in translation which, as Sugawara indicates, accounts for the many collections published in English of Fitzgerald's short stories (Sugawara in Stanley 1980). Despite learning English beginning in secondary school, Japanese are "hardly able to understand such intricate textures of English as Fitzgerald's" and therefore the average Japanese tends to read Fitzgerald in Japanese translation" (J219). Both *The Great Gatsby* and *Tender Is the Night* were translated and published in 1957, followed in 1970 by the translation of *This Side of Paradise* and in 1977 by *The Last Tycoon*, (*The Beautiful and Damned* remains untranslated). Between 1955 and 1995, 52 short stories appeared in translation in various collections, many by several different translators as, for example, "Babylon Revisited" which has been translated 13 times. *The Great Gatsby* has been retranslated 10 times. Kiyohiko Tsuboi provides an insight into the process of translating English into Japanese, which explains the multiplicity of translations:

> Translation is one of the indices of foreign literature's popularity, since the Japanese language is quite different from other languages, even from Chinese and Korean. It is virtually impossible to transliterate English to Japanese. The process of translation is a kind of alchemy. First, we read a sentence and understand the meaning, and then through a complex process in the brain, we produce a Japanese sentence close to the original English. There is no perfect translation (J219).

In addition to the translations of Fitzgerald's writings, many translations have been accomplished of the work on Fitzgerald by American scholars. Books by A. Scott Berg, Matthew J. Bruccoli, Humphrey Carpenter, Tom Dardis, Richard Lehan, Nancy Milford, Arthur Mizener, Edwin Moseley and Andrew Turnbull are now all available to the Japanese in translation. (J88-J97). Japanese scholars utilize these books in translation and many others in English to support and develop their scholarship, as the annotations attest.

The many translations both reflect and support the development of Fitzgerald's reputation in Japan. At the beginning of this recent period between 1980 and 2000, some of the translations were performed by Haruki Murakami, a young and increasingly influential Japanese writer. Murakami translated some of Fitzgerald's stories and "My Lost City" in *The Crack-Up*. As Yukiko Tokunaga explained, "Murakami is popular among the young people for his easy, friendly, intimate style" (Tokunaga, 21 Apr 2001), and his influence, according to Tsuboi, "has been far greater than mere scholars' efforts" (J219).

Near the end of this period, in 1996, the year of Fitzgerald's Centennial, two major Fitzgerald publishing events occurred in Japan. *The Selected Works of F. Scott Fitzgerald* in nine volumes of facsimile reprints of the first editions, edited by Kiyohiko Tsuboi, was published by Hon-no-tomo-sha in Tokyo to promote additional Japanese scholarly research on Fitzgerald (J71). Also, in 1996, Sadao Nagaoka published *The Lectures on F. Scott Fitzgerald*, a biography which also contains a "minutely and meticulously compiled bibliography of articles, translations, and books published in Japan" (J219). Prof. Nagaoka also translated the bibliography into English for the purpose of this present study (J86).

Kenji Inoue wrote in 1984, "As his works have since the 1950s become popular in Japan, Fitzgerald studies have become a major 'industry' for Japanese academics" (J127). With over 600 items in Nagaoka's Bibliographical Center, it would appear that more has been written in Japan on Fitzgerald than in any other one country, except the United States. What have the Japanese had to say about him?

The 1980 edition reveals early trends in the Japanese response: "While much of it is repetitious because there is no interuniversity organization of American literature publications, much also contributes to the Fitzgerald canon" (Stanley, 1980, 197). As Miner says, 'Japanese professors of English literature are, after all, Japanese. They possess a perspective on literature, American included, that no other nation can lay claim to'" (Miner in Stanley 195-96). Categories of critical approaches between 1950 and 1969, the years covered in the 1980 volume, that do overlap with criticism elsewhere include biography, textual studies of *The Great Gatsby* and *Tender Is the Night*, psychological studies on Fitzgerald, and comparison studies of Fitzgerald and Hemingway. Approaches that seem particularly pertinent to a postwar Japan are "the influence of Fitzgerald in the creation of a generation gap in Japanese life" (Stanley 197) and "a demand for guides to personal success" (Schwantes as quoted in Stanley 196).

An overview of current scholarship between 1980 and 2000 includes the familiar categories of biography intertwined with psychological studies of his work which is generally seen as autobiographical. These studies focus primarily on *The Great Gatsby* but also on his short stories and other novels, several comparing Fitzgerald with other writers, including Hemingway, some seeking to establish the influence of other writers on him and others discussing his influence on other writers, and several examining patterns of imagery, and point of view, reflecting his double vision. Kenji Inoue writes in 1984, "As the studies widen, the problem is that the subject has become monotonic, frequently focusing on themes such as the American dream and its failure/breakdown, double vision, and such. In particular, studies of *The Great Gatsby* dominate the whole industry" (J127). Most of these essays are in fact on *The Great Gatsby*, on Nick's double vision, and on the failure of the American Dream, but in this period, many have been written from an American Studies point of view on the American culture of the 1920s, including several that are primarily gender studies. The writing on Fitzgerald that is indigenous to Japan is both by Haruki Murakami, the well-regarded Japanese writer, and by scholars about Fitzgerald's influence on Murakami (J85).

Kiyohiko Tsuboi explained in Princeton why the Japanese are uniquely interested in Fitzgerald's life:

> Having had the tradition of the self-destructive, self-revealing or self-exposing novel, so-called Watakushi Shosetsu (I novel or Ich Roman), Fitzgerald's way of exposing himself in *The Crack-Up* and other works was understood and accepted by the Japanese. Fitzgerald's candid honesty toward himself, his sincere commitment to the truth of life, and his tragically romantic life, his unfulfilled inner desire under the cover of "the greatest, gaudiest spree," and his never ceasing quest for the meanings of life, found great compassion and understanding among the Japanese. The translations of Zelda Fitzgerald's *Save Me the Waltz* and *Zelda* by Nancy Milford, *Selected Letters of Fitzgerald*, and *Scott Fitzgerald* by Andrew Turnbull have helped as well (J219).

Yukiko Tokunaga agrees that the Japanese have been drawn to Fitzgerald for his Romanticism and for what they perceive as his corresponding weakness (Tokunaga, 21 April 2001).

Nearly all of the full-length studies and collections on Fitzgerald in Japan are wholly or at least in part biographical: Yuko Hoshino's *Life Story: Scott Fitzgerald—Exile from Paradise* (J80); Taiwa Izu's *The Novels of F. Scott Fitzgerald: The World of Self-Projection* (J81); Yoichiro Kobori's *Scott Fitzgerald: The Man and His Work* (J83); Nobuo Morikawa's *Fitzgerald—His Adolescence of Love and Wandering* (J84); Haruki Murakami's *The Scott Fitzgerald Book* (J85); Sadao Nagaoka's *The Lectures on F. Scott Fitzgerald* (J86); and Kiyohiko Tsuboi's *A Touch of Disaster—F. Scott Fitzgerald: His Life and Works* (J87). Several of these rely on American biographies.

Many essays are also biographical. Seiwa Fujitani has written of Fitzgerald's use of his past in his writing specifically his alcoholism (J111) and his image of the Japanese based on a Japanese servant he and Zelda once had (J112). Kazuo Shimizu writes on his days in New York (J201), as does Haruki Murakami in "a cinematic vision of young Fitzgerald and his first visit to New York City in 1906" (Murakami, 1983). Murakami writes about his visits to several of the places in which Fitzgerald lived, including the Garden of Allah (Murakami, 1983) and Montgomery, Alabama (Murakami, 1986), and the pilgrimage he made to Rockville, Maryland (Murakami, 1984). Writing of Fitzgerald's attractiveness (Murakami, 1980), Murakami also writes of the fact that he destroyed his youth and that of his beautiful wife, Zelda (Murakami, 1983). Norio Shimamura sees a reflection in his writings of his own process of breaking down (J200), and Yoshitaka Naruse discusses the writer's need to describe his failure (J184). Hiroshi Nagase argues that *Tender Is the Night* best reflects Fitzgerald's conflicting romanticism and Catholic morality, leading to his crack-up and rebirth in writing *The Last Tycoon* (J174).

Several essays also discern autobiographical elements in his stories. Haruo Sato examines how his life affected the writing of "May Day," "The Rich Boy," and "Babylon Revisited" (J199). Osamu Hamaguchi has also written on the autobiographical nature of "Babylon Revisited" (J119), and Masanori Baba sees the older Fitzgerald as a continuation of Charlie Wales's beliefs (J102). Yoshio Ito writes on the autobiographical elements in "The Sensible Thing" (J130), and Haruo Sato on Fitzgerald's pessimism about his financial circumstances as reflected in several short stories (J198).

Other scholars see Fitzgerald's familial relationships in several of his characterizations or in letters from and to family members. Junko Fujimoto writes about his feelings toward his parents as reflected in *The Great Gatsby* and *Tender Is the Night,* (J107), and from an interview with Scottie, Toshifumi Miyawaki writes about how Scott and Zelda appeared to her (J159). Finally, Hiroshi Narasaki examines Fitzgerald's letters to Scottie (J180).

Much more scholarship has, of course, been written on Fitzgerald's work. In terms of the characterizations in his fiction, Yukimi Masui sees Daisy as a potentially tragic character who cedes her life to others, ending up empty (J151). Nobuaki Matsumura focuses on Nick's descriptions of both Gatsby who he believes has the passion and decisiveness that he lacks himself and of Daisy who he depicts through images of material beauty (J153). Muneyuki Kato argues that the metamorphosis of Nick's judgment from tolerance to judgment is based on Daisy's keeping secret her killing of Myrtle Wilson (J142).

Several essays focus on the imagery and symbolism in *The Great Gatsby.* Taiwa Izu finds that Gatsby seems to live by moonlight and in fact is killed during bright summer sunlight (J138). Hideaki Hatayama concentrates on glasses and the green light in *Gatsby* (J120) whereas Shuji Muto comments on the drifting motion in *Gatsby* (J166) and Hidehiro Nakao writes on the pervasiveness of jazz (J178). Tadatoshi Saito analyzes the various images of Christ in *Gatsby* (J196). Yoshitada Kobayashi considers the symbolism of colors in the novel (J143).

In analyzing the themes of *Gatsby,* Yumiko Hirono and Toshinobu Fukuya reflect on the complex time scheme (J123) and Junko Fujimoto sees Fitzgerald's obsession with time in the various images of clocks and watches (J105). Kazuyoshi Ohata is also concerned with the sense of passing time in *Gatsby*

(J193). Several writers consider the novel from a religious point of view. Shinichi Morimoto reflects on Fitzgerald's depiction of a bustling society where values are confused and God is lost (J163). Hirotsugu Inoue believes Gatsby practiced idolatry in worshipping money (J126). As is to be expected, most scholars see the major theme of the novel as the passing of the idealistic American Dream and the ascendancy of a materialistic version. Both Yoshitaka Naruse (J181) and Nobuko Shinohara (J204) discuss the passing of the old agrarian, egalitarian dream and the corresponding emergence of the business-oriented dream of the American 1920s. Nobuo Kamioka analyzes the economic differences among the various geographical regions, seeing the Jeffersonian agricultural fundamentalism and self-sufficiency of the Midwest as ideal (J140).

Yoshio Nakamura writes of the subtle difference between the sentimental and the romantic Gatsby (J176). Interestingly, Yukinari Nakano argues that Gatsby's idealistic dream redeemed Daisy from despair, but the materialistic dust that floated in the wake of his dream ironically led him to his death (J177). Tatsura Iwasaki sees Fitzgerald as a "true believer" in the innocence of the dream (J132), and Shinohara argues that idealism is the only remnant left of the dream (J204). Haruki Murakami has also written on Fitzgerald's Romanticism as reflected in his belief in the American Dream (J85).

Most scholars who consider Fitzgerald's technique in *Gatsby* reflect on his use of a double vision: Kiyohiko Tsuboi sees the employment of a double vision as a modernist technique (J226). Several others, such as Shinji Watanabe, look at it in *Gatsby* specifically in terms of the tactics of a self-controlled narrative (J231), and Eiichi Hayakawa sees Nick as contradictory (J121). Taiwa Izu's book is subtitled *The World of Self-Projection* in which he sees the technique as emerging from Fitzgerald's own double vision (J81). In "Class and the American Dream in *The Great Gatsby*," Koji Kotani examines the opposing views of wealth in the novel (J149), and Takashi Tasaka examines the oxymorons in the novel that emphasize this double vision (J210). In other studies of Fitzgerald's technique, Takashi Sasaki analyzes his approach in writing short stories that then become novels, (J197), and Yoshitada Kobayashi has published 18 articles on the color symbolism in Fitzgerald, including in *The Great Gatsby* (J143-148).

Japanese scholars also have written on *Tender Is the Night*. Nobuko Shinohara writes on the conflict of values in *Tender* (J203), Yoshitaka Naruse sees Dick's crack-up coming about because of his allowing himself to be seduced by the rich (J182). Yumi Nagaoka argues that the second version of *Tender* is better because it emphasizes the prevailing theme of disruption and disintegration (J170). Junko Fujimoto believes that in their brightness and dark aftertaste, carnivals symbolize both the hope and disillusionment in both *The Great Gatsby* and *Tender Is the Night* (J103). Fujimoto also sees Paris as a place of meaning in *Tender Is the Night* as the Paris visit by Nicole and Rosemary creates the climax of the novel (J108). Yoshitada Kobayashi considers the symbolism of colors in the novel (J144).

Several scholars have written about Fitzgerald's other novels. Both Itaru Yamaguchi (J235) and Taiwa Izu (J137) believe that in developing a new perspective in writing *The Last Tycoon,* Fitzgerald was celebrating a rebirth as a writer. Takashi Tasaka writes of oxymorons and double vision in *The Last Tycoon* (J211), and Yoshitada Kobayashi considers the symbolism of colors in the novel (J147). Three scholars write positively of *This Side of Paradise,* including Yoshio Nakamura who sees intellectual unity in Amory's somewhat puritanical outlook that only increases his flexibility, thus giving the novel consistency (J175). Taiwa Izu sees Amory as Fitzgerald's Adam on his way to experience (J139), and Yoshitaka Naruse argues that Amory transcends his selfishness (J183). Finally, Yoshitada Kobayashi considers the symbolism of colors in *This Side of Paradise* (J148). In *The Beautiful and Damned,* Reiko Uefuji believes Fitzgerald developed too many themes that obscure the central one (J228), but Taiwa Izu gives the novel credit for being an important "transition" (J133) in Fitzgerald's growth in consideration of formal structure. Yoshitada Kobayashi considers the symbolism of colors in *The Beautiful and Damned* (J145).

Many of the essays on Fitzgerald's short stories focus on their relationship to the novels, particularly on *The Great Gatsby.* While Itaru Yamaguchi writes on Fitzgerald's Catholicism in "Absolution" (J232), Yoshio Ito describes the close relation between "Absolution" and *Gatsby* (J131), and Itaru Yamaguchi compares time in *Gatsby* to that in "Winter Dreams" (J234) and sees Dexter Green's sense of time as more fragile than Gatsby's (J233). In "Dispossessed Dick and Philippe," Junko Fujimoto contends that "Philippe"'s medieval theme foreshadows Dick as a king with "magic power" before being disposed (J104). Nobuaki Matsumura believes the stories written between the Jazz Age and *Tender Is the Night* indicate the author's growing maturity (J154).

Other scholars focus on the parallel themes in the stories: Tadashi Miyazawa says that while "The Offshore Pirate" appears trivial, it has the author's themes (J161). Tadashi Miyazawa writes on the rapid change of time in "Tales of the Jazz Age" (J162), and Kazuyo Ishikawa, on illusions about a rich girl in "Winter Dreams" (J128). Osamu Hamaguchi writes of Charlie Wales's failure in "Fitzgerald's Babylon Revisited: Charlie's Atonement for His Past Sin" (J119), and Sawako Taniyama describes Fitzgerald as a critic of consumption, not only in "Babylon Revisited" but also in "Winter Dreams" and "The Rich Boy." Sawako argues that the author frowned on adultery, sloth, and excess and saw hope in plain and modest men like Nick and reformed debauchers like Charlie (J208). Taiwa Izu also writes of Fitzgerald's ambivalence towards wealth in "The Rich Boy" (J135). Motoko Fukaya focuses on the relationship between the myth of happiness, consumption and accumulation in "Emotional Bankruptcy" (J116).

Emi Nagase argues that contrasting and contradictory themes permeate "The Ice Palace," "The Jelly-Bean," and "The Last of the Belles" (J172). Yoshio Ito also discerns in "The Sensible Thing" a sense of the delicate balance between opposites, Fitzgerald's double vision (J130). As well, Taiwa Izu sees his double vision of wealth in "The Diamond as Big as the Ritz" (J136) and in "The Rich Boy" as well (J135).

The final category of essays on his short stories focuses on Fitzgerald's characterizations. Kayoko Miyauchi writes about the new image of the heroine in "Winter Dreams" (J157) and on the new type of hero in "Babylon Revisited" (J158). Kiyohiko Tsuboi argues that "Philippe, Count of Darkness" is less convincing because the protagonist is modeled on the Hemingway hero or modern man, yet the setting is medieval (J221). Itaru Yamaguchi traces Gordon Sterrett's deterioration in "May Day" (J236) while Masanori Baba believes that Fitzgerald saves Charlie Wales from the barbaric world through his sense of community (J102).

Japanese scholars have thoroughly investigated Fitzgerald's life and work. Several write about his plays and one, his poetry. Kiyohiko Tsuboi has discovered that the earlier play mentioned in *The Captured Shadow* as the prototype for the play in the story of the same name turns out to be fictional (J224). Yukiko Tokunaga believes even the early Princeton play, *Fie! Fie!, Fi-Fi!* anticipates the themes of his later work, and she argues that *The Vegetable* deserves more attention for its chronological proximity to *The Great Gatsby* and for the theatrical elements in the novels (J216). Chiaki Ohashi also writes about "Paternal Values in *The Vegetable*" (J190). (See discussion of gender below.) Finally, Miyuki Aoyama believes Fitzgerald's poetry is not great but does reflect his substance (J99).

Nobuyoshi Aoki considers the Fitzgerald filmography. He has discovered 40 movies and TV shows, both silent and sound, that bear some relationship to Fitzgerald and his work (J98). Sadao Nagaoka claims that *The Last Time I Saw Paris* interested the Japanese in Fitzgerald after the war (J167). Haruki Murakami's *The Scott Fitzgerald Book* (J85) includes an article on the Jack Clayton film of *The Great Gatsby*. Kiyohiko Tsuboi informed the Centennial Conference-goers at Princeton that the film versions of *The Great Gatsby* (1974) and *The Last Tycoon* (1977) attracted large audiences (J219). Kazuo Shimizu sees in Fitzgerald's own radio scripts not novels and short stories rewritten for broadcasting but sample pieces or sketches by Scott that show the limits of his script-writing (J202).

A sizeable category of Japanese writing on Fitzgerald reflects scholars' efforts to both discern other writers' influence on the author and his influence on other writers. Takashi Tasaka believes that Shelley and André Maurois gave Fitzgerald the means to deepen Gatsby's Platonic conception of himself (J209). Seiwa Fujitani sees the image of a mother praying for her son in both *The Captured Shadow* and in Hemingway's "Soldier's Home" as one Stephen Crane had originally used in *George's Mother*, and Fujitani concludes that Crane influenced both writers (J114). Kenjiro Arai sees the influence of Henry James's *The American* on *The Great Gatsby* but whereas Newman is a realist and uses experience to mature, Gatsby does not (J100). Fitzgerald once wrote that he felt a profound sympathy for Sherwood Anderson's work, and Kyoichi Watanabe writes of Anderson's influence on Fitzgerald's thought (J230). Iwao Nishio believes that "Babylon Revisited" was influenced by Hemingway's *Farewell to Arms* (J185).

As for Fitzgerald's influence on other writers, Kiyohiko Tsuboi sees John O'Hara in *Doctor's Son* using the same narrative technique and time scheme as Fitzgerald used in *The Great Gatsby* (J223). Kiseko Minaguchi discerns the presence of Fitzgerald in Bobbi Ann Mason's "In Country" (J155). Toshifumi Miyawaki depicts Murakami, McInerney and Beattie as Fitzgeraldians (J160), and Eiji Saito agrees that he influenced McInerney and Murakami, but also John Irving and C.D.B. Brian (J195). Junko Fujimoto (J106) believes Fitzgerald's sense of sorrow and emptiness in New York City is present in McInerney's *Bright Lights, Big City.* Koji Ishizuka asserts that though Scott and Zelda clearly influenced Tennessee Williams in his *Clothes for a Summer Hotel,"* Williams doubles himself in his representation of Fitzgerald (J129).

Still other Japanese scholars compare Fitzgerald to other writers. Toshinobu Fukuya writes on Ahab and Gatsby as tragic heroes whose crazed actions are seen as sublime by the narrators (J117). In "The Final Destiny of Narcissists, Dorian Gray and Jay Gatsby," Hirotsugu Inoue see both characters as narcissists who could not recognize reality (J124). Kiyohiko Tsuboi describes the protagonists of both Steinbeck's "Cup of Gold" and *The Great Gatsby* as engaged in a quest for self-accomplishment (J222). Koji Kotani compares Gatsby to Faulkner's Sutpen because both are typical American success stories with mysterious sources who are blinded by the magnificence of the dream. Whereas Fitzgerald likes the beauty of the dream, however, Faulkner prefers the drama of society and history (J150). Nobuaki Namiki also compares Thomas Sutpen and Gatsby as men obsessed with dreams (J179). Kiyohiko Tsuboi sees Fitzgerald's double vision also present in Faulkner's "That Evening Sun." (J222). Kigen Okamoto compares Fitzgerald and Hemingway in their concern to recapture objects and experiences—the fact as it is (J194). Hirotsu Inoue sees Robert Cohn and Charlie Wales as heroes who failed in middle age because they didn't make a choice that led to a traditional middle class life (J125). Kiyohiko Tsuboi compares *The Great Gatsby* and *Look Homeward, Angel* for their uniqueness as confessional novels (J225), and Tsuboi also sees *This Side of Paradise* and *Look Homeward, Angel* as different kinds of novels: the former is a novel of selection, the latter a novel of saturation (J227).

An American Studies approach to Fitzgerald represents a departure for Japanese scholars in the decades of the 1980s and 1990s. Several essays focus on the new economy experienced in the 1920s. Nobuo Kamioka analyzes the varied regional economics reflected in *The Great Gatsby* (J140). Sadao Nagaoka and Kiyohiko Tsuboi discuss American publishing practices (J169). The resulting society is typified by Fitzgerald's depiction of New York City as degraded, barbaric, over-determined Hirotoshi Baba sees Fitzgerald's New York as an urban wasteland, a tragic vision of American civilization (J101).

Takayuki Tatsumi sees in Fitzgerald's description an over-determined image of the city, carrying connotations of the East, women and success (J213). In various articles, urban society is depicted as emotionally bankrupt (J116), as a social vacuum with no limits, resulting in a loss of identity on the border between the body and the machine (J206). Women are seen as predatory beings who adeptly survive in the new society (J212). In his fragmented vision, Fitzgerald is seen to reflect a modernist ethos (J213).

Consumption, accumulation, commercialism, financial success are the goals of the society. Motoko Fukaya sees *The Beautiful and Damned* as "A Fable of the Society of Consumption" (J115), Niimi Sumiko analyzes "Love and Desire in the Era of Mass Consumption" in *The Great Gatsby* (J205), and Motoko Fukaya reflects on "Emotional Bankruptcy Through Accumulation" in the short story "Emotional Bankruptcy" (J116). Shin-ichi Morimoto writes on Fitzgerald's godless America (J163), while Baba Masanori believes that Charlie Wales can withstand the barbaric quality of the modern world (J102).

Class has become an issue in this new era. Mamoru Totake writes on the Jazz Age, seeing Gatsby as standing for American idealism but becoming a victim of the new establishment being formed (J218). Tetsuo Uenishi writes of the modernization of gangs, who have become more business-like and even gentlemanly. Gatsby, Uenishi writes, has reduced himself to this image of Jews in the 20s (J229). Takayuki Tatsumi describes the difference between two billionaires, Gatsby and Monroe Stahr: the former is a Romantic egoistic billionaire whereas Stahr is a modernist charismatic figure (J212). In his "Reexamination of the Beginning of Jazz Age," Toshinobu Fukuya emphasizes the growth of a new meritocracy between May 1919 and the beginning of the 1920s (J118).

"Self-creation," "copying," "self-naming," "self-made man" are also words and phrases associated with the identity of the new citizen in Japanese interpretations of Fitzgerald's works. Masatoshi Miyashita writes on self-naming in American culture (J156), Sanae Fujino on "Money and Identity in *The Great Gatsby*" (J109), Yosuke Murakami on *The Great Gatsby* as a critique of self-made man" (J165), and Takako Tanaka on "Body, Copy, Art" in *Tender Is the Night* (J206).

Two inventions relatively recent to the Jazz Age, the automobile and the telephone, bear much of the symbolism of the novels according to several scholars. Takako Tanaka analyzes how the cost of an automobile reflects the station in life of the characters in *Gatsby* and in 1920s American society (J207). Taiwa Izu sees the care with which one drives reflecting one's moral virtue (J134). Takaai Niwa concludes that in *Gatsby*, Fitzgerald was the first writer to give an important role to the motorcar (J186). Emi Nagase sees a contradictory role for the telephone as a communication medium as it "obstructs communication among the characters" (J173).

Many of the studies written between 1980 and 2000 focus on gender. Takaki Hiraishi asserts that capitalist society associates schizophrenia with gender, and from that point of view, with her endless momentum, Nicole trespasses several traditional codes, including the gender code (J122). Seiwa Fujitani writes on the image of women in Fitzgerald's short stories as arising from the conflict between Scott and Zelda (110). Kayoko Miyauchi describes that image as reflecting materialism, reality, wealth, and hedonism (J157). Mizuho Terasawa believes Fitzgerald's women characters substitute for the ideal mother who can secure the hero's omnipotence and narcissism (J214). Yukiko Tokunaga sees Daisy as a victim but as too reticent to tell her story (J217), and interestingly, believes that Daisy was oppressed, that Myrtle was a rebel, that only Jordan could speak in the male world, and that only Myrtle could have narrated Daisy's story but Daisy kills her (J215). Emi Nagase appears to disagree in arguing that Daisy's voice represents her radical sentiments against her traditional surroundings and is strong enough to convey both her romantic feelings and her inner fragility (J171).

Junko Fujimoto writes of the father-and-son theme in Fitzgerald and argues that there are no strong fathers in *The Great Gatsby* and *Tender Is the Night*. In one of three essays he has written on Fitzgerald's hierarchical and paternal values, Chiaki Ohashi sees Amory searching for paternal figures, Nick locating his hierarchical and paternal values in the paterrnal Mid-West, and Monroe Stahr himself embodying paternal values which are ultimately conquered and degraded by urban/ modern values (J187). In a second article, Ohashi argues that women degrade men's moral hierarchy (J191). In his third article, Ohashi believes that in *The Vegetable*, a balance is achieved between the validity and nonvalidity of paternal values (J190). Matsumura Nobuaki's take is that gender ambiguity and reversal prevail in Fitzgerald's work: the protagonists are passive, the women more assertive. Men like the ideal of women, but not the women themselves (J152).

Chiaki Ohashi has also written several essays on Zelda's short stories written between 1928 and 1930. In "Zelda's Girls" and "Girl Stories," Ohashi sees Zelda's characters as having "means of self-expression, but lacking the energy and strategy to achieve self-actualization" (J188, J189). In "The Figurative Language of Zelda Fitzgerald," Ohashi argues that "not objecting to the paternal/patriarchal values frontally, but transgressing the enclosure of the system" Zelda obtains pleasure which can be observed in her use of figurative language that eludes our attempts at its classification (J192). Haruki Murakami also comments on Zelda's life in *The Scott Fitzgerald Book* (J85).

What appears most indigenous and valuable in the Japanese reception of Fitzgerald is the industriousness that Japanese scholars bring to the study of Fitzgerald in Japan: the Bibliographical Center, the Fitzgerald Club of Japan, created by Profs. Nagaoka and Tsuboi in 1989, which meets "every year to discuss Fitzgerald and enjoy his literature (and) publish *The Fitzgerald Club of Japan Newsletter*" (J219) and which is also responsible for the Bibliographical Center. Also indigenous to Japan are the 1996 publication of facsimiles of

Fitzgerald's first editions by Kiyohiko Tsuboi in *The Selected Works of F. Scott Fitzgerald* and the publication of the contents of the Bibliographical Center (J86), which also appeared near the end of this current assessment of work on Fitzgerald between 1980-2000.

A final indication of an author's reputation in any country is the extent to which his or her works are taught in universities. As Tsuboi informs us, "(Fitzgerald's) stories are taught in freshman English classes in colleges and universities, and his novels are taught in upper-level classes for English majors" (J219). Fitzgerald's reputation in Japan appears assured.

REFERENCES

Miner, Earl. *English Criticism in Japan: Essays By Younger Japanese Scholars on English and American Literature.* Tokyo: University of Tokyo Press, 1972.

---. "A Cinematic Vision of Young Fitzgerald and His First Visit to New York City in 1906." *Suntory Quarterly* (14 Jan. 1983): 40-49.

---. "Scott Fitzgerald and the Garden of Allah." *Suntory Quarterly* (16 Sept. 1983): 52-63.

---. Montgomery, Alabama—A Strangely Cozy Place in the Sun." *Marie Claire Japan* (5 Nov. 1986): 73-85.

---. "A Pilgrimage to Rockville, Maryland." *Suntory Quarterly* (19 Nov. 1984): 28-39.

---. "Fitzgerald's Attractiveness." *The Asahi* (11 Dec. 1980): culture page.

---. "An Author Who Consumed His Youth and That of His Beautiful Wife, Zelda Fitzgerald." *Women Who Have Molded History* VI—*in the Name of Wives.* Shuei-sha (Aug.1983): 239-80.

Nagaoka, Sadao. "Fitzgerald Bibliographical Center in Japan." *Fitzgerald/Hemingway Annual* (1979): 145-46.

---. Letter to author, 20 March 1995.

---. *Some Positivistic Studies on F. Scott Fitzgerald's Life and Works (The Study Jottings of F. Scott Fitzgerald).* Eiho-sha, June 2003.

Schwantes, Robert S. *Japanese and Americans: A Century of Cultural Relations.* New York: Harper and Brothers, 1955.

Stanley, Linda C. *The Foreign Critical Reputation of F. Scott Fitzgerald: An Analysis and Annotated Bibliography.* Westport: Greenwood Press, 1980.

Sugawara, Seiji. "F's Reputation in Japan." *Fitzgerald/Hemingway Annual* (Fall 1961): 70.

Tokunaga, Yukiko. Personal interview. 21 April 2001.

Tsuboi, Kiyohiko. "The Reception of F. Scott Fitzgerald in Japan," *Fitzgerald/Hemingway Annual* (1979): 141-43.

---. *Works on F. Scott Fitzgerald in Japan.* Graph prepared for Fitzgerald Centennial Conference, Princeton, 1996.

---. *Japanese Translations of F. Scott Fitzgerald.* Chart prepared for Fitzgerald Centennial Conference, Princeton, 1996.

Parenthetical citations to entry numbers refer to annotated references in this chapter.

TRANSLATIONS/EDITIONS

J1.   Fitzgerald, F. Scott. "The Bridal Party." *America Sentan Bungaku Sosho-Sentan Tanpen-shu* [*American Trend Literature Series—Trend Short Stories*] 1930.

J2.   Fitzgerald, F. Scott. "At Your Age." *Gendai America Tanpen-shu* [*Contemporary American Short Stories*] 1933.

J3.   Fitzgerald, F. Scott. *Ame no asa Paris ni shisu.* Trans. Kô Shimuzu. Tokyo: Mikasa shobô, 1955; Trans. Yoshide Iijima. Tokyo: Kadokawa-shoten, 1955. Revised edition, 1968. [Includes "Babylon Revisited," "May Day," and "Crazy Sunday"].

J4.   Fitzgerald, F. Scott. *Babylon Revisited and Winter Dreams.* Intro. and Notes by Ikuo Uemura. Tokyo: Kenkyu-sha, 1955. In English.

J5.   Fitzgerald, F. Scott. *Fuyu no yume.* Trans. Kazuyo Nishi and Sakae Morioka. Tokyo: Eihô-sha, 1956.

[Includes "Winter Dreams," "Bernice Bobs Her Hair," "Absolution," "The Diamond as Big as the Ritz"]

J6.   Fitzgerald, F. Scott. "Babylon Revisited," "The Cut-Glass Bowl," "Absolution." Trans. Junshu Jijima. Tokyo: Kadodawa-shoten, 1957; ed. and Notes by Toshisaburo Koyama and Kenichi Haya; Tokyo: Nan'un-dô, 1958. Reprinted 1959.

J7.   Fitzgerald, F. Scott. *Idainaru Gatsby* [*The Great Gatsby*]. Trans. Takashi Nazaki. Tokyo: Kenkyu-sha, 1957.

[Includes "Babylon Revisited" and "The Rich Boy"]

J8.   Fitzgerald, F. Scott. *Rakuen no Kochiragawa* [*This Side of Paradise*]. Trans. Katsuji Takamura. Tokyo: Areci Shuppan-sha, 1957.

[Includes *This Side of Paradise, Tender Is the Night*, "Babylon Revisited," "Family in the Wind," and "Winter Dreams"]

J9.   Fitzgerald, F. Scott. *Yume awaki seishun* [*The Great Gatsby*]. Trans. Saburo Onuki. Tokyo: Kadokawa-shoten, 1957.

J10.   Fitzgerald, F. Scott. *F. Scott Fitzgerald: The Crack-Up*. Tokyo: Nan'un-do, 1958. In English.

[Includes "Sleeping and Waking," "The Crack-Up," and "Handle With Care"].

J11.   Fitzgerald, F. Scott. *F. Scott Fitzgerald: May Day*. Ed. And Notes by Toshisaburo Koyama and Kenichi Haya. Tokyo: Nan'un-do, 1958. Reprinted 1959. In English.

J12.   Fitzgerald, F. Scott. *Yufukuna seinen*. Trans. Yokichi Miyamoto and Reijimi Nagakawa. Tokyo: Nan'un-do, 1958.

[Includes "May Day," 'The Rich Boy," "Sleeping and Waking," and "The Crack-Up"].

J13.   Fitzgerald, F. Scott. *F. S. Fitzgerald: Babylon Revisited*. Notes by Yoshitaka Sakai. Tokyo: Nan'un-dô, 1959. Reprinted 1960. In English

J14.   Fitzgerald, F. Scott. *Yoru wa yasashi [Tender Is the Night]*. Trans.
        Rikuo Tangiguchi. Tokyo: Kadokawa-shoten, 1960.

J15.   Fitzgerald, F. Scott. *Two Short Stories of F. S. Fitzgerald*. Ed. and Notes
        by Mitsuo Yoshida. Tokyo: Shohaku-sha, 1960. In English

J16.   Fitzgerald, F. Scott. *The Great Gatsby*. Ed. and annot. by Naotaro
        Tatsunakuchi and Nobuyuki Kiuchi. Tokyo: Kairyudo's Mentor Library
        11, 1960. In English

J17.   Fitzgerald, F. Scott. *F. Scott Fitzgerald: A Night at the Fair and Forging
        Ahead*. Tokyo: Intro. and Notes by Yoshihide Ueki. Yamaguchi-shoten,
        1961. In English

J18.   Fitzgerald, F. Scott. *The Baby Party and Gretchen's Forty Winks*. Ed.
        and Notes by Hiroshi Yamamoto. Tokyo: Gakusei-sha, 1962. In English

J19.   Fitzgerald, F. Scott. *F. Scott Fitzgerald: The Diamond as Big as the Ritz*.
        Intro. and Notes by Toshisaburo Koyama. Tokyo: Yamaguchi-shoten,
        1962. In English

J20.   Fitzgerald, F. Scott. *Three "Basil" Stories by F. Scott Fitzgerald*. Intro.
        and Annot. by Akio Atsumi. Tokyo: Kenkyu-sha, 1964. In English

J21.   Fitzgerald, F. Scott. *The Short Stories of F. Scott Fitzgerald*. Ed. and
        Notes by Tamotsu Nishiyama. Tokyo: Eicho-sha, 1968. In English

[Includes "The Sensible Thing" and "The Rough Crossing"]

J22.   Fitzgerald, F. Scott. *Francis Scott Fitzgerald: The Ice Palace and
        Magnetism*. Ed. and Notes by Shuichi Motoda and Akira Kataoka.
        Tokyo: Eicho-sha, 1968. In English

J23.   Fitzgerald, F. Scott. *F. Scott Fitzgerald: The Ice Palace and Absolution*.
        Ed. and Notes by M. Kashahara and T. Tasaka. Tokyo: Kabun-sha, 1969.
        In English

J24. Fitzgerald, F. Scott. *This Side of Paradise.* Intro. by Makoto Nagai. Tokyo: Aoyamu, 1970. In English

J25. Fitzgerald, F. Scott. *Babylon Revisited and Other Stories.* Fumi Adachi. Annotation. Hokusei-do, Jan. 1976. 92 + vii.

J26. Fitzgerald, F. Scott. *F. S. Fitzgerald—Short Stories.* Ed. Katsuji Takamura. Eicho-sha, Feb. 1977. 143.

J27. Fitzgerald, F. Scott. *The Last Tycoon.* Trans. Toshinori Yoneda. Mikasa-shobo, Apr. 1977. 236.

J28. Fitzgerald, F. Scott. *The Last Tycoon.* Trans. Shinchiro Innui. Hayakawa Literary Books, July 1977. 298.

J29. Fitzgerald, F. Scott. *The Last Tycoon.* Trans. Saburo Onuki. Kadokawa Literary Books, Sep. 1977. 291.

J30. Fitzgerald, F. Scott. *The Pat Hobby Stories.* Eds. Toshisaburo Koyama and Ashihara (Hosogoshi) Kazuko. Sanshu-sha, Mar. 1978. 61 + xxxi.

J31. Fitzgerald, F. Scott. *"Last Kiss" and Other Stories.* Eds. Takashi Tasaka and Yoshiya Chiba. Shinozaki-shorin, Apr. 1978. 75+ xxii.
[Contains "Jacob's Ladder," "The Swimmers," and "Last Kiss"]

J32. Fitzgerald, F. Scott. *The Great Gatsby.* Tran. Yoichi Moriya. Obun-sha Literary Books, Aug. 1978. 306.

J33. Fitzgerald, F. Scott. *The Vegetable.* Eds. Susumu Kawanishi and Inui Mikio. Tsurumi-Shoten, Dec. 1978. 145 + xviii.

J34. Fitzgerald, F. Scott. *Babylon Revisited (and Other Stories).* Trans. Yoichi Moriya. Obun-sha Literary Books, Aug. 1979. 203.

J35. Fitzgerald, F. Scott. "The Long Way Out." *Modern American Masterpieces.* Ed. Yuzaburo Shibuya. Kinsei-do, Dec. 1979.

J36. Fitzgerald, F. Scott. *The Great Gatsby (Another Novel and Other Stories)*. Trans. Takashi Nozaki and Numazawa Koji. Shuei-sha Edition: *The Collected Works of the World*, Vol. 76. Nov. 1979, 458.

J37. Fitzgerald, F. Scott. F. Scott Fitzgerald: The Collapse and Revival of the American Dream: Lighting Up Literary Works in the 1920s." *The Umi* [*The Sea*] XII.12 (Dec. 1980). 297-355.

[Contains "Lees of Happiness," "The Ice Palace," and "An Alcoholic Case".]

J38. Fitzgerald, F. Scott. *My Lost City and Other Stories*. Trans. Haruki Murakami. Chuokoron-sha, May 1981. 215.

[Contains "Lees of Happiness," "Lo, the Poor Peacock," "The Ice Palace," "An Alcoholic Case," "Three Hours Between Planes," and "My Lost City."]

J39. Fitzgerald, F. Scott. *Selected Stories and Essays of F. Scott Fitzgerald (I)*. Eds. Akio Atsumi and Kenji Inoue. Arechi Publishing Co., May 1981. 245.

J40. Fitzgerald, F. Scott. *Selected Stories and Essays of F. Scott Fitzgerald (II)*. Eds. Akio Atsumi and Kenji Inoue. Arechi Publishing Co., July 1981. 220.

J41. Fitzgerald, F. Scott. *Selected Stories and Essays of F. Scott Fitzgerald (III)*. Eds. Akio Atsumi and Kenji Inoue. Arechi Publishing Co., Oct. 1981. 226.

J42. F. Scott Fitzgerald. "Financing Finnegan." *20th Century Short Stories: American Authors*. Eds. Yasuo Hashiguchi and Takahiro Kamogawa. Shohaku-sha, Mar. 1982.

J43. Fitzgerald, F. Scott. *Letters of F. Scott Fitzgerald—Selected from His Life of Love and Disaster*. Ed. and trans. Sadao Nagaoka and Kiyohiko Tsuboi. Arechi Publishing Co., July 1982. 201.

J44. Fitzgerald, F. Scott. "The Last of the Belles." *Modern American Authors*. Annotated by Yoichiro Kobori and Yasuhiro Ishikawa. Yumi Press, Apr. 1983.

J45.   Fitzgerald, F. Scott. "Two Families" and "Antibes." *Living Well Is the Best Revenge*. Ed. Calvin Tomkins. Trans. Minami Aoyama. *Reproport* (May 1984): 5-13, 104-151.

J46.   Fitzgerald, F. Scott. "The Sensible Thing." *Modern American Masterpieces*. Eds. Yoshi Ito, Hisashi Egusa, Mitsuo Kato, and Chitoshi Nishimura. Asahi Pub. Co., 1984. 122.

J47.   Fitzgerald, F. Scott. "The Baby Party." *New American Models*. Annotated by Yuzaburo Shibuya. Kinsei-do, Dec. 1984.

J48.   Fitzgerald, F. Scott. *The Letters of F. Scott Fitzgerald to His Daughter*. Ed. Kayoko Miyauchi. Introduction: "Charms of Fitzgerald" by Haruki Murakami. Tokyo: Sansyu-sha. 1985. 97

J49.   Fitzgerald, F. Scott. "The Last of the Belles." *Images of Women in Literature*. Ed. Katsumi Kamioka. New Currents International Co., Feb. 1987.

J50.   Fitzgerald, F. Scott. "Three Hours Between Planes." Trans. Hiroshi Takami. *Esquire* [*Japanese Edition*] II.1 (Apr. 1988): 217-237.

J51.   Fitzgerald, F. Scott. "What Became of Our (Flappers and) Sheiks?" Trans. Toshifumi Miyawaki. *Eureka: Poetry and Criticism* XX.14 (Dec. 1988): 51-245.

J52.   Fitzgerald, F. Scott. "Eulogy on the Flapper." Trans. Toshifumi Miyawaki. *Eureka: Poetry and Criticism* XX.14 (Dec. 1988): 51-245.

J53.   Fitzgerald, F. Scott. "The Pampered Men." Trans. Toshifumi Miyawaki. *Eureka: Poetry and Criticism* XX.14 (Dec. 1988): 51-245.

J54.   Fitzgerald, F. Scott. "Looking Back Eight Years." Trans. Toshifumi Miyawaki. *Eureka: Poetry and Criticism* XX.14 (Dec. 1988): 51-245.

J55.   Fitzgerald, F. Scott. "The Bridal Party." Trans. Koji Numazawa.

Eureka: Poetry and Criticism XX.14 (Dec. 1988): 51-245.

J56.   Fitzgerald, F. Scott. "The Ice Palace." *American Eves in Short Stories.* Eds. Keisuke Tanaka and Yasuko Idei. Eihô-sha, Jan. 1988: 35-71.

J57.   Fitzgerald, F. Scott. "Tarquin of Cheapside." Trans. Yasuhiko Terakado. *Eureka: Poetry and Criticism* XX.14 (Dec. 1988): 51-245.

J58.   Fitzgerald, F. Scott. "Teamed with Genius." Trans. Kazuko Tsutsumi. *Eureka: Poetry and Criticism* XX.14 (Dec. 1988): 51-245.

J59.   Fitzgerald, F. Scott. "The Freshest Boy." Trans. Akio Atsumi. *Eureka: Poetry and Criticism* XX.14 (Dec. 1988): 51-245.

J60.   Fitzgerald, F. Scott. "Letters" extracted from *Letters to His Daughter.* Trans. Hiroshi Narasaki. *Eureka: Poetry and Criticism* XX.14 (Dec. 1988): 51-245.

J61.   Fitzgerald, F. Scott. *The Great Gatsby.* Trans. Saburo Onuki. Kadokawa Literary Books, June 1989. 251.

J62.   Fitzgerald, F. Scott. *The Great Gatsby.* Trans. by Takashi Nozaki. *Selected Literary Works of the World America* II. Shuei-Sha Gallery, Oct. 1989. 9-146.

J63.   Fitzgerald, F. Scott. *Fitzgerald's Short Stories.* Trans. Takashi Nozaki. Shincho Literary Books (paperback), Aug. 1990. 291.

J64.   Fitzgerald, F. Scott. *Babylon Revisited and Other Stories.* Trans. Koji Numazawa. Shuei-sha Literary Books (paperback), Dec. 1990. 265.

J65.   Fitzgerald, Zelda. *Zelda Fitzgerald: The Collected Writings.* Trans. Minami Aoyama and Kiyomi Sasame. Ed. Matthew J.Bruccoli. Sinchosha, 1991; 2001.

J66.   Fitzgerald, F. Scott. *Babylon Revisited.* Ed. ChiakiYokoyama. Kodansha English Literary Books, Jan. 1991. 212.

J67.   Fitzgerald, F. Scott. "Babylon Revisited." Trans. Haruki Murakami.
        The Shincho Apr. 1991: 210-233.

J68.   Fitzgerald, F. Scott. *Fitzgerald's Short Stories.* Trans. Yasuki Saeki.
        Iwanami Literary Books, Apr. 1992. 432.

J69.   Fitzgerald, F. Scott. *The Baby Party and Other Stories*, retold by Stephen
        Waller, annotated by Kuniyoshi Ishikawa. Tokyo: Nan'un-do + Penguin
        Series (11) Mar. 1993. 91. In English

J70.   Fitzgerald, F. Scott. *The Great Gatsby.* Trans. Takashi Nozaki. Shuei-
        sha Literary Books, Oct. 1994. 319.

J71.   Fitzgerald, F. Scott. *The Selected Works of F. Scott Fitzgerald.* 9 vols.
        Ed. Kiyohiko Tsuboi. Tokyo: Honnotomo-sha, 1996.

[All the books published during Fitzgerald's lifetime are completely reproduced
in this selected collection. They are all the first editions—first issues, except
bindings. The posthumous publications are excluded.]

J72.   Fitzgerald, Zelda. "Southern Girl." Trans. Chiaki Ohashi. *Baika
        Review*, Vol. 30, 1997.

J73.   Fitzgerald, Zelda. "The Original Follies Girl." Trans. Chiaki Ohashi.
        Baika Review, Vol. 31, 1998.

J74.   Fitzgerald, Zelda. "Mis Ella." Trans. Chiaki Ohashi. *Baika Review*, Vol.
        32, 1999.

J75.   Fitzgerald, Zelda. *Short Stories of Zelda Fitzgerald: the Works and
        Commentary.* Trans. and introduction Chiaki Ohashi. Osaka: Osaka
        Kyoiku Tosho, 1999.

J76.   Fitzgerald, Zelda. "A Couple of Nuts." Part I. Trans. Chiaki Ohashi.
        Baika Review, Vol. 33, 2000.

J77. Fitzgerald, Zelda. *Zelda Fitzgerald: The Collected Writings*. Ed. Matthew J. Bruccoli. Trans. Minami Aoyama and Kiyomi Sasame. Sincho-sha, 1991, 2001.

J78. Fitzgerald, Zelda. *Save Me the Waltz*. Trans. Minami Aoyama. Tokyo: Shobun-sha, 1974. 249.

BOOKS: FULL-LENGTH STUDIES AND COLLECTIONS

J79. Adachi, Fumi. *F. S. Fitzgerald Kenkyu* [*A Study of F. S. Fitzgerald*]. Hokusei-do, Sep. 1975. 214 + v.

One of the earliest book-length works on Fitzgerald but depends on the previous introductory studies in Japan.

J80. Hoshino, Yuko, ed. *Life Story: Scott Fitzgerald—Exile from Paradise*. Media Factory Inc., June 1992. 141.

This is a story of the life of Fitzgerald as told by the author, making use of the past translations and studies published in Japan.

J81. Izu, Taiwa. *Fitzgerald no Chohen Shosetsu* [*The Novels of F. Scott Fitzgerald: The World of Self-Projection*]. Tokyo: Oshi-sha, December 1988. 282.

Almost all of Fitzgerald's fiction is autobiographical. However, Fitzgerald did not write his own biography, but fictionalized his own experiences into novels and stories. How does he make his own experiences into fiction? How does he project himself into the protagonist's situation? How does he sublimate his personal life into universal art? Point of view is very important especially in the case of autobiographical fiction like Fitzgerald's. Izu discusses point of view in *This Side of Paradise, The Beautiful and Damned, The Great Gatsby, and Tender Is the Night*, appending a discussion on the narrative techniques of the Pat Hobby stories.

J82. Karita, Motoshi, ed. *The Literature of F. Scott Fitzgerald and the Death of the American Dream*. Arechi Shuppan-sha., Mar. 1982. 228.

Thirteen scholars, a writer and a movie producer contributed. See essays by individual writers: Kiyohiko Tsuboi, "In the Wake of Tradition;" Sadao Nagaoka, "Aspiration and Frustration—Fitzgerald's Life;" Takashi Tasaka,

"The Style of Fitzgerald;" Yukio Rizawa, "Fitzgerald's Sense of His Home Town;" Makoto Nagai, *This Side of Paradise, The Beautiful and Damned;*" Motoshi. Karita, *"The Great Gatsby;"* Hiroshi Nagase, *"Tender Is the Night, The Crack-Up;"* Izu Taiwa, *"The Last Tycoon;"* Katsuji Takamura, "Short Stories;" S. Nagaoka, "Women to Whom Fitzgerald Was Attached;" Kigen Okamoto, "Fitzgerald and Hemingway;" Haruki Murakami, "Tender Is the Night—Two Versions;" Toshio Kanazeki, "Fitzgerald and His Interest in Money;" Kiyohiko Tsuboi, "Fitzgerald's Plays and Movies;" Tomio Kuriyama, "Fitzgerald in Hollywood;" Ichiro Ishi, "Fitzgerald: Letters to His Daughter;" Masaru Orake, "About Fitzgerald Studies."

J83. Kobori, Yoichiro. *Scott Fitzgerald: hito to sakuin* [*Scott Fitzgerald: The Man and His Work*]. Yumi-shobo, July 1987. 265.

Kobori, who traveled widely in the U.S. following Fitzgerald's trek from St. Paul to Malibu, discusses his major literary works.

J84. Morikawa, Nobuo. *Fitzgerald—His Adolescence of Love and Wandering.* Maruzen-Books, Apr. 1995. iv + 263.

A biographical essay of Fitzgerald based on Japanese translations of American biographies.

J85. Murakami, Haruki. *The Scott Fitzgerald Book.* TBS Britannica, Apr. 1988. 284.

Murakami, a writer influenced by Fitzgerald, writes about five places where Fitzgerald lived: New York, Hollywood, Rockville, Montgomery, and St. Paul and makes some comments on the two versions of *Tender Is the Night,* Zelda's life, the movie of *The Great Gatsby* (Robert Redford) and the translation of "On Your Own" and " The Rich Boy."

J86. Nagaoka, Sadao. *Tokkou Fitzgerald* [*The Lectures on F. Scott Fitzgerald*]. Tokyo: Kobian Press, Mar. 1996. 303.

This biographical work consists of three parts: Part I gives a detailed documentation of Fitzgerald's life and familial background, using newspaper articles and letters, and also comparing other Fitzgerald biographies. Fitzgerald's "spectatorial" relation to the First World War suggests Fitzgerald became a volunteer not because of his patriotic enthusiasm but rather because of his desire to escape from his break with Ginevra King and from his academic failure at college. Part II demonstrates close readings of Fitzgerald's works, including commentaries on their Japanese translations. Fitzgerald's writing and revising "Babylon Revisited" in the context of Zelda's mental breakdown enabled him gradually to distance himself from his emotional involvement with the excruciating experience of her collapse. In the revised version of "Crazy Sunday," Fitzgerald smoothes the temporal order of events and by so doing, enhances the psychological aspect of the story. Part III focuses on Fitzgerald's relationship to Sheilah Graham. He appropriated Sheilah's life experiences in his own work, *The Last Tycoon*.

J87.   Tsuboi, Kiyohiko. *Hametsu no Kage* [*A Touch of Disaster—F. Scott Fitzgerald: His Life and Works*]. Apollon-sha, Dec. 1976. 310.

The "crack-up" essays reflect the "touch of disaster" detected in Fitzgerald's early life that made his tragic end inevitable. His tendency to dramatize himself and his world made his works dramatic as well as tragic.

Japanese Editions of American Studies and Collections

J88.   Berg, A. Scott. *Maxwell Perkins: Editor of Genius*. Trans. Suzuki Chikara. Soshi-sha,, July 1987. 5-14 & passim.

J89.   Bruccoli, Matthew J. *Scott and Ernest: The Authority of Failure and the Authority of Success* (New York: Random House, 1978). Trans. Kigen Okamoto and Yoshiharu Takayama. Kyoto: Apollon-sha, 1983.

J90.   Carpenter, Humphrey. *Geniuses Together: American Writers in Paris in the 1920s*. Trans. Ken Mori. Heibon-sha, Mar. 1995. 307-316.

J91.   Dardis, Tom. *Some Time in the Sun*. Trans. Kenji Iwamoto and Takashi Miyamoto. Sanrio Co. Ltd., Nov. 1982. 29-117.

J92.   Dardis, Tom. *The Thirsty Muse—Alcohol and the American Writer*. Trans. Hiroshi Seki and Tadaaki Akita. Topaz Press, Apr. 1994. 137-222.

J93.   Lehan, Richard. *The Great Gatsby—The Limits of Wonder*. Boston: Twayne Publishers, 1990. Trans. Taiwa Izu. Oshi-sha, Sep. 1995. 246.

J94.   Milford, Nancy. *Zelda*. Trans. Kichinosuke Ohashi. Tokyo: Shincho-sha, 1974. 430.

J95.   Mizener, Arthur. "F. Scott Fitzgerald, *Tender Is the Night,*" *Twelve Great American Novels.* Trans. Kigen Okamoto. Hyoron-sha, Mar. 1980. 171-197.

J96.   Moseley, Edwin M. *F. Scott Fitzgerald: A Critical Essay.* Trans. Muneharu Kitagaki. Sugu-shobo, Jan. 1980. 90.

J97.   Turnbull, Andrew. *Scott Fitzgerald.* Trans. Sadao Nagaoka and Kiyohiko Tsuboi. Kobian-shobo, Sept. 1988. 404.

ESSAYS/CHAPTERS/NOTES/CONFERENCE PAPERS

J98.   Aoki, Nobuyoshi, ed. "Filmography of F. Scott Fitzgerald." *Eureka: Poetry and Criticism* XX.14 (Dec. 1988): 51-245.

A list of about forty movies and TVM's, silent and sound, produced and projected, which have some relationship to Fitzgerald and his work. Short commentaries, with some names of actors added.

J99.   Aoyama, Miyuki. "F. Scott Fitzgerald and His Poetry." *American Literature* [The Tokyo Branch of the American Literature Society of Japan] 44 (Oct. 1984): 24-33.

Fitzgerald wrote poetry as well as fiction. Influenced by Keats, Tennyson and others, he earnestly continued to write poems until the end of his life. In 1981 *F. Scott Fitzgerald: Poems 1911-1940* was published by Bruccoli Clark. Once his poems are read, he can no longer be thought of as a mere talented but careless and fickle playboy of the Jazz Age. Fitzgerald was a much more serious and complicated writer. Although many of his poems are criticized for lack of lyricism and perception, they reflect his concerns with his real world. Especially after the Great Depression in 1929, even though discouraged, he revealed a sense of moral responsibility. Although Fitzgerald was not a great poet, his poetry was reflects his substance.

J100.   Arai, Kenjiro. "On the Evil of (Henry James's) *The American* and *The Great Gatsby.*" *Annual Journal of Faculty Research* [Bunka Women's U] 11 (Jan. 1980): 255-265.

The American (1877) written by Henry James and *The Great Gatsby* (1925) have much in common in the development of their protagonists. Fitzgerald is certainly influenced by James. The novel technique of point of view that James employed, Fitzgerald also uses in *The Great Gatsby*. Also, Gatsby moves through the same trajectory that Christopher Newman does—Innocence (Goodness) to Experience (Facing Evil) to Growth (or Collapse). Why does Newman grow up to be a mature person, while Gatsby collapses in the end? Both Newman and Gatsby start with innocence, but they differ in the field of experience. In facing mental evil, Newman is a practical man and therefore can see the difference between a vision and the reality of life; on the other hand, in facing material evil, Gatsby is a romanticist and therefore cannot see reality.

J101. Baba, Hirotoshi. *"The Great Gatsby* and the City" [Synopses of the Reports of the Symposium at the 40th Annual Convention of the English Literary Society of Kyushu 1987]. *Kyushu American Literature* 29 (1988): 74-75.

The Great Gatsby is constructed upon the opposition between the small town life of the Midwest and the chaotic metropolis: all Western characters, to various degrees, show their inability to fully adapt to city life. In his depiction of New York as an urban waste land, the writer joins John Dos Passos and Nathanel West in expressing through the degraded city a "tragic vision of American civilization."

J102. Baba, Masanori. "'Babylon Revisited'—Charlie Wales's Sense of Community Within the Modern World." *Papers of Kyushu Women's U Parts of Humanities and Social Science* XXVII.1 (Dec. 1991): 1-9.

Charlie Wales's recovery from the past is genuine. First of all, Fitzgerald explicitly refers to Wales's belief in character. Moreover, when Charlie remembers his past at the end of Part I, we know, as Arthur Mizener writes, that even during his wildest days, he was conscious that he was ignoring his family whom he really loved. By depicting his love of his family and the familial tragedy without any moral judgment, Fitzgerald succeeds in intimating Charlie's effort to stifle his grief and renew his life. Part II and Part III of the story dramatize Charlie's renewed character from his subjective point of view. Part IV, however, is the most important part because Charlie's character is shown from an objective viewpoint. In contrast to Lorraine, Charlie, who offers reconciliation to Marion in spite of their mutual antipathy, shows a sense of community that can withstand the barbaric quality of the modern world.

J103. Fujimoto, Junko. "Carnivals in F. Scott Fitzgerald's Works." *English and Literature—Foreign Languages and Literature: Faculty of Literature Annual of Teikyo U* 24 (Feb. 1993): 401-422.

Fitzgerald was attracted to carnivals, fairs and other festivities throughout his life. He liked their brightness and conviviality as well as their dark aftertaste. In almost all his works, he uses images of carnivals to symbolize both man's hopes and dreams and his subsequent disillusionment. In *The Great Gatsby*, Gatsby's house, brightly lighted like 'a World's Fair' and then deserted after Gatsby's death, depicts this before and after carnival atmosphere. In *Tender Is the Night*, the local Agiri Fair, where Nicole has a nervous breakdown, is one of the most important scenes in the novel. On the way home from the fair, Nicole's hand disturbs Dick's driving, and they have a dangerous accident on the mountain road, suggestive of Dick's emotional and mental exhaustion.

J104. Fujimoto, Junko. "'Deposed' Dick and Philippe: From *Tender Is the Night* to 'Philippe—The Count of Darkness.'" *Alice: Studies in Literature & Language* 12 (Dec. 1992): 14-32.

Fitzgerald wrote four short stories that would be a novel with a hero like Hemingway and a little village of Villefranche on the Riviera for the setting. Though these short stories have been neglected as Fitzgerald's 'failure,' they clearly are important in relation to his way of using many medieval images in his works, especially in *Tender Is the Night*. Dick Diver is a king with his 'magic power' in his own kingdom when Rosemary Hoyt meets him on the beautiful Riviera beach for the first time. Everyone around him thinks he is the center of the universe. Dick, however, gradually loses his power over others who once feel comfortable with him, including Nicole, his wife. Near the end of the novel Dick has to leave the Riviera, his former kingdom, as the result of his divorce, losing everything, like a deposed king. To this very place Fitzgerald's strong and young hero, Philippe, returns to rebuild his own kingdom taken by foreign savages. In this situation, Fitzgerald's own hope, hope from the very bottom of desperation, can be detected. Fitzgerald also wrote about his interests and thoughts from his own life during those years in Europe in these short stories. Therefore, they should not be neglected and should be studied along with *Tender Is the Night*.

J105. Fujimoto, Junko. "Seeking Eternal Youth—Fitzgerald and 'Time.'" *Teikyo Women's College Annual* 17 (31 Jan. 1997): 125-133.

Fitzgerald seems to be obsessed with 'Time' because he strongly admires youth and strength. Here discussion on 'Time' in Fitzgerald's works goes along with the myths, in which Time is stronger than any other gods or goddesses, even than Fate who can control man's fate. As Gatsby hopes in vain, time cannot go backward, and man is just aging as it passes. Fitzgerald's obsession with time appears in so many descriptions of time, watches, and clocks, and each description has its own meaning. For example, when Gatsby meets Daisy at

Nick's house, a clock on the mantelpiece falls, and everyone there thinks it is broken. This episode suggests that men cannot control time though they often hope to make it go backward. There are many descriptions of time and clocks in *Tender Is the Night*, as well. Fitzgerald had his idea that men cannot do anything against Time through all his life, which made him strongly long for the eternal youth.

J106. Fujimoto, Junko. "Looming Shadow of Fitzgerald in Jay McInerney's *Bright Lights, Big City*." *Teikyo Women's College Annual* 18 (31 Jan. 1998): 249-267.

Undoubtedly, modern American writers are influenced by writers of the Lost Generation, and McInerney is no exception. In his *Bright Lights, Big City*, not only does McInerney describe the youth in New York of his time as Fitzgerald did, but he seems to be influenced in many ways by Fitzgerald's works. Their ideas about human life seem to be similar. McInerney's hero comes to New York, hoping for success, but he fails in his work, and his life changes when his mother dies of cancer. He ceases to be able to work effectively, and then his wife walks out on him after her success in modeling. Subsequently, he plays around in New York without much pleasure because he feels that he is not the kind of guy who should be where he ends up each morning. McInerney describes the hero's despair and hope in the last scene during which he is walking down the street watching people start to work in the early morning. This scene clearly reminds the reader of the last scene of *The Great Gatsby* because McInerney also describes the sorrow, emptiness and disillusionment behind the bright life in New York.

J107. Fujimoto, Junko. "Fathers and Sons/Daughters Seen in F. Scott Fitzgerald." *English and Literature: Faculty of Literature Annual of Teikyo U* 30 (31 Jan. 1999): 77-85.

The father-and-son theme in which the son can overcome the conflict between his father and himself has been the subject of many American novels. However, Fitzgerald's heroes can never overcome that kind of conflict because there are no strong fathers for them to overcome. Rather, his heroes seek surrogate fathers, but they cannot defeat or move beyond these surrogate fathers. His heroines, on the other hand, can overstep their fathers, actual or surrogate, at the end. As we know, Fitzgerald's father was gentle but weak and his mother was eccentric. This may be the reason why Fitzgerald seems to have sought a strong father figure throughout his life and dismissed any trace of a mother. In addition, he writes about a hero who cannot become a perfect, or strong father, either. Fitzgerald used his own experiences and those of his friends, which interestingly complicates the father-and-son theme in *The Great Gatsby* and *Tender Is the*

Night.

J108. Fujimoto, Junko. "F. Scott Fitzgerald's Paris" *Alice: Studies in
Literature & Language* 20 (1 Mar. 2001): 1-20.

This essay examines Fitzgerald's feelings toward Paris using the Paris section of
Tender Is the Night as a guide. For Fitzgerald, Paris was a fascinating carnival-
like place or, as Hemingway called it, a "moveable feast." But it was never a
pleasant nor comfortable place that he had always anticipated. Fitzgerald writes
his love and hate toward Paris in this section. He created 'his Paris' through his
impressions and imagination, even if he mentioned many factual places. That is,
Paris is used as a way of explaining his characters' behavior and emotions, not
as a mere setting but, with its brightness and charms, a place of meaning in
itself. When Nicole and Rosemary pass the rue des Saints-Pères, they find out
that they once lived on this street. This scene reminds us of Nicole's
uncomfortable experience with her father and of Rosemary's infatuation with
Dick, at first, her perfect father figure. Ironically, neither of these fathers are like
saints at all. Fitzgerald uses these actual names of Paris that seemingly have
meanings as sorts of symbols. This Paris section can be said to be the climax in
the novel, and readers surely detect Fitzgerald's intricate skill in writing this
section.

J109. Fujino, Sanae. "Money and Identity in *The Great Gatsby*." *Shoin Review*
[Shoin College] 9 (Dec. 1993): 37-53.

The explosion of consumerism and optimism in the Twenties was fueled by an
unprecedented prosperity and industrial development but also derived from the
need to exorcise the atrocities of WWI. This generated an excessive trust in
money and the endless possibilities its possession seemed to imply. In *The Great
Gatsby* there is an abundance of monetary terms and a display of materialism,
best exemplified by Gatsby himself and his attempt to achieve his goals through
his dedication to the frontier mentality of self-realization. Yet, frontier values
don't completely work in the East and in a society that for the first time in its
history is now predominantly urban and industrial. While the Buchanans are
perfectly at ease in such mechanism of money and power, Gatsby ignores the
limits of wealth and overestimates money's power to "remake one's identity,"
thus failing in his attempt to gain full acceptance into the world of the rich.

J110. Fujitani, Seiwa. "Change of Women's Image in F. Scott Fitzgerald's
Short Stories." *Faculty of Letters Review* [Otemon Gakuin U] 25 (Dec.
1991): 181-197.

Three kinds of girls are found in Fitzgerald's short stories: flappers who flirt and
discard "all the sad young men," girls who help middle-aged men in the process

of collapse, and girls who are emotionally bankrupt. A flapper like Judy Jones in "Winter Dreams" is typical of Fitzgerald's female image. However, these flappers disappear after 1929, when Zelda's psychological problems became serious. The conflict between Scott and Zelda gave rise to a new image of woman.

J111. Fujitani, Seiwa. "Fitzgerald and Alcoholism. *Alcoholism and American Literature*. Eihosha (25 Feb. 1999): 85-134.

How did alcohol affect Fitzgerald in writing stories and novels? Unlike Hemingway, Fitzgerald could not drink much, but he tried to, and as a result, he became an alcoholic in his thirties. Alcohol inspired him, however, in his twenties. He wrote many stories for magazines, and those stories also appeared in his earlier novels. However, Fitzgerald lost interest in human beings after becoming an alcoholic. There is a difference in his portraits of women from the 1920s and those of the 1930s. Fitzgerald did not illustrate his heroines deliberately as he had, for example, in "Winter Dreams." His poetic descriptions and his fantasies disappeared. An alcoholic does not admit that he is an alcoholic, but Fitzgerald does in *The Crack-Up*. By illustrating the depletion of imagination and his difficult situation caused by alcohol, he tries to be a novelist.

J112. Fujitani, Seiwa. "F. Scott Fitzgerald and the Japanese, Tana." *Review of English Culture Association*, .9 (Mar. 2000): 97-102.

Fitzgerald's image of Japanese people can be seen in his depiction of the two Japanese characters that appear in his stories: Tana in *The Beautiful and Damned* and Mr. Utsuonoma in "Forging Ahead," one of *The Basil and Josephine Stories*. Zelda also depicts the Japanese, Tanka, in *Save Me the Waltz*. Fitzgerald and Zelda had a model for these Japanese characters. When they moved to Westport, Connecticut in May of 1920 and lived there until September, they hired "a small enthusiastic Japanese," Tana, whose real name may be Tanaka. Fitzgerald's impressions of him reflect the image of the Japanese at that time: speaking English poorly, working hard, and dreaming of success.

J113. Fujitani, Seiwa. "Mistakes in Fitzgerald's Biography: Fitzgerald's Correct Address in Syracuse." *Bulletin of Otemon Gakuin U. English Literature Association* 3 (Mar. 1994): 147-150.

Fitzgerald's biography owes much to *The Ledger*. However, his memory of his childhood is not accurate. His father, Edward Fitzgerald, moved three time within Syracuse, New York, from 1901 to 1903. The address in 1901 was not "Mrs. Peck's apartment (sic) on East Genesee Street," but Mrs. Peck's apartment 603 (now 607) on West Genesee Street. The address in 1902 is not "the Kassou" on James Street, but The Kasson, suite 2, 512 (now 735) on James Street. Concerning the address in 1903, *The Ledger* only says "a flat on East Willow Street." Its concrete address is a flat with no name, 613 (now 735) on East Willow Street.

J114. Fujitani, Seiwa. "A Study of the Influence of One Writer's Depiction of a Scene on Other Writers in the Works of Stephen Crane, Ernest Hemingway and F. Scott Fitzgerald." *Faculty of Letters Review* [Otemon Gakuin U] 27 (Nov. 1993): 161-177.

Through one scene common to the works of three novelists, the influence of a picture is shown.. Referring to "Soldier's Home," Fitzgerald said in *Bookman* that he was impressed by the scene where the mother asks her son, who has "all the bitter world in his heart, to kneel down beside her in the dining room in Puritan prayer." Fitzgerald comments that "a picture—sharp, nostalgic, tense— develops before your eyes." Two years later, Fitzgerald uses this "picture" in "The Captured Shadow," where a mother prays for her son. However, Stephen Crane had already illustrated this scene in *George's Mother*. To Crane, a novel was "a succession of sharply outlined pictures which pass before the reader like a panorama, each leaving its definite impression." Crane's method of "showing" the story through pictures was adopted by Hemingway and Fitzgerald.

J115. Fukaya, Motoko. "A Fable of the Society of Consumption: Fitzgerald's *The Beautiful and Damned*." *English Literature* [The English Literary Society of Waseda U] 77 (10 Mar. 1999): 43-57.

The purpose of this paper is to reevaluate *The Beautiful and Damned*. This novel has been considered not to be worth reading, as trash, mainly because it describes a frivolous, rich couple, Anthony and Gloria, wasting their time and money on drinks and parties, and fulfilling their wants with material things; in short, it is an exhibition of the material desires of snobs. But we have to listen to the question the novel puts before us: why do they want and waste so many things? It seems that Fitzgerald tried to answer this question by choosing a snobbish couple as protagonists on purpose and showing how in their search for happiness they are controlled to the point of exhaustion by their material desires. Using Thorstein Veblen's and Jackson Lears's theories of the consumption society, The *Beautiful and Damned* can be seen as a fable of snobs entangled in the desire system of a consumption society. Fitzgerald wanted to emphasize in this novel that however "beautiful" the promise of such a society, it turns out to be "damned" once one is entangled in its emptiness.

J116. Fukaya, Motoko. "Emotional Bankruptcy through Accumulation:
Fitzgerald's 'Emotional Bankruptcy' in an Era of Mass Consumption."
American Literature [The American Literature Society of Japan] 61 (1
June 2000): 32-39.

The title of Fitzgerald's minor story, "Emotional Bankruptcy," has been used as
a keyword which conveys depletion or loss, a familiar theme in his works. This
paper makes it clear, however, that the emotional bankruptcy Fitzgerald tried to
describe is not mere depletion, but depletion through accumulation. It seems
paradoxical to paradoxical to become bankrupt through accumulation, but
Josephine Perry bankrupts emotionally by accumulating too many kisses from
her suitors. She always wants what she does not have and pursues it, but the
moment she wins it, she gets bored and looks for more. At last, she has had
everything she wanted, only to discover that she does not know what to want
next, though she still wants something more. Sociologists such as Jean
Baudrillard and Jackson Lears show us through their research that the myth of
happiness causes consumers to accumulate material things only to find in
emptiness that perfect satisfaction will not come no matter how much they
accumulate. This mechanism of mental distress is quite similar to that of
Josephine. Emotional bankruptcy is not a problem peculiar to one of Fitzgerald's
heroines, but a problem shared among all consumers. Fitzgerald was aware at
the beginning of the 1920's that emotional bankruptcy was an ethos of those
who lived in the mass-production/consumption era.

J117. Fukuya, Toshinobu. "Ahab and Gatsby: the Tragic in the Lineage of
American Heroes." *Yaseel* 2 (Aug. 1998): 33-42.

Ahab in *Moby Dick* and Gatsby in *The Great Gatsby* finally collapse upon
themselves in struggling against the differences between their dreams and their
realities. Their collapses do not make the stories of the two heroes tragic; rather
the tragedy results from the two narrators' sympathies for the sublimities
underlying the crazed actions of the heroes. In *The American Adam* R. W. B.
Lewis insists that the myths of innocent American heroes can be enriched by
including the tragic realities. Ahab and Gatsby, the tragic heroes representative
of American literature, reflect the realities of the social changes in America and
thus strengthen the lineage of American tragic heroes.

J118. Fukuya, Toshinobu. "The Reexamination of the Beginning of the Jazz
Age." *Circles* 2 (Aug. 1999): 49-59.

Fitzgerald defines the period of the Jazz Age in "Echoes of the Jazz Age" as
follows: "The ten-year period that, as if reluctant to die outmoded in its bed,

leaped to a spectacular death in October, 1929, began about the time of the May Day riots in 1919." While this early date for the inception of the Jazz Age is unexpected, for Fitzgerald, its beginning was about more than the dissipated hedonism of flapper girls and the Charleston. He found space for the growth of a new meritocracy in American society in the time lag between May in 1919 and the beginning of the 1920s. Without this breakthrough, the challenges faced by Fitzgerald's heroes in scaling the wall of social class would have been impossible.

J119.   Hamaguchi, Osamu. "Fitzgerald's 'Babylon Revisited': Charlie's Atonement for His Past Sin." *The Bulletin of the Faculty of School of Education* [Hiroshima U] II.7 (Dec. 1984): 9-19.

Fitzgerald's "Babylon Revisited" is one of his most autobiographical short stories. His own experiences and impressions are clearly seen in the protagonist's fruitless struggle to establish a home with his estranged daughter. But, however closely it may be related to the author's private life, the fact remains that the story is a literary work, fictionalized through his artistic imagination. Assuming that a literary work is given a "superindividual" existence (see Shuichi Motoda, *Analysis and Technique of Short Stories*, Kaibunnsha, 1981), we can arrive at a satisfactory understanding of it by our careful reading and analysis of the work itself. By examining some of Fitzgerald's techniques and characterizations apparent in this story, the true meaning of Charlie Wales's tragedy and the origins of the pathetic mood of this story can be explored.

J120.   Hatayama, Hideaki. "Under the Illusion of 'Glasses' and the 'Green Light.'" *Essays on American Literature* 7 (Sep. 1985): 20-27.

Gatsby's tragedy is, in a metaphorical sense, caused by his red-green blindness and astigmatism. The "green light" on Daisy's deck doesn't mean "walk" but "stop"; his success and love, like a castle in the air, is nothing but a nightmare distorted by his excessive romanticism and the American dream of success. After he returns to the Midwest, the narrator Nick Carraway notices "a quality of distortion" in the East, which was "beyond my eyes' power of correction." As Jordan said, remembering a conversation they had about driving a car, Nick was also "another bad driver" Nick (Care-way?) was more or less safe but Gatsby's tragedy can be regarded as being caused by his bad driving through life without any awareness of "a quality of distortion." An oculist's billboard above the gray land, "Doctor T. J. Eckleburg" with "a pair of enormous yellow spectacles" has a symbolic role in the text: from Fitzgerald's viewpoint, a cynical warning to the characters about an eye, or insight, or how to drive a life in a distorted world. And Gatsby's "green light" is through the historical perspective overlapped with "a fresh, green breast of the new world" of colonial days. The American dream is suspended between progress "walk" and regress "stop."

J121. Hayakawa, Eiichi. "The Narrator's Function in *The Great Gatsby*."
       Arthurian and Other Studies—Festschrift Presented to Shunichi Noguchi.
       Woodbridge, Suffolk; Rochester, New York: Boydell & Brewer, 1993.
       69-75.

Gatsby, who is revealed as an eminently contradictory character when observed objectively, becomes, thanks to Nick's perspective, a great mythical figure because of his dual role as both character and narrator. Nick shows all his idiosyncrasies in the way he generalizes and in his "inability to reserve judgment"; even though he does not willingly lie or falsify facts, he tends to manipulate the significance of certain events, thus influencing the reader's perception of Gatsby. One of the clearest examples is Nick's interpretation and justification of Gatsby's dream, as well as his conflation of himself, Gatsby, the reader, and the author in the general 'we' at the end of the novel.

J122. Hiraishi, Takaki. "Gender is the Night: *Yoru wa Yasashi* no shihon-
       shugi, bunretsu-sho, gender [Gender is the Night: Capitalism,
       Schizophrenia, and Gender in *Tender Is the Night*]." *Bungaku America
       Shihon-shugi* [*Literature and American Capitalism*]. Eds. Masashi
       Orishima, Takaki Hiraishi, and Shinji Watanabe. Tokyo: Nan-un-do,
       1993: 281-294.

The association of gender with schizophrenia is characteristic of modern, capitalist society in *Tender Is the Night*. Capitalism drives human beings into schizophrenia in its constant, circulatory movements from one code to another, from coding to decoding, as analyzed in Deleuze and Guattari's *Anti-Oedipus*. Following their postulation of schizophrenia as the by-product of capitalism, Nicole can be seen as a schizophrenic figure who freely trespasses traditional codes. In *The Great Gatsby* as in *Tender*, women embody the schizophrenic decoding with their capricious impulses and plurality of desire. Moreover, it is money that enables their free-floating acts. Thus, women, the schizophrenic, and money are inextricably interrelated in Fitzgerald. For him, wealth and female gender are associated in equal terms. However, *Tender* also embraces the reversal of gender relation between Dick and Nicole. Thus, the decoding function of capitalism inevitably brings out the vacillation of gender codes. As a figure of endless momentum, Nicole's split personality, in parallel with Zelda's, puts male characters under her power. Fitzgerald, himself, is "feminine," that is, schizophrenic. His addictive habit of drinking not to mention, writing of *Tender*, too, indicates a schizophrenic aspect, with the plot depending on emotional impulses and accidental events rather than on logical consequence and coherence. Divided between Nicole and Rosemary, Dick, too, drives into night, into death, which is nothing but the ultimate decoding from every code of life.

J123. Hirono, Yumiko and Fukuya, Toshinobu. "Time in *The Great Gatsby*." *Bulletin of the Faculty of Education Yamaguchi U* 46.1 (December 1996): 121-33.

The narration of *The Great Gatsby* is presented as Nick's recollection of the events of the summer he met Gatsby. Rearranging the narrative order of these events, Fitzgerald constructs a complicated time scheme that makes "time" in his work an especially important element. Therefore, the meaning of "time" relative to the central theme of *The Great Gatsby* must be clarified, particularly how the distance between the past and the present changes for Gatsby during the progress of the story. The narrator's sense of time also changes with his spiritual development. Finally, Gatsby's challenge to recover his past is closely connected with the "American dream."

J124. Inoue, Hirotsugu. "The Final Destiny of Narcissists, Dorian Gray and Jay Gatsby." *Studies in Comparative Culture* 31 (March 1996): 1-12.

Dorian Gray in *The Picture of Dorian Gray* by Oscar Wilde and Jay Gatsby are extraordinary lovers of themselves, equal to Narcissus in the Greek mythology. Fascinated at his portrait drawn by Basil Hallward Dorian fell into intense love with Sybil who called him "Prince Charming." On the other hand, Gatsby was fascinated by Daisy whom he met while he was in military service. Discovering upon his return to the States that she had married Tom Buchanan, Gatsby tried desperately to get Daisy's love back. But he was in love not with the real Daisy but with the one whom his illusion created, symbolized by a single green light at the end of her dock. Loving his idea of Daisy fiercely, he was deeply attached to himself who he thought was loved by her. Both heroes had one thing in common, an extraordinary fascination with themselves. Consequently they could not recognize reality as it really was.

J125. Inoue, Hirotsugu. "Robert Cohn and Charles Wales: Frustration in Middle Age." *Language and Culture* [International Language and Culture Institute, Sapientia U 2 (March 1999): 1-19.

Both Robert Cohn in Hemingway's *The Sun Also Rises* and Charles Wales in Fitzgerald's "Babylon Revisited" are heroes of failure in their middle age, in spite of the possibility they had of reaching self-realization. They both suffered from a poor self-image due to their lack of a sense of achievement. Cohn says, "I can't stand to think my life is going so fast and I'm not really living it." At 34, he is at a loss. As Charlie Wales revisits Paris, he realizes that he "spoiled this city for myself. I didn't realize it, but the days came along one after another, and then two years were gone, and everything was gone, and I was gone." Self-pity took possession of Wales as he realizes his wealth spoiled him. Neither character can accept himself as he really is. The sense of failure they have in common arises from the inability they had in the past to work hard to earn a living, to cope with a lifelong partner peacefully and prudently, and to confront their inner selves realistically.

J126. Inoue, Hirotsugu. "The Tragi-comical Image of Jay Gatsby, Or the Struggle of a Man Who Pronounced a Death Sentence upon God." *Bulletin of Kobe Kaisei Women's College and Junior College* XXVII (December 1988): 65-84.

The tragi-comical image of Jay Gatsby is seen in the failure of his efforts to acquire Daisy, whom he identified as a goddess, as his partner in life and in fact in being murdered due to her betrayal. A man with an extraordinary gift for hope, Gatsby had an infinite capacity to fulfill his dream but failed in doing so. Denying God, the creator of the universe, Gatsby served the Goddess whom his passion created out of some heightened sensibility he had to the promises of life. His tragic ending was a punishment for the sin of idolatry. He was sincere to his inner self but made himself a victim of the dream, which can be seen as laughable.

J127. Inoue, Kenji. "Fitzgerald [Fitzgerald Studies in Japan]." *Eigo-seinen: The Rising Generation.* [Extra Number "Studies in English and American Literature in Japan . . . The Status Quo and Problem to Solve,"] June 1984: 109-111.

As his works have become more and more popular since the 1950s, Fitzgerald studies have become a major "industry" for Japanese academics. From 1930 to 1983, critical studies of Fitzgerald written by Japanese scholars reached 401, including five monographs. As the studies increase, the problem is that the subjects have become monotonous,+- frequently focusing on themes such as the American dream and its failure/breakdown, double vision, and such. In particular, studies of *The Great Gatsby* dominate the whole industry.

J128. Ishikawa, Kazuyo. "A Study of Fitzgerald's 'Winter Dreams.'" *Bulletin of Nagoya Women's College* 28 (Mar. 1982): 317-320.

"Winter Dreams" follows the life of a boy of modest origins who ascends the social ladder through work and financial success; he is then able to obtain the rich girl he had become infatuated with years before, only to lose her again. In the end, hearing of her sad present life from a friend, he realizes that her exceptionality had been mostly an illusion, which he had created himself.

J129. Ishizuka, Koji. "Scott to Zelda no *yurrei geki*: T Williams no *Hotel heno natsufuku sugata de* [Scott and Zelda's *Ghost Play*: T. Williams' *Clothes for a Summer Hotel*]." *Eureka* 20.14 (Dec. 1988): 202-205.

Tennessee Williams's play, *Clothes for a Summer Hotel*, draws Scott and Zelda's relationship. However, as its subtitle "A Ghost Play" suggests, it is not a realistic representation of their life. As in his other plays, Williams inscribes his personal narrative onto the mythical figures of Scott and Zelda. Williams, in his own decline and habit of drinking, doubles himself in his representation of Fitzgerald. The reflection of Williams' sister, Rose, can also be seen in the figure of Zelda.

J130. Ito, Yoshio. "The Sensible Thing." *Modern American Masterpieces*.
    Eds. Yoshio Ito, Hisashi Egusa, Mitsuo Kato, and Chitoshi Nishmura.
    Tokyo: Asahi Press, April 1985. ix+122.

Fitzgerald is among those writers who describe themselves directly in their works. "The Sensible Thing" is a typical example. His experiences in his youth are clearly reflected in this story, which recalls the troubled process of his engagement and marriage to Zelda Sayre. Initially, Fitzgerald was filled with delight at his engagement, but he suffered later when she broke it off. In his agony, he devoted himself to completing his first novel, *This Side of Paradise,* the success of which enabled him to marry Zelda after all. In "The Sensible Thing," we find a similar situation between the lovers. The story ends with the young lovers back together; nevertheless, the protagonist George O'Kelly vaguely feels the sweet and shining days of his youth have disappeared forever. In this fashion, Fitzgerald's better works always depict the light and shadow of youth Fitzgerald has a sense of the delicate balance between opposites—glory and disappointment, intoxication and disillusion, for example—and this sense is frequently called his "double vision."

J131. Ito, Yoshio. "On 'Absolution.'" *The Bulletin of Fuji Women's College*
    I.17 Sapporo (Jan. 1980): 1-15.

Fitzgerald's short story titled "Absolution" was first written as the prologue of his masterpiece, *The Great Gatsby*. It was published independently, however, because Fitzgerald intended to keep a sense of mystery about Jay Gatsby's boyhood in the novel. Fitzgerald had a preference for writing short stories that shared motifs and themes with his novels. Therefore, "Absolution" is closely related to *The Great Gatsby*, and it also can be studied with reference to other short stories such as "Winter Dreams" or "The Rich Boy Although "Absolution" is one of the shortest stories among his works, Fitzgerald's mastery of technique enables the reader to sense the story's extension in both time and space.

J132. Iwasaki, Tatsuru. "The American Dream and Nightmare—Chiefly on *The Great Gatsby.*" *New Currents of English Language and Literature* (Dec. 1987): 71-79.

In his *American Dreams, American Nightmares,* David Madden says, "Those who say yes (to the American dream) I call the true believers. . . . Those who say no I call atheists." From this viewpoint, Fitzgerald could be seen as a true believer, even had he only written *The Great Gatsby.* Gatsby believes in the American dream and almost realizes it, which on the one hand seems to make Fitzgerald a true believer, but on the other, as Fitzgerald does not allow Gatsby to accomplish his dream, readers may doubt that he is in the category of true believers. Based not on Gatsby, but on Nick, the narrator, however, who has been looking for something innocent in Gatsby (though he fails to put it into words), Fitzgerald reaffirms his belief in the American dream, which is based on a kind of innocence.

J133. Izu, Taiwa. "*The Beautiful and Damned* as a Novel of 'Transition'" *Eigo to Eibei Bungaku* [*English and English-American Literature*], Yamaguchi U] 20 (Dec. 1985): 127-144.

The Beautiful and Damned, Fitzgerald's second novel, is the least evaluated and discussed of his five novels. It is a novel of 'transition' from the first novel, *This Side of Paradise,* to the third novel, *The Great Gatsby.* It may not be a good literary work, but it shows Fitzgerald's growth as a novelist, particularly in his consideration of formal structure.

J134. Izu, Taiwa. "'Careless Driving' in *The Great Gatsby.*" *Eigo to Eibei Bungaku* [*English and English-American Literature,* Yamaguchi U] 29 (Dec. 1994): 229-239.

It is said that there were, on the average, two cars for every three families in America in the early twenties. The Jazz Age was, in this sense, the age of motorization. In *The Great Gatsby,* the car is not only a means of transportation but also a signifier that suggests the character and function of its owner and driver. Almost all the main characters own and drive their cars and are essentially careless drivers. Many traffic accidents occur, and the accident Daisy causes is fatal. "Careless driving" reflects the moral carelessness of the drivers.

J135. Izu, Taiwa. "F. Scott Fitzgerald and Wealth—A Note on 'The Rich Boy.'" *Eigo to Eibei Bungaku* [*English and English-American Literature.* Yamaguchi U] 24 (Dec. 1989): 215-228.

Fitzgerald had an ambivalence for, or "double vision" toward wealth; he is both fascinated and disgusted by it. "The Rich Boy" is dominated by cool objectivity, and Fitzgerald's ambivalence cannot be recognized here because of the detachment of an anonymous narrator.

J136. Izu, Taiwa. "A Fantasy of Wealth—A Note on 'The Diamond as Big as the Ritz." *Eigo to Eibei Bungaku [English and English-American Literature.* Yamaguchi U] 28 (Dec. 1993): 229-241.

Fitzgerald's ambivalent attitude toward wealth is seen in "The Diamond as Big as the Ritz." Although John T Unger is fascinated by the Washingtons' kingdom of wealth, the cool voice of the third-person narrative describes it critically.

J137. Izu, Taiwa. *"The Last Tycoon*: In Search of Fitzgerald's Rebirth." *Fitzgerald no Bungaku [The Literary World of Fitzgerald].* Ed. Motoshi Karita. Tokyo: Arechi Shuppansha, Mar. 1982. 105-117.

Monroe Stahr is a strong hero in the movie industry who presents many contrasts with Fitzgerald himself in Hollywood. Why did he write a novel about a strong hero when he himself was regarded not as a great novelist but as a mere scenario writer? From this viewpoint, the author's biographical background, the composition and structure of the novel, the first-person-narrator's point of view, and the rhetoric of narration suggest the possibility of Fitzgerald's rebirth as a novelist in Hollywood.

J138. Izu, Taiwa. "Moonlight in *The Great Gatsby*." *Eigo to Eibei Bungaku [English and English-American Literature,* Yamaguchi U] 32 (Dec. 1997): 339-351.

Gatsby appears at the night when the moon is out. As a character, he is a moonlit person of mystery. As Nathaniel Hawthorne indicates, moonlight offers "a neutral territory, somewhere between the real world and fairy-land, where the Actual and the Imaginary may meet." Moonlight creates a "neutral territory," for Gatsby, a stage of romance where he can metamorphose himself from a suspicious gangster into a mysterious hero. He is essentially a hero of romance who happens to stray into the world of the novel. He cannot live in the day so he is killed in the sunlight in the end.

J139. Izu, Taiwa. "In Search of Fitzgerald's Adam: A Note on *This Side of Paradise*." *English and English-American Literature* [Yamaguchi U] 19 (Dec. 1984): 133-147.

Fitzgerald's first novel is immature and fragmentary, so loosely constructed that we can hardly call it a novel; yet, in Amory Blaine one can see, not only the author's reflection, but also the precursor of all later Fitzgerald male protagonists. Amory is thus an American Adam on his way to experience: he starts out as a typical narcissistic egotist who projects his own desires and aspirations on the world. The four women that he gets involved with are his Eves, and they prefigure the women of his later novels; Amory idealizes his women as 'Golden Girls' and then inevitably falls prey to disillusionment. Finally, as he matures, Amory shows also his moralistic side, which anticipates a character like Nick and his decent moral stand against the corruption of the rich.

J140. Kamioka, Nobuo. *"The Great Gatsby* to mittu no keizai taisei [*The Great Gatsby* and Economic Systems in Three U.S. Regions]." *Eigo Seinen: The Rising Generation* . CXXXVIII.5 (Aug. 1992): 210-214.

Gatsby's dream has been seen as the modern version of the American Dream/frontier spirit and its tragedy as a dilemma between spirituality and materialism. This dilemma can be considered from the vantage point of regional economic contrasts. Nick's narrative aligns the opposition between the East and the West with that of innocence and moral corruption. But to evaluate the 'westerner' Gatsby's success in NY, Nick's narrative voice is tinged with incoherence. The North-South contrast in Fitzgerald's short story "The Ice Palace" and also the representation of New York in "The Rich Boy," correspond to the relation of and correspondence to the East-West contrast in *The Great Gatsby*. Furthermore, Daisy represents the elements of the South—the tradition of stability, land and family—which in turn overlap with the values of the Midwest, in opposition to disorder, corruption and capitalism in the East. *Gatsby* posits Jeffersonian agricultural fundamentalism and self-sufficiency of the midwest as an ideal. The fact is, however, that the West and the South were both commonly immersed in capitalism—and this very contradiction is the core dilemma of the American dream, and also of Gatsby's dream.

J141. Kato, Mitsuo. "The World of Fitzgerald (1): 'The Ice Palace' and Its Description of Nature." *Culture and Language* 32.2 (31 Mar.1999): 47-73.

The opening paragraph of "The Ice Palace," which describes the hot summer scenes of a southern town, makes all the more distinctive the characteristics of the northern winter locked in snow and ice. The description of those scenes is an indispensable factor in immortalizing this story. Born and brought up in the north, Fitzgerald subtly describes the winter scenes printed on his memory in the forms of sketches, inerasable archetypes, or perverse inner pictures. Those natural descriptions are detailed and accurate and stimulate infinitely the formation of associated pictures in the readers' minds. All are depicted in sentences of precisely selected words and phrases that glitter superbly and flow like poetry, giving us an unforgettable emotion. Culture, living styles and customs and climate itself also change with the time and when this happens people's passions and their lives are left somewhere back in the past.

J142. Kato, Muneyuki. "Daisy Buchanan's Secret and Nick Carraway . . . An Interpretation of *The Great Gatsby*." *Journal of the Faculty of Literature* [Kitakyushu U] 33 (Mar. 1984): 1-30.

Nick's tolerant habits of mind which, through Daisy's refusing to acknowledge her secret, metamorphosed into a severe judgmentalism that he could no longer contain, gave birth to the novel.

J143. Kobayashi, Yoshitada. "The Color Symbolism in *The Great Gatsby* by F. Scott Fitzgerald." *Memoir* [School of Education, Ehime U] II. 15 (Feb. 1983): 51-63.

Colors are one of the main symbolic patterns used in the book. White, in spite of its traditional association with purity, is here more closely related to Daisy's and Jordan's emptiness and dullness; blue also seems to lose its connections to seas and serene skies; yellow evokes decadence and corruption, rather than gold and cheerfulness; the green light symbolizes fresh desire and hope, but in the last part of the novel both prove unattainable; gray, with its vagueness and opacity casts a gloomy atmosphere on the novel, while black more directly suggests crime and vice; silver and gold represent superficial perfection disguising moral emptiness; finally, red is Gatsby's blood at the end, while its variant pink suggests health and richness. Thus, all colors are presented in the novel within an ambiguous symbolism of positive and negative connotations.

J144. Kobayashi, Yoshitada. "The Color Symbolism in *Tender Is the Night* by F. Scott Fitzgerald," *New Currents of English Language and Literature.* Tokyo: New Currents International Co., Ltd. (Dec. 1988): 58-71.

White is fascinating to Dick and at the same time it gives him an unpleasant feeling through Nicole's betrayal. Though blue which is connected with the eyes of Dick or his ancestors is the hopeful color, the color as well implies gloom, misery and sadness, and it is often used under the influence of *yellow* which alludes to madness or money. Therefore, it may be said that *yellow* interrupts Dick's entrance into the hopeful territory which is symbolized by *blue*.

J145. Kobayashi, Yoshitada. "The Description of Color Words in *The Beautiful and Damned* by F. Scott Fitzgerald," *Memoir* [School of Education, Ehime U] II. 22 (Feb. 1990): 69-94.

The novel is seen in grays and whites. Gray is in use as the color which represents the house inviting the disaster in Marietta where Anthony and Gloria live after their honeymoon. Gray also appears as the color of Gloria's eyes which symbolizes her obstinate personality in connection with "granite," suggesting her desperate and gloomy life after her marriage to Anthony. White, which stands for cleanliness and neatness, is used as the color of Anthony's small apartment in New York which helps to turn the misfortune to their advantage. White is also the color of the dress that Gloria wears when she visits Anthony's apartment for the first time and of the clothes which Dorothy has on when she becomes acquainted with Anthony in the army. Finally, morbidly, whiteness is associated with weirdness, ominousness, fearfulness and pennilessness.

J146. Kobayashi, Yoshitada. "F. Scott Fitzgerald and Color Words," *New Currents of English Language and Literature*. Tokyo: New Currents International Co., Ltd. (Sep. 1994): 76-82.

Three color words, white, blue and gray, rank above other color words in the frequency with which Fitzgerald uses them in his work. Fitzgerald appears to have a deep attachment to white, which is especially embodied in New York City, "the glittering white city." Zelda's eyes, which were said to be the bluest in Montgomery and in the State of Alabama, became deeply rooted in his mind and influenced him even when he wrote a novel. Further, the frequency of gray is comparatively high because of his experience of the bitter trials of life and his sense of the shadow of the dismal historical period in which he lived.

J147. Kobayashi, Yoshitada. "The Image of Color Words in *The Last Tycoon* by F. Scott Fitzgerald," *New Currents of English Language and Literature*. Tokyo: New Currents International Co., Ltd. (Jan. 1990): 70-83.

Silver is closely to Kathleen for whom Stahr is patiently searching, and it gives the whole story a brilliant atmosphere, connecting with her belt and with the grunions. But this color, which verges on white, also suggests the cold heart of Stahr who remembers his dead wife's face so often that he cannot propose to Kathleen. White, forming the background around Kathleen and functioning as the color which describes her neatness, cleanliness and holiness, is used together with lights to emphasize the brightness, but at the same time it evinces anxiety, distress, contempt, and old age.

J148. Kobayashi, Yoshitada. "Various Phases of Color Words in *This Side of Paradise* by F. Scott Fitzgerald," *Memoir [School of Education, Ehime*

UJ II. 21 (Feb. 1989): 161-178.

White is used almost exclusively in reference to New York City and students' clothes which is probably related to Fitzgerald's admiration for the innocence of the young people of the City. However, more important, white also takes on the connotation of an ill omen which appears in the descriptions of Dick's dead face and Eleanor's small devilish, witch-like figure. One of the themes in the novel seems to be an inexplicable disquiet beyond the "gray bulwarks of civilization" that young people hold in their mind.

J149. Kotani, Koji. "Class and the American Dream in *The Great Gatsby*." *Studies in Languages and Cultures* . 10 (Mar. 1999): 95-103.

A close analysis of Nick's complex class consciousness brings to light Fitzgerald's opposing views of wealth: the realistic perception of the power structure inherent in wealth and the romantic idealization of wealth as a representation. This double vision is reflected in Nick's portrait of Gatsby. While his metaphorical and rhetorical language presents a glorified picture of Gatsby as an embodiment of the myth of the American dream, it also conceals the paradoxical structure as an indispensable basis of the myth; that is, the American dream, although predicated on the existence of class structure in American society, creates an illusion of equal opportunity, and by so doing hides the power structure in the class system.

J150. Kotani, Koji. "Gatsby's Dream and Sutpen's Dream." *Kyushu American Literature* [Synopses of the Reports of the Symposium at the 40th Annual Convention of the English Literary Society of Kyushu, 1987] 29 (1988): 77-80.

Both Gatsby and Thomas Sutpen, the protagonist of Faulkner's *Absalom, Absalom!*, embody the typical "American success story," which they achieve through hard work and self-discipline. In both cases the source of their wealth is mysterious, and rumors contribute to the characters' mythical, but questionable, status. Gatsby and Sutpen are both blinded by the magnificence of their dream, but while Fitzgerald shows a greater fascination for the timeless beauty of the dream, Faulkner is more concerned with the "human drama" of history and society.

J151. Masui, Yukimi. "Fitzgerald's Elaboration on Daisy's Charm." *Journal of the College of Arts and Sciences* [Chiba U] B.23 (Nov. 1990): 343-349.

The characterization of Daisy in *The Great Gatsby* fascinates Gatsby and Nick; her charm is described as something beyond words, and hinted at symbolically and metaphorically, through the use of colors and images. While white and yellow point at Daisy's "nothingness" and shallowness, yet she is also a tragic character, suspended as much as is Gatsby, between a purely materialistic charm and a more spiritual one. Unlike Gatsby, Daisy abandons her youthful dreams and infatuations and lets others direct her life; this is why Nick and the author judge her negatively at the end of the novel and include her among the corrupted and careless rich.

J152. Matsumura, Nobuaki. "Romance no shuyaku ni narenai otoko tachi: F. Scott Fitzgerald no egaku dansei tachi ni kansuru ichi-kousatsu [All the Sad Young Men; or, Men Who Cannot Be the Hero of Romance: A Note on Fitzgerald's Male Characters]." *Shuryu*. [English Literary Society of Doshisha U] 55. (Feb. 1994): 35-50.

Gender ambiguity and gender reversals pervade Fitzgerald's works, characterizing Nick Carraway in *The Great Gatsby*, Amory Blaine in *This Side of Paradise*, Dick Diver in *Tender Is the Night*, and Jacob Booth in "Jacob's Ladder." Each work registers male passiveness in contrast to the aggressiveness of female characters, who challenge the Victorian codes of female propriety and are better at decision-making and steering their way in the modem pragmatic world. While American women in the 20s began to liberate themselves from traditional constraints of femininity, men were often unable to attain masculine identities and to deal with the harsh reality of a capitalist society. Fitzgerald's men cannot love women: instead, they love and desire images of women, rather than the women in reality.

J153. Matsumura, Nobuaki. "Nick no kataru Gatsby, Nick no kataru Daisy ni tsuite [Gatsby and Daisy in Nick's words]." *Shuryu* [English Literary Society of Doshisha U] 52 (Mar. 199): 131-147.

Although Nick attests to his reliability as an objective observer and narrator, certain biases are working in his view of other characters, and it is therefore important to read Gatsby and Daisy apart from Nick's point of view. For example, in his narrative, Nick describes Daisy solely in terms of images. Instead of describing her in empirical detail, Nick forms Daisy's image allusively, in the way which W. Iser calls "ideation"—image-making without the direct perception of the object. As such, Daisy's image—especially her voice "full of money"—evokes in the viewer the dream and wish for wealth and material beauty. She thus becomes the symbol of material success and frivolous high bourgeoisie in Nick's and Gatsby's views which may well imply their mutual inability to understand reality. Nick eminently lacks heterosexual romantic desire as evidenced by his passivity and indecisiveness, which in turn motivates in him an admiration and sympathy for Gatsby as a vicarious embodiment of what Nick lacks in himself.

J154. Matsumura, Nobuaki. "Transitional Stories of F. Scott Fitzgerald—Three Stories in Bits of Paradise." *Annual Report of Doshisha Women's College of Liberal Arts* 42.1 (Dec. 1991): 199-219.

Three short stories from the late Twenties and early Thirties were collected for the first time in 1973 in *Bits of Paradise*. Even though Fitzgerald didn't include them in any collection during his lifetime, a lot of their themes, situations, and characters are similar to those in *Tender Is the Night* and therefore give an interesting insight into the transition between the Jazz Age and the more mature later production of the writer. In "Jacob's Ladder" the protagonist is not one of the young romantics of Fitzgerald's early fiction, but a bachelor in decline, who becomes infatuated with a much younger woman, thus anticipating Dick Diver's fate. "The Swimmers" deals with serious issues like the relationship between money and power, and the nature of America and its opposition to Europe. Finally, in "A New Leaf" Fitzgerald gives a pessimistic account of the decline of an alcoholic, whose addiction will prevent his marriage to the woman he loves, and will eventually destroy him.

J155. Minaguchi, Kiseko. "Bobbi Ann Mason's Intertexts." *Bulletin of Teikyo U Junior College* 13 (Jan. 1993): 29-50.

In the context of contemporary worldwide upheavals, Bobbie Ann Mason's issues of disruption and unification confront us as more than mere rhetoric. In her earlier work, she tried capturing the ephemeral ambience of a split between the individual and the family arena before she demonstrates a noteworthy breakthrough in a post-Vietnam novel "In Country." Mason's thematic and technical preoccupation with the sense of alienation establishes a transtextual identity with the concerns embraced by other writers, especially F. Scot Fitzgerald. Mason is aligned with Porter and Welty who depict the universal issue of dis-unification of the basic paradigm of personal relationships. A transition is epitomized in "A New Wave Format," reminiscent of the concept of balancing that Fitzgerald addressed in "The Crack-up." With "In Country" Mason allows a young girl to challenge Fitzgerald's apathetic elegy with rock-n-roll empathy toward her uncle's post-war Veteran distress. Mason's phonetic strategy of working with dialectic apprehension resonates with Colwin, but her perception of a break in sexuality and sanity echoes Fitzgerald and Plath.

J156. Miyashita, Masatoshi. "An Introduction to the American Penchant for Changing One's Name (Re)Naming." *Language and Culture* 17 (1989): 177-194.

The act of self-naming is popular in American culture and represents a "secularized version" of the Puritan idea of conversion: by renaming oneself the individual tries to create a new and more authentic identity. This can be observed in Emerson, as well as in characters like Gatsby and Clyde Griffiths from *An American Tragedy*; with Malcolm X and Ralph Ellison, the act of self-naming becomes problematic and exposes the "inherent violence of naming."

J157. Miyauchi, Kayoko. "The 'New Woman' in F. Scott Fitzgerald's 'Winter Dreams.'" *Aoyama Gakuin Joshitankidaigaku Kiyo* [*Bulletin of Aoyama Gakuin Women's Junior College*] 44 (Nov. 1990): 1-18.

Dexter Green, despite his wholehearted love of Judy Jones, is played with, treated coolly, rejected in his wooing, and finally deserted by his love. Their relationship does not develop as equal loving partners. While Dexter admires and adores the extremely beautiful rich girl, who is the symbol of plutocracy and hedonism, they symbolize contrasting approaches to life such as romanticism vs. materialism, idealism vs. reality, poverty vs. wealth, work ethic vs. hedonism, and faithfulness vs. slovenliness. By depicting Judy as a typical flapper of high society who resists the traditional social order and moral restrictions, Fitzgerald creates a new image of the heroine, an image that captures the mentality of the youth of the Jazz Age accurately

J158. Miyauchi, Kayoko. "A Study of Fitzgerald's 'Babylon Revisited.'" *Aoyama Gakuin Joshitankidaigaku Kiyo* [*Bulletin of Aoyama Gakuin Women's Junior College*] 41 (Nov. 1987): 17-33.

Why is this work evaluated most highly of some 70 short stories written by Fitzgerald? The specific background, the technique, the structure, the style and the personalities of the characters offer a clue. He uses the method of condensing a long past within a short period of the present, of structuring a plot that holds off solutions to many riddles, and of constructing a surprising ending, the same techniques used for *The Great Gatsby*. Fitzgerald successfully depicts a completely new type of hero, one who has found the essence of life, for Charlie Wales is utterly different from Fitzgerald's other protagonists who yearn for wealth, fame and a beautiful rich girl. He has a maturity that is apparent in the memory that he cherishes for his dead wife and in his love for his daughter. In the 1920s, America was befuddled with an unprecedented economic boom which engulfed Charlie Wales, who is affected by deep regrets and self-accusation.

J159. Miyawaki, Toshifumi. "Musume kara mita Scott to Zelda [Scott and Zelda in the Daughter's Eyes]." *Eureka* 20.14 (Dec. 1988): 114-18.

Scottie's lecture on her father shows Scott's and Zelda's parental affection for their daughter. In Scottie's teens, however, the family begins to suffer crises, such as Zelda's hospitalization for mental disturbances and Scott's alcoholic addiction and the decline of his literary career. The letters frequently exchanged between Scott and Scottie during the daughter's attendance at school indicate his fatherly concern: he gave her detailed advice and recommendations concerning what books to read or what classes to take. But sometimes his concern for his daughter went too far, became almost obsessive. This was because Scott, in his literary decline and Zelda's mental breakdown, wanted his daughter to avoid repeating such a catastrophic way of life.

J160. Miyawaki, Toshifumi. "Fitzgerald no gendai-sei: Murakami Haruki, Jay McInerny, Ann Beattie [Contemporaries of Fitzgerald: Haruki Murakami, Jay McInerny, and Ann Beattie]." *Eureka* 20.14 (Dec. 1988): 70-75.

Fitzgerald's works demonstrate a rare capacity for viewing the world objectively while keeping a keen sensibility toward it. His writings, *Gatsby* in particular, offer the ways to lead life in a big city. Although some of his works have the consistent theme of the American Dream, their plots and focuses are mostly within the domain of secular and everyday life in the city. Another appealing aspect to the contemporary reader is that Fitzgerald anticipates the coming of age of visual culture, especially of cinema. His writings foresee the cultural shift from letters to visual images projected on screen, which may dilute the viewer's sense of reality and identity. Writing amid the rapid cultural shift of the 1920s, Fitzgerald detects the difficult relationship that exists between culture and identity. In this sense, Fitzgerald is indeed a precursor of minimalist novelists of the new lost generation such as Murakami, McInerney, and Beattie.

J161. Miyazawa, Tadashi. "'The Offshore Pirate': the Realities in 'This Unlikely Story.'" *The Bulletin of Kobe Women's Junior College* 25 (Mar. 1992): 83-96.

"The Offshore Pirate" in *Flappers and Philosophers* is a fanciful romance of a young man and woman. While Fitzgerald is very good at showing us a witty and dream-like love romance, he soberly perceives the future of flappers represented by Ardita Farnam. She is rebellious and likes a man with "an imagination and the courage of his conviction," but she is rather realistic when it comes to her own marriage and the author hints that the courage "will tarnish her beauty and youth." Fitzgerald also sees through the characteristic mentality of the very rich, something outsiders cannot share. These are the themes Fitzgerald repeatedly dealt with in his literary career, and though this story is considered trivial, it is possible to find indications of his themes.

J162. Miyazawa, Tadashi. "*Tales of the Jazz Age* as the Jazz Age Fables: Time and Change." *Mukogawa Literary Review* 32, (Mar. 1996). n. pag.

Fitzgerald had to pad his second collection of short stories with earlier works including those written in his college days because of the delay of his second novel and the production of his play, *The Vegetable: or from President to Postman*. Indeed some of these works are trivial, but Fitzgerald offers them "into the hands of those who read as they run and run as they read," and shows the rapid change of time in which nothing can remain the same. "May Day" deals with a chaotic 24 hours after World War I, and "The Jelly-Bean," "O Russet Witch!" and "The Lees of Happiness" describe abortive romantic feelings as time goes by. "The Curious Case of Benjamin Button" makes the reader aware of time because the protagonist grows younger toward the end of his life. "The Diamond as Big as the Ritz" not only criticizes the materialistic American dream but also the American myth in which America is an exceptional paradise uninfluenced by time and change.

J163. Morimoto, Shin-ichi. "F. Scott Fitzgerald: Roaring and Restlessness without God." *The Review of Studies in Christianity and Literature* 12 (May 1995): 81-89.

While America was in a boom caused by World War I, Fitzgerald suddenly became popular for *This Side of Paradise*. Many young people were attracted by the licentiousness of the protagonist, Amory Blaine. Fitzgerald was obliged to write a large number of short stories too rapidly. In one essay he compared himself to a cracked plate and closed with a passage from *St. Matthew*: "But if the salt hath lost its savour, wherewith shall it be salted?" He died at the age of forty-four. A female painter in *Tender Is the Night* has nervous eczema and lies in bed just in order to suffer. This character seems to stand for the distressed author. "Something must come of it" is her appeal, though her voice can find "only remote abstractions." Fitzgerald wrote in *This Side of Paradise* that there was no God in Amory's heart. Both through his works and life itself, Fitzgerald dramatically shows us the destiny of a bustling society where the values are confused and God has been lost.

J164. Morioka, Yuichi. "Enchantment and Disillusion—*The Great Gatsby* as a City Novel." *Studies of Language and Culture*, 1982. n pag.

To Nick, New York is the core of the sophisticated East endowing him with a blissful feeling of being in the center of the world. The idealized image of the metropolis is shattered when he meets Gatsby, experiences his world, and sees it die out. Gatsby is to him the embodiment of the great city as he sees it with all its charms and mysteries and confusion. After Gatsby's death, Nick returns to his Middle West, with the newly-found ability to see the East and the West in their true perspective.

J165. Murakami, Yosuke. "*The Great Gatsby* as a Critique of the Self-Made Man." *The Scientific Reports of The Kyoto Prefectural U.—Humanities* 34 (Nov. 1982): 29-39.

The Great Gatsby should be read as an indictment of the myth of the self-made man. The reader becomes progressively aware of this through Nick, who first admires Gatsby, and later sees his tragic flaws. Gatsby is the prototype of the self-made man: in recreating himself, he erases his inconvenient past and changes his heritage. In his dream of self-accomplishment, Gatsby refuses any limits of time and space and tries to shape reality according to his own conception; yet this results in his being totally uprooted from society. He is incapable of any real human connection and ultimately of love, as even his desire for Daisy is actually a form of self-love. He becomes a prisoner of the artificial image of himself that he created, and all his parties and sociability are only a mask for his illegal activities, which sustain him financially but ironically prevent him from really entering the social class he aspires to belong to. Thus the famous final pages, with the evocation of the American Dream, cannot be read without an ironic overtone, which points to the tragic failure of man's attempt to exist in a social vacuum and without limits.

J166. Muto, Shuji. "Drift and Motion—Fitzgerald's *The Great Gatsby*." *Journal of Literature of Chuo U* 52 (Mar. 1983): 23-43. (Rpt. in *American Literature in the 1920s—Tracing the Drifters*. Tokyo: Kenkyusha Publishing Co: 1-34.)

D.H. Lawrence referred to emigrants to the New World as people who made "a great drift" from the old European authority. The theme of drift, therefore, is one of the persistent themes in American literature, and especially eminent in the 1920s—in Dos Passos, Cather, O'Neill, Hemingway, and Fitzgerald. In *The Great Gatsby*, the "valley of ashes," "the grey land" over which the spasms of bleak dust "drift endlessly," is a symbolic scene of the American Waste Land, where energy turns to dust and waste drifts aimlessly. Daisy was, before marriage, one of the fresh faces who "drifted here and there like rose petals blown by the sad horns around the floor." Her husband, Tom, would, Nick felt, "drift forever seeking . . . for the dramatic turbulence of some irrecoverable football game." Gatsby, who would seem to have no elements in common with these characters, eventually turns out to be one of the drifters. His body drifting in the pool is at the mercy of "a small gust of wind." He is incredibly but inseparably connected with the ashen figure of Wilson as members of the same drifting family. Except for the narrator, Nick, the characters are all drifters who "beat on, boats against current, borne back ceaselessly into the past."

J167. Nagaoka, Sadao. "Fitzgerald and Japan." Paper delivered at First

International F. Scott Fitzgerald Conference. Hofstra University, 24 Sep. 1992.

See Chapter Introduction.

J168. Nagaoka, Sadao. "How Fitzgerald's Works Were Introduced to Japan— Post and Pre-World War II." *Eureka: Poetry and Criticism* XX.14 (Dec. 1988): 51-245.

The Japanese publication of "The Bridal Party" in 1930 appears with an introduction that merely emphasizes a frivolous image of the Jazz Age and of the author himself. The editor of the second short story to be published in Japan, "At Your Age" (1933), offers a more favorable view of Fitzgerald, praising the author's insightful description that gives an accurate account of the Jazz Age. In 1940, *This Side of Paradise* is referred to in the Japanese translation of F. L. Allen's *Only Yesterday* (1930). Another reference to Fitzgerald is seen in *America Bungaku-fukkou no Danmen* [*A View of American Literary Renaissance*] (ed. Matsuo Takagaki, 1939), which again associates the author with the frivolity of the Jazz Age. Published in 1946, Takashi Sugiki's *America Bungaku Shiron* [*Essays on American Literature*] includes an essay titled "'Mayoeru Jidai' no Ko Fitzgerald ni tsuite [Fitzgerald, A Child of 'the Lost Generation']," which gives a deeper understanding of Fitzgerald. Jinichi Uekusa published a brief essay on the author in *Eiga no Tomo* [*Friends of Films*] in May 1950. Binichi Ueki's "America Realism no Ichi-danmen [A View of the American Realism]" (in *Takigawa* 3 (May 1950) introduces *The Great Gatsby* in detail.

J169. Nagaoka, Sadao and Kiyohiko Tsuboi. "Scott Fitzgerald's Tormented Paradise." *The Discovery of Genius—Maxwell Perkins and His Writers.* Arechi Publishing Co., Nov. 1983. 21-51.

The authors discuss the modern American publishing system: publishing houses, editors and agents. They also discuss the relation between Perkins and his writers: Fitzgerald, Lardner, Hemingway, Morley Callaghan, Thomas Wolfe, Rawlings, Davenport, Sherwood Anderson, and James Jones, with a short biography of Perkins.

J170. Nagaoka (Kawahata), Yumi. "A Note on *Tender Is the Night* (1): The First and Final Edition." *Gakuen* [The Institution of Modern (Japanese) Culture, Showa Women's U] 604 (Mar. 1990): 83-93.

The final edition of the novel is the one that best reflects the author's original intention. Although the use of flashback in Book Two of the first edition enhances the sense of suspense and mystery for the reader's reading of the revelation of Dick's past and reality, the chronological structure of the final edition accentuates Dick's story as the history of his rise and fall. Considering the fact that the subject of the novel is the disruption and disintegration of American society itself as symbolized in Dick, and hence Western culture as a whole, the structure of the final edition emphasizes the subject better. The use of Rosemary's innocent point of view to observe Dick from outside in the middle of the final edition also has an effect to foreshadow his decline.

J171. Nagase, Emi. "Daisy's 'Voice' in *The Great Gatsby.*" *Shujitsu Eigaku Ronso* [*Shujitsu English Studies,* Shujitsu Women's U] 10 (Mar. 1992): 71-114.

The Great Gatsby is 'a story of Daisy and Jordan', although most of the studies on *The Great Gatsby* have been centered on the male characters and have regarded its heroine as an evil woman. Jordan is characterized as a new woman for the age who lives her life according to her own standards. Daisy is a somewhat conventional woman as her life is based on her home and her radius of action is limited. Daisy's "voice" represents her radical sentiments against her traditional surroundings, and is strong enough to convey both her romantic feelings and her inner fragility.

J172. Nagase, Emi. "A Study of Fitzgerald's Tarleton Trilogy." *Shujitsu Eigaku Ronso* [*Shujitsu English Studies,* Shujitsu Women's U] 15 (Mar. 1996): 41-60.

Fitzgerald's works often comprise contradictory and contrasting themes at the same time—for example, the themes of money and love, of success and failure, of a dream and its loss, of the north and the south, of the east and the west, and so on. Fitzgerald's uses of symbols in the "Tarleton Trilogy" are as follows. First, Fitzgerald's contrasting motif is seen in the descriptions of "cold snow and the artificial light" and "the natural light of the warm sun" which symbolized the North and the South in "The Ice Palace." Second, the contrasting colors of white and gray equate the old South and the new South in "The Jelly-Bean." Third, the descriptions of various sounds including human voices exemplify the charmed old South in "The Last of the Belles." What is common to the three stories is that Fitzgerald's sentiments toward the South are the same as his sentiments toward women. The author himself once had a romantic attachment to the South (the women), but during the nine blank years between the second story and the third, Fitzgerald lost his yearning for the South as he also lost his yearning for women.

J173. Nagase, Emi. "The Fifth Guest—Fitzgerald's Use of 'Telephone Call' in
The Great Gatsby." *Shujitsu Eigaku Ronso* [*Shujitsu English Studies,*
Shujitsu Women's U] 16 (Mar. 1997): 99-130.

The Great Gatsby describes the early 20th century American culture satirically
by means of various modern devices; for example, cars, trains, a hydroplane,
telephones, a juicer, an electric oven, and so on. In *The Great Gatsby,* the
telephone, which was one of the representative products of the modern age,
plays an important role in representing Fitzgerald's criticism of civilization. The
telephone was popular among American people as one of the communication
media of the period; Fitzgerald's descriptions of the telephone were elaborated,
and the frequency of its use was increased when Fitzgerald's corrected the
galleys. The telephone in *The Great Gatsby* plays a contradictory role as a
communication medium as it obstructs communication among the characters.

J174. Nagase, Hiroshi. "*Tender Is the Night, The Crack-Up.*" *The Literature of
F. Scott Fitzgerald and the Death of the American Dream.* Ed. Motoji
Karita. Arechi Pub. Co., 1982: n. pag.

Tender Is the Night takes its title from a Keats poem. Set amidst the romantic
social world of the French Riviera which evokes the world of beauty and
sensuality which Keats so loved, the protagonist, Dick, exhausts and ruins
himself in both mind and body while trying to save the various tormented and
suffering characters in the novel. It is the novel in which Fitzgerald's two facets
as an Irish romanticist and a Catholic moralist are most clearly expressed. The
poor reception of *Tender Is the Night* led to Fitzgerald's own mental, physical,
and economic breakdown. His state of mind at the time is candidly recorded in
three articles represented by "The Crack-up." These three articles have been
criticized as nothing more than effeminate grumblings but taken from the
perspective of his Catholic elements, these essays serve as a sort of Catholic
confession and can be said to have opened the path for his rebirth in the writing
of *The Last Tycoon.*

J175. Nakamura, Yoshio. "Intellectual Unity in *This Side of Paradise.*"
Bulletin of the Faculty of Liberal Arts, Humanities (Nagasaki U) 33.2
(Jan. 1993): 35-48.

This Side of Paradise has been criticized by many critics as immature, as having
no intellectual unity. But John B. Chambers evaluates the novel highly because
he thinks it has "a coherent intellectual foundation," and Thomas J. Stavola
thinks it has the central theme of self-fulfillment. Although these critics try to
value it highly, their ways of evaluation mask a constraint as if they were

shutting us in a small closed space, for they are not flexible in their way of thinking about the hero Amory's puritanical nature. True, Amory is somewhat puritanical, but such a disposition does not necessarily determine a puritanical way of living. On the contrary, it enables him to live flexibly and correspond freely to changing situations, the consistency of which I think is what forms the identity of Amory. In this respect, the novel is coherent from beginning to end and has its own merit.

J176. Nakamura, Yoshio. "Sentimental Gatsby and Romantic Gatsby."
    Bulletin of the Faculty of Liberal Arts (Humanities) [Nagasaki U] 35. 1
    (July 1994): 79-90.

Is Gatsby a sentimental person or a romantic? According to Amory, hero of *This Side of Paradise*, a sentimentalist "thinks things will last," while "a romantic person hopes against hope that they won't." Many critics seem to think that Gatsby is a sentimentalist. For example, Robert Emmet Long said that Gatsby and Lord Jim resemble each other in their propensity for cherishing grand dreams about their future. But it seems to me that they are very different even in their ways of dreaming, because Jim seeks self-glorification and loses sight of himself in the process, while Gatsby's dream is not so self-centered and he knows thoroughly what he is doing. In other words, Jim becomes a victim of traditional heroic dreams, while Gatsby is a conscious constructor of his own dream, who "hopes against hope" he can destroy the actual situation of Daisy's marriage to Tom. Of course, it cannot be denied that he is a sentimentalist but it is certain that he is also a romantic person.

J177. Nakano, Yukinari. "On *The Great Gatsby*—a False Civilization and
    Gatsby's Death." *Bulletin of Osaka College of Music* 32 (Dec. 1993):
    175-194.

By describing all characters as feeling lonely, nihilistic and uneasy, Fitzgerald produces the decadent atmosphere of the twenties. But Gatsby's presence and conduct, as against that of Tom and Daisy, make him the symbol of romanticism and heroism personified. In addition, as romanticism, including heroism, is the idealistic basis of belief in the American Republic, Gatsby can be interpreted as the ultimate symbol of the American Republic. That is, he has the same rich imagination as Dutch sailors who fixed their eyes on "a fresh, green breast of the new world." He was born and raised under the influence of Benjamin Franklin's guiding principle in life. In brief, he belongs to that exceptional nation, "the Republic" which has vanished from the new world. As his primitive traits, definitely traceable to romanticism, made her uneasy, they set him apart from her at the end. This width and depth of the split between Gatsby and Daisy clearly shows that the circumstances of idealistic Americanism (moral virtue) have changed substantially by the influence of realistic ideology (material values) of the materialistic American Dream. Consequently, his heroism for redeeming her from her own despair ironically drove him to death.

J178. Nakao, Hidehiro. "Jazz and *The Great Gatsby*—F. Scott Fitzgerald as a Scribe of the Jazz Age." *The Bulletin of Arts and Science* [Meiji U] 234 (Mar. 1991): 33-60.

F. Scott Fitzgerald, who named the 1920s the Jazz Age, defined the word "jazz" as follows: "The word jazz in its progress towards respectability has meant first sex, then dancing, then music" ("Echoes of the Jazz Age"). As his definition suggests, Jazz meant much more than it does now. Out of nine chapters of *The Great Gatsby*, seven songs are mentioned in six chapters. The first song, "Jazz History of the World," which might vaguely predict Gershwin's "Rhapsody in Blue," is a fictitious "yellow cocktail music" played by the full orchestra. The second is "The Sheik of Araby" (1921). "The Love Nest" (1920) and "Ain't We Got Fun?" (1921) are quoted together in Chapter 5, contradicting the situation where Gatsby confuses the end with the means. The fifth is "Three O'Clock in the Morning" (1922) whose sentimental waltz tune vexes Gatsby. "Beale Street Blues" (1917) played by the wailing saxophones brilliantly represents Daisy's "artificial world" when she meets Gatsby for the first time. The last song is "The Rosary" (1898). Wolfsheim, the man behind the scene, whistles this religious and popular piece "tunelessly." His performance symbolizes the grotesque noise beneath the cultural sentimentality. F. Scott Fitzgerald as a Jazz Age scribe records the "Jazz" sounds so exquisitely that each song depicts a different aspect of the spirit of the age.

J179. Namiki, Nobuaki. "Thomas Sutpen to Jay Gatsby: Yume ni tsukareta otoko tachi [Thomas Sutpen and Jay Gatsby: The Men Obsessed with Dreams]." *Eigo Seinen [The Rising Generation]* 134 (June 1988): 128-132.

What Thomas Sutpen and Gatsby have in common are elements of "American innocence" and the self-made man. In both cases, a dream—particularly, the ambition for wealth—overwhelms and controls the two characters. They are both so-called "flat characters," who do not change in the course of novel and keep setting themselves aloof from their past, society, and the outside world, which eventually causes their tragedies. *Gatsby* and Sutpen have common, complex structures that connect experience and narration, dream and reality.

J180. Narasaki, Hiroshi. "Letters to the Daughter." *Eureka* 20.14 (Dec. 1988): 197-201.

Introduction of Fitzgerald's letters addressed to his daughter, Frances Scott Fitzgerald (Scottie), with excerpts. The article cites several letters that were sent from Scott to his daughter, who lived apart from her parents. They show Fitzgerald's almost maternal concern for his daughter, with affection which Zelda, because of her mental disturbances, could indicate to her daughter fully. In these letters, Fitzgerald gives Scottie detailed advice and suggestions for school, classes to take, books to read, and life in general.

J181. Naruse, Yoshitaka. "American Dreams—Their Formation and Changes." *The Hiyoshi Review of the Faculty of Business and Commerce* [Keio U, Yokohama, Japan] 27.XVII-1 (Jan. 1981): 1-29.

In *Letters from an American Farmer,* written in the latter half of the 18th century, the first realization of a dream by ordinary people in America is shown as a form of "the most complete society". Success in that society does not mean acquisition of wealth by a few people but rather, the egalitarian position of small independent farmers. This is the prototype of the American dream in a sense that the dream is one of earthly success. Showing people these concrete examples of success, many early advocates of success told them that they could achieve respectability by observance of puritan ethics. So long as wilderness existed, the concept held true, but once the frontier disappeared, this model was no longer a valid ideal. The dream came to be sought after in the world of business for the most part. However, the number of people who were fortunate enough to succeed by themselves was very small, and therefore, writers began to indicate that the American dream is merely a myth by describing the failure of heroes in their works.

J182. Naruse, Yoshitaka. *"Tender Is the Night*: A Carnival in a Boom Society." *The Hiyoshi Review of English Studies* [Keio U, Yokohama, Japan] 1 (June 1985): 66-88.

Dick Diver's marriage appears to be based on his love for Nicole and also his wish for her recovery through his own affectionate psychiatric treatment. But there is a more important reason than his love and desire to cure her. He has his subconscious desire for property in order to realize his ideal: to carry out psychiatric research without worrying about money and to achieve scholarly breakthroughs. Certainly at first he resists Nicole's use of her money for their life, but he is soon seduced by the rich life which his wife supports. Dick's surrender to the high life shows his mental deterioration because a person like him with stoicism and integrity should overcome any kind of temptation as long as his mind functions normally. Dick's crack-up comes out of his association with the rich, especially with his wife Nicole. More specifically, his crack-up is closely connected with the particular circumstances of American society during the boom of the twenties. In a society without faith and value an innocent person like Dick cannot retain his sanity.

J183. Naruse, Yoshitaka. *"This Side of Paradise*: Amory Blaine's Search for
Self and His Attitude of Resistance to Society." *The Hiyoshi Review of
English Studies* [Keio U, Yokohama] 4 (Oct. 1986): 49-69.

Amory Blaine searches for the meaning of life in his youth. The main object of
his quest is to discover himself. In the process he loses love for Rosalind
Connage, which makes him both aware of and critical of the social system. In
this sense his attitude of resistance to society is suggested though the description
of his love. The course of the protagonist's self-discovery is discussed both as an
effort to retrieve his real self and as a struggle to abandon his selfishness. This
egotism is not merely a part of him but also the most vital ingredient, and
therefore he can hardly relinquish it. Through the relationship with Monsignor
Darcy whom he respects, however, he decides to become a person who
incessantly attempts to improve and develop himself by undergoing experiences.
This resolution later leads him to the realization that he has to become a man
indispensable for others, not by denying his selfishness but by transcending it.
This is the answer to his search for self-discovery.

J184. Naruse, Yoshitaka. "Scott Fitzgerald: Why Fitzgerald Depicts His
Frustration." *The Hiyoshi Review of the Faculty of Business and
Commerce* [Keio U, Yokohama, Japan] 33 (Feb. 1984): 58-76.

Even after the great success of his first novel, Fitzgerald continues to have
interest in writing about the frustration of his protagonists; he not only depicts
Anthony's alcoholism and Gatsby's death but he plans to depict the ruin of a
main character through murdering his mother in a subsequent novel "Our Type."
One of the reasons for such a literary tendency is because he has experienced
frustration since his childhood; the failure of his father in business, his lost love
for Ginevra King, his love for Zelda Sayre which he nearly loses, and his loss of
the presidency of the Triangle Club. These experiences make him sympathetic
with failures, but such a quality is seen in him even in his childhood; his early
rejection of his father changes into his reconciliation with him. His support for
weak animals in the battle between strong animals and weak ones in a story for
children shows evidence that he has naturally the quality which makes him write
about failures.

J185. Nishio, Iwao. "Fitzgerald and Hemingway—Chiefly on the Technique of
'Babylon Revisited.'" *Studies in Liberal Arts* [The Faculty of Political
Science and Economics, Waseda U] 97/98 (Mar, 1995): 181-200.

Fitzgerald and Hemingway had developed their styles before they first met in
Paris in 1925; they were beyond imitation. Nevertheless, other forms of
influence were possible, both personal and aesthetic. Both *A Farewell to Arms*
and "Babylon Revisited" resemble each other in many points of composition,

images and symbols. Both are divided into five parts respectively, and the five-part structure could be compared to the five acts of a dramatic tragedy. Each part contains a number of incidental scenes that do little to advance the plot, but rather provide a realistic lower-keyed contrast to the intensity of the tragic action. It would be worth notice that Fitzgerald acknowledged the specific aesthetic influence of Hemingway on *Tender Is the Night* (1934) in his letter to Hemingway, June 1, 1934.

J186. Niwa, Takaaki. *"The Great Gatsby* and the Motorcar." *The Review of English Literature* [Division of English, Faculty of Integrated Human Studies, Kyoto U] LXV (Mar. 1993): 81-101.

Nick's story mentions lots of cars, from Gatsby's custom-built Rolls-Royce of "rich cream color" to George Wilson's "dust-covered wreck of a Ford." Significantly, the cars serve as the indices of the *dramatis personae*'s status and personalities. Gatsby's Rolls-Royce, for instance, speaks all about its owner's taste. In addition, his restless and romantic nature is tactfully shown when he balances himself on the "dashboard" of his gorgeous machine. Tom's "blue coupe" tells of his snobbish taste for aristocratic British culture, while his driving manners testify to his true colors. Nick's "old Dodge" goes well with his conservative mentality, together with his preference for safe trains over unsafe automobiles. Moreover, the age's own traits—blind, careless, and irresponsible—are represented by a series of car accidents, where, first, one of Gatsby's guests drops his car in the gutter too drunk to back it out; then, Jordan drives so badly as to flip a passerby's coat button, appalling Nick with her bold justification; and finally, Daisy kills Myrtle when driving Gatsby's car only to fly away selfishly with Tom, putting everything on her innocent admirer. Indeed, *The Great Gatsby* is the first major American novel to give a very important role to the motorcar.

J187. Ohashi, Chiaki. "Fitzgerald and His Paternal Values." *Baika Literary Bulletin, English and American Literature and Language* 25 (Dec. 1990): 123-137.

In the absence of the father figure in *This Side of Paradise,* we see Fitzgerald's criticism of urban/modern situations. The hero, Amory Blaine, keeps searching for the paternal figure, the God, or the hierarchy of values that can guide him through the modern world where the arbitrariness or the relativity of values dominate. His mother, Beatrice, symbolizes the maternal values that subsume one by forgiveness and permissiveness, not by forbidding or ordering. The narrator Nick Carraway makes it explicit at the beginning of *The Great Gatsby* that the basis for his moral judgments is in the paternal Mid West. And at the end, having learned in New York just how much absurdity the arbitrariness of values brings about, he goes back home for his private salvation. In this novel the paternal values are presented outside the urban/modern society. In *The Last Tycoon* there is presented no spatial paternal periphery. The hero, Monroe Stahr, an embodiment of the paternal values, is conquered and degraded by urban/modern values of the capitalist society.

J188. Ohashi, Chiaki. "'Girl Stories' by Zelda Fitzgerald." *Baika Literary Bulletin* 32 (1998): n. pag.

From 1928 through 1930 Zelda Fitzgerald wrote six short stories, which give us a glimpse into the predicaments that Zelda was in at the time. In "The Girl the Prince Liked," no matter how much influence the heroine has on her society, she remains just a wealthy housewife. She is left with nothing to be proud of except for a brief affair with the Prince, just like Zelda had nothing to be proud of except being the wife of "Prince Scott." In "The Girl with Talent" the heroine wavers between career and domesticity, and finally gives up her brilliant success as a dancer. She has means of self-expression, but lacks the energy and strategy to achieve self-actualization. "Poor Working Girl" deals with a girl who fails to go to Broadway and learn acting. Her goals are not hindered by some inescapable situations but blurred by her own inability to cope with reality. Zelda Fitzgerald and her heroines all break away from the social codes and try to substitute them with their own codes, which are far from being valid.

J189. Ohashi, Chiaki. "Zelda Fitzgerald's 'Girls.'" Ed. Masahiro Minai. *Aspects of Fiction*. Tokyo: Eihosha, 1999.

From 1928 through 1930 Zelda Fitzgerald wrote six short stories, which give us a glimpse into the predicaments that Zelda was in at the time. In "The Original Follies Girls," Zelda depicts a flapper dancer who dies in the end after giving birth to a child. The heroine represents romanticism, which comes to an end the moment it materializes. The "originality" of her way of life is imitated and meaninglessly repeated everywhere, which reflects Zelda's own status as the queen of the flappers. "Southern Girl" is similar to Scott's "The Ice Palace," but the denouement is quite opposite. The heroine, once rejected by the rigid family of the North, goes through the process of assimilation, and finally finds happiness in a married life there. From a feminist point of view the situation is a step backwards. In "A Millionaire's Girl," the actress heroine is married to a millionaire by "tactics" that she didn't really intend, and the prospect of their married life is rather bleak. This ironic twist of fate is meant to be an innuendo to Scott's relationship with a Hollywood movie actress.

J190. Ohashi, Chiaki. "Paternal Values in *The Vegetable*," *Baika Literary Bulletin*. 33 (1999): n. pag.

The Vegetable is Fitzgerald's only published full-length play. The book has received a few mixed reviews since its publication, but further study is needed, especially of its thematic continuity to the author's other works. On its most superficial level, *The Vegetable* is a political satire of Harding and his administration, but it is, as Perkins wrote Fitzgerald, "double edged satire" wielded on those who share the idea of democracy that everybody ought to want to rise in the world. On a deeper level it questions paternal values, like in the previous novels, where the author makes most of women's symbolic potential as the destroyer of patriarchal/paternal systems, and, accordingly, as supporter of the economic systems of the new era. A president is a symbol of the ultimate patriarch. The story does not, in the end, elevate or put down patriarchal/paternal systems. Jerry's ultimate vocation, delivering letters, signifies literature as a third alternative. The play gave Fitzgerald a new perspective, a precarious balance between the validity and the invalidity of patriarchal/paternal values, which is conspicuous in his later works.

J191. Ohashi, Chiaki. "Two Worlds in Fitzgerald's *Tender Is the Night*."
       Baika Review (Department of English, Baika Womens' College) 26
       (1993): n. pag.

Tender Is the Night shows Fitzgerald's major concern over the validity of paternal values, by which term I mean ones with an idea of absoluteness and hierarchy. In his novels Fitzgerald describes such values either through such paternal figures as a priest (Monseignor Darcy) or a self-made man (Monroe Stahr), or through a patriarchal community outside the boundary of the city (the Midwest in *The Great Gatsby*). Paternal values are a countermeasure for Fitzgerald against the arbitrary/relative values promoted by the industrialization and urbanization of America. There are also two worlds of paternal values in *Tender Is the Night*. Dick Diver first embodies such values but gradually gives in to the values of the *haute bourgeoisie*, which tries to subsume and annul him. And in more than any other of his novels, Fitzgerald is aware here of the gender metaphor. In the first part of the first edition of the novel, Dick is depicted like a king presiding over his own realm in Riviera. The father role he plays for his wife and Rosemary presently gives way, however, to his self-indulgence, while women in this novel serve as "seducers;" ones with economical independence who degrade a man out of his moral, aesthetic hierarchy.

J192. Ohashi, Chiaki. "The Figurative Language of Zelda Fitzgerald." *Baika
       Literary Bulletin* 34 (2000): n. pag.

Zelda Fitzgerald's style is noted for its loose structure and immature technique, which nevertheless has much allure and effect. Reflecting these two sides, her use of figurative language is the most conspicuous feature of her writing. Figurative language in her stories, which Zelda wrote to become independent from Scott, includes truly modernistic expressions, which are ironically connected with the plight of the heroines, where they try in vain to break away from the paternal values. Zelda's autobiographical *Save Me the Waltz* abounds in modernistic and surrealistic language. With her marriage, Alabama breaks away from her stern father, in search of self-actualization. But at his death, finding herself afield and lost, she tries to recover herself in the lost relationship with her father. Zelda's unrestrained use of figurative language is effective in describing the heroine's unsuccessful flight from paternal logos. Zelda lacked the insights needed to turn her dissatisfaction into social indictment. This in turn gave her freedom from rigid ideology. Not objecting to the paternal/patriarchal values frontally, she transgresses the enclosure of the system, often invading the realm of insanity, the pleasure of which can be observed in her use of figurative language that eludes our attempts at its classification.

J193. Ohata, Kazuyoshi. "An Elegy to a Passing Youth . . . On *The Great Gatsby.*" *Essays on American Literature* 7 (Sep. 1985): 12-19.

Almost everything about the hero of this story is told to readers through Nick's view tinged with a strong sense of Midwestern moral values. Therefore, the extent of what readers find out about Gatsby is confined within Nick's moral values and his changing consciousness toward Gatsby. What matters most here is what Nick comes to find out about a young man newly rich and how he evaluates the young man's extraordinarily romantic vision of the future. Taking a close look at Nick's consciousness, however, readers are sure to find there is something pathetic drifting through Nick's entire narration, for his final evaluation of Gatsby's life in the last chapter is painted with a strong feeling of loss. It is because the author's sense of values is reflected respectively in Gatsby and Nick; in a sense they are the other selves of Fitzgerald himself. It could be said that Fitzgerald deplored the loss of the romantic dream, which once existed in himself, through Nick's narration tinged with a traditional moral sense. *The Great Gatsby* is an elegy to the passing youth of the author himself.

J194. Okamoto, Kigen. "F. Scott Fitzgerald's Short Stories and Hemingway." *Keonan Joshi Daigaku Kenkyu Kiyou* [*Konan Women's U Research*] 26 (Mar. 1990): 1-18.

Although some critics have tended to discuss only Fitzgerald's influence on Hemingway, Hemingway influenced Fitzgerald's short stories in the 1930s. Although the styles of these two authors are very different—one is decorative and the other is concise—both have a common artistic concern with 'the fact as it is'—or how to recapture objects and experiences in novelistic representation. Thus in the relationship that developed between them, each author defined himself alongside and against the other in terms of artistic creation. Also, each author inscribes each other's figure in his fiction, such as the image of Fitzgerald in Hemingway's "The Snows of Kilimanjaro,"' and the other way around in Fitzgerald's "Finnegan." These mutual inscriptions are at once sarcastic and self-reflexive, in that they are representations of artist-figures in the struggle of artistic creation.

J195.   Saito, Eiji. "Fitzgerald no kodomo tachi [Fitzgerald's Children]." *Nami* [*Wave*] XXI.11 (August 1987): 16-18.

Jay McInerney, John Irving, Haruki Murakami, and C.D.B. Brian have all been influenced by Fitzgerald. For Brian, author of *The Great Dethriffe*, Fitzgerald and the "rolling twenties" are almost mythical figures in comparison to the monotonous late twentieth century. This ambivalence of adoration and defeat toward Fitzgerald and his era is the undercurrent of Brian's novel.

J196.   Saito, Tadatoshi. "The Image of Christ in *The Great Gatsby*." *Studies in English and American Literature* [Japan Women's U] 28 (Mar. 1993): 57-71.

The Great Gatsby makes quite a few allusions to Biblical images and develops the idea that Gatsby is the American version of Christ, parodying him in various ways. For instance, the valley of ashes between West Egg and New York reminds us of the valley full of dry bones in *Ezekiel*, and the eyes of Doctor T.J. Eckleburg as well as representing the eyes of God are a parody of the wheels Ezekiel saw in his vision. As a boy, the young Jay Gatsby imagined that he was "a son of God" and that he must be about His Father's business. As the business of America has been said to be business, Gatsby a Christ was about America's business, in the process dying a vicarious death for Daisy, whose voice was full of money.

J197.   Sasaki, Takashi. "From Winter Dreams to the American Dream: Fitzgerald's *The Great Gatsby* and Its Esquisse." *Doshisha American Studies* [Center for American Studies, Doshisha U] 21 (Mar. 1985): 53-66.

Fitzgerald's *The Great Gatsby* (1925) and "Winter Dreams" (1922), which the author himself called "a sort of first draft of the *Gatsby* idea," represent a *tableau* and its *esquisse,* as the story's development of a personal dream becomes a sketch of the American Dream developed in the novel. Both protagonists of the respective works, Dexter Green and Jay Gatsby, are bright and ambitious young men who associate their dreams of wealth and position with a rich and beautiful woman, only to find that they attain nearly everything they want at the cost of the love that made it all worth wanting. Together with the same geographical context of the East and West and the same historical backdrop of World War I, both works explore the romantic dream and the disillusion inherent in it. Despite these similarities, however, the great advance of the novel over the story is obvious, not only in terms of its artistic techniques, but also in terms of the nature of the dreams the hero explores. The "American Dream" is a personal dream that embodies a vision which is simultaneously in and out of time and space, is represented by a meaningful symbol, and crystallized by the strong will of the hero in the process of his pursuit of his "unutterable vision."

J198. Sato, Haruo. "Fitzgerald's Ledger, or Sensitivity to the Promises of
        Life." *Eureka* 20.14 (Dec. 1988): 98-105.

Fitzgerald's short story "Financing Finnegan" discloses the destitution of a once well-known writer, which may well reflect the author's own financial circumstances. "Finnegan" and the essays in "The Crack-Up" express Fitzgerald's view of his own life in an objective and insightful way, the life in which he literally worked for the publishing industry for the purpose of making a considerable amount of money. Although these writings express ironic humor, resignation, and self-pity, they are also invested with what Nick Carraway calls "a heightened sensitivity to the promises of life." In the ending of "Finnegan," the narrator expresses an optimistic view of Finnegan's future. This combination of tragedy and revived optimism inherent in Fitzgerald's works can also be seen in the ledger that he recorded during his career. The ledger shows how, in his later phase, Fitzgerald made his living mainly from short stories and from his collaboration with Hollywood, but also how he earlier had led a luxurious life that exceeded his income. The author's unquenchable optimism about money and life as seen in his ledger is indispensable to his writings.

J199. Sato, Haruo. Introduction. *Babylon Revisited and Other Stories by F.
        Scott Fitzgerald*. Trans. Koji Numazawa. Shuei-sha Literary Books,
        1990. 265.

Unlike Hemingway, Scott Fitzgerald was a true pessimist all his life, the budding of which appears in the writing of his first published poem "Football" in the school journal. Generally, he began not as an A class novelist but as the first commercial short-story writer that modern America produced. As a novelist, his clumsy writing improved considerably owing to Maxwell Perkins, his editor, and Edmund Wilson, the incipient but sharp critic who both criticizes and appreciates Fitzgerald's talent, referring to him as an old woman who is extremely proud of a diamond that someone left her but who doesn't know what to do with it. Wilson's criticism worked well enough to urge Fitzgerald to write his third novel, *The Great Gatsby*, far more seriously. The three stories of this collection make a representative volume: "May Day" is a refreshing breath after the Victorian naturalism from Europe. "The Rich Boy" is a mature piece that makes the reader think of what wealth represents to modern youth. "Babylon

Revisited," the title story, may be associated with Fitzgerald's straits in caring for Zelda but also experiencing a upsurge in writing ability.

J200. Shimamura, Norio. "The Heat and the Sweat and the Life—An Essay on F. Scott Fitzgerald." *English Language and Literature* [English and American Literary Society, Tokyo: Chuo U Press] 23 (Mar. 1983): 155-182.

Fitzgerald's life was, as he himself recognized in one of his personal memoirs, "a process of breaking down." Another memoir shows how his early success gave him a "mystical conception of destiny as opposed to will-power." He lived in a delicate balance between two such opposed ideas: the former required stoicism and morality, effort and determination, and the latter required only the appreciation that "life is a romantic matter." In fact, the works of Fitzgerald suggest that he was, from the beginning of his career, partaking of a dualistic world: "success" and "failure," "right" and "wrong," "inner life" and "garnished front." Therefore, his literature can be said to reflect the fear of his own downfall caused by his losing balance in this world of duality.

J201. Shimizu, Kazuo. "F. Scott Fitzgerald and His Disappointed Days in New York: Through 'Babes in the Woods.'" *The Ryukoku Journal of Humanities and Sciences* XII.1 (Aug. 1990): 67-79.

A comparison of two versions of "Babes in the Woods" shows Fitzgerald's changing image of his heroines. Isabelle, in the story entitled "Babes in the Woods' in *The Nassau Literary Magazine,* is modeled on Fitzgerald's childhood sweetheart, Ginevra King, an archetypal figure of the flapper to be. In *This Side of Paradise,* the "second version" of "Babes in the Woods," Isabelle becomes the more sophisticated character.

J202. Shimizu, Kazuo. "F. Scott Fitzgerald and His Radio Scripts: on 'The Great Game.'" *The Ryukoku Journal of Humanities and Sciences* [Ryukoku U] XV.2 (Feb. 1994): 97-113.

Princeton U owns Fitzgerald's radio scripts. Titled "Home to Mother," "Broadcast Number Thirteen," and "The Great Game," they are not Scott's novels and short stories rewritten for broadcasting, but are sample pieces or sketches by Scott. "The Great Game"(also known as "Let's Go Out and Play") is written in "an effort to promote peace education," but as it is not always "a powerful plea for peace," it shows the limits of his script-writing.

J203. Shinohara, Nobuko. "Conflicts of Values in F. Scott Fitzgerald's *Tender Is the Night*." *Bulletin of Shikoku Women's U* X.1 (Dec. 1990): 75-95.

The reasons for Dick's downfall correspond to Fitzgerald's tragic idea of the inevitability of a 'crack-up' under stressful circumstances that cannot be sustained beyond a certain limit. While Gatsby dies at the apex of his dreams, thus preserving them untouched, Dick represents the tragedy of maturity and the corruption of one's ideals. Many contradictions bring about Dick's decline: one is his own inner conflict between his desire for pleasure and his puritanical value system. The others are more related to the society in which he lives: Nicole deprives him of his "masculine values" (independence and strength) and leaves him emotionally drained and at the mercy of others. Finally, there is a social conflict between Dick's middle class background and the "leisure class" of the billionaire Warren family: Dick tries unsuccessfully to enter the society of the rich, but is instead destroyed by their corrupted ways and lack of values.

J204. Shinohara, Nobuko. *The Great Gatsby*—A Romance of the American Dream." *Bulletin (of) Shikoku Women's U* [Shikoku U since 1992] VII.2 (Mar. 1988): 217-230.

The Great Gatsby is a reflection on the social and economical context of the 1920s in America. The Jazz Age was an era of unprecedented affluence and enthusiasm that saw the beginning of a society of consumerism and hedonism. Fitzgerald participated in such a climate, but was also able to see its limits and tragic outcome, especially in the collapse of universal and traditional values and in the moral relativism typical of the time. Daisy and Tom are perfect specimens of such a ruthless world of money and material interest; Gatsby, while partaking of the same cult of superficial success and easy wealth, can still retain his ability to dream, and this is what confers upon him some kind of superiority in the eyes of Nick: his undying idealism thus remains the only value left in an otherwise completely commercialized society.

J205. Sumiko, Niimi. "Love and Desire in an Era of Mass Consumption: A Study of *The Great Gatsby*." *Love and Death in the American Literature Cinematized Today.* Ed. Japan Malamud Society, Hokuseido, 1998. n. pag.

According to Freud, money is as solid as gold, but Fitzgerald revealed an age in which gold had became fluid. He lived through an age when accumulation gave way to quick earning and spending. Although such transition of vision took place over the past two centuries, the fact remains that the pursuit of money symbolizes the basic human incentive: that is, Eros. The hero of Fitzgerald's novels does not seek money so much as position at the top of the social hierarchy, and the heroine becomes the symbol of that position. In writing about the romance of money and its mysterious power, Fitzgerald dealt with the central spirit of a transitional American age.

J206. Tanaka, Takako. "Fitzgerald's *Tender Is the Night*: Body, Copy, and Art." *Journal of Humanities and Social Sciences* 4 (1998): 1-12.

In *Tender Is the Night*, Fitzgerald reveals his artistic concern with the machine age. He examines the relationship of the original work of art to its copy through the mechanical process of reproduction. He also compares culture with nature. Rosemary's body is attractive, but to Dick Diver, she is more appealing as a film actress. Rosemary represents the hard-working middle-class American mass culture. Nicole on the other hand is original, extremely wealthy and suffering from the trauma of incest. However, she is tired of being treated like a work of art by Dick, and courts the American "copy culture" to escape from her mental ordeal. With talented Dick dishonored and disappearing into anonymity, the author seems to acknowledge his despair of the modern era. Fitzgerald, however, is also sensitive to the allure of the mass popular culture. His ambition in *Tender* is to grasp the threat and fascination of a person's loss of identity on the border between the body and the machine, between an individual and a mass. To be a copy in the machine culture is a failure, according to Fitzgerald, but to catch the allure and the pain of being at the border is a work of art.

J207. Tanaka, Takako. "The Automobile and Four American Novels of the 1920's." *The Jimbun Ronshu* [*Journal of Cultural Science*] [Kobe U of Commerce] XXIV.2 (Dec. 1988): 27-44.

Fitzgerald, Hemingway, and Faulkner reacted to the U.S automobile culture in the 1920's during which the advertisers of automobiles changed their emphasis from the practical value of cars to the fashionable. Fitzgerald is acutely aware of the glamour of the automobile as a symbol. In *The Great Gatsby*, a Rolls Royce is an appropriate symbol of the wealthy class for Gatsby and also represents his confidence in his ability to control time and space. Fitzgerald suggests Gatsby's mistaken idea of time by juxtaposing the image of a boat to that of an automobile. Yet, he acknowledges that Gatsby's high ideal transcends the desire for commodity goods. Hemingway, on the other hand, wants to keep an automobile just as an automobile. What matters to Hemingway's hero is to keep a good command of a car, but this often turns out to be more difficult than he expects. Faulkner describes the guarded response of the Southern rural community to the automobile culture, though he betrays his fascination with the speed of a car, which seems to refute all the burdens of the past.

J208. Taniyama, Sawako. "Things Go Glimmering: Fitzgerald as Critic of Conspicuous Consumption." *New Perspective* 27.2 (November 1996): 18-22.

F. Scott Fitzgerald knew the destructive side of the seemingly carefree Roaring 20's, particularly the conspicuous consumption that drove it. In stories like "The

Rich Boy," "Winter Dreams," and "Babylon Revisited," one finds not only the abuses of wealth and its consequences, but also the psychological pain caused by the desire for riches and the glamour that it can buy. Fitzgerald was at heart a traditional moralist, strongly influenced by his conservative Irish Catholic background. He hated the frivolous rich children of the 20's not for their wealth and power but for their lack of earnestness. Fitzgerald frowned on adultery, on sloth and on excess. He found the modern liberated woman, the young society "flapper," a monster. Fitzgerald saw hope in plain and modest men like Nick Carraway (*The Great Gatsby*) and reformed debauchers like Charlie ("Babylon Revisited") who have abandoned frivolous pleasure for real work and family happiness.

J209. Tasaka, Takashi. "The Desire of the Moth for the Star: Shelley, A. Maurois and Fitzgerald." *Eigo Seinen: The Rising Generation.* (Kenkyusha) CXLIII.11 (Feb.1998): 664-666.

Shelley and A. Maurois influenced the writing of *The Great Gatsby*. The overt resemblance is between Shelley's aspiring to the star moths ("One Word") and the image of Gatsby wearing colorful shirts and holding his arms toward the green light. The covert one is the influence of his reading experience of Shelley's *Alastor* and A. Maurois's *Ariel* on the concept of Gatsby's dream. Both writers give Fitzgerald the means to deepen Gatsby's Platonic conception of himself beyond the shallow conception in the Gatsby-cluster stories such as "Winter Dreams" and "The Sensible Thing."

J210. Tasaka, Takashi. "Fitzgerald's Style." *Fitzgerald no Bungaku Amerika no Yume to sono Shi [The Literature of F. Scott Fitzgerald American Dream and Its Death].* Tokyo: Arechi-Shuppan, 1982. 37-49.

Based on Richard Ohmann's supposition that stylistic preferences reflect cognitive preferences, one can argue that Fitzgerald's contradictory expressions, especially oxymorons, like "a warm chill", a "white darkness," and "yawned gracefully," reflect his sense of the double vision. The artistic and functional effects of oxymorons in *Gatsby* are also discussed, including the flexibility of meanings: the smallest units in the language of the novel function as indicators of its meaning as a whole.

J211. Tasaka, Takashi. "Shiroi Yami: Oxymoron no sekai—Fitzgerald no buntai [The White Darkness: The World of Oxymoron—Fitzgerald's Style]." *Eigo Seinen: The Rising Generation* 32 (July 1986): 158-162.

As a phrase from Fitzgerald's notebook for *The Last Tycoon* exemplifies well, his style is an oxymoron, a contradictory combination of languages that is set against the mutual expectancy of language, and thus constantly hovering between two contradictory meanings. The oxymoronic figures that appear in his various texts symbolically represent Fitzgerald's way of perception and imagination: to see through the substance behind the appearance of things, and also to embrace the mutually exclusive aspects of things. At the core of the author's artistic design, this rhetorical device has an intimate relation with the subjects of his stories. Nick Carraway best embodies this so-called "double vision" that accommodates realism and romanticism in his ambivalent reaction to other characters and the East itself, registering simultaneous enchantment and repulsion toward them. Behind this double vision lies Fitzgerald's ambivalent feelings toward his own parents, and more important, Keats's influence on artistic creation—the negative capability," which allows an artist to stand between two opposite things, and hence to see both sides without making an ultimate judgment.

J212. Tatsumi, Takayuki. "Echoes of the Oz Age: A Note on Post-Gatsby Billionaires." *Geibun-Kenkyu* [*Studies in Arts and Literature*]. Keio-Gijuku Daigaku Geibun-Gakkai [Keio U Society of Arts and Literature]. 75 (December 1998): 105-123.

Fitzgerald is a representative man of the Jazz Age who was persistently obsessed with the image of the American billionaire. And yet, a casual glance at the critical difference between Jay Gatsby and Monroe Stahr discloses the way the Jazz Age was disrupted not only by the Great Depression but also by the Hollywood Gold Rush, which took place with the advent of talkies in 1926. Gatsby as a Romantic egoistic billionaire becomes old-fashioned and is replaced by a modernist charismatic figure like Stahr, who dominates the very network of film industry. What is more, during the Jazz Age William Randolph Hearst became so powerful as the king of media, that he inspired Fitzgerald to create Stahr in *The Last Tycoon* (1940), and Orson Welles to produce a masterpiece *Citizen Kane* (1941).

J213. Tatsumi, Takayuki. "Motto romantic ni: Fitzgerald no 'My Lost City' [Make It More Romantic: Fitzgerald's 'My Lost City']." *Eureka* 20.14 (Dec. 1988): 135-141.

As exemplified in *The Great Gatsby* and "My Lost City," the city carries an almost over-determined connotation of the East, women, and success. Embodying these conflated images, New York itself becomes a symbol of the American dream in the early twentieth century. However, the city is the place not only of success but also of failure. In the 1920s, the decade of economical boom and panic, New York epitomizes this tension between successful perfection and devastating collapse. Fitzgerald's aesthetics stand on this teetering edge between success and failure. In this sense, the "romantic" 1920s are more closely associated with literary romanticism than the modernism of the day. While modernism is characterized by the collapse of the world as an organic whole and by the attempt to produce a fragmented world view, romanticism is characterized by the impulse to create new values even from absences, just as Fitzgerald invests the period of the post-war discord with the new values of the Jazz Age. When the dream is ephemeral, vulnerable to disillusionment and destruction, this romanticism is all the more preciously "romantic" as *The Great Gatsby* and the author's own life insinuate.

J214. Terasawa, Mizuho. "Naze kare ha kanemochi no bijo ni hikarerunoka?: 'Zennou no hahaoya' tankyu no bungaku [Why Does He Prefer Rich, Beautiful Women?: Literature in Search of the 'Omnipotent Mother']." *Eureka* 20.14 (Dec. 1988): 106-113.

The question of whether Fitzgerald's male protagonists can obtain a rich beautiful woman is a capital wager for their lives and even identities. Fitzgerald's mother, who was a socially isolated figure, inculcated in him the importance of wealth in determining one's fate; thus, her doting love incubated in his ego the sense of narcissistic omnipotence. Accomplishing literary success in his early twenties, Fitzgerald preserves this sense of omnipotence almost intact. And yet the dissatisfaction he inevitably confronts in reality could easily threaten his whole identity as a center of the world. It is because of this unconscious struggle to bridge this gap between reality and ego ideal that Fitzgerald writes fiction, wielding his imagination to signify life and reality in his own way. Alongside the desire for money as a way to the perfection of self, the desire for beautiful women is also part of this fantasizing function. Those beautiful women sought by Fitzgerald's male protagonists are in fact substitute figures of the author's ideal mother who can satisfy and secure his omnipotence and narcissism. But this psychological need to keep the fantasy of self against the anxiety of disillusion is also a universal phenomenon, and cannot be limited to Fitzgerald.

J215. Tokunaga, Yukiko. "Daisy and Myrtle: A Study on *The Great Gatsby*." *KanSai American Literature* [The Kansai American Literature Society] 29 (Nov. 1992): 46-58.

The women in *The Great Gatsby* respectively represent the difficulty for women in speaking in the patriarchal society. The comparison between Daisy and Myrtle, especially their experiences of confinement, reveals that while Daisy is a typically oppressed woman whose utterance is lost, Myrtle is a rebel who is punished for her very utterance. Androgynous Jordan alone is allowed to speak in the male-dominated world, but because of her "masculinity" she fails to adequately narrate Daisy's story. Not Jordan, but Myrtle could have been the only true narrator of Daisy's story, but by killing Myrtle, Daisy loses her narrator forever.

J216. Tokunaga, Yukiko. "On *Fie! Fie! Fi-Fi!* and Other Early Plays: Re-evaluating F. Scott Fitzgerald as a Playwright." *Osaka International University Journal of International Studies* 12.3 (Mar. 1999): 19-34.

Fitzgerald's theater has been mostly neglected or dismissed by critics. His earliest plays, while being juvenile experiments written for a dramatic club in St. Paul, show his serious interest for the theater, both as a playwright and as an actor, since the beginning of his writing career. His most noteworthy theatrical work is *Fie! Fie! Fi-Fi!*, a musical comedy written for the Triangle Club at Princeton. The play anticipates themes and situations which Fitzgerald later explored in the novels, such as the critique of the American dream, the relationship between Europe and America, the love between a poor boy and a rich girl. His career as a playwright ends early on after the disastrous failure of *The Vegetable*. The comedy, despite its obvious flaws, deserves closer attention, given its chronological proximity to *The Great Gatsby* and the inclusion in Fitzgerald's early novels of theatrical elements.

J217. Tokunaga, Yukiko. "Reading of Daisy's Story: A Study of *The Great Gatsby*." *Journal of Kanazawa Women's U* [Faculty of Letters] 4 (Dec. 1990): 78-85.

Discussions about Daisy used to be focused on her irresponsibility, her corruption, or her malignity, before the feministic essays, in the 1970s, such as those of Joan S. Korenman and Leland S. Person Jr., brought forth the Daisy who was a victim herself. But it is Daisy's peculiar, and sometimes obstinate, reticence that makes it difficult for readers to know what she herself thinks or how she feels. She seldom expresses what is inside herself. Her mouth is firmly shut even at the critical moments. Contrary to her once predominant image as an egotistic femme fatale, however, Daisy's own story which has been buried in the text reveals neglect and confinement.

J218. Totake, Mamoru. "The Jazz Age and Fitzgerald." *America Bungaku to Jidai Henbo* [*A New Perspective of American Literature*]. Ed. Shigeo Hamano. Tokyo: Kenkyusha, Apr. 1989. 191-203.

The evaluation of Fitzgerald by Japanese academics and his general readership here has changed greatly in recent times. While originally his books were highly valued as representative of the Roaring Twenties, many critics now dismiss *The Great Gatsby* as a mere love story, lowering it to the level of melodrama. However, a careful reading of *The Great Gatsby* will lead readers into the writer's deep insights into American history and culture. Despite his native country being founded on the ideals of freedom and equality, in the 1920s there was a privileged and exclusive social class known as "The Establishment" in the eastern United States. This clearly contradicts the idealism on which the nation was founded. This novel targets America's hypocrisy by examining the nature of a hero who possesses "romantic readiness," the naiveté, sensitivity and pioneer spirit, that "transcendental idealism" on which America is purported to be founded, only to become its victim.

J219. Tsuboi, Kiyohiko. "The Belated, But Not Too Late, Arrival of F. Scott Fitzgerald in Japan." Paper delivered at F. Scott Fitzgerald Centennial Conference. Princeton University, 21 Sep. 1996.

See Chapter Introduction.

J220. Tsuboi, Kiyohiko. "Fitzgerald's Revision of 'Tarquin of Cheapside.'" *Persica* [Journal of the English Literary Society of Okayama] 3 (Dec. 1976). 123-37.

The first published version of Fitzgerald's early story "Tarquin of Cheapside" and the version later included in *Tales of the Jazz Age* are worthy of comparison. Despite what Fitzgerald himself and some of his editors claimed, the story undergoes a substantial revision and expansion, making it "more plausible, realistic, and dramatic." It is interesting, though, that the author incorporates and re-uses most of the material he cuts in other parts of the story, rather than eliminating it.

J221. Tsuboi, Kiyohiko. *"Philippe, Count of Darkness* by F. Scott Fitzgerald." *Persica* [Journal of the English Literary Society of Okayama] 5 (Jan. 1978): 25-33.

Philippe, Count of Darkness, which Fitzgerald planned after *Tender Is the Night*; was published as a cycle of stories in a magazine but the novel itself remained unfinished. It is one of Fitzgerald's few attempts at historical fiction. The story, set in Medieval France during the chaotic situation of the 9th century, symbolically alludes to Hitler and the turmoil in contemporary Europe. The protagonist, modeled on Hemingway, is intended to embody the 'modern man' as Fitzgerald attempted to move away from the autobiographical romantic heroes of many of his other works. Yet the coexistence of such diverse material with the use of American slang is unresolved, and the novel remains one of the author's less convincing texts.

J222. Tsuboi, Kiyohiko. "Steinbeck's *Cup of Gold* and Fitzgerald's *The Great Gatsby*." Steinbeck Monograph Series 8 (1 May 1978): 40-47.

The two books present many similarities, especially in the way the protagonists are engaged in a quest for self-accomplishment, and in doing so idealize the objects of their desire. Both authors invest their stories with a variety of mythological and literary references, using among others the story of Troilus and Cressida, the grail legend, and the Faustian myth, to present their protagonists' ceaseless quest for a woman. The main difference lies within the two writers' presentation of the American Dream: whereas Fitzgerald admires its powerful idealism and romantically regrets its failure, Steinbeck presents it as an illusion, and has his character abandon all his ideals in exchange for wealth.

J223. Tsuboi, Kiyohiko. "The Composition of 'Doctor's Son' by John O'Hara." *Transactions of Okayama U School of Letters* (Dec. 1987): 145-154.

In "Doctor's Son" by O'Hara we find the same narrative techniques and time scheme as those of *The Great Gatsby*, probably due to his deep attachment to Fitzgerald.

J224. Tsuboi, Kiyohiko. "A Play by F. Scott Fitzgerald : *The Captured Shadow*." *Chushikoku American Literature Studies.* 18 (no date): 3-13.

The Captured Shadow published in *Saturday Evening Post* is derived from his boyhood play of the same name. However, the close comparison between the original play and the play referred to in the short story of the same name reveals that Fitzgerald fictionalized the fact (the original play) in the story, contrary to the popular concept that Fitzgerald drew a story directly out of his own experience.

J225. Tsuboi, Kiyohiko. "Autobiographical Heroes in the Works F. Scott Fitzgerald and Thomas Wolfe." *Heroes in the American Literature.* Ed. Yoshiaki Koshikawa. Tokyo: Seibi Do, 1991, 1999. 42-50.

Heroes in *The Great Gatsby* and *Look Homeward, Angel* are unique in that they are self-exposing and confessional in the tradition of American literature.

J226. Tsuboi, Kiyohiko. "Narrator and Time in the Works of F. Scott Fitzgerald and William Faulkner." *In the Beginning Was the Word: Language and Literature.* Festschrift in honor of Dr. H. Ono on his Retirement. Eds. Yoshinori Umedu et al. Tokyo: Eicho-sha, 1993. 238-47.

One of the characteristic narrative techniques in *The Great Gatsby* is the double vision. The same kind of technique is found in Faulkner's "That Evening Sun." Both writers manipulate the time sequences in their writings as is often observed in the writers of Modernism.

J227. Tsuboi, Kiyohiko. "Wolfe and Fitzgerald: Similarities and Differences."
*Studies in Thomas Wolfe: A Tribute from Japan to Thomas Wolfe's
Centennial.* Eds. T. Kodaira and H. Tsunemoto. Tokyo, Kinsei-Do,
2000. 49-66.

Maxwell Perkins helped F. Scott Fitzgerald and Thomas Wolfe create *This Side
of Paradise* and *Look Homeward, Angel.* Both were romantic modernists and
wrote about themselves and America. Wolfe, however, is a writer of saturation,
while Fitzgerald is selective. Similarity is also found in the editing of their
posthumous publications. Perkins asked Edmund Wilson to edit Fitzgerald's
unfinished novel, *The Last Tycoon.* After the relative failure of *Tender Is the
Night* (1934), Fitzgerald had planned to revise it but he left it only partly revised.
Malcolm Cowley edited and published it as the author's final version, but which
is the better of the two versions remains controversial. Wolfe's editor, Edward
Aswell at Harpers, freely edited, added, and deleted from the bulk of his
posthumous manuscripts and published *The Web and the Rock* and *You Can't
Go Home Again.* His editing met with scholarly discussions on their
authenticity.

J228. Uefuji, Reiko. "A Study of *The Beautiful and Damned*: Centering on Its
Themes." *Humanities Review* [The Journal of the Literary Association of
Kwansei Gakuin U] XXXI.3 (Jan. 1982): 89-103.

The Beautiful and Damned is often criticized as a failure because its theme is
obscure. Although at the beginning Fitzgerald's intention to tell how young and
attractive Anthony Patch and his beautiful wife Gloria collapsed through
dissipation was clear, it had become less focused by the time the novel was
finished. Fitzgerald had added too many other themes to the story: for instance,
the aristocratic sense of the American wealthy class, the revolt of the young, the
conflict between the North and the South, and the war. When he wrote the
novel, he devoted much more care to the detail of the book, as he himself
admitted. This coupled with its technical problems obscured the central theme.

J229. Uenishi, Tetsuo "The Jewish Gang in *The Great Gatsby.*" *Chiba Review*
[English Literature Association, Chiba U] 16 (Nov. 1994): 1-18.

The very common dream of Gatsby's winning a woman and money is explained
by an episode in American history. The story is based on the Fuller-McGee case,
a contemporary Wall Street scandal. It is easy to see parallels between Gatsby's
life and the life of the main offender, Edward Fuller, and between the character
of Gatsby's boss Meyer Wolfsheim and that of Arnold Rothstein allegedly
behind the case. In the 1920s the New York underworld underwent a drastic
shift toward modernization. Prohibition introduced the bootleg business which
turned old ethnic neighborhood gang groups into modern universal complex

systems like big businesses. Underworld people tried to adjust themselves to the new situation and behave like business executives. This modernization is well represented by Rothstein who then established a modern syndicate in the New York underworld and appeared to be a solid gentleman. What Gatsby really did is to reduce himself to a Jew, forgetting his stock is Nordic. This standpoint is consistent with the characterization of Wolfsheim, which emphasizes his Jewishness.

J230. Watanabe, Kyoichi. "Sherwood Anderson's Literary Influence on F. S. Fitzgerald in Thought." *The English Department Review of Hirosaki Gakuin College* 12 (Mar. 1988): 2-14.

As writers whom Sherwood Anderson influenced, Hemingway and Faulkner have been pointed out. But Anderson also influenced Fitzgerald. Some of Fitzgerald's works bear the trace of Anderson's influence. Fitzgerald wrote in his letters that he felt a profound sympathy for Anderson's works. Subsequently, Hemingway impulsively wrote *The Torrents of Spring* in which he seems to have satirized the fact that Fitzgerald imitated Anderson's works.

J231. Watanabe, Shinji. "Self-controlled Narrative and Its Three Tactics: Towards the Dream of Gatsby." *Eigaku-Ronko* [*English Studies*] (Tokyo Gakugei U) 14 (Feb. 1983): 38-52.

Fitzgerald succeeded as an objective novelist only in *The Great Gatsby* because the narrator Nick Carraway developed the rare strategy of the self-controlled narrator who reserves judgments and evades questioning or any criticism. This strategy, while making this novel amoral because it gives no clear judgment as to Gatsby's job, Daisy's behavior, or Nick's love game with Jordan, comprises three tactics in order to make the novel consistent and dedicated to the dream of Jay Gatsby: the use of chance and accident, the use of deception, and the sense of balancing. The first tactic keeps the plot simple, avoiding side plots and descriptions of complicated human relations; the second suggests some immoral aspects in the novel, leaving nothing true except Gatsby's dream; and the last brings in parallel discoveries and avoids a break-up of the plot. The strategy based on three tactics make *The Great Gatsby* not a masterpiece, but a well-wrought novel.

J232. Yamaguchi, Itaru. "'Absolution' and *The Great Gatsby*: On Fitzgerald's Catholicism." *Hiroshima Shudai Ronshu* [*Hiroshima Shudo U Studies*]. (Hiroshima Shudo U). 24 (December 1983): 115-136.

This essay is an attempt to investigate the relationship between F. Scott Fitzgerald and Catholicism, which is often apt to be neglected, mainly by comparing his short story, "Absolution," with *The Great Gatsby*. The Catholic element is central to "Absolution," which was to have been a prologue of *The Great Gatsby*. While it is almost absent in the novel, Fitzgerald's Catholicism is shown through Rudolph Miller's conflicts between the Catholic ethos that disciplines him and the aesthetic pathos he has in his mind. Fitzgerald failed to offer a final solution as a way out of the conflicts at the end of the story. From this it can be assumed that the failure forced him to avoid emphasizing the Catholic element in the novel, where Gatsby has no religious conflicts. In spite of the failure, however, Fitzgerald salvaged "Absolution" from the discarded version of *The Great Gatsby*, for it was a literary confession of his own at an early stage of his life as a writer. As the conflicts are to be found again in his later works, the Catholic ethos continually dominated his moral vision in his life and art.

J233. Yamaguchi, Itaru. "Distinctive Characteristics of 'Winter Dreams': In Comparison with *The Great Gatsby*." *Hiroshima Shudai Ronshu* [*Hiroshima Shudo U Studies*]. (Hiroshima Shudo U). 33 (Mar. 1993): 119-135.

F. Scott Fitzgerald once described one of his earlier short stories, "Winter Dreams," as "a sort of first draft of the *Gatsby* idea." Having accepted this comment, critics lay emphasis on the similarities between "Winter Dreams" and *The Great Gatsby*. This comparative analysis of the two stories, however, reveals that their qualitative differences have more weight. While *The Great Gatsby* is almost immaculate in art and thought, "Winter Dreams" has some flaws deriving from Fitzgerald's handling of the problem of point-of-view. The coherence of the narrative voice of the story is somewhat marred by the writer's own interventions. Because of the flaw, however, we can perceive the immediacy with which he attempted to convey the meanings of the protagonist's illusions. Fitzgerald underlines the greatness of Gatsby's transcendental qualities: the colossal vitality of his illusions is timeless. The central stress of "Winter Dreams" is placed on the fragility of Dexter's illusions. It reflects the writer's more pathetic vision of the human condition.

J234. Yamaguchi, Itaru. "The End of 'Winter Dreams' and Time." *Hiroshima Shudai Ronshu* [*Hiroshima Shudo U Studies*]. (Hiroshima Shudo U). 35.1 (Sept. 1994): 71-96.

Dexter Green laments the loss of something in himself at the end of "Winter Dreams." The lamentation has given rise to various interpretations, mainly because what Dexter finally lost is left unclear. The key to a better understanding of the elusive ending is to investigate the effects of time on Dexter's dreams. While yearning for the timeless ecstasy stirred by Judy Jones' beauty, Dexter longs to achieve financial success. The double-focused dreams enmesh him in tangled emotions. By giving up Judy, he resolves to keep her beauty of the past alive in his heart. The imaginative present, however, does not last unchanged. Paradoxically, Dexter's imaginative power sustaining his sense of being "magnificently attuned to life" gradually decreases with the passing of time before he knows it while he rises high in the real world. It is this power that he finally finds he has lost. At the end of "Winter Dreams," through dramatizing the tension between reality and the inner springs of life, Fitzgerald stresses the inevitable decline of man's imaginative power with the inexorable passage of time. In spite of its painfulness, however, Dexter's realization of the decline seems to include a chance of maturing his true self.

J235. Yamaguchi, Itaru. "F. Scott Fitzgerald's New Perspective in *The Last Tycoon*." *Hiroshima Daigaku Bungakubu Kiyo* [*Hiroshima U Department of Literature Studies*] (Hiroshima U) 41 (Dec. 1981): 221-236.

In writing *The Last Tycoon*, Fitzgerald started to take a new attitude as a writer in spite of or rather because of his personal degeneration and the social breakdown of the United States in the 1930s. Fitzgerald characterizes Monroe Stahr as a much more realistic figure than Jay Gatsby. He feels it necessary to lay more emphasis on the role of Stahr in a social context. He tries to embody a much wider vision, which the American writers at the social crisis of the 30's needed, than that in *Gatsby*. The process of the struggle and defeat in the novel is placed in a historical context. Fitzgerald identifies the inhumanity of Hollywood with the crisis in which the American society was losing the great American spirit in the early 20th century, though he believes that it will never be lost, for the paradoxical coexistence of the traditional spirit and the progressive one is the essence of the American society. The main purpose of *Tycoon* seems to be to make the readers notice that the recognition of this essence is fading out.

J236. Yamaguchi, Itaru. "A Study of 'May Day': With Special Reference to Gordon Sterrett's Deterioration." *Hiroshima Shudai Ronshu* [*Hiroshima Shudo U Studies*]. (Hiroshima Shudo U) 26 (Dec. 1985): 31-35.

In "May Day," Fitzgerald seems to have managed to achieve objectivity by overcoming his tendency to confuse his individual life with his fiction. However, we can find his own inner conflict still lurking in the story. Gordon is uncertain of the possibility of re-establishing his identity, which poverty has split into an ideal self aspiring to the higher social class and a real self in miserable conditions. The uncertainty not only reflects Fitzgerald's own but also shows his fault. Another cause of Gordon's deterioration lies in his inner vulnerability. When his leisure-class friends' withdrawal from him leaves it up to him to restore his split identity, he falls into isolation and despair. At the end of the story Gordon commits suicide on the table holding "his drawing materials" which had sustained his illusory self. The lyrical note of the desperate state in the most devastating form of vulnerability shows that the writer could not find a final solution to his obsessive conflict at least at the time of "May Day."

BOOK REVIEWS/NEWS ARTICLES/RADIO PROGRAMS

J237. Tsuboi, Kiyohiko. Review of *The Life of F. Scott Fitzgerald : Some Sort of Epic Grandeur* by Matthew Bruccoli. *Eigo Seinen* [*The Rising Generation*]. CXX VII Kenkyusha, 1982.6: 228.

Prof. Bruccoli's meticulousness based upon the facts is highly praiseworthy.

TEACHER/STUDENT GUIDES AND EDITIONS

J238. Nozaki, Takashi, ed. 20th Century Ebeibungaku Annai: Fitzgerald [A Study Guide to English and American Literature: Fitzgerald]. N. p., n. pag.

Study guide for university students.

MUSICAL AND FILM PRODUCTIONS

J239. *The Great Gatsby: A Musical Based on the Novel of F. Scott Fitzgerald.* Scripted and directed by Shinichiro Koike. Produced by Takarazuka Review Co. Aug. 8-Sept. 17, 1991; Dec. 3-26 in Tokyo.

The program contains M. J. Bruccoli's review and K. Tsuboi's commentary.

Canada

In his essay "Canadian Images," written for Malcolm Bradbury's *The Atlas of Literature*, Greg Gatenby writes that the Expo '67 Fair in Montreal created in Canada

> a newly energized *zeitgeist* which entered writing, spawning a fresh generation of poets, playwrights, short story writers and novelists. Most were young, and able to explore a past largely denied them, a present which was virtually unwritten. The fact that Toronto was near-virgin literary ground proved a major stimulus. Groups formed, new magazines began. An early road-block was the attitude of established Canadian publishing houses, who seemed to believe that every good writer fled the country—Mavis Gallant, Brian Moore and Mordecai Richler all did in the 1950s—and that any that remained were by definition second-rate" (Gatenby, 1996, 308).

Gatenby further offers that "the cultural developments of the sixties and seventies were sorely needed; the results have been formidable" in terms of Canadian writers being published in Canada, a literary festival of world repute, good literary magazines, and major writers. Gatenby concludes, "Between 1967 and 1980 the whole nature of English-Canadian experience and its cultural texture transformed" (308).

Michael Nowlin, a Fitzgerald scholar from the University of Victoria, confirms that there has been "a firm entrenchment of Canadian literature in university literature departments since the 70s." Nowlin claims that the shift to Canadian literature has occurred at the expense of the study of American literature rather than of British literature (Nowlin, 20 June2003). He adds, "Graduate students seem less interested in (and remarkably ignorant about) canonical American literature around here, though many seem eager to learn about African-American, ethnic-American, and American women writers, etc. Too often they are reading the latter, it seems to me, apart from their relation to dominant literary figures and trends and apart from the nationalistic literary field in which their work emerged" (Nowlin, 8 Sept. 2003). Nevertheless, Fitzgerald's work seems to be read in both high schools and universities in Canada (Nowlin, 20 June 2003), including in French-speaking and -reading areas, if a review written in French of books on Fitzgerald is a sufficient indication (C33).

Since 1980, Canadian scholars have written numerous articles about Fitzgerald's work and have participated in the various International Fitzgerald Conferences beginning in the early 1990s (C20, C27). One strand of scholarship particularly pertinent to Canadian interests has focused on the filmscript that Malcolm and Margerie Lowry wrote for *Tender Is the Night,* much of the commentary concentrating more on the Canadian novelist's cinematic treatment of the novel than on Fitzgerald's work, but the contrasts made between the two authors' work do offer insight into Fitzgerald's intent in writing the novel. Other critical work on Fitzgerald reflects trends in scholarship elsewhere in the world: influences by other writers on Fitzgerald; influences by Fitzgerald on other writers; humor (or lack thereof) in his works, sexual identity, politics, and roles; class; and race and ethnicity. Several essays analyze *Tender Is the Night,* both those on Lowry's filmscript and others on the novel itself. Most, of course, are on *The Great Gatsby,* and some are on the stories.

Malcolm Lowry scholarship is "relatively prominent" in Canada (Nowlin 20 June, 2003), and nine articles, introductions, and prefaces are on Malcolm and Margerie Lowry's filmscript of *Tender Is the Night.* Miguel Mota and Paul Tiessen, editors of *The Cinema of Malcolm Lowry: A Scholarly Edition of* Tender Is the Night (1990), wrote an introduction indicating that the filmscript is more Lowry than Fitzgerald but that Lowry intended his work to be an homage to the other writer (C16). In a 1993 piece in the *Malcolm Lowry Review,* Paul Tiessen, editor, presents "A Few Items Culled From What Started Out To Be a Sort of Preface," in which Malcolm and Margerie Lowry argued that *Tender Is the Night* is a "near failure as a novel" but that unlike *The Great Gatsby* which was fully realized as a book, *Tender* leaves room to move creatively within it" (C13). Tiessen also wrote an introduction to the Lowrys' "Preface" in which he claims the Lowrys believed Fitzgerald intended to write a tragic novel, even though he didn't accomplish his intention (C30).

In addition to his and Tiessen's introduction to the scholarly edition, Miguel Mota has written two essays on the subject. In "The Tyranny of Words," Mota claims that Lowry's work on *Tender Is the Night* is his struggle for personal redemption through the redemptive possibilities he saw reflected in Dick's consciousness (C14). In "'We Simply Made One Up,'" Mota agrees that Lowry's filmscript, which never resulted in a film, is not a professional screenplay as such but suggests it is instead a celebration of a "cinematic imagination" (C15).

Other scholars have also written about the Lowry screenplay. Chris Ackerley explores its literary qualities (C1), Bill Hagen discusses Lowry's use of expressionistic film techniques (C8), Kieron O'Hara asserts that none of the humor Lowry embedded in *Through the Panama* finds its way into the filmscript, which is not great because it is not funny enough (C21). Finally, Audrie Rankin argues that Lowry sees Dick as heroic because he breaks through conflict to explore deeper areas of subconscious thought (C26).

Among several influence studies, Ralph Curry and Janet Lewis discuss Fitzgerald's use of Stephen Leacock's "situational nonsense" in several of his earlier works, including "The Cruise of the Rolling Junk." Scenes in *The Great Gatsby* also parallel the humor in elegant circles that Leacock lampoons (C3). In another comment on Fitzgerald's humor, Doug Crowell claims that Andy Kaufman has been influenced by *The Great Gatsby* and Jay Gatsby himself in one of his routines (C2). Joseph Griffin discerns the influence of Stephen French Whitman in *The Beautiful and Damned* and that of H. L. Mencken and Joseph Conrad on *Gatsby* (C32). Michael Nowlin also asserts that Mencken's *Defense of Women* caused Fitzgerald to remorselessly deflate the aestheticized vision of Woman in *The Beautiful and Damned* (C20).

Two essayists argue for Edith Wharton's influence on both *The Beautiful and Damned* and *The Great Gatsby*. Helen Killoran sees *The Glimpses of the Moon* as a significant influence on *Gatsby*, particularly in the character of "Owl Eyes" who resembles Wharton's Mr. Buttles (C11). The scenes, details, theme, form, and technique of Wharton's *The Spark* also influenced Fitzgerald's writing of *Gatsby*, according to Michael Peterman. (C23). Alice Hall Petry claims that Warren G. Harding is James Gatz's mentor (C24). Finally, Julie Jones informs us that Fitzgerald influenced Elena Garro in her writing of *Reencuentro de personajes* as one character endlessly reads *Tender Is the Night*, believing her destiny to be inscribed in its pages.

Eleven of the essays are on *The Great Gatsby*; of the 15 on *Tender Is the Night*, nine are on Lowry and Lowry's screenplay. Two essays are on *The Beautiful and Damned*, and three on are on the short stories. In addition to the essays on *Gatsby* discussed above under humor and influence, Paul Giles examines the Catholic ideology "secularly resonant" in the novel (C7), Alberto Lena is concerned with Tom Buchanan's decadence (C12), and David O'Rourke argues for Nick Carraway's reliability as a narrator (C22).

Reflecting the preoccupations of an American studies approach, considerations of sexuality are reflected in the remaining three essays on *Gatsby* which examine, respectively, the sexual undertone of an ambiguous sexuality in most of the characters (C5), three dominant types of sexual roles among the characters (C29), and forms of homosexuality in both Nick and Gatsby (C31). Judith Fetterley also examines *Tender Is the Night* for its sexual politics (C4), Jacqueline Tavernier-Courbin in her two essays on *Tender Is the Night* writes of desire as a motivating factor in the novel (C27, C28), and Michael Nowlin sees modernist irony and feminized men as inextricably entwined (C18).

Also reflecting the current American studies trend in global literary scholarship are two essays on race and ethnicity in some stories and novels Nowlin writes of Fitzgerald's ambivalence about race in "Head and Shoulders," "The Offshort Pirate, "The Diamond as Big as the Ritz," and *The Beautiful and*

Damned (C19), and Julie Jones argues that Fitzgerald demonstrates an ethnocentric view of Latin Americans in his characterizations of Francisco and Luis Campion in *Tender Is the Night* (C10).

In addition to Nowlin's essay mentioned above on racial ambivalence in three short stories (C19), Curry and Lewis write of Stephen Leacock's influence on two of Fitzgerald's prep school stories and also "Jemima" and "The Usual Thing" (C3). Finally, Helge Norman Nilsen writes of the ironic, dual image of Anson Hunter in "The Rich Boy" (C17).

Crossing borders are several non-Canadian scholars who have been published in Canadian journals. Helge Norman Nilsen (C17) is a Norwegian scholar published in the Canadian publication *International Fiction Review* as was American scholar Edward Wasiolek (C31). *Thalia: Studies in Literary Humor* also published Doug Crowell (C2), who teaches at Texas Tech. Judith Fetterley, another American scholar, was published in *Mosaic: A Journal for the Interdisciplinary Study of Literature* (C4), and Helen Killoran and Alice Hall Petry appeared in *Canada Review of American Studies* (C11, C24).

Jacqueline Tavernier-Courbin and Michael Nowlin have also participated in several of the international Fitzgerald conferences held every other year since 1992. At the 1994 International Hemingway/Fitzgerald Conference in Paris, Jacqueline Tavernier Courbin presented on "The Influence of the French Background on Nicole's Recovery." For the Princeton Centennial Conference in 1996, Michael Nowlin read a paper on "'Profound Banalities:' Castration and the Marriage Plot in The Beautiful and the Damned." For the Nice Conference in 2000, Jacqueline Tavernier Courbin presented "'The Edouard Jozan Affair' by Scott and Zelda Fitzgerald" and Michael Nowlin looked at "*Tender Is the Night's* Black Gentleman."

Canadian literary studies are therefore on the cusp both of a relatively new pride in indigenous literature and interest in the global trend toward American studies approaches to American literature. Michael Nowlin received the F.E.L Priestly Prize in 2001 for his "F. Scott Fitzgerald's Elite Syncopations: The Racial Make-up of the Entertainer in Early Fiction" published in *English Studies in Canada*, the organ of ACCUTE (Association of Canadian College and University Teachers of English, sponsor of the Prize (C19). Nowlin might best represent Canadian scholarly thought when he writes

> I don't think being a Canadian gives me that unique a perspective on Fitzgerald studies—perhaps it makes me less reverent towards the kinds of American ideals that Fitzgerald's work is often praised for evoking, since I've never internalized these to the extent that many Fitzgerald scholars seem to have done (especially from an earlier generation). I love Fitzgerald's writing and find him a remarkably interesting man; I am deeply interested in American literature and history and enjoy visiting the United States, but have no desire to be American (Nowlin).

REFERENCES

Gatenby, Greg. "Canadian Images." *The Atlas of Literature*, general editor Malcolm Bradbury. London: De Agostini Editions; Don Mills, Ontario: General Publishing Co Ltd., 1996; Rpt 1997.

Nowlin, Michael. E-mail to author. 20 June 2003.

Parenthetical citations to entry numbers refer to annotated references in this chapter.

ESSAYS/CHAPTERS/NOTES/CONFERENCE PAPERS

C1.   Ackerley, Chris. "Notes Towards Lowry's Screenplay of *Tender Is the Night*." *The Malcolm Lowry Review* 29/30 (1991/92): 31-50.

These notes explore the literary qualities of Lowry's screenplay of *Tender Is the Night*: its use of allusion, its echoing of Lowry's other works, and the idiosyncratic intonation of so many apparently commonplace words and phrases. They consist of citations of proper names, such as Philoctetes, Kraft-Ebbing, and Diderot; of works of literature, such as *Thus Spake Zarathustra*, several Shakespeare plays, works by Freud and other psychoanalysts, the *Oedipus* cycle, and *The Sun Also Rises*; of musical compositions by both jazz and classical composers, such as Beiderbecke and Ravel; films like *The Cabinet of Dr. Caligari*; places, such as the Café Chagrin in Paris; and terms and phrases from Fitzgerald himself, such as "the Conradian legend that the sea exists."

C2.   Crowell, Doug. "Why is Andy Kaufman Funny?" *Thalia: Studies in Literary Humor* 7.1 (Spring-Summer 1984): 35-44.

The author cites a Kaufman stand-up routine, in which, dressed in a tuxedo, he reads authoritatively and with great seriousness from *Gatsby* over classical music to a bewildered, then delighted audience. This is a "Gatsby-like" thing to do. There is risk inherent in it, which makes Gatsby the perfect icon for Kaufman.

C3.   Curry, Ralph, and Janet Lewis. "Stephen Leacock: An Early Influence on F. Scott Fitzgerald." *Canadian Review of American Studies* (7 Jan. 1976): 5-14.

In 1917 Fitzgerald sent a letter to Leacock accompanying two "Leacock school" stories he'd written: "Jemima, a story of the Blue Ridge mountains, by John Phlox Jr" and "The Usual Thing" by "Robert W. Shamless [sic]," which have counterparts in Leacock's *Nonsense Novels*. Fitzgerald had previously published two Leacockian stories in his prep school paper: "A Luckless Santa Claus" (1912) and "The Trail of the Duke" (1913), both parodies in which the central characters are doomed to social failure by their indecisive natures. He would further imitate Leacock in undergraduate pieces written in 1916 and 1917, and later still in a three-part article titled "The Cruise of the Rolling Junk." Both writers delighted in situational nonsense, and the use of language that is deliberately absurd; Fitzgerald also used Leacockian incongruity to heighten the comedy of low life. Fitzgerald's later, serious fiction largely turns away from the fun-poking of Leacock; still it is sometimes thrown into the mix—Gatsby's outlandish flannel suit, absurd names like Clarence Endive. Scenes in *Gatsby* parallel the tension in elegant circles that Leacock lampoons.

C4.   Fetterley, Judith. "Who Killed Dick Diver? The Sexual Politics of *Tender Is the Night.*" *Mosaic: A Journal for the Interdisciplinary Study of Literature* 17.1 (Winter 1984): 111-28.

At the heart of the novel is the anxiety-ridden perception that culture, not biology, is destiny, that nothing protects a man from experiencing the fate of woman in our society except his culturally determined power to impose that fate on her. In what finally became a mutually antagonistic struggle for survival between him and Zelda, Scott based his claim to be the one "saved" on his role as the professional writer and on the psychological and economic consequences of that role. He did not see Zelda as different in kind from himself—and at least one doctor perceived Scott as equally sick and in need of treatment—but holding the trump cards of institutionalized sexism helped him retain his claim to the role of the sane one.

C5.   Fraser, Keith. "Another Reading of *The Great Gatsby.*" *English Studies in Canada* 5 (1979): 330-43.

The quality of concealment in *Gatsby* causes us to read over scenes we are meant to read through, such as the exchange between Nick and Mr. McKee in Chapter 2. Another, similar sexual undertone lies in the fact that cars, symbols of masculinity, are in *Gatsby* poorly driven by women. Nick deliberately cultivates ambiguity. In his encouragement to the reader to "reserve all judgements" he may be pleading his own case. His "personal affairs" are never accounted for, nor is his relationship with women. What is Nick hiding? An uncertain sexuality. The theme of bisexuality is discoverable in *The Satyricon*, to which Fitzgerald was drawn. And it is Encolpio, the ambivalently sexual narrator of *The Satyricon*, who provides a model for Nick. Both fail with women, but not for lack of trying, and both describe their odysseys as parodies.

C6. Gervais, Ronald J. "The Socialist and the Silk Stockings: Fitzgerald's Double Allegiance." *Mosaic: A Journal for the Interdisciplinary Study of Literature* 15.2 (June 1982): 79-92.

In his major works, biography, and correspondence dating from the post-World War I "Red Scare" through the 1930s, Fitzgerald reveals a two-mindedness toward Marxist ideology, what he called a "double allegiance to the class I am part of, and to the Great Change I believe in." Unable to reconcile these two loyalties, he developed in his work an attitude toward Marxism that was neither embrace nor rejection, but the ability "to hold two opposed ideas in the mind, at the same time, and still retain the ability to function." Fitzgerald depicts lovingly the charm and grace of capitalism's upper classes, yet consistently states his conviction, born of personal resentment and a sense of historical necessity, that they are doomed. Not entirely enthusiastic about this prospect, and with "no faith in the future of my kind in the supposedly classless society," Fitzgerald creates in his art a strategy of literary debate that permits him to deal with his ambivalence.

C7. Giles, Paul. "Aquinas vs. Weber: Ideological Esthetics in *The Great Gatsby*." *Mosaic: Journal for the Interdisciplinary Study of Literature* 22.4 (Fall 1989): 1-12.

Catholic ideology is secularly resonant in *Gatsby* in its contemplation of the power of powerlessness and its near-parody of the American dream. André Le Vot refers to Gatsby's "spiritual intactness" and discusses Nick's elevating of Gatsby into transfigured splendor. An underlying ambiguity, and ambivalence relates to the uncertain social status of American Catholicism in the 1920s. In *Gatsby*, elements of Catholic assimilation are combined with those of Catholic alienation, consumer culture is sanctified, and Daisy almost religiously idolized. Symbolism abounds: "incarnation," "vision," "perishable breath." There is clear emphasis on transubstantiation between material and metaphysical planes. Fitzgerald's implicit discourse of Catholicism produces cultural undertones that pull the novel in directions it may not otherwise have taken.

C8. Hagen, Bill. "Malcolm Lowry's 'Adjustable Blueprint': The Screenplay of *Tender Is the Night*." *The Malcolm Lowry Review* 29/30 (1991/92): 51-63.

James Agee, Jay Leyda, Christopher Isherwood, and MGM producer Frank Taylor received Lowry's screenplay with enthusiasm. Two scenes in Lowry's adaptation use traditional 1950 industry practices and also provide enough rich material to suggest potential scenes according to current 'art film' standards. In the Villa Diana party scene, Lowry attempted to create unity of effect by transforming psychological perspective into visual imagery and to merge that imagery into the flow of dialogue, as in *Under the Volcano*. Lowry's aim was to portray human relationships in the context of a larger vision that reveals human beings less in control than they think. In a second scene, Lowry's version of the sanitorium sequence, Dick Diver remembers Nicole's case, within which her mind displays its disorder and she begins to respond more positively to Dick's attention. Within her sequence are realistic flashbacks, abstract puppet or animated sequences which allegorically represent her mental state, and a discourse of images—some recalled, some spontaneous—in response to Diver's comments. Lowry was influenced by German expressionistic films such as *The Cabinet of Dr. Caligari* (1919) and *Sunrise* (1927) and American films *Citizen Kane* (1941) and *Spellbound* (1945) by Hitchcock. The screenplay anticipates the work of Ingmar Bergman, especially the beginnings of *Wild Strawberries* (1957) and *Persona* (1966). Considerable culling and refinement would be necessary even in the best scenes.

C9.   Horne, Lewis B. "The Gesture of Pity in *Jude the Obscure* and *Tender Is the Night*." *Ariel: A Review of International English Literature* 11 Feb. 1980: 53-62.

Jude's whispering Job's curse on his own life in *Jude the Obscure* and Dick Diver's blessing of the beach with a papal cross from his hotel balcony before returning to America in *Tender Is the Night* are both judgments. In each situation, a deserted man of certain good qualities moves into obscurity, vacating a place once marked in some manner as his. A new time has come, one with which neither man can contend. Yet the disappearance of each man signifies that something valuable is lost, perhaps irrevocably. Both novels depict qualitative and metaphysical changes in the spirit and nature of time. The two heroes suffer the advent of a new era inimical to the qualities with which each man was born and nurtured. In the life of each is dramatized the waning effectiveness of the altruistic impulse.

C10.   Jones, Julie. "Text and Authority in Elena Garro's 'Reencuentro de personajes'." *Canadian Review of Comparative Literature* 18.1 (Mar. 1991): 41-50.

Reencuentro revolves around a cast of Mexican expatriates whose sense of self is defined by a long-ago encounter with Fitzgerald and their conviction that they are described in *Tender Is the Night*. Garro cannibalizes Fitzgerald to satirize a Latin America that looks abroad for definition. She argues that there is a close link between national identity and great works of fiction, and additionally asserts that Fitzgerald invented the whole modern era. One character in *Reencuentro* endlessly rereads *Tender Is the Night*, believing her destiny to be inscribed in its pages. Another is identified by Garro with Francisco, and another with Luis Campion, both used by Fitzgerald to point up a theme of moral decay. Implicit in *Reecuentro* is Garro's criticism of Fitzgerald's ethnocentric view of Latin Americans.

C11.   Killoran, Helen. "An Unnoticed Source for *The Great Gatsby*: The Influence of Edith Wharton's *The Glimpses of the Moon." Canada Review of American Studies* 21.2 (Fall 1990): 223-4.

A friendship between Wharton and Fitzgerald resulted in a visit, letters, book-swappings, dialogue written by Fitzgerald for the 1923 screenplay of Wharton's *The Glimpses of the Moon* and, probably, Wharton's substantial influence on *The Great Gatsby*. Fitzgerald borrows an image from *Moon*—Mr. Buttles wiping his glasses—for his own character, "Owl Eyes," the only one of Gatsby's acquaintances to attend his funeral. He perhaps names Nick Carraway after *Moon*'s Nick Lansing. Lansing is referred to as "Old Nicks" by his friends, a slang term for the devil.

C12.   Lena, Alberto. "Deceitful Traces of Power: An Analysis of the Decadence of Tom Buchanan in *The Great Gatsby." Canadian Review of American Studies* 28.1 (1998): 19-41.

Tom Buchanan is one of the pivotal characters in *The Great Gatsby*, embodying the decadence of the upper classes. An analysis of his wealth and character are instrumental in understanding the limits of Fitzgerald's fascination with riches. Tom is a consumer, not a producer. Veblen added that the leisure of men like Tom was as obtrusive as their consumption. Nick emphasizes Tom's connection with sports and the "predatory life." Tom is careless in two senses: by smashing things up and further by not caring about the consequences of his actions. Finally, Tom's not being familiar with Nick's bond business shows his removal from the sources of production. As a result, the leisure class is a symbol of obsolescence and decay. Tom's main physical characteristic is his muscularity. Nick emphasizes on the other hand his "simple mind." *The Great Gatsby* is pervaded by ambiguity regarding the decadence of the West for Fitzgerald believed that culture follows money and those individuals he criticizes in his novels are wealthy without the concomitant cultural responsibility. *The Great Gatsby* thus represents the halfway mark in Fitzgerald's intellectual development.

C13.   Lowry, Malcolm and Margerie. "A Few Items Culled From What Started Out To Be A Sort of Preface." Ed. Paul Tiessen. *The Malcolm Lowry*

Review 33 (1993): 48-66.

Fitzgerald had at the back of his mind some kind of great tragedy and was divided as to how to write it. He was further divided by personal disaster, and the sober conclusions of psychoanalysis served further to adulterate any heroic quality in it. The novel lacks any clear dramatic line or integration. Its near failure as a novel is that, unlike *The Great Gatsby*, it was not fully realized as a book and leaves much room to move creatively within it, which gives a great advantage to the film writer. Fitzgerald is meticulous with his foreground and background in order to conceal the disorderliness of the whole. The subterranean part of the book contains a law of cause and effect. In a time of censorship, the incest motif could not be introduced, but Nicole's madness is as equally an integral part of the structure as is the incest, and is more consistently organic. In the end, Fitzgerald has stripped Dick of any tragic stature. The book is a tragedy with Dick Diver as Moby Dick, the buried intention having been to make him, both on the constructive and destructive side, a sort of archetypical American.

C14. Mota, Miguel. "The Tyranny of Words: Malcolm Lowry's *Tender Is the Night.*" *Canadian Literature* 154 (1997): 10-26.

Lowry's work on the *Tender Is the Night* filmscript became central to his career as a writer and essential in his struggle for personal redemption, differing markedly from the novel in its Expressionist film ethic. Lowry was enchanted by the protean capability of words to create the self but also threatened by the possibility that they are the product of an autonomous, authoritative subjectivity existing nowhere but in language and vulnerable to other discourses of authority. Words become objects in the filmscript, graphic representations of Dick's consciousness, what Lowry sees as consciousness of humanity and its redemptive possibilities. Lowry creates a tyranny of words and other objects as well, such as Nicole's Isotta.

C15. Mota, Miguel. "'We Simply Made One Up': The Hybrid Text of *Tender Is the Night. A Darkness That Murmured: Essays on Malcolm Lowry and the Twentieth Century.* Eds. Fredrick Asals and Paul Tiessen. Toronto: U. of Toronto P, 2000. 128-38.

The critical response to the Lowry film script adaptation of *Tender Is the Night* will to a significant extent be determined by an assessment of its generic status, which is, however, unclear since the script is not a conventional shooting script for an actual Hollywood production, and has been taken to task on these grounds. Other than a 'professional' screenplay, though, Lowry's text might be seen as a celebration of a cinematic imagination enacted within a literary context that never hesitates to play with generic conventions. The Lowrys' composition, though nominally a film script, is in effect a literary hybrid, a dialogue of genres that in many ways typifies Lowry's post-*Volcano* work. However, it has as much right to be considered a serious literary work as any of the later fiction. The work moves significantly beyond the conventional bounds of the film script genre, mixing it, with what is in effect the epistle and the critical literary essay, offering readings not only of Fitzgerald's novel but also of film aesthetic and history.

C16. Mota, Miguel, and Paul Tiessen. Introduction. *The Cinema of Malcolm Lowry: A Scholarly Edition of* Tender Is the Night. Eds. Miguel Mota and Paul Tiessen. Vancouver: U of British Columbia P, 1990. xiii, 262.

Absorbing the best of both European and American cinemas, Lowry has enlarged and enlivened our sense of cinema's potential and achievement through his films and writings. Though never produced as a film, Lowry's 1949-50 filmscript is a complex essay on Fitzgerald and his work and an essay and variation on Lowry's *Under the Volcano*, incorporating Lowry's thoughts on Jung, America, tragedy, the human soul, and the creative process. In arguing that his script possessed as much artistic integrity and legitimacy as any other serious work of art and that his de/reconstruction of Fitzgerald's work should be thought of as an act of homage to Fitzgerald, Lowry was reflecting his specific sense that the story would actually work best in film form. However, the resulting "Lowry-text" within the filmscript is mainly a record of Lowry's own voice—a text within which is registered only here and there a smattering of Fitzgerald's words—extensively reflecting his published and other unpublished writing and at the same time playing upon the films he loved and upon film in general. It is a self-portrait showing Lowry in the act of creating not only art but also audience. The aesthetic of the text is a critique and restatement, an illustration and enlargement, of his literary practice.

C17. Nilsen, Helge Norman. "A Failure to Love: A Note on F. Scott Fitzgerald's "The Rich Boy." *International Fiction Review* 14.1 (Winter 1987): 40-43.

Fitzgerald, who imposed a strong personal perspective of American society on *The Great Gatsby*, finds even more room for his point of view in his later short story, "The Rich Boy" (1926), through a narrator who is both relatively detached from the title character and also conveniently anonymous. In this way the reader is inclined to take criticism of Anson Hunter, a second-generation "rich boy" of "stunted development" who is superficial, self-indulgent, lacking in moral virtue and, above all, a failure at deep personal relations, as the indictment of an "implicit author." Hunter's relationship with Paula, a woman capable of the "intuitive understanding of the meaning of love," is, the only thing that would have "saved" Hunter from the superficiality inherent in his ilk. The American infatuation with the rich—and an accompanying lack of desire to find fault with them—allows an ironic, dual image of Hunter as affable charmer and pathetic, isolated "victim" of his own emotional stagnation.

C18. Nowlin, Michael. "'The World's Rarest Work': Modernism and Masculinity in Fitzgerald's *Tender Is the Night*." *College Literature* 25.2 (Spring 1998): 58-77.

This essay examines Dick Diver in terms of Fitzgerald's own famed sense of division between being an entertainer and a serious artist in order to show how that division derives from contradictory aspects of modernism inseparable from masculine anxieties about vocation and identity. Hostility to America's burgeoning popular culture industry pervades the novel, which originated as a story about a run of the mill Hollywood employee and became the story of a psychiatrist-savior who is also an artist figure, a producer of what Fitzgerald calls "the world's rarest work." The novel ends up revealing the shortcomings of high modernist aspirations in the face of an irresistible foe, exemplified most obviously in actress Rosemary Hoyt's seduction of Diver. Exposed as a Father-imposter and as feminized a subject as any of his patients, Diver can only fall back on a modernist irony that the novel reveals as hollow.

C19. Nowlin, Michael. "F. Scott Fitzgerald's Elite Syncopations: The Racial Make-up of the Entertainer in the Early Fiction." *English Studies in Canada* 26.4 (December 2000): 409-443.

F. Scott Fitzgerald's earlier work—including "Head and Shoulders," "The Offshore Pirate," *The Beautiful and Damned* and "The Diamond as Big as the Ritz"—harbours the racial meanings of his major fiction. From the outset of his career, and in response to his own overnight popularity, Fitzgerald critically engaged the notion of 'whiteness' by representing as irresistible the allure of a darker, melting-pot America. 'Whiteness,' however, also grounded Fitzgerald's resistance to the role of commodified entertainer and the licentiousness of the jazz age. Thus, while Fitzgerald's celebration of modern times necessitated a critical view of white supremacy, his moralistic denunciation of it depended on an elegiac evocation of an older world where racial boundaries were more firmly in place.

C20. Nowlin, Michael. "Mencken's Defense of Women and the Marriage Plot of *The Beautiful and Damned*." In *F. Scott Fitzgerald in the Twenty-First Century*. Eds. Bryer, Prigozy, and Stern. Tuscaloosa: University of Alabama Press, 2003. 104-120. Earlier version delivered at International Fitzgerald Centennial Conference, Princeton, 1996.

Though scholars have long recognized Mencken's influence on *The Beautiful and Damned*, little regard has been given to the ways in which Mencken may have helped Fitzgerald articulate the radically unsentimental views of heterosexual relations we find in that novel, specifically through his 1919 work, *In Defense of Women*. Mencken—whom Fitzgerald undoubtedly had in mind when he named his first collection of stories *Flappers and Philosophers*—may have functioned like the philosopher Apollonius in Keats's "Lamia" for the temperamentally romantic Fitzgerald, for in no other novel does he so remorselessly deflate the phantasmic, aestheticized ideal of Woman. He does so by deploying a marriage plot that displays a woman in all her "damned" domestic actuality.

C21.   O'Hara, Kieron. "'You Do Not Know Why You Dance:' Comedy in *Under the Volcano, Through the Panama,* and *Tender Is the Night." The Malcolm Lowry Review* 31/32 (1992-93): 68-84.

Whereas *Under the Volcano* is a very funny book, Lowry's film script of *Tender Is the Night* is deficient in humor and therefore is unilluminated by the light that Lowry's art casts over the darker areas of thought and life. Perhaps Lowry's *Through the Panama* most resembles aspects of *Tender Is the Night*. Lowry's novel is funny on many levels including the puns on the names of important cultural figures. The protagonist journeys to hell locked in the canal as Lowry has Dick Diver's hyper-awareness take the form of an extended commentary on a dream in which a cliff represents integrity and an abyss desire. Another common theme between the two works is the idea of a canal as a ship, and in each work great play is made with the enjoyment of the metaphysical Hell. The journey through this canal is mad, comic symbolism but in *Tender Is the Night* he uses genuinely heavy-handed symbolism of the seaspray as the unconscious. For Lowry comedy and tragedy are inseparable. The Consul is a likeable fellow for all his comic tragedy but Dick is repellent and it is difficult to care about his demise. Lowry's *Tender Is the Night* is not great because it is not funny enough, and makes us wonder why Dick didn't kill himself immediately if he's having such a rotten time.

C22.   O'Rourke, David. "Nick Carraway as Narrator in *The Great Gatsby." International Fiction Review* 9.1 (Winter 1982): 57-60.

Critics interested in the role of Nick Carraway as narrator in *The Great Gatsby* may be divided into two rather broad groups: those who see Nick as reliable, basically honest, and ultimately changed by his contact with Gatsby, progressing from innocence to experience before finally locating a moral vision; and those who hold that Nick is unreliable, a sentimentalist at least, and possibly dishonest and immoral. Hence, the novel is either a deceptively tricky novel, or one that is artistically flawed in both character and structure. It would be naïve to expect a slow-thinking, sentimental, and occasionally dishonest narrator to be totally reliable, particularly when exacerbated by drink and the inauthenticity of East

Egg, which is why the reliability of Nick's narration is so surprising. His slow-thinking is channeled into caution, his dishonesty is rare and ultimately acknowledged, and his break with Jordan signals an astute, if slow to crystallize, moral sense.

C23. Peterman, Michael A. "A Neglected Source *for The Great Gatsby:* The Influence of Edith Wharton's *The Spark.*" *Canadian Review of American Studies* (8 Jan. 1977): 26-35.

The influence of Joyce, Cather, and Conrad on the novel have been noted, but the influence of Wharton (as a follower of Henry James) was largely ignored by critics and by Fitzgerald himself after its publication. *The Spark*—the third of the four *Old New York* novellas—is, however, more influential for Fitzgerald than *Ethan Frome* or *The Custom of the Country*. It bears many striking resemblances to *Gatsby* in matters of scene, detail, theme, form, and technique. Despite the cogency of Wharton's remarks about *Gatsby* which Fitzgerald appreciated at the time of its publication, he turned away from her after 1925 perhaps because many influential critics had decided that she was the literary equivalent of tufted furniture and gas chandeliers.

C24. Petry, Alice Hall. "James Gatz's Mentor: Traces of Warren G. Harding in *The Great Gatsby.*" *Canadian Review of American Studies* 16.2 (Summer 1985): 189-196.

Dan Cody conjures with his name alone images of an American hero and the American frontier; more than that Cody is similar to the ultimate American hero, the President of the United States, specifically, Warren G. Harding. They are alike in appearance, intellect, and personal habits; both are wealthy, inveterate travelers, heavy drinkers, ladies' men. Cody's mistress/nemesis bears an uncanny resemblance to Harding's wife. The relationship between Gatsby and Cody smacks of the one between two members of Harding's Ohio Gang who had an intense, complex, father/son relationship. As the scandal-ridden Harding was a poor role model for America, so was Cody a disastrous role model for Gatsby, providing him with only a criminal education. Prior to *The Great Gatsby*, Fitzgerald's play *The Vegetable or, From President to Postman* showed striking parallels between Harding and the play's protagonist, Jerry Frost.

C25. Probert, K. G. "Nick Carraway and the Romance of Art." *English Studies in Canada* 10.2 (June 1984): 188-208.

The character of Nick makes use of three types of traditional romance in his attempt to understand Gatsby's life. First, the Odyssean seafaring romance, evidenced by nautical imagery and Gatsby's sailing voyages: Nick, restless and compulsive, can be equated to Ulysses. Next, the Arthurian quest romance, whose motifs in *Gatsby* include references to a "grail," an "invisible cloak," a "king's daughter," as well as Gatsby's chivalry and Daisy's idealized maidenhood. Like *Gatsby*, Arthurian stories treat the destructive power of love (adultery) and the corruption of ideals, and contemplate the collapse of a dream kingdom. Finally, medieval romanticized forms, namely Chaucer's *Troilus and Criseyde*: romantic encounters are arranged during rain storms, the narrator is unable to love, the heroes are apotheosized. In witnessing all this, and also legendizing Gatsby within a romantic framework in order to give meaning to his career, Nick—whose motives must be suspect—illustrates the dangers of contemporary idealism, heroism and romance-writing.

C26.   Rankin, Audrie. "Malcolm Lowry's *Tender Is the Night*: Form, Structure, Spirit." *The Malcolm Lowry Review* 31/32 (1992/93): 85-111.

The most obvious way in which Fitzgerald's novel jibes with Lowry's adaptation is in his treatment of the protagonist as a character independent of his creator. Whereas at the end, Fitzgerald's Diver fades from the picture, Lowry's remains a tangible presence—heroic, distinctive, responsible, fallible. In order to portray his heroic character, Lowry drew on Bertolt Brecht's epic style and estrangement theory. Lowry uses frequent and subtle use of typestyle and other graphic material especially in the telegram "Would you consider my buying your life? Please reply immediately," which serves to pinpoint the climax of the novel in Dick's decision to accede. The effect of the two foci—the image and captions—is to slow the reader down, to make the text physically more demanding both visually and emotionally. Lowry believed conflict is all important—in learning about the self, about discipline, and about the human condition. Print, whether subtitle or caption, may also be the means through which Dick breaks through the surface tension and explores the deeper area of subconscious thought. Lowry is concerned with the aesthetics of writing, as well as with the instruction of the novice in the audience.

C27.   Tavernier-Courbin, Jacqueline. "The Influence of France on Nicole Diver's Recovery in *Tender Is the Night*." *French Connections: Hemingway and Fitzgerald Abroad*. Eds. Gerald J. Kennedy and Jackson R. Bryer. New York: St. Martin's 1998: 215-32. Earlier version delivered as paper at Hemingway/International Conference, Paris, 1994.

France offers Nicole a society accepting of sexual desire and provides her with a man who does not question his own physical desires. Provence and the Côte d'Azur are hedonistic backgrounds that nudge her toward recovery by bringing her closer to an acceptance of human nature and allow her to come to terms with her own sensuality. Her involvement with Barban is a symptom of her recovery. His primitivism does not violate her nature—he loves her without controlling her—and her relationship with him reveals her true self. Nicole, commonsensical sensualist, belongs more to France than to mental illness, and in her discarding of puritan manners, more to the Riviera than Chicago, or a mental institution. The Latin need for periods of contemplative silence—a stark contrast to the American need for activity—is congenial to Nicole, as is the naturally erotic setting of the Mediterranean.

C28. Tavernier-Courbin, Jacqueline. "Sensuality as Key to Characterization in *Tender Is the Night*." *English Studies in Canada* 9.4 (Dec. 1983): 452-67.

Sexual desire is the undercurrent in the relationships between the characters in *Tender*. Rosemary's eroticism for Dick is aroused by the realization that his and Nicole's relationship is one of active love; she wants her share of their physical passion. But there can be no satisfactory consummation of Rosemary's desire for Dick because, to give way to her, he would lose the strength that attracts her. In contrast, Tommy's desire for Nicole is purely erotic, for he is confronting life with his openly physical attraction. For her part, Nicole does not idealize her relationship with Tommy, relishing its pure sexuality, and this is a sign of her mental health. Her relationship with Dick, motivated by psychological disturbance, was doomed once she recovered. Dick's sexuality is of the mind and for that reason is destructive; Tommy's is instinctive, and therefore fulfilling. The final success of Tommy and Nicole lies in their acceptance of a basic instinct of life.

C29. Thornton, Patricia Pacey. "Sexual Roles in *The Great Gatsby*." *English Studies in Canada* 5 (1979): 457-68.

Fitzgerald refines the themes of sexual confusion and role reversal in *Gatsby*. In Gatsby's guest list, women are defeminized (Francis Bull), men are emasculated (Ernest Lilly). Fitzgerald's couples are more like twins than lovers, and he created three sets, representing three dominant types of sexual roles: Tom and Daisy—traditional yet fragile masculine/feminine roles; Gatsby and Myrtle—new sexual stereotypes, at home in a new era of machines and sensuality; and Nick and Jordan—androgynous. *Gatsby* witnesses the failure of the traditional sexual relationship of masculine dominance (Tom and Daisy); forecasts the problems of experimental sexuality (Gatsby and Myrtle); and sees Jordan's androgyny fail due to the fact that she chooses the worst from both sexes. Nick succeeds, however, as an androgynous ideal, having chosen the most virtuous traits of the sexes.

C30. Tiessen, Paul. Introduction to "A Few Items Culled From What Started

Out To Be A Sort of Preface." *The Malcolm Lowry Review* 33 (1993): 48-66.

Malcolm and Margerie Lowry wrote a "sort of preface" for their 1950 film script of *Tender Is the Night*, which they addressed to Frank Taylor, one of the publishers of Lowry's *Under the Volcano* who had recently become an MGM producer and was eager to produce a film based on Fitzgerald's novel. Although the final version of the script is a "work of literature," the film would have run to six hours. The script has never been published. The preface considers the role of the serious novelist and also the serious adapter in a Hollywood seemingly impervious to art and also in the context of what the Lowrys saw as Fitzgerald's "apparent but unfulfilled intentions" to write a tragic novel.

C31. Wasiolek, Edward. "The Sexual Drama of Nick and Gatsby."
      International Fiction Review 19.1 (1992): 14-22.

Nick, ostensibly fair and judicious in his role as narrator, is perhaps less than fair in his comparison of Gatsby and Tom Buchanan. What defines Gatsby is his idealistic, non-sexual love for Daisy which explains Nick's defense of Gatsby and his abhorrence for Tom. Gatsby's fleeing from "dirty" women is a form of homosexuality, and Nick's own homosexuality is blatant in his dislike for the "aggressive masculinity" of Tom and his "dirty" kind of love. Nick is an enabler of both Gatsby's relationship with Daisy and Tom's relationship with Myrtle. The two men represent for Nick good and bad fathers—Gatsby loves, whereas Tom denies that love. Nick, ultimately, is a voyeur, wanting to have it both ways and calling his strategy honest. In the end, it is Nick and Gatsby against the world and then, ultimately left without Gatsby, Nick reconciles with Tom, the reviled father.

BOOK REVIEWS/NEWS ARTICLES/RADIO PROGRAMS

C32. Griffin, Joseph. "Faulkner, Hemingway, Fitzgerald and Dos Passos:
      Some Recent Studies." *Canadian Review of American Studies* 13.2 (Fall
      1982): 253-265.

Robert Emmet Long looks at the cultural and literary influences on *Gatsby* in the first book-length study of the novel, *The Achieving of* The Great Gatsby. The book discusses *fin de siècle* romantic echoes, the impact of Stephen French Whitman's novel *Predestined: A Novel of New York* on *The Beautiful and Damned*, and the impact of H.L. Mencken and Joseph Conrad on Fitzgerald.

Gatsby is placed in the context of its time and similarities are drawn between Fitzgerald and his peers.

C33.   Tavernier-Courbin, J. "Autour de F. Scott Fitzgerald." Review of *The Price Was High: The Last Uncollected Stories of F. Scott Fitzgerald.* Edited with Introduction by Matthew J. Bruccoli; *The Notebooks of F Scott Fitzgerald,* Edited by Matthew J. Bruccoli; and *The Foreign Critical Reputation of F Scott Fitzgerald: An Analysis and Annotated Bibliography,* by Linda C. Stanley. *Canadian Review of American Studies* 12.3 (Winter 1981): 397-404.

Of the stories collected in *The Price Was High,* "In the Darkest Hour" is "perhaps less interesting" but none is mediocre. "More Than Just a House" and "Lo, the Poor Peacock" are even excellent. Characters and situations have an "intense reality" and it is "impossible not to sympathize with both." Furthermore, *"Indecision," "Flight and Pursuit,"* and *"On Your Own" announce Tender Is the Night. The Notebooks* are reserved for specialists as they are largely documentary of the periods when he wrote Tender Is the Night, The Crack-Up, and The Last Tycoon. Also include are the notes he wrote for The Last Tycoon. Stanley's volume is a "remarkable work" of annotations concerning the foreign reputation of Fitzgerald but for each country they are also preceded by a "long and excellent introduction." Her analyses are "conscientious and intelligent." The annotations for each work and each article are sufficiently developed that the reader understands how the ideas evolve. Candles and Carnival Lights offers a new interpretation of Fitzgerald's work based on the dichotomy established by Saint Augustine between the city of man and the city of God. The author concludes that Fitzgerald is profoundly religious, which shows him in a new light, "but her approach . . . deforms more than it reveals of an extremely complex life and work, which cannot be reduced to a unique perspective."

DISSERTATIONS

C34.   Doyle, Kegan R. *The Blood of Numbers: Sacrificial Violence in the Fiction of F. Scott Fitzgerald and Nathanael West.* Diss. U. of Toronto, 1995.

C35.   Ruppel, James Robert. *Narcissus Observed: the Pastoral Elegiac in Woolf, Faulkner, Fitzgerald, and Graeme Gibson.* Doctoral Diss. U. of Toronto, 1977.

TEACHER/STUDENT GUIDES

C36. *The Great Gatsby*. Cole Notes.

One of best selling Cole Notes of 1997.

C37. *The Last Tycoon*. Audio Book. Narrator: Lloyd Bochner and Cast.
Length: Abridged 2 hours. Publisher: Scenario Productions.

C38. Kehrli, Kathy. *"The Great Gatsby* by F. Scott Fitzgerald." Suite Book
Committee Recommendations. Suite University: Your place for online
learning! Suite101.com.

Index

ABOUT THE AUTHOR

LINDA C. STANLEY is Professor of English at Queensborough Community College, City University of New York. She is also the author of *The Foreign Critical Reputation of F. Scott Fitzgerald: An Analysis and Annotated Bibliography* (Greenwood Press, 1980).